Praise for *The War That Must Never Be Fought*

"This important book is a collection of thoughtful papers written by a stellar cast of experienced students of today's dilemma posed by nuclear weapons and deterrence policy. Recognizing the unimaginable devastation to humanity and the planet we all inhabit in the event of a failure of this policy, either by deliberate action or human error, the authors add valuable insights into policies and initiatives that nations should pursue in a global effort to reduce existing dangers of entering into The War That Must Never Be Fought."

—**Sidney D. Drell** is a senior fellow at the Hoover Institution at Stanford University and a professor emeritus of theoretical physics at Stanford's SLAC National Accelerator Laboratory, where he served as deputy director.

"More than an assertion, The War That Must Never Be Fought *calls for a robust public debate of the dilemmas of nuclear deterrence. It challenges us all to decide what kind of a world we want and to participate in getting there. The articles included provide a balanced and thoughtful catalyst for beginning that discussion."*

—**William J. Perry** was the 19th secretary of defense, and is a senior fellow at the Hoover Institution and the Freeman Spogli Institute of International Studies at Stanford University.

"In 2007, I joined with George Shultz, Henry Kissinger, and Bill Perry in warning that 'unless urgent new actions are taken, the U.S. soon will be compelled to enter a new nuclear era that will be more precarious, psychologically disorienting, and economically even more costly than was Cold War deterrence.' That new nuclear era is fast approaching. In this book, a talented group of global experts explores the role of nuclear deterrence in today's world. Can nations move together toward a new, safer, more stable form of deterrence with decreasing nuclear risks and an increased measure of security for all nations? The answers are varied and provide the reader with provocative arguments that should stimulate a much-needed debate. The bottom line, in my view, can be found in the warning given to us by President Reagan in his 1984 State of the Union message: 'A nuclear war cannot be won and must never be fought.'"

—**Sam Nunn** is a former US senator, cochairman of the Nuclear Threat Initiative, and an Annenberg Distinguished Visiting Fellow at the Hoover Institution, Stanford University.

THE WAR
THAT MUST
NEVER
BE FOUGHT

Dilemmas of Nuclear Deterrence

The Hoover Institution gratefully acknowledges the following foundations for their significant support of this publication:

THE WILLIAM AND FLORA HEWLETT FOUNDATION
THE FLORA FAMILY FOUNDATION

THE WAR THAT MUST NEVER BE FOUGHT

Dilemmas of Nuclear Deterrence

Edited by
George P. Shultz and James E. Goodby

HOOVER INSTITUTION PRESS
STANFORD UNIVERSITY   STANFORD, CALIFORNIA

The Hoover Institution on War, Revolution and Peace, founded at Stanford University in 1919 by Herbert Hoover, who went on to become the thirty-first president of the United States, is an interdisciplinary research center for advanced study on domestic and international affairs. The views expressed in its publications are entirely those of the authors and do not necessarily reflect the views of the staff, officers, or Board of Overseers of the Hoover Institution.

www.hoover.org

Hoover Institution Press Publication No. 658

Hoover Institution at Leland Stanford Junior University,
Stanford, California 94305-6010

First printing 2015
23 22 21 20 19 18 17 16 15   9 8 7 6 5 4 3 2 1

Manufactured in the United States of America

The paper used in this publication meets the minimum Requirements of the American National Standard for Information Sciences—Permanence of Paper for Printed Library Materials, ANSI/NISO Z39.48-1992. ⊛

Cataloging-in-Publication Data is available from the Library of Congress.
ISBN: 978-0-8179-1845-3 (pbk. : alk. paper)
ISBN: 978-0-8179-1846-0 (e-pub)
ISBN: 978-0-8179-1847-7 (mobi)
ISBN: 978-0-8179-1848-4 (PDF)

Contents

Preface

George P. Shultz

The year 2015 is the seventieth anniversary of the first nuclear explosion. It took place at a desert test site at Alamogordo, New Mexico, on July 16, 1945. The city of Hiroshima was obliterated by an atom bomb on August 6, 1945, and Nagasaki was destroyed on August 9. I was a Marine Corps captain at the time, on a troop ship in the Pacific bound for the United States where we expected to regroup and return to the Pacific for the invasion of Japan. We heard about Hiroshima and then Nagasaki while on the ship. None of us had ever heard of an atom bomb or had any idea what it was. By the time we arrived in California the war in the Pacific was over. When I saw the photographs of the two cities I was shocked at the devastation from one bomb, and I realized that something entirely new had entered human history. Warfare would change. Some of the chapters in this book discuss the subsequent history, but I recall it this way:

> At the outset of the nuclear age, the American strategist Bernard Brodie wrote that "thus far the chief purpose of our military establishment has been to win wars. From now on its chief purpose must be to avert them." President Eisenhower followed that precept and cut the US defense budget, especially for ground forces, while building a modest

nuclear deterrent force. The idea behind this was that war could be averted only by "the certain inescapable power to inflict swift, and crushing retaliation," as Winston Churchill said. But Brodie's and Eisenhower's premise was challenged as strategists, mostly American, debated how war could be averted when two bitter adversaries had large numbers of nuclear weapons. President Kennedy warned of a choice between "holocaust and humiliation." He added scores of new ballistic missiles and built up US conventional forces.

After Kennedy's success in resolving the Cuban Missile Crisis in 1962, the Soviet leadership forced Nikita Khrushchev to resign from his leadership position and adopted a massive nuclear buildup program. The numbers of nuclear weapons multiplied and the premise that war must be and could be averted by threatening nuclear retaliation had turned into a nuclear arms race. Each side claimed that it did not want war but could prevail if a nuclear war occurred.

Some of us painted a somewhat different picture in 2011. In an op-ed published by the *Wall Street Journal* on March 7, 2011, William Perry, Henry Kissinger, Sam Nunn, and I wrote:

As long as there has been war, there have been efforts to deter actions a nation considers threatening. Until fairly recently, this meant building a military establishment capable of intimidating the adversary, defeating him or making his victory more costly than the projected gains. This, with conventional weapons, took time. Deterrence and war strategy were identical.

The advent of the nuclear weapon introduced entirely new factors. It was possible, for the first time, to inflict at the beginning of a war the maximum casualties. The doctrine of mutual assured destruction represented this reality. Deterrence based on nuclear weapons, therefore, has three elements:

- It is importantly psychological, depending on calculations for which there is no historical experience. It is therefore precarious.
- It is devastating. An unrestrained nuclear exchange between superpowers could destroy civilized life as we know it in days.
- Mutual assured destruction raises enormous inhibitions against employing the weapons.

The logic was impeccable if one accepted the premise that nuclear weapons could deter only if they were seen to be capable of being used "successfully" on a large scale in warfare. A strategy of prevailing in a protracted nuclear war became the official policy of the United States at the end of the Carter administration. The idea was that deterrence would work only if the United States could respond to an enemy nuclear attack with a controlled nuclear response of its own, holding enough nuclear weapons in reserve to be able to respond to yet another nuclear attack from the enemy, and so on until the enemy's nuclear forces were eliminated.

The technical ability to launch with one missile a number of independently targetable nuclear warheads made it possible to strike several targets with one missile. The advance of technology also permitted much greater accuracy in the delivery of these warheads and, consequently, the number of potential military targets also multiplied. This created incentives to launch a first disarming strike. The side that used its nuclear weapons first could theoretically gain an edge. By the time Ronald Reagan became president of the United States in 1981, there were twenty-four thousand bombs and warheads in the US nuclear arsenal; the Soviet Union had about thirty thousand. There was no end in sight. Many missiles and bombs on both sides were on high alert, ready to launch.

Ronald Reagan came into office with the deep sense that threatening millions of human lives and the destruction of civilization was immoral. He saw that nuclear deterrence was flawed in its very essence and that this error had led to a whole edifice of reasoning about deterrence that also was flawed. I became his secretary of state in 1982 and soon became familiar with his strategic thinking. Early in my tenure in office, my late wife, O'Bie, and I spent part of a snowy weekend at the White House with President Reagan and Nancy Reagan. I came to realize then that he intended to engage directly with the Soviet leadership on what he saw as a life-or-death issue, not only for the United States but for humanity in general. He felt that he had to rebuild US defenses first, but that when that had been set in motion he wanted a constructive, broad-based dialogue with Soviet leaders. I shared his views and worked to support his objectives.

In his 1984 State of the Union address, the president spoke directly to the people of the Soviet Union. He said,

There is only one sane policy, for your country and mine, to preserve our civilization in this modern age: A nuclear war cannot be won and must never be fought. The only value in our two nations possessing nuclear weapons is to make sure they will never be used. But then would it not be better to do away with them entirely?

His words were met with disbelief by the establishment at the time. But the president met with a new Soviet general secretary, Mikhail Gorbachev, in Geneva in 1985. They issued a statement that echoed his State of the Union address: "a nuclear war cannot be won and must never be fought."

In October 1986, President Reagan and I sat across a small table from Gorbachev and his foreign minister, Edouard Shevardnadze, in Reykjavik. We discussed the possibility of eliminating all nuclear weapons; no public posturing by the president or the general secretary, just private talks between national leaders.

We failed to reach an agreement in Reykjavik but President Reagan succeeded in enlarging the envelope of thinking about nuclear weapons very considerably. Not coincidentally, 1986 was the peak year for numbers of nuclear bombs and warheads globally. Today, the numbers are less than a third of what they were then.

The Reykjavik meeting led directly, in 1987, to a US-Soviet treaty that eliminated a whole class of intermediate-range nuclear weapons. Now, nearly thirty years later, that treaty's future is in doubt as Russia appears poised to deploy weapons systems prohibited by the treaty. The problem it dealt with remains: those weapons had the potential for dividing Europe from the United States by posing, in the starkest terms, the perennial question of whether the United States would risk an attack on itself by defending European allies. The deployment in Europe of intermediate-range weapons of our own and NATO cohesion and resolve proved to be a turning point in ending the Cold War.

Today, the prospect of a Europe whole and free, which the end of the Cold War seemed to promise, is itself being threatened as Russian President Putin pursues his dangerous policies toward Ukraine. Those actions clearly violate the principles of the Helsinki Final Act and the terms of the arrangements, signed by Russia, that led Ukraine to send all the nuclear warheads on its territory to Russia for dismantlement.

When my colleagues, Henry Kissinger, William Perry, Sam Nunn, and I began our series of appeals in 2007 for serious attention to the nuclear threat, we thought that the goal of a world free of nuclear weapons would motivate nations to accept a series of restraints that would move the world, step-by-step, toward the total elimination of nuclear weapons. In our article of March 7, 2011, we asked: "Does the world want to continue to bet its survival on continued good fortune with a growing number of nuclear nations and adversaries globally?" We realized that the incidence of errors in nuclear operations is low, but that the risks are extremely high.

In a book I edited with Dr. Sidney Drell, entitled *The Nuclear Enterprise,* we listed the thirty-two "Broken Arrow" incidents that were recorded between 1950 and 1980. These are incidents that jeopardize the safety of US nuclear weapons. Several serious incidents have been reported in the US press very recently. And safety procedures probably are not better in other nuclear-armed nations, to say the least. It would be foolish to entrust the well-being and safety of humanity to a wager that nuclear deterrence can go on forever without any chance of mistakes or errors in judgments.

From the beginning of our series of appeals, my colleagues and I stressed that the world is a complicated place. We highlighted the regional conflicts that would have to be settled. We stressed that a world without nuclear weapons would not be the world as it is, minus nuclear weapons. Steps that will create the conditions for a world without nuclear weapons are essential. Several chapters in this book provide perspectives of the regions where conflicts have driven decisions to acquire nuclear weapons: Northeast Asia, South Asia, and the Middle East. Other chapters deal with the situation in Europe, the cockpit of the Cold War confrontation.

When President Obama took office, he endorsed the goal of a world without nuclear weapons and in a speech in Prague asked for agreement on several implementing steps. One of his prime goals was a new US-Russian treaty that would reduce the numbers of US and Russian warheads below the ceilings mandated in the Strategic Offensive Reductions Treaty of 1992 and in the first START agreement initiated by President Reagan.

Obama's negotiating team succeeded in negotiating a treaty called "New START"; it was ratified by the US Senate in 2010 by a 71–26 vote. It created a new and very effective verification system and mandated a modest reduction in strategic nuclear weapons.

Why has it been so difficult to do these relatively simple things, and what does this tell us about nuclear deterrence and about the goal of a world free of nuclear weapons? It shows that negotiated treaties on cooperative security are inherently difficult to do because they tend to challenge the status quo. This is precisely what Reagan and Gorbachev set out to do. They succeeded because they provided strong leadership and because their people were ready for change.

Nuclear weapons were, and are, the gravest threat to humanity's survival. Their effect in preventing wars has been overrated and reports of the damage they cause tend to be brushed aside. New studies show the major impact of their use on the climate and agriculture beyond all the other effects that we knew about previously. To depend on nuclear deterrence indefinitely into the future, especially when other means of deterrence are available, is foolhardy. On December 7, 2014, Pope Francis sent a letter to a conference in Vienna on the humanitarian impact of nuclear weapons. He wrote that "nuclear deterrence and the threat of mutually assured destruction cannot be the basis for an ethics of fraternity and peaceful coexistence among peoples and states. The youth of today and tomorrow deserve far more."

The world has lately taken a turn for the worse with one result being a rising threat of nuclear proliferation. Here at Stanford University's Hoover Institution, we take pride in what we have done to rekindle the flame of hope that burned so brightly at Reykjavik in 1986. In 1996 and again in 2006, we convened conferences commemorating the 1986 Reykjavik meeting. In January 2007, Secretary Kissinger, Secretary Perry, Senator Nunn, and I wrote and published the first of several articles that called for a world without nuclear weapons. The public response in the United States and abroad was swift and enthusiastic. It was a moment in history when people around the world obviously hungered for precisely that inspiration, for that infusion of hope. We cannot allow that moment to be squandered.

GEORGE P. SHULTZ
The Thomas W. and Susan B. Ford
Distinguished Fellow
Hoover Institution, Stanford University
Stanford, California

Acknowledgments

The text of this book benefited enormously from the work of our copy editor, Barbara Egbert, who has a remarkable gift for finding felicitous ways to express complex ideas. Barbara Arellano, the managing editor, was an invaluable source of advice regarding the realities of bringing a book to the point of publication and faced every impossible requirement with good cheer and workable solutions. The production editor certainly lived up to his title: Marshall Blanchard's capacity to keep track of the details of complicated editorial issues thrown at him every day, combined with a clear grasp of the total picture, enabled him to produce a high-quality book from a manuscript in what must be record time. Jennifer Navarrette, our design expert, used her artistic skills to give us a book cover that captures graphically a major concern of this book—humanity's stewardship of the earth. Summer Tokash, program coordinator at Hoover, helped us launch this project in 2012 with her leadership in organizing a conference on the themes developed in this book. To all of these outstanding partners in this enterprise, the editors extend their heartfelt thanks.

It also needs to be said that each and every one of the brilliant people who contributed their knowledge, their insights, their judgments, and their writing skills to this book were unusually cooperative and clearly dedicated to the accurate and nuanced expression of their analyses of the nuclear issues before us. We will always be grateful to them.

Introduction to Part One

"Deterrence in the Age of Nuclear Proliferation" was the title of an article published in the *Wall Street Journal* on March 7, 2011. It was written by George P. Shultz (one of the co-editors of this volume) together with William J. Perry, Henry A. Kissinger, and Sam Nunn. That title could also be applied to Part One of this book and, in a sense, to the book as a whole because we intend to explore how nuclear deterrence should be understood seventy years after the first nuclear explosions. Fundamentally, as was asserted in "Deterrence in the Age of Nuclear Proliferation," nuclear deterrence has three elements:

- It is importantly psychological, depending on calculations for which there is no historical experience. It is therefore precarious.
- It is devastating. An unrestrained nuclear exchange between superpowers could destroy civilized life as we know it in days.
- Mutual assured destruction raises enormous inhibitions against employing the weapons.

The judgment expressed in this article was that "from 1945 to 1991, America and the Soviet Union were diligent, professional, but also lucky that nuclear weapons were never used." And a question was posed: "Does the world want to continue to bet its survival on continued good fortune with a growing number of nuclear nations and adversaries globally?"

In many regions of the world, neighbors are seen as enemies, memories of war remain a vivid presence in the public mind, and armed conflict is an imminent possibility and an ever-present fear.

In such places, nuclear weapons are seen as agents of safety or as instruments of oppression, depending on whether or not one's nation possesses them. The United States, fortunately, is not in that position. But the view that nuclear deterrence is crucial to the safety of the nation is commonplace among Americans, as well. Americans have in their collective consciousness a vision of a long and bloody war ended by the use of two atomic bombs and of a World War III forestalled by the judicious threat of mutual assured destruction.

Behind these popular judgments lies an elaborate rationale for the existence of nuclear weapons.

Confronted unexpectedly with a new weapon that promised incredible destruction if ever used in warfare, the world's major powers—and, first of all, the United States—were forced to develop ideas that would justify the production, deployment, and possible use of such weapons. Many of these ideas were derived from earlier theories about the psychological effects of attacks from the air. Others simply hypothesized how nations should react when faced with the possibility of nuclear devastation.

Gradually, it became the accepted truth that:

- Nuclear weapons deterred war between those major nations that possessed them, like the United States and the USSR.
- Nuclear weapons wielded benevolently in defense of allies would prevent an increase in the numbers of nuclear-weapon states.
- Nuclear weapons prevented conventional war, at least between those states that possessed them.

Although not a part of deterrence thinking, a prevalent theory was that nuclear weapons bestowed prestige on nations that possessed them and guaranteed them a seat at the "high table."

In Part One of this book, deterrence theories developed in the Cold War are challenged. In the first chapter, a skeptical scholar asks for evidence that these theories are really valid and questions the added value which nuclear weapons may bring to deterrence provided by other means.

The next two chapters review the utility of nuclear weapons. Using American experience as evidence, chapter 2 emphasizes the fundamental importance of the political context in determining the possibilities for changes in national policies regarding deterrence and especially for changes in the purposes of a nuclear arsenal. Challenges to the status quo are rare but one of them, put forward by President Reagan and General Secretary Gorbachev, led to the end of the Cold War and to a sharp decline in the global holdings of nuclear weapons. Hopes that nuclear weapons could be eliminated were raised by this experience but the persistence of faith in the power of nuclear deterrence remains. Nevertheless, the utility of nuclear weapons as a deterrent has a very limited scope, as is also explored in chapter 2.

Chapter 3 describes near misses and close calls in managing nuclear arsenals. Considering the large role luck has played in averting deadly nuclear accidents, a realist concludes that there is a strong case— particularly for the United States—for a world without nuclear weapons.

Readers will judge for themselves how convincing the case is for reduced reliance on nuclear weapons. What is indisputable is that there is a clear need to reexamine notions from the Cold War, or an even more distant past, which no longer fit present circumstances.

CHAPTER 1   # A Bet Portrayed as a Certainty: Reassessing the Added Deterrent Value of Nuclear Weapons

Benoît Pelopidas

"Concepts, first employed to make things intelligible, are clung to often when they make them unintelligible."

William James[1]

The Argument

A world free of nuclear weapons has been seen as an exercise in utopian dreaming.[2] It took the credentials of realists like Secretaries Shultz, Perry, and Kissinger and Senator Nunn to bring this goal back to the front of the

---

1. William James, "The compounding of consciousness," in *The Writings of William James: A Comprehensive Edition,* ed. J. J. McDermott (Chicago: University of Chicago Press, 1977), 560. (Original work published in 1909.)

2. Harold Brown and John Deutch, "The Nuclear Disarmament Fantasy," *Wall Street Journal,* November 19, 2007; Harold Brown, "New Nuclear Realities," *The Washington Quarterly* 31, no. 1 (Winter 2007–2008). This framing of the discussion in terms of reality versus utopia or fantasy is topical and can be found in most countries. In the French case, for example, one of the leading articles against this goal was Tiphaine de Champchesnel, "Un monde sans armes nucléaires. L'utopie du zéro" (A World without Nuclear Weapons: The Utopia of Zero), *French Yearbook of International Relations,* vol. 11, 2010. This builds on my op-ed, "Why nuclear realism is unrealistic," *Bulletin of the Atomic Scientists,* September 26, 2013.

US political scene.[3] But framing the discussion in terms of utopia versus reality is deceptive because in actuality both supporters and critics of this goal hold to a vision of the world as they think it ought to be. On the one hand, setting a goal of a world without nuclear weapons while there are still approximately seventeen thousands of them in the world today is clearly ambitious.[4] On the other hand, those who reject this goal and want to continue to rely on the threat of nuclear retaliation have to assume that this strategy will work perfectly until the end of days.[5] There is no third future.[6] Either nuclear weapons remain in numbers higher than necessary to create a global-scale disaster and we have to rely on deterrence and hope for the best or we reach very low numbers or zero and the issue then will be to make sure that they are not rebuilt. Even if a

---

3. Martin Senn and Christoph Elhardt, "Bourdieu and the bomb: Power, language and the doxic battle over the value of nuclear weapons," *European Journal of International Relations* 20, no. 2 (June 2014): 316–340.

4. See Ploughshares Fund's report based on the compiled estimates of Hans Kristensen and Robert Norris for the *Bulletin of the Atomic Scientists,* December 2012, http://www.ploughshares.org/sites/default/files/resources/Stockpile-Report-082814.pdf.

5. We are much more demanding with nuclear weapons used for deterrence than we are with any other technology: they are not allowed to fail once if failure means the launch of a nuclear weapon. Moreover, proponents of nuclear deterrence expect the strategy of deterrence to work forever. It is worth repeating that the original proponents of nuclear deterrence combined with a focus on sovereign states saw this as a "tentative, second-best, and temporary" solution. See Daniel Deudney, *Bounding Power: Republican Security Theory from the Polis to the Global Village* (Princeton: Princeton University Press, 2007), 247.

6. A third future would contemplate the breaking of the so-called nuclear taboo and the conventionalization of the use of nuclear weapons. It would not only require that the weapons are used but that this use leads to a move away from deterrence toward preventive war as a strategy. This is only one possible consequence of the use of nuclear weapons and, so far, it is not considered likely. See Mark Fitzpatrick, "The World After: Proliferation, Deterrence and Disarmament if the Nuclear Taboo is Broken," Institut Français des Relations Internationales, Proliferation Paper 31 (Spring 2009); and George H. Quester, *Nuclear First Strike: Consequences of a Broken Taboo* (Baltimore: Johns Hopkins University Press, 2006).

credible missile defense system could be built, it would not constitute a third future; it would just be another parameter in the choice between these two futures.[7]

Proponents of a world without nuclear weapons use the rhetoric of only two possible futures: either getting to zero or nuclear proliferation.[8] But getting to very low numbers versus trusting nuclear deterrence forever reflects a more fundamental truth. This depiction of future choices does not make any assumption about the pace of proliferation or the connection between nuclear disarmament and nuclear proliferation.

If the only two available futures are getting to zero (or very low numbers) and relying on luck forever, which future ought to be realized? This is not a question of realism or utopia. It is a question of political choice: we either wager on perpetual luck or we wager on the ability of people to adjust to new international environments. Which future do you choose as a goal before putting your forces into the battle to "bring the 'is' closer to the 'ought'"?[9] Maybe the proponents of nuclear deterrence assume that a

---

7. The current projects about missile defense do not intend to replace nuclear deterrence but to complement it, contrary to President Ronald Reagan's original idea. So even if a credible missile-defense system could be built, the reliance on nuclear deterrence would still exist. And the jury is still out on whether missile defense would facilitate the elimination of nuclear weapons. A good approach to this debate can be found in Tom Sauer, *Eliminating Nuclear Weapons: The Role of Missile Defense* (New York: Columbia University Press, 2011).

8. A recent example of this common argument can be found in Scott Sagan, "A call for global nuclear disarmament," *Nature* 487, (July 5, 2012): 31. He writes, "The choice is . . . between a world free of nuclear weapons or one with many more nuclear states."

9. This is George Shultz's expression in Harry's Last Lecture on May 19, 2009, at Stanford University: "The power of the ought," borrowing the title of Max Kampelman's presentation for the twentieth anniversary of the Reykjavik Summit on October 11, 2006, at the Hoover Institution. See also Steven P. Andreasen, "Introduction: Closing the Gap Between the 'I' and the 'Ought,'" in *Reykjavik Revisited: Steps Toward a World Free of Nuclear Weapons,* ed. George P. Shultz, Steven P. Andreasen, Sidney D. Drell, and James E. Goodby (Stanford: Hoover Institution Press, 2008).

civilization-destroying disaster will happen before nuclear weapons are used, so that their priorities lie elsewhere, but this bet is not made explicit or maybe they imply that future nuclear weapons use is inevitable and can be limited. Those are debatable assumptions which should be made explicit and become part of the conversation. Once this is done and the proponents of nuclear deterrence acknowledge the fundamental problem of global nuclear vulnerability, the burden of proof will be shared more equally and the ethical and political questions about which future we want to strive for will be fruitfully reopened.

The Case for Nuclear Deterrence

In this paper, I address three of the most frequently used arguments for maintaining a significant measure of dependence for international security on nuclear deterrence both globally and regionally:[10]

1. Nuclear weapons have deterred great powers from waging war against each other, so a world without nuclear weapons will lead to, or at least might encourage, great-power war.
2. The US nuclear umbrella has deterred nuclear proliferation, so the reduction of the US nuclear arsenal will undermine the credibility of US extended deterrence and create additional incentives for nuclear proliferation.
3. Nuclear weapons have deterred other powers from invading the territory of those states that possess nuclear weapons and thus

---

10. A fourth objection I do not address here would emphasize that nuclear weapons are an incomparable instrument for coercive diplomacy. Todd S. Sechser and Matthew Fuhrmann convincingly rebut this objection in a recent study showing that nuclear weapons do not provide more leverage than conventional weapons in crisis situations. See "Crisis Bargaining and Nuclear Blackmail," *International Organization* 67, no. 1 (January 2013): 173–195.

leaders of countries with relatively weak conventional capabilities will keep their weapons as an equalizer. A version of this argument focuses on dictatorial regimes or "rogue states" whose very existence depends on their having nuclear weapons.

I argue that none of these arguments holds.

These three arguments for acquiring and keeping nuclear arsenals rest on the power of these weapons to deter an action, whether a great-powers war, nuclear proliferation, or invasion of and regime change in weaker nations. But deterrence of such an action is most often based on the credibility of a set of national capabilities that include all the non-nuclear assets of a nation, including its credibility as an ally. Therefore, deterrence should not be identified with nuclear weapons and defined by them as has become the habit, almost unconsciously.[11] The *added* deterrent value of nuclear weapons,[12] rather than their deterrent value per se, has to be reexamined, keeping in mind that conventional weapons and other factors (economic, as an example) can have a deterrent effect with a much higher credibility of actual use.[13]

After showing that these arguments are not as convincing as their frequency suggests, I will delineate opportunities which advocates for a nuclear-free world should exploit on their way to advancing their goal, based on the decoupling of nuclear weapons and deterrence.

---

11. Patrick Morgan and George Quester remind us that the concept of deterrence predates the invention of nuclear weapons and show how mutual nuclear deterrence as we know it was not codified before the late 1950s and early 1960s. See "How History and the Geopolitical Context Shape Deterrence" in *Deterrence: Its Past and Future,* ed. George P. Shultz, Sidney D. Drell, and James E. Goodby (Stanford: Hoover Institution Press, 2011).

12. This builds on Steven P. Lee's notion of the "marginal deterrent value" of nuclear weapons in *Morality, Prudence, and Nuclear Weapons* (Cambridge, UK: Cambridge University Press, 1993), 132ff.

13. Ibid., 124–129.

One cannot state for certain that great-power war will be more likely in a world without nuclear weapons

The most intimidating critique of the goal of a world free of nuclear weapons is that it would make the world safe for further war among great powers. Its most eloquent proponent was probably Winston Churchill, who warned his fellow citizens: "Be careful above all things not to let go of the atomic weapon until you are sure and more than sure that other means of preserving peace are in your hands."[14] In other words, according to Kenneth Waltz, "abolishing the weapons that have caused sixty-five years of peace would certainly have effects. It would, among other things, make the world safe for the fighting of World War III."[15] This common belief is summarized in the famous October 2009 *Time* magazine article: "Want peace? Give a Nuke the Nobel."[16]

I will show three major flaws in this statement. First, it assumes that we can know for sure what caused peace and neglects several competing hypotheses explaining the absence of great-power wars. Second, it thus assumes that nuclear weapons are either the only, or at least a necessary, cause of great-power peace. Third, it assumes a stark contrast between the world of the last seventy years, which have appeared relatively "peaceful," and a world without nuclear weapons that would be war-prone.

---

14. Quoted by Margaret Thatcher at Lord Mayor's banquet, November 10, 1986, http://www.margaretthatcher.org/document/106512; and most recently by Bruno Tertrais, "The Illogic of Zero," *The Washington Quarterly* 33, no. 2 (April 2010): 136.

15. Kenneth N. Waltz, "The Great Debate," *The National Interest,* September–October 2010, 92.

16. David Von Drehle, "Want peace? Give a Nuke the Nobel," *Time,* October 11, 2009.

The "nuclear peace" is only a risky hypothesis among others

We cannot know for sure what caused the absence of great-power wars over the last seventy years.[17] We are left with dueling counterfactuals and the need to bet and trust.[18] The opponents of the goal of a world without nuclear weapons create a false dichotomy between what we know for a fact and what we hypothesize. On the one hand, they argue, is the hard fact of the nuclear peace; on the other hand are other hypotheses or counterfactual reasonings. But the nuclear peace is not a fact. It is a hypothesis trying to link two observable facts: the existence of nuclear weapons in the world since 1945 and the absence of war between the United States and the Soviet Union during the same period. The fact is that the idea of the nuclear peace and competing explanations share the same status: all are hypotheses, requiring a rerun of the history of the last seventy years without nuclear weapons to see whether war would have broken out. The

17. One might say sixty-six years if the reference point is the Soviet Union acquiring nuclear weapons. The date changes again if delivery vehicles enter the assessment. In any case, the problem here is that high subjective confidence is not a good indicator of validity and that experts are not rewarded for admitting the limits of validity of their knowledge—quite the opposite. Daniel Kahneman, *Thinking, Fast and Slow* (New York: Farrar, Straus, and Giroux, 2011), chap. 20 and pp. 262–263.

18. The social science literature testing this only reaches probabilistic conclusions that are irrelevant in a realm in which one failure would be intolerable. Robert Rauchhaus confirms, for example, that possession of nuclear weapons by multiple parties to a crisis makes them less likely to enter a crisis, in "Evaluating the Nuclear Peace Hypothesis: A Quantitative Approach," *Journal of Conflict Resolution* 53, no. 2 (April 2009): 269. There are three fundamental problems with this type of finding: (1) The validity of such a finding given the limited number of cases we have and the limited duration of the nuclear age; (2) the amount of what we don't know about the past; and, (3) the past's questionable relevance for the future. For further analysis of these points, see James G. March, Lee S. Sproull, and Michal Tamuz, "Learning from Samples of One or Fewer," *Organization Science* 2, no. 1 (February 1991); and Benoît Pelopidas, *Renoncer à l'arme nucléaire: La séduction de l'impossible?* (Giving up Nuclear Weapons Ambitions: The Seduction of the Impossible?) (Paris: Sciences Po University Press, forthcoming).

nuclear peace hypothesis is no less a counterfactual than its rivals.[19] It faces the challenge of proving a negative. In these circumstances, faith in the nuclear peace becomes a bet or a matter of trust.[20]

Moreover, we know that complex and tightly coupled systems like nuclear weapons are doomed to fail eventually, even if the frequency of failure is very low. This is because their complexity and tight coupling don't allow for anticipating and testing of every possible failure.[21] Given this epistemological challenge, which relies ultimately on the trust one puts in one potential cause of peace at the expense of the others and on the expected timing of nuclear versus non-nuclear disasters, at least one question arises: is seventy years a high enough standard of evidence for us to surrender our fate to nuclear weapons forever?[22]

---

19. John Mueller, "Epilogue: Duelling Counterfactuals," in *Cold War Statesmen Confront the Bomb: Nuclear Diplomacy since 1945*, ed. John Lewis Gaddis, Philip H. Gordon, Ernest R. May, and Jonathan Rosenberg (Oxford: Oxford University Press, 1999); and Richard Ned Lebow, *Forbidden Fruit: Counterfactuals and International Relations* (Princeton, NJ: Princeton University Press, 2010), 13.

20. The claim that the nuclear peace hypothesis is true results from a common fallacy which consists in turning a correlation between two variables into a causal relationship. Cognitive psychology shows how common this is given that intuition "automatically and effortlessly identifies causal relations between events, sometimes even when the connection is spurious." Kahneman, *Thinking, Fast and Slow*, 110; see also 75, 114–118.

21. See Charles Perrow, *Normal Accidents: Living with High Risk Technologies* (Princeton, NJ: Princeton University Press, 1999), chap. 2; Scott Sagan, *The Limits of Safety: Organizations, Accidents, and Nuclear Weapons* (Princeton, NJ: Princeton University Press, 1993); and Matthew Rendall, "Nuclear Weapons and Intergenerational Exploitation," *Security Studies* 16, no. 4 (October 2007). Drell and Goodby rightly characterize the view that nuclear deterrence will always work as "an exercise in wishful thinking," in Sidney Drell and James Goodby, "The Reality: A Goal of a World without Nuclear Weapons is Essential," *Washington Quarterly* 31, no. 3 (Summer 2008): 29. This critique was particularly strong in the late 1970s and early 1980s.

22. Assuming validity and reliability is a common mistake psychologists call "the law of small numbers." In our judgments about the validity of claims, we tend to pay more

The limits of nuclear deterrence as a peacemaker[23]

Critics of abolition portray a world without nuclear weapons as war-prone and believe that nuclear weapons are a necessary and sufficient cause for great-power peace. This is only the latest instance of an idea that has repeatedly been proven wrong, since at least 1860: the expectation that the unprecedented destructiveness of a new weapon system and the threat of its use will put an end to war. This was wrong for dynamite, submarines, artillery, smokeless powder, the machine gun, and poison gas.[24] Was nuclear deterrence a necessary and sufficient cause for peace among great powers? Most critics of the idea of a world without nuclear weapons maintain that it was. They argue that the nuclear-armed

---

attention to the content of messages than to information about their reliability. See Daniel Kahneman, *Thinking, Fast and Slow,* chap. 10.

23. The idea of a nuclear peace has been challenged for several years. See Evan Luard, *War in International Society: A Study in International Sociology* (London: I. B. Tauris, 1986), 396; Michael MccGwire, "Nuclear Deterrence," *International Affairs* 82, no. 4 (June 2006): 784; Michael MccGwire, "Deterrence: The Problem, Not the Solution," *International Affairs* 62, no. 1 (Winter 1986); John Mueller, "The Essential Irrelevance of Nuclear Weapons: Stability in the Postwar World," *International Security* 13, no. 2 (Fall 1988); John Vasquez, "The Deterrence Myth: Nuclear Weapons and the Prevention of Nuclear War" in *The Long Postwar Peace: Contending Explanations and Projections,* ed. Charles Kegley (New York: HarperCollins, 1991); Ken Berry, Patricia Lewis, Benoît Pelopidas, Nikolai Sokov, and Ward Wilson, "Delegitimizing Nuclear Weapons: Examining the Validity of Nuclear Deterrence," James Martin Center for Nonproliferation Studies, Monterey Institute of International Studies, May 2010; and Steven Pinker, *The Better Angels of Our Nature: Why Violence Has Declined* (New York: Viking, 2011), 268–278.

24. For a condensed presentation of these arguments, see James Lee Ray, "The Abolition of Slavery and the End of International War," *International Organization* 43, no. 3 (Summer 1989): 429–430. Kenneth Waltz recognizes the exception he is arguing for when he labels nuclear weapons as "the only peacekeeping weapon the world has ever known," in "The Great Debate," 92. The proponents of the previous weapons in the list said the same thing.

states never fought a war against each other.[25] This can now be proven wrong. The 1969 border clash between China and Russia[26] and, more recently, the 1999 Kargil crisis between India and Pakistan show that the conventional wisdom that a nuclear-armed state cannot be attacked is historically inaccurate. Moreover, nuclear-armed states have been attacked by non-nuclear-weapon states on multiple occasions. US troops were attacked by Chinese forces in 1950 in Korea and by Vietnamese forces in the 1960s and 1970s; Israel was attacked by Syria and Egypt in 1973 and by Iraq in 1991; and in 1982, Argentina invaded the British Falkland Islands.[27] This narrows down the claims for nuclear weapons as peacemakers. More importantly, even this narrower claim needs to be reexamined taking into account two facts: (1) avoidance of several nuclear disasters was due to luck and cannot be explained by nuclear deterrence; and (2) deterrence as a strategy has favored more risk-prone strategies and in some cases made war possible instead of preventing it.

Luck is too often taken as a confirmation that nuclear deterrence kept the peace.[28] But luck should not be misread as successful deter-

---

25. Waltz, "The Great Debate"; Bruno Tertrais, "In defense of deterrence," Institut Français des Relations Internationales, Proliferation Paper 39, Fall 2011: 9; Robert Rauchhaus, "Evaluating the Nuclear Peace Hypothesis," 268.

26. David Holloway, "'Czech-mating' China? The Sino-Soviet Crisis of 1969," in *Historie Prožité Minulosti,* ed. Jiří Kocian, Milan Otáhal, and Miroslav Vaněk (Prague: Institute of Contemporary History, 2010).

27. T. V. Paul, *The Tradition of Non-Use of Nuclear Weapons* (Stanford, Stanford University Press, 2009), 145.

28. The argument based on luck is decisive. Indeed, Paul Schroeder, who argued in favor of managing the nuclear danger without abolishing the weapons, recognized this: "If since 1945 only luck had kept the world from nuclear holocaust then one would have to join . . . cries for some drastic action to turn things around." See Paul Schroeder, "Does Murphy's Law Apply to History?" *Wilson Quarterly* 9, no. 1 (1985): 87. I would argue that it is the case even if luck was the only reason why we avoided disaster in one single case. There is no need for luck to be the only cause of non-use of nuclear weapons to justify a call for change in nuclear policy.

rence.[29] More accurately, as Thomas Schelling noted, leaders of nuclear-weapon states can make threats that "leave something to chance"[30]—recognizing that things could spiral out of control and nuclear weapons could be used even if they do not intend to use them—to make those threats more credible. But including luck in a successful deterrence strategy, as if you could control it, is both a conceptual confusion and a retrospective illusion.[31] Luck was on our side this time, but this is not a consequence of purposeful action. For example, during the night of October 26–27, 1962, at the height of the Cuban missile crisis, an American U-2 spy plane strayed into Soviet airspace over the Arctic. Soviet fighter jets scrambled to intercept the U-2 while F-102 interceptors were sent to escort it home and prevent Soviet MIGs from freely entering US airspace. Given the circumstances, the F-102s conventional air-to-air missiles had been replaced with nuclear-tipped ones and their pilots could decide to use nuclear weapons. According to Scott Sagan in *The Limits of Safety*, "the interceptors at Galena were armed with the nuclear Falcon air-to-air missiles and, under existing safety rules, were authorized to carry the weapons in full readiness condition in any 'active air defense'

29. On this problem, see Benoît Pelopidas, "We all lost the Cuban missile crisis," in *The Cuban Missile Crisis: A Critical Reappraisal,* ed. Len Scott and R. Gerald Hughes (London: Routledge, 2015).

30. Thomas C. Schelling, *The Strategy of Conflict* (Cambridge, MA: Harvard University Press, 1960), chap. 8.

31. Because past crises did not escalate and turn into nuclear war, we are prone to what psychologists call "hindsight bias" or "narrative fallacy," which retrospectively will create a false causal relation between crisis management and the favorable outcome of the crisis which avoided nuclear war. Some of these consequences could only be known retrospectively; claiming hindsight is an overstatement. We are also likely to believe that we can learn more than we should from the favorable outcome of crises because we misunderstand the role of luck. See Kahneman, *Thinking, Fast and Slow,* chap. 19. On this confusion, see Benoît Pelopidas, "The theorist who leaves nothing to chance," paper presented at the 2014 International Studies Association conference, Toronto, March 29, 2014.

mission."[32] Fortunately, the spy plane turned back and the Soviet jets held their fire.[33] There are many other instances in which deterrence cannot account for favorable outcomes.[34] Robert McNamara was direct about the role of luck during the Cuban missile crisis:

> According to former Soviet military leaders, at the height of the crisis, Soviet forces in Cuba possessed 162 nuclear warheads, including at least 90 tactical warheads. [And the United States. was not aware of that at the time.] At about the same time, Cuban President Fidel Castro asked the Soviet ambassador to Cuba to send a cable to Soviet Premier Nikita Khrushchev stating that Castro urged him to counter a U.S. attack with a nuclear response. Clearly, there was a high risk that in the face of a U.S. attack, which many in the U.S. government were prepared to recommend to President Kennedy, the Soviet forces in Cuba would have decided to use their nuclear weapons rather than lose them. Only a few years ago did we learn that the four Soviet submarines trailing the U.S. Naval vessels near Cuba each carried torpedoes with nuclear warheads. Each of the sub commanders had the authority to launch his torpedoes. The situation was even more frightening because, as the lead commander recounted to me, the subs were out of communication with their Soviet bases, and they continued their patrols for four days after Khrushchev announced the withdrawal of the missiles from Cuba. The lesson, if it had not been clear before, was made so at a conference on the crisis held in Havana in 1992. . . . Near the end of that meeting, I asked Castro whether he would have recommended that Khrushchev use the weapons in the

---

32. Sagan, *The Limits of Safety*, 137.

33. Ibid., 135-138.

34. One of the most recent lists can be found in Martin E. Hellman, "How Risky is Nuclear Optimism?" *Bulletin of the Atomic Scientists* 67, no. 2 (2011). See also Michael Dobbs, *One Minute to Midnight: Kennedy, Khrushchev, and Castro on the Brink of Nuclear War* (New York: Alfred A. Knopf, 2008), 303ff.

face of a U.S. invasion, and if so, how he thought the United States would respond. "We started from the assumption that if there was an invasion of Cuba, nuclear war would erupt," Castro replied. "We were certain of that. . . . [W]e would be forced to pay the price that we would disappear." He continued, "Would I have been ready to use nuclear weapons? Yes, I would have agreed to the use of nuclear weapons." And he added, "If Mr. McNamara or Mr. Kennedy had been in our place, and had their country been invaded, or their country was going to be occupied . . . I believe they would have used tactical nuclear weapons." I *hope* that President Kennedy and I would not have behaved as Castro suggested we would have. . . . Had we responded in a similar way the damage to the United States would have been unthinkable. But human beings are fallible [emphasis added].[35]

This fascinating account shows how lack of information, misperception, and ideology could have led to disaster if we had not been lucky. But false information, lack of information, and misperceptions were not the only reason why luck was the decisive cause of the positive outcome of the Cuban missile crisis. Limits of safety, limits of command and control, and organizational problems also have to be taken into account. As Scott Sagan wrote:

Many serious safety problems, which could have resulted in an accidental or unauthorized detonation or a serious provocation to the Soviet government, occurred during the crisis. None of these incidents led to inadvertent escalation or an accidental war. All of them, however, had the potential to do so. President Kennedy may well have

---

35. Robert S. McNamara, "Apocalypse Soon," *Foreign Policy* 148 (May–June 2005): 33. Dean Acheson proposed this interpretation as early as 1969. He explained the positive outcome of the Cuban missile crisis as due to "plain dumb luck." He explained the positive outcome in *Esquire,* February 1969, 76.

been prudent. He did *not*, however, have unchallenged final control over U.S. nuclear weapons.[36]

Most-recent studies show that sloppy practices in nuclear weapons management have occurred at all levels of decision-makers, leaders, nuclear safety and security teams, and top-level military personnel in most nuclear-weapon states. They also show the limits of learning from past sloppy practices. Confidence in perfect nuclear safety is still a matter of wishing for the best and relying on luck.[37] One telling example of this occurred at Minot Air Force Base in North Dakota in 2007. This offers a well-documented case of multiple sloppy practices and suggests the limits of learning after the incident was identified. On August 29–30, 2007, six US nuclear-armed cruise missile warheads were mistakenly flown to Barksdale Air Force Base in Louisiana. They had been placed by mistake under the wings of a B-52; the weapons had not been guarded appropriately during a thirty-six-hour period. Had the plane experienced any problems in flight, the crew would not have followed the proper emergency procedures.[38] After this widely publicized case of sloppy

---

36. Sagan, *The Limits of Safety*, 116.

37. Eric Schlosser, *Command and Control: Nuclear Weapons, the Damascus Accident, and the Illusion of Safety* (New York: Allen Lane, 2013); and Patricia Lewis, Heather Williams, Benoît Pelopidas, and Sasan Aghlani, "Too Close for Comfort: Cases of near nuclear use and options for policy," Chatham House, Royal Institute of International Affairs, April 2014, http://www.chathamhouse .org/sites/files/chathamhouse/home/chatham/public_html/sites/default/files /20140428TooCloseforComfortNuclearUseLewisWilliamsPelopidasAghlani.pdf.

38. This included jettisoning the cruise missiles if necessary. This involved sloppy practices at multiple levels. First, the original movement plan was changed and this change was not reported in the documents produced for the internal coordination process at Minot. "As a consequence, one of the originally scheduled pylons of cruise missiles had not been prepared for tactical ferry. [Second] When the breakout crew accessed the storage facility, they did not properly verify the status of the weapons in the facility as required by established procedure and they failed to note that the missiles on one of the pylons on their internal work document still contained nuclear warheads. Although procedure requires three subsequent verifications (by

practices,[39] US Secretary of Defense Robert Gates emphasized the need for responsibility in handling nuclear weapons: "The problems were the result of a long-standing slide in the Service's nuclear stewardship. . . . For your part, you must never take your duties lightly. There is simply no room for error. Yours is the most sensitive mission in the entire US military."[40] Change and improvement were supposed to follow, but even on the base where the incident took place and where the Secretary of Defense came to give his speech, it was necessary to repeat the order to leave no room for error. In April 2013, one officer from the 91st Missile Wing at the same Air Force Base in North Dakota was punished for sleeping on the job while having the blast door open behind him. (Sleeping wasn't prohibited on a twenty-four-hour shift, but leaving the blast door open was.) He was one of two missile officers sanctioned that year for such a fault and he told his superiors that it wasn't the first time.[41] Air Force officers told the Associated Press that such violations of the safety procedures had happened more often than just in the two documented cases.[42] The limits of safety, the limits of command and control, and the persistence of sloppy practices even in the US nuclear forces suggest that the role of luck is likely to have been even more important than we can document here.

---

three different groups) of the payload installed in those cruise missiles, those procedures were not followed." The quotes for the account of this particular accident are taken from the unclassified account available in the February 2008 report from the Defense Science Board Permanent Task Force on Nuclear Weapons Surety, entitled *Report on the Unauthorized Movement of Nuclear Weapons.*

39. George P. Shultz, William J. Perry, Henry A. Kissinger, and Sam Nunn, "Toward a Nuclear-Free World," *Wall Street Journal,* January 15, 2008, http://www.nuclearsecurityproject.org/publications/toward-a-nuclear-free-world.

40. Global Security Newswire, "Gates stresses nuclear responsibility at Minot Air Force Base," December 2, 2008, http://www.nti.org/gsn/article/gates-stresses-nuclear -responsibility-at-minot-air-force-base/.

41. Robert Burns, "Officers In Charge Of Nuclear Missiles Left Blast Door Open: Air Force Officials," *Associated Press,* October 22, 2013.

42. Ibid.

There are no reliable records of nuclear weapons accidents or close calls in most nuclear-weapon states.

Another reason why nuclear weapons cannot be considered as a necessary and sufficient cause for peace among the great powers is that they have encouraged more risk-prone behavior which, in some cases, made war possible. In other words, nuclear deterrence can require leaders to get closer to the brink of disaster to make their deterrent threat more credible. "The most recent research has confirmed this argument and established that a significant deterrent effect against conventional conflict requires regional states to adopt an asymmetric escalation posture, which puts pressure on the command and control system and increases the risk of accidental use."[43] One case in which nuclear deterrence arguably favored more risk-prone behavior is Kennedy's strategy of deterrence in 1961. After Khrushchev's ultimatum on Berlin, Kennedy hoped to deter him from escalating the crisis. So he emphasized, both privately and publicly, US nuclear superiority and his willingness to conduct a nuclear first strike. The result was an increase in the tension between the two countries in the months leading to the Cuban missile crisis.[44] Longer term, the strategies of deterrence developed by the two superpowers from the late 1950s to October 1962 created a spiral of escalation in which the deployment of forces or their overestimation for the sake of deterrence led to an

---

43. Vipin Narang, "What Does It Take to Deter? Regional Power Nuclear Postures and International Conflict," *Journal of Conflict Resolution* 57, no. 3 (2012).

44. Richard Ned Lebow and Janice Gross Stein, *We All Lost the Cold War* (Princeton, NJ: Princeton University Press, 1994), chap. 2; see also Vojtech Mastny, "Introduction: new perspectives on the Cold War Alliance" and "Imagining War in Europe: Soviet Strategic Planning," in *War Plans and Alliances in the Cold War: Threat Perceptions in the East and West*, ed. Vojtech Mastny, Sven G. Holtsmark, and Andreas Wenger (New York: Routledge, 2006), 3, 38. A recent review of the historical evidence on the Soviet side of the crisis is Sergey Radchenko, "The Cuban Missile Crisis: Assessment of New, and Old, Russian Sources," *International Relations* 26, no. 3 (September 2012).

increased threat perception.[45] It is interesting to note that this risk-prone behavior, caused partly by the strategy of nuclear deterrence, does not come only from a high risk perception. For instance, the crisis between the United States and the Soviet Union after the 1973 war in the Middle East was based on a low risk perception and faith in nuclear deterrence. Convinced that its adversary would not risk a nuclear escalation, each nation sought unilateral advantages that exacerbated the crisis.[46]

More importantly, a relationship of mutual nuclear deterrence at the strategic level creates opportunities for low-intensity conflicts. Even worse than the 1973 Middle East confrontation was the Kargil crisis between India and Pakistan in 1999, which killed a thousand soldiers. The nuclear arsenals of both countries and the beliefs associated with them contributed to the crisis instead of preventing it. Contrary to the optimistic readings of the proponents of deterrence who focus on the fact that there was no escalation[47] or simply do not count it as a war,[48] the Pakistani generals thought that their nuclear arsenal gave them the ability to send troops beyond the Indian border without risking retaliation from India.[49] They were

---

45. Dominic D. P. Johnson, *Overconfidence and War: The Havoc and Glory of Positive Illusions* (Cambridge, MA: Harvard University Press, 2004), chap. 5; Richard Ned Lebow, "Conventional vs. Nuclear Deterrence: Are the Lessons Tranferable?" *Journal of Social Issues* 43, no. 4 (1987): 179.

46. Lebow and Stein, *We All Lost the Cold War,* chap. 10 and 13.

47. Tertrais, "In defense of deterrence," 9, note 5.

48. Scott Sagan and Alexander Montgomery focus on this fallacy and its effects in "The Perils of Predicting Proliferation," *Journal of Conflict Resolution* 53, no. 2 (April 2009): 304, 321–322.

49. S. Paul Kapur, "Revisionist ambitions, conventional capabilities, and nuclear instability: Why Nuclear South Asia is not like Cold War Europe," in *Inside Nuclear South Asia,* ed. Scott Sagan (Stanford: Stanford University Press, 2009); Timothy Hoyt, "Kargil: the nuclear dimension," in *Asymmetric Warfare in South Asia: The Causes and Consequences of the Kargil Conflict,* ed. Peter Lavoy (Cambridge, UK: Cambridge University Press, 2009), 144.

wrong, and war broke out.[50] Before getting nuclear weapons, they had never attempted such an aggression.

The "long peace" was not that peaceful . . . a world without nuclear weapons will not be unprecedentedly war-prone

For nuclear deterrence advocates, the Cold War is portrayed as the "long peace" whereas a world without nuclear weapons would be war-prone. Both sides of this statement seem to be wildly exaggerated. On the one hand, the "long peace" was neither all that peaceful nor all that exceptional. It existed only in a limited space, and proxy wars killed several million people during the Cold War.[51] It was not that exceptional if defined as the avoidance of an all-out great-power war, which has been a pretty rare event.[52] On the other hand, a world without nuclear weapons may well be much less war-prone than people assume. In a widely quoted article, Schelling wrote: "One can propose that another war on the scale of the 1940s is less to worry about than anything nuclear. But it might give pause to reflect that the world of 1939 was utterly free of nuclear

---

50. S. Paul Kapur shows that the nuclearization of India and Pakistan increased the frequency and intensity of conflicts between the two countries. See Kapur, *Dangerous Deterrent: Nuclear Weapons, Proliferation and Conflict in South Asia* (Stanford: Stanford University Press, 2007), 122–127; Kapur, this volume. For a contrarian position and Kapur's defense, see Sumit Ganguly and S. Paul Kapur, *India, Pakistan, and the Bomb: Debating Nuclear Stability in South Asia* (New York: Columbia University Press, 2010).

51. Odd Arne Westad, *The Global Cold War: Third World Interventions and the Making of Our Times* (Cambridge, UK: Cambridge University Press, 2005). Cold War studies are partly responsible for maintaining this illusion of the long peace. As Holger Nehring notes: "While attracting attention from many different fields and profiting from interdisciplinary inspiration, Cold War studies . . . might have lost sight of one of the key elements of the 'Cold War': its war-like character." See Nehring, "What Was the Cold War?" *English Historical Review* 127, no. 527 (August 2012): 923, 925.

52. Randolph M. Siverson and Michael D. Ward, "The Long Peace: A Reconsideration," *International Organization* 56, no. 3 (Summer 2002).

weapons, yet they were not only produced, they were invented, during war itself and used with devastating effect."[53]

There are at least three counter-arguments to the idea of a radical contrast between the "long nuclear peace" and a war-prone world without nuclear weapons.

The first: yes, abolishing nuclear weapons is not abolishing war. However, the ability to reconstitute nuclear weapons would create a "virtual deterrent" effect.[54] Moreover, in a world without nuclear weapons, the support for measures to prevent or respond to a breakout would, arguably, be much greater than it is today.[55] Leaders in this world would probably remember Schelling's story and learn from it. As Sagan said, "In a nuclear-free world, the former nuclear-weapons states would have far stronger *mutual* incentives to punish and reverse any new state's decision to acquire atomic bombs. Ironically, it is precisely because nuclear-weapons states have such large arsenals today that they sometimes succumb to the temptation to accept new proliferators. In a disarmed world, such complacency would be more obviously imprudent."[56]

The second counter-argument is included in the quote of Schelling's work: yes, another war of the size of 1940 is less to worry about than anything nuclear. This is because of the speed of the destruction caused by a nuclear war, which would be much more difficult to stop if it ever

---

53. Thomas C. Schelling, "A World without Nuclear Weapons?" *Daedalus* 138, no. 4 (Fall 2009): 125, 127.

54. The original idea of "virtual arsenals" or "weaponless deterrence" comes from Jonathan Schell in his book *The Abolition* (New York: Alfred A. Knopf, 1984). See also Sidney D. Drell and Raymond Jeanloz, "Nuclear Deterrence in a World without Nuclear Weapons"; and Christopher A. Ford, "Nuclear Weapons Reconstitution and its Discontents: Challenges of 'Weaponless Deterrence'" and David Holloway, "Deterrence and Enforcement in a World Free of Nuclear Weapons," in *Deterrence: Its Past and Future.*

55. Holloway, "Deterrence and Enforcement," 342; and Sagan, "The Great Debate," 90.

56. Sagan, "The Great Debate," 90.

started, and of the duration of the radiation effects that would follow the war if anyone survived.

The third counter-argument would be that a world without nuclear weapons will not be achieved overnight, so changes that would happen between now and then need to be considered. One is a macro-trend toward a steady decline in the number of armed conflicts between states, at least since 1945, a trend that became stronger after 1989.[57] Then comes the "Norman Angell rebuttal,"[58] suggesting that four years before the most destructive war man had ever experienced, theoreticians also saw the end of war and an increase in economic interdependence that was supposed to make war too costly. It is also true that the idea of the changing character of war has appeared every one or two generations in the last two centuries.[59] However, the trend is observed by most analysts even if they disagree on the causes.[60] Another interesting trend is the recognition that UN peace-keeping operations are more successful than previously

---

57. John Mueller, *Retreat from Doomsday: The Obsolescence of Major War* (New York: Basic Books, 1990); Joshua S. Goldstein, *Winning the War on War: The Decline of Armed Conflict Worldwide* (New York: Dutton Books, 2011); Steven Pinker, *The Better Angels of Our Nature: Why Violence Has Declined* (New York: Viking, 2011); Richard Ned Lebow, *Why Nations Fight: Past and Future Motives for War* (Cambridge, UK: Cambridge University Press, 2010); Christopher J. Fettweis, *Dangerous Times? The International Politics of Great Power Peace* (Washington, DC: Georgetown University Press, 2009); Azar Gat, "The Changing Character of War," in *The Changing Character of War*, ed. Hew Strachan and Sibylle Scheipers (Oxford: Oxford University Press, 2011), 44; John Horgan, *The End of War* (New York: McSweeney's, 2012),133–137.

58. Norman Angell was an English journalist and Labor Member of Parliament who argued in 1909 that a major war would be futile and would not pay, due to major economic interdependence among nations. His book, *Europe's Optical Illusion,* was republished in 1910 under the title *The Great Illusion: A Study of Military Power and National Advantage* (London: G. P. Putnam's sons, 1910) and often retrospectively portrayed as claiming that World War I was impossible.

59. Gat, "The Changing Character of War," 27.

60. The declining trend in the frequency of war among great powers is still visible if you shift the threshold for war from the standard one thousand battle deaths to

thought and rather inexpensive.[61] These are obviously not irreversible—the fear that climate change would reverse this trend and create wars has been expressed widely[62] as well as fear of a war in the Taiwan strait[63]—but they suggest policies to keep this trend downward.

Nuclear proliferation risks are not likely to increase if the size of the US nuclear arsenal decreases[64]

The second key critique of the goal of a world without nuclear weapons is based on the idea that positive nuclear security guarantees, or the so-called "nuclear umbrellas," are necessary to prevent proliferation. Therefore, shrinking the size of the US arsenal would simply decrease the credibility of extended nuclear deterrence and, thus, create additional incentives for nuclear proliferation.[65] If so, getting to zero might not be achievable or desirable, as it would spur proliferation.

---

twenty-five. Andrew Mack, roundtable on Steven Pinker's *The Better Angels of our Nature,* ISA, San Diego, Calif., April 3, 2012.

61. Goldstein, *Winning the War on War;* interview of the author with Joshua S. Goldstein, San Diego, April 4, 2012. He observed that every US household pays $700 a month to fund the military, including pensions, and only $2 a month for UN peacekeepers, who are chronically underfunded and suffer from a lack of resources.

62. A famous voice is Colin S. Gray, *Another Bloody Century: Future Warfare* (London: Weidenfeld & Nicolson, 2005), 82–83.

63. Lebow, *Why Nations Fight,* 223.

64. Some of the arguments in this section will also appear in Benoît Pelopidas, "The Nuclear Straitjacket: American Extended Nuclear Deterrence and Nonproliferation," in *The Future of US Extended Deterrence: NATO and Beyond,* ed. Stéfanie von Hlatky and Andreas Wenger (Washington, DC: Georgetown University Press, forthcoming 2015).

65. Here, by credibility, I mean credibility in the eyes of the protégé/ally and those of the potential attacker. I ignore the technical issue of stockpile reliability as well as that of the confidence of US policymakers in that reliability. On these issues, see Benjamin

The idea that extended nuclear deterrence deters proliferation has been stated in official US policy documents even before the 2001 *Nuclear Posture Review*[66] and has been US official policy at least since then. In December 2008, the Report of the Secretary of Defense Task Force on DoD Nuclear Weapons Management stated, "The United States has extended its nuclear protective umbrella to 30-plus friends and allies as an expression of commitment and common purpose as well as a disincentive for proliferation."[67] On page 7, this report also quotes the 1998 annual defense report stating that "Nuclear forces remain an important disincentive to nuclear, biological, and chemical proliferation." The same idea is expressed in a May 2009 report requested by Congress: "During the Cold War, proliferation was strongly inhibited by the relationships of extended deterrence established by the United States (and also by the Soviet Union)."[68] The May 2009 report to Congress also states that:

> [The United States] must continue to safeguard the interests of its allies as it does so. Their assurance that extended deterrence remains credible and effective may require that the United States retain

Sims and Christopher R. Henke, "Repairing Credibility: Repositioning nuclear weapons knowledge after the Cold War," *Social Studies of Science* 42, no. 3 (June 2012).

66. In a comment on the *Nuclear Posture Review* he has heavily influenced, Keith Payne wrote: "[The United States] extended nuclear deterrence commitments— it nuclear umbrella—permit friends and allies to forgo seeking their own independent nuclear capabilities or alternatives. This is perhaps the single most important inhibitor of the pace of global proliferation today." Keith B. Payne, "The Nuclear Posture Review: Setting the Record Straight," *Washington Quarterly* 28, no. 3 (Summer 2005): 148.

67. US Department of Defense, "Report of the Secretary of Defense Task Force on DoD Nuclear Weapons Management, Phase II: Review of the DoD Nuclear Mission, 2008," iv.

68. United States Institute of Peace, *America's Strategic Posture. The Final Report of the Congressional Commission on the Strategic Posture of the United States* (Washington, DC: United States Institute for Peace Press, 2009), 8.

numbers or types of nuclear capabilities that it might not deem necessary if it were concerned only with its own defense.

This idea was expressed quite clearly in a Council on Foreign Relations April 2009 report entitled *US Nuclear Policy:*

> Although the United States does not need nuclear weapons to compensate for conventional military weaknesses, other states are not in a similar position—they may consider acquiring nuclear weapons to deter attacks. The United States has the responsibility to assure allies through extended deterrence commitments. This assurance helps convince many of these allies not to acquire their own nuclear weapons. . . . A related pillar, necessary to maintain the credibility of the U.S. nuclear deterrent for as long as it is needed, is to ensure that the U.S. nuclear arsenal is safe, secure and reliable.[69]

The text of the *Nuclear Posture Review* restates the same two arguments about the role of extended nuclear deterrence—it is meant to reassure allies and in the process deter proliferation:

> The United States will retain the smallest possible nuclear stockpile consistent with our need to deter adversaries, reassure our allies. . . . By maintaining a credible nuclear deterrent, . . . we can reassure our non-nuclear allies and partners worldwide of our security commitments to them and confirm that they do not need nuclear weapons capabilities of their own.[70]

This argument persists because people generalize from a few cases in which a positive nuclear security guarantee actually played a role in the

---

69. Council on Foreign Relations, "US Nuclear Weapons Policy," 2009: 5. These points are reaffirmed on pages 8, 14–16, 81, 90–91.

70. Department of Defense, "Nuclear Posture Review Report," April 2010: 39, 7.

decision not to go for the bomb—Germany, Japan[71]—and because it has not received the careful historical analysis it deserves.[72]

As a critique of this argument, I propose three points:

1. The idea that a decrease in the size of the US nuclear arsenal will lead to a wave of proliferation wrongly assumes the existence of a pressing desire for the bomb waiting for more favorable conditions. This expectation has been proven wrong for several decades.

2. An extended nuclear deterrence guarantee has historically not been a necessary condition for states to give up nuclear-weapon ambitions.

3. The existing studies fail to isolate the role of nuclear weapons among other factors in the security guarantee they discuss. As a consequence, they underestimate the credibility problem of extended nuclear deterrence and overestimate the demand for such a nuclear guarantee, which has been perceived as more threatening than reassuring in important cases.

At the state level, the present and foreseeable demand for nuclear weapons is limited

The argument that without a credible nuclear security guarantee states would have additional incentives to develop their nuclear arsenals

---

71. Daniel Deudney explicitly focuses on these two cases when he makes the argument that the extended nuclear deterrence commitment played a major role in non-proliferation decisions. See Daniel Deudney, "Unipolarity and nuclear weapons," in *International Relations Theory and the Consequences of Unipolarity*, ed. G. John Ikenberry, Michael Mastanduno, and William C. Wohlforth (Cambridge, UK: Cambridge University Press, 2011), 305, 307.

72. David Holloway notes this lack of historical analysis of the role of extended deterrence in what he calls "the proliferation objection" to a world without nuclear weapons in "Deterrence and Enforcement," 353, note 19.

assumes an implicit desire to go for the bomb. It suffers from what I call the nuclear straitjacket. In this perspective, the ultimate security guarantor has to be nuclear. This approach neglects the possibility of a non-nuclear understanding of security. This is a strong bias given that the most generous estimate of the number of states that have ever had nuclear-weapon-related activities totals only forty.[73] Most states, as a matter of fact, have never expressed any interest in developing nuclear weapons even if academic and governmental forecasts have announced cascades of proliferation at least since the late 1950s.[74] Moreover, among those states that have had any form of nuclear-weapons-related activities, more have given up before or after building a nuclear arsenal (twenty-nine) than have kept their arsenals (nine).[75] It is worth noting that two recent authoritative analyses reject the idea of a wave of proliferation following the possible acquisition of nuclear weapons by Iran.[76] Moreover, recent studies of the management of nuclear-weapons programs show that, contrary to conventional wisdom, the rate of failure has increased over time and the time

---

73. Details about these numbers can be found in Benoît Pelopidas, "The Oracles of Proliferation: How Experts Maintain a Biased Historical Reading that Limits Policy Innovation," *Nonproliferation Review* 18, no. 1 (March 2011). Forty is the most pessimistic estimate of nuclear-weapons-related activities. See http://thenuclearworld .org/wp-content/uploads/2012/01/Benoit_Pelopidas_oracles_of_proliferation _NPR2011-3.pdf.

74. Ibid.

75. Ibid., 306. (To add up to forty, the list would have to include Iran and Syria.)

76. William Potter, with Gaukhar Mukhatzhanova, eds., *Forecasting Nuclear Proliferation in the 21st Century: A Comparative Perspective, Volume 2* (Stanford, CA: Stanford University Press, 2010); James J. Wirtz and Peter Lavoy, eds., *Over the Horizon Proliferation Threats* (Stanford, CA: Stanford University Press, 2012). These two books cover Argentina, Australia, Brazil, Burma, Egypt, Indonesia, Iran, Japan, Ukraine, South Africa, Taiwan, Turkey, South Korea, Syria, Saudi Arabia, Venezuela, and Vietnam. In the most recent of these two studies, only one case, Saudi Arabia, is considered as very likely to go for the bomb. See James Russell, "Nuclear Proliferation and the Middle East's Security Dilemma: The Case of Saudi Arabia," in *Over the Horizon Proliferation Threats*.

needed to lead a nuclear-weapon program to completion has increased.[77] So the idea that decreasing the size of the US nuclear arsenal would create additional incentives for proliferation underestimates important factors: the lack of desire for these weapons in the first place and the frequency of nuclear reversal in midcourse, on top of the managerial and technological obstacles to developing a nuclear-weapon program, which remain very strong.

Extended nuclear deterrence has neither been necessary nor sufficient to deter proliferation

A positive nuclear security guarantee has not been a necessary or sufficient condition for all states to give up nuclear weapons ambitions. In other words, some states have given up nuclear weapons plans despite the lack of a positive nuclear security guarantee or "nuclear umbrella" (South Africa, Libya, Ukraine, Sweden[78] and all the states that had not

---

77. Jacques Hymans, *Achieving Nuclear Ambitions: Scientists, Politicians, and Proliferation* (Cambridge, UK: Cambridge University Press, 2012).

78. Analysts reluctant to consider Ukraine, Belarus, and Kazakhstan as nuclear-weapon possessors focus on the issues of launch codes, satellites, and testing. Here, I will focus on Ukraine as an example. To be considered as possessing a nuclear arsenal, Ukraine would have needed access to the launch codes for its missiles and would have had to become able to change the targets of that same arsenal. The experts I met agreed that the Ukrainians could have obtained the codes had they been given enough time. (Interview with Robert Nurick, Washington, DC, April 4, 2008; interview with Nikolai Sokov, Monterey, Calif., November 13, 2009.) James E. Goodby mentions a "strong presumption that if [Ukraine] chose to keep the nuclear weapons within its borders, it could have done so." See "Preventive Diplomacy for Nuclear Nonproliferation in the Former Soviet Union," in *Opportunities Missed, Opportunities Seized: Preventive Diplomacy in the Post-Cold War World,* ed. Bruce W. Jentleson (New York: Rowman & Littlefield, 2000), 110. It is true that Ukraine had neither an independent satellite system to monitor missiles nor a testing site, yet Christopher Stevens argues that nuclear warheads would have remained viable without testing until at least 2010, whereupon computerized tests could have been carried out. See Christopher Stevens, "Identity Politics and Nuclear Disarmament: The Case of Ukraine," *Nonproliferation Review* 15, no. 1 (March 2008). He

expressed interest in developing these weapons in the first place) while others have developed nuclear weapons in spite of a nuclear security guarantee (France and Great Britain).[79]

It is true that Ukraine and Libya received some form of security assurances but, in spite of what the Ukrainian leadership said for domestic purposes, the security assurances Ukraine received from Russia, the United Kingdom, and the United States on December 5, 1994, are nowhere close to a promise of extended nuclear deterrence and were ignored by Russia in 2014.[80] Moreover, the results of recent research across cases are contradictory and do not allow us to conclude that any strong relationship exists between a positive nuclear security guarantee and national nuclear-weapons decisions.[81]

---

also points out that US and Russian experts believed that the Ukrainians had the capacity required to ensure the security of nuclear warheads.

79. The complete analysis of those two early cases and their relevance can be found in Pelopidas, "The Nuclear Straitjacket."

80. The memorandum and an analysis of the negotiation can be found in Goodby, "Preventive Diplomacy for Nuclear Nonproliferation," 123–126 and 128–129. [See footnote 78.]

81. The key insights of this body of literature are the inconsistency of the results, the lack of statistically significant correlation between the relationship with a nuclear-armed state and nuclear-weapons-related behavior, and the skepticism of qualitative case studies regarding such a connection. Some studies suggest that a security guarantee offered by a nuclear-armed power has only a limited effect on a state's decision to explore a nuclear weapons option. See Philipp C. Bleek, "Why do states proliferate? Quantitative analysis of the exploration, pursuit, and acquisition of nuclear weapons," in *Forecasting Nuclear Proliferation in the 21st Century: Volume 1, The Role of Theory,* ed. William Potter, with Gaukhar Mukhatzhanova (Stanford, CA: Stanford University Press, 2010), 179–180; Erik Gartzke and Dong-Joon Jo, "Determinants of nuclear weapons proliferation," *Journal of Conflict Resolution* 51, no. 1 (2007); Sonali Singh and Christopher Way, "The correlates of nuclear proliferation: a quantitative test," *Journal of Conflict Resolution* 48, no. 6 (December 2004). After rectifying a methodological problem in Singh and Way, Sagan and Montgomery show that their result was not statistically significant, in "The Perils of Predicting Proliferation." However, Sagan is right to object that these results might be due to selection effects in "The Causes of Nuclear Proliferation," *Annual Review of Political Science* 14

The counter-argument would be to say that even if these conditions were not necessary across cases, it is enough if they were decisive in a few key cases, like Germany and Japan. It is true that German rearmament was a key concern in the post-World War II years and the Germans were suspected of seeking nuclear weapons. Similarly, after the end of the Cold War, the same fear reemerged and the German chancellor Helmut Kohl gave credit to what I called the nuclear straitjacket. He explained that Germany would not develop its own nuclear weapons because it trusted the US "nuclear umbrella."[82] We are therefore expected to think that extended nuclear deterrence kept Germany from going nuclear in the past and the same is supposed to be true for Japan, whose officials

---

(June 2011): 233. Other studies suggest opposite results and argue that pacts with nuclear-armed states would increase the risk of proliferation rather than decrease it. See, for example, Harald Müller and Andreas Schmidt, "The Little-Known Story of Deproliferation: Why States Give up Nuclear Weapons Activities," in *Forecasting Nuclear Proliferation in the 21st Century: The Role of Theory*. But even in this case, the authors recognize that the link is only weak. This is in line with the skepticism of the qualitative literature regarding this type of correlation. Etel Solingen insists on the weakness of the correlation between positive nuclear security guarantees and nonproliferation and Jacques Hymans and T. V. Paul emphasize the variation in the effects of alliances on nuclear proliferation decisions from one case to the other. See Etel Solingen, *Nuclear Logics: Contrasting Paths in East Asia and the Middle East* (Princeton, NJ: Princeton University Press, 2007), 12–14, 25–27, 256; Jacques Hymans, *The Psychology of Nuclear Proliferation: Identity, Emotions, and Foreign Policy* (Cambridge, UK: Cambridge University Press, 2006), 42–43, note 79; T. V. Paul, *Power Versus Prudence: Why Nations Forgo Nuclear Weapons* (Montreal: McGill Queens University Press, 2000), 53–154. Only Maria Rublee offers a more favorable analysis of positive nuclear security guarantees. She argues that if there is internal debate, such guarantees can be decisive and convince the supporters of an independent nuclear-weapon capability. See Maria Rost Rublee, *Nonproliferation Norms: Why States Choose Nuclear Restraint* (Athens, GA: Georgia University Press, 2009), 202–203. However, even she does not argue for a systematic effect across cases. A good systematic review of this subset of literature can be found in Jeffrey W. Knopf, "Varieties of Assurance," *Journal of Strategic Studies* 35, no. 3 (2012): 389–394.

82. Interview with Helmut Kohl, *Le Figaro*, May 6–7, 1992.

emphasize so strongly the nuclear component of the alliance.[83] It certainly played a role, but it is necessary to keep in mind that, first, it is hard to discern how policies were affected exclusively by the nuclear component of the security guarantee and, second, the utility of future nuclear options may be seen in a different light than they were in the past. [See chapters 13 and 14 in this volume regarding Korea and Japan.]

For example, the most detailed study on the German case argues that German nuclear policy decisions were not determined primarily by concerns about extended deterrence but rather about its foreign policy situation in NATO. For Bonn, showing that it was able to exercise a nuclear option was an opportunity for influence within NATO.[84] Decades later, the nuclear nonproliferation treaty has affected German perceptions of appropriate behavior and the Fukushima nuclear accident has crystallized the progress of an anti-nuclear culture which has played a strong role in German nuclear policy after the Cold War.[85] Similarly, in the case of Japan, the nuclear security guarantee appears as a necessary but not sufficient cause for nonproliferation.[86]

---

83. The Taiwanese and South Korean rollbacks are better explained by other variables. See Solingen, *Nuclear Logics*.

84. Catherine McArdle Kelleher, *Germany and the Politics of Nuclear Weapons* (New York: Columbia University Press, 1975). Matthias Küntzel agrees that the purpose of Germany's policy was to reach a threshold status and to keep a nuclear weapons option open in *Bonn and the Bomb: German Politics and the Nuclear Option* (London: Pluto Press, 1995). There is disagreement on this issue though, and Beatrice Heuser makes the case for what I called the nuclear straitjacket in the German case, at least until Bonn signed the NPT. She argues that short of national nuclear forces, the German leadership advocated a NATO nuclear force and/or a European one. See Beatrice Heuser, *NATO, Britain, France and the FRG: Nuclear Strategies and Forces for Europe 1949–2000* (New York: St. Martin's Press, 1997), 125–126.

85. Harald Müller, "Nuclear Weapons and German Interests: An Attempt at Redefinition," Peace Research Institute Frankfurt, report 55, 2000: 10; Tom Sauer and Bob van der Zwaan, "US Tactical Nuclear Weapons in Europe after NATO's Lisbon Summit: Why their Withdrawal is Desirable and Feasible," *International Relations* 26, no. 1 (March 2012): 88–89.

86. Rublee, *Nonproliferation Norms*, 96.

So the nuclear security guarantee cannot be judged to have been a necessary or sufficient condition for nonproliferation across cases. Even when it played a role, the coupling of deterrence with nuclear weapons makes it hard to separate out what that role was.

The coupling of extended deterrence and nuclear weapons overestimates the role of these weapons in nonproliferation policy

The assessments of extended nuclear deterrence as a nonproliferation tool analyze the value of the nuclear component as a subset of the total value of the security guarantee that is offered. This leads to overstating the role of nuclear weapons in nonproliferation policy in two ways: (1) every security guarantee offered by a nuclear-armed state is implicitly considered as a nuclear security guarantee,[87] neglecting the central problem of credibility that plagues extended nuclear deterrence; and (2) the demand for nuclear security guarantees on the part of the protégé is mischaracterized.

Extended nuclear deterrence suffers from a basic credibility problem.[88] Its advantage vis-à-vis deterrence by conventional means comes from the higher level of anticipated damage if the nuclear threat is executed, but the credibility of this threat is dubious since its aim is to protect an ally and not necessarily the homeland of the protecting state. The tradition of

---

87. On the inability of most studies to conceive of a non-nuclear security strategy as purposive and deliberate as opposed to a default option, see Benoît Pelopidas, "Reversal and Restraint," in *Handbook of Nuclear Proliferation and Policy*, ed. Nathan Busch and Joseph F. Pilat (London: Routledge, 2015). The biased premise and the conclusion it necessarily leads to are condensed in the following sentence by Bruno Tertrais: "Security guarantees by a nuclear-armed state, potentially involving the use of nuclear weapons to protect an ally, have played an important role in preventing proliferation." See Tertrais, "Security Assurances and the Future of Proliferation," in *Over the Horizon Proliferation Threats*, 240.

88. Timothy W. Crawford, "The Endurance of Extended Deterrence: Continuity, Change, and Complexity in Theory and Policy," in *Complex Deterrence: Strategy in the Global Age*, ed. T. V. Paul, Patrick Morgan, and James Wirtz (Chicago: University of Chicago Press, 2009).

non-use of nuclear weapons makes this lack of credibility more of a fact every day.[89] This credibility deficit is best captured by the words of Henry Kissinger, who confessed at a meeting of American and European defense experts that, as national security adviser and secretary of state, he had often repeated the promise of extended deterrence to NATO allies. Then, he added:

> If my analysis is correct, these words cannot be true. And we must face the fact that it is absurd to base the strategy of the West on the credibility of the threat of mutual suicide. Therefore, I would say— which I might not say in office—the European allies should not keep asking us to multiply strategic assurances that we cannot possibly mean, or, if we do mean, we would not want to execute, because if we execute we risk the destruction of civilization.[90]

Even if this statement has a specific purpose and has to be understood in context, it is a candid acknowledgement of the credibility problem of extended nuclear deterrence: the protector who pretends to use nuclear weapons to protect an ally either does not mean what he says or, if he means it, will not want to keep his promise when the time comes because it is too risky. In the end, the credibility of extended nuclear deterrence pledges never seems to be credible enough to dissuade those nations that decided to go for the bomb from doing so.

Beyond the underestimation of the credibility problem, the need for extended nuclear deterrence as a nonproliferation tool is overestimated because analysts misunderstand the demand for positive nuclear security

89. For an argument about the role of the taboo in decreasing the credibility of extended deterrence pledges, see George Perkovich, "Extended Deterrence on the Way to a Nuclear-Free World," paper for the International Commission on Nuclear Non-proliferation and Disarmament, May 2009, http://icnnd.org/Documents/Perkovich_Deterrence.pdf.

90. Henry A. Kissinger, "The Future of NATO," *Washington Quarterly* 2, no. 4 (Autumn 1979).

guarantees: they assume that such a demand does exist on the part of the protégé and that it will not coexist with an independent deterrent. None of these claims is supported by the historical record.

There have been numerous cases in which the presence of such a guarantee in the form of nuclear weapons deployed on foreign soil was perceived as more threatening than protecting. The type of security guarantee that is requested is not necessarily of a nuclear nature and pretending to offer a "nuclear umbrella" can be counterproductive.[91] Good examples of a rather widespread fear would be Norway and Libya.

As a NATO member since 1954, Norway benefits from a nuclear umbrella. However, in December 1957, Prime Minister Einar Gerhardsen unexpectedly announced at a NATO summit in Paris that his country would not accept the deployment or storage of nuclear weapons on its soil in peacetime.[92] By doing so, the prime minister avoided turning his country into a target of Soviet nuclear forces. Before speaking at the NATO summit, he had assured the Soviet Union that Norway would not authorize American troops to supervise nuclear charges on its soil.[93] This fear is not unique. In the early days of the Cold War, when British Prime Minister Clement Attlee was informed that if nuclear weapons had to be

---

91. One critical problem here is that positive and negative assurances can be in tension since the efforts to increase the credibility of the pledge of extended nuclear deterrence require affirmation of a readiness to use them, which is contradictory to the idea of negative security assurances. Bruno Tertrais shows it well in "Security Assurances and the Future of Proliferation." See also Knopf, "Varieties of Assurance," 388–389.

92. When they decided to be among the founding members of NATO, Norwegian authorities also made clear that they would not accept permanent basing of foreign forces on their soil either. Simon Duke, *United States Military Forces and Installations in Europe* (New York: Oxford University Press, 1989), 217.

93. Astrid Forland, "Norway's Nuclear Odyssey: From Optimistic Proponent to Nonproliferator," *Nonproliferation Review* 4, no. 2 (Winter 1997): 12–14.

used against the Soviet Union, they would be launched from British terri-tory, he tried to convince President Truman to do otherwise.[94]

As for Libya, it should have been a perfect case for the nuclear straitjacket—either an independent national deterrent or an extended nuclear security guarantee—given the length of the pursuit of nuclear weapons by Colonel Moammar Gadhafi[95] and the fact that his life had been threatened by the United States.[96] The current historical knowledge about the Libyan case suggests, however, that Tripoli received no pos-itive nuclear security guarantee. It is true that it received two security guarantees from those with whom it negotiated the dismantlement of its so-called weapons of mass destruction program, none of which had any-thing to do with extended nuclear deterrence. The first one was offered during negotiations around the settlement of the Lockerbie case in the late

---

94. Nicholas Wheeler, "The Attlee Government's Nuclear Strategy, 1945–1951," in *Britain and the First Cold War,* ed. Anne Deighton (New York: St. Martin's Press, 1990). Such a fear and opposition to a "nuclear umbrella" can be found in Sweden and New Zealand.

95. Gadhafi started the nuclear-weapons program only a few months after taking power in 1969 and ended it in 2003. See Rublee, *Nonproliferation Norms,* 152; Solingen, *Nuclear Logics,* 213, 215; Malfrid Braut-Hegghammer, "Libya's Nuclear Turnaround: Perspectives from Tripoli," *Middle East Journal* 62, no. 1 (Winter 2008): 59–61; Harald Müller, "The Exceptional End to the Extraordinary Libyan Nuclear Quest," in *Nuclear Proliferation and International Security,* ed. Morten Bremer Maerli and Sverre Lodgaard (London: Routledge, 2007), 78; Wyn Q. Bowen, *Libya and Nuclear Proliferation: Stepping Back from the Brink* (London: Oxford University Press, 2006), 52; David Albright, *Peddling Peril: How Secret Nuclear Trade Arms America's Enemies* (New York: Free Press, 2010), 49; William Langewiesche, *The Atomic Bazaar: The Rise of the Nuclear Poor* (New York: Penguin, 2007), 171.

96. The operation El Dorado Canyon in 1986 can be considered as at attempt at killing the Libyan leader given the amount of effort to determine where he would spend the night the evening before the attack. Leif Mollo, *The United States and Assassination Policy: Diluting the Absolute,* MA thesis, Naval Postgraduate School, Monterey, Calif., December 2003: 15–16 ; Ward Thomas, *The Ethics of Destruction, Norms and Force in International Relations* (Ithaca, NY: Cornell University Press, 2001), 75–77; and Pelopidas, *Renoncer à l'arme nucléaire,* 216–220.

1990s.[97] It consisted in implicitly assuring the Gadhafi regime that it was not under threat. The second one was not formalized before June 2006. That was more than two and a half years after Libya officially announced it had given up on nuclear weapons, even if one could argue that the discussions on the terms of this letter started just before the official announcement.[98] In this letter, signed by the British and then the Libyan authorities, London committed itself to help satisfy Tripoli's needs in terms of conventional defense and to actively seek an action from the United Nations Security Council if Libya were attacked by biological or chemical weapons.[99] Neither of these guarantees can be presented as a positive nuclear security guarantee. The only nuclear component of these declarations reaffirms the negative security guarantee the United Kingdom provided to the non-nuclear NPT member states in April 1995.

This does not mean that security considerations did not contribute to Libya's decision to give up nuclear, biological, and chemical weapon programs. The security considerations were focused on regime survival.[100] Gadhafi's son Saif al-Islam was explicit about the need for security guarantees, but focused on the conventional level. In 2004, he reported the commitments of the United States and the United Kingdom in the following terms: "They said we, the West, and the international society will

---

97. On December 21, 1988, a bomb was detonated on board Pan Am flight 103 from Frankfurt to Detroit and parts of the plane crashed onto Lockerbie, Scotland, killing more than 270 people. After a two-year investigation, an arrest warrant was issued for two Libyan nationals.

98. Wyn Q. Bowen, "Libya, nuclear rollback and the role of negative and positive security assurances," in Security Assurances and Nuclear Nonproliferation, 12.

99. Ibid., 1.

100. Braut-Hegghammer, "Libya's Nuclear Turnaround," 71; Bowen, "Libya, nuclear rollback and the role of negative and positive security assurances," 9–11; Bruce Jentleson and Christopher Whytock, "Who 'Won' Libya? The Force-Diplomacy Debate and its Implications for Theory and Policy," International Security 30, no. 3 (Winter 2005–2006): 56, 74; Harald Müller, "The Exceptional End to the Extraordinary Libyan Nuclear Quest," 88-89; Solingen, Nuclear Logics, 216.

be responsible for the protection of Libya" and will provide "necessary defensive weapons."[101]

Not only does the nuclear straitjacket wrongly assume that demand for a positive nuclear security guarantee exists—it also falls into the opposite trap of neglecting that such a demand can coexist in various ways with a national nuclear-weapon program. For example, it fails to capture the thinking of decision-makers in France and the United Kingdom when their nuclear-weapons programs were developed.[102] In both cases, the leaders never thought their choice was *either* a national nuclear-weapons capability *or* a positive nuclear security; they contemplated combinations of both.

Non-democratic leaders can give up nuclear weapons for regime survival

The third recurring critique of the goal of a world without nuclear-weapons states is that it is not feasible because states with relatively weak conventional arsenals will never give up their nuclear arsenals.[103] A specific

---

101. Carla Ann Robbins, "In giving up arms, Libya hopes to gain new economic life," *Wall Street Journal,* February 12, 2004.

102. Pelopidas, "The Nuclear Straitjacket."

103. The three cases would be Israel, France, and Pakistan. A chapter is dedicated to each country in Barry Blechman and Alexander Bollfrass, eds., *National Perspectives on Nuclear Disarmament* (Washington, DC: Henry L. Stimson Center, 2010). See also Avner Cohen, "Israel's Nuclear Future: Iran, Opacity, and the Vision of Global Zero," and Venance Journé, "France's Nuclear Stance: Independence, Unilateralism, and Adaptation," in *Getting to Zero: The Path to Nuclear Disarmament,* ed. Catherine McArdle Kelleher and Judith Reppy (Stanford, CA: Stanford University Press, 2010); and Devin T. Hagerty, "The Nuclear Holdouts: India, Israel, and Pakistan," in *Slaying the Nuclear Dragon: Disarmament Dynamics in the Twenty-First Century,* ed. Tanya Ogilvie-White and David Santoro (Athens, GA: University of Georgia Press, 2012); James M. Acton, *Deterrence during Disarmament: Deep Nuclear Reductions and International Security* (Abingdon, UK: Routledge, 2011); Malcolm Chalmers, Andrew Somerville, and Andrea Berger, eds., *Small Nuclear Forces: Five Perspectives* (London: Royal United Services Institute, 2011).

version of this argument is used as the scarecrow intended to stop the conversation about the goal of a world without nuclear weapons: dictators with nuclear weapons will never give them up. This section will assess this particular critique. The most frequently quoted supporting evidence for this argument is that dictators have learned the lesson from Libya. On December 19, 2003, President George W. Bush officially welcomed Colonel Gadhafi's decision to give up weapons of mass destruction with the following words:

> Today in Tripoli, the leader of Libya, Colonel Muammar al-Gaddafi, publicly confirmed his commitment to disclose and dismantle all weapons of mass destruction programs in his country. . . . And another message should be equally clear: leaders who abandon the pursuit of chemical, biological, and nuclear weapons, and the means to deliver them, will find an open path to better relations with the United States and other free nations. . . . As the Libyan government takes these essential steps and demonstrates its seriousness, its good faith will be returned. Libya can regain a secure and respected place among the nations, and over time, achieve far better relations with the United States. . . . Old hostilities do not need to go on forever.[104]

The so-called WMD programs were dismantled with the help of the United States, Russia, and the United Kingdom.[105] Less than ten years

---

104. BBC News, transcript of President George Bush's statement in Washington on Libya's dismantling of WMD, December 20, 2003, http://news.bbc.co.uk/2/hi/americas/3336159.stm.

105. Jack Boureston and Yana Feldman, "Verifying Libya's Nuclear Disarmament," *Trust & Verify* 112, Verification Research, Training and Information Centre, London, 2004; Joseph Cirincione, Jon Wolfsthal, and Miriam Rajkumar, *Deadly Arsenals: Nuclear, Biological, and Chemical Threats,* 2nd ed. (Washington, DC: Carnegie Endowment for International Peace, 2005). One has to recognize that his long quest for nuclear weapons had led to very little success. For a summary of the Libyan program's failures and shortcomings, see Hymans, *Achieving Nuclear Ambitions,* 239–243. However, I argued elsewhere that these were not enough to pretend that Libya was not a

later, members of the armed forces of the National Transition Council captured Gadhafi and beat him to death after his convoy was bombed by NATO forces. Many constituencies of the nuclear conversation seem to have learned the same lesson from this episode: if you are not a US ally, keep your nuclear weapons or get a few quickly. Otherwise, your survival as a ruler is not assured. Pundits and proliferation analysts, civilian and military alike, have publicly expressed this lesson from the Libyan story.[106] The efforts by US officials to disconnect Libyan disarmament from the fall of the Gadhafi regime did not convince observers.[107] The North Koreans were the first ones to express skepticism publicly. "The situation in Libya is a lesson for the international community," said a spokesman for the North Korean Foreign Ministry, unnamed by the North's news agency. "It has been shown to the corners of the earth that Libya's giving up its nuclear arms, which the US liked to chatter on about, was used as an invasion tactic to disarm the country. . . . Having one's own strengths was the only way to keep the peace."[108] This is not an isolated statement. Iran's religious leader, Ayatollah Ali Khamenei, addressing the population for

---

serious proliferator: it did not give up when the sanctions and the technological impediments were the strongest. See Pelopidas, *Renoncer à l'arme nucléaire*.

106. Among others, see Andrew J. Pierre, "If Gaddafi Had The Bomb," *Huffington Post,* August 4, 2011; Waltz, "The Great Debate," 92. Kenneth N. Waltz and Mira Rapp-Hopper, "What Kim Jong-Il Learned from Qaddafi's Fall: Never Disarm," *The Atlantic,* October 24, 2011; Gus Lubin, "Why The Libyan War Means That No Country Will Ever Give Up Its Nuclear Weapons Again," *Business Insider,* March 24, 2011; Norman Cigar, "Libya's Nuclear Disarmament: Lessons and Implications for Nuclear Proliferation," US Marine Corps University, Middle East Studies (January 2012): 12–13.

107. "Where they're at today has absolutely no connection with them renouncing their nuclear program or nuclear weapons," said Mark Toner, a State Department spokesman, in March 2011. Quoted in Mark McDonald, "North Korea Suggests Libya Should Have Kept Nuclear Program," *New York Times,* March 24, 2011.

108. Korea JoongAng Daily, "Libyans should have kept nukes, says Pyongyang," March 24, 2011, http://koreajoongangdaily.joinsmsn.com/news/article/article .aspx?aid=2933884.

the Persian New Year, said that Gadhafi's concessions to the West over Libya's nuclear program showed that Iran was right to continue to reject any curb to its nuclear development.[109] As Norman Cigar wrote in a paper for the US Marine Corps University, "The sense of legitimacy of a country's previous acquisition of nuclear weapons or its efforts to do so will increase, in part thanks to a more understanding environment, especially among countries with similar concerns."[110]

Advocates for a world without nuclear weapons seem to face a conundrum. The end goal becomes impossible to achieve because no dictator will ever give up nuclear weapons. Therefore, it should not be desired. It is true that the United States has never attacked a nuclear-armed adversary to overthrow its regime and only one nuclear-armed state has suffered military attacks aiming at least at changing the regime: Israel.[111]

---

109. Robin Pomeroy, "Don't Bomb Libya, Arm Rebels, Says Iran's Khamenei," Reuters, March 21, 2011, http://www.reuters.com/article/2011/03/21/us-iran-khamenei -idUSTRE72K50L20110321.

110. Cigar, "Libya's Nuclear Disarmament," 13.

111. In 1973, it was well-known that Israel had developed such a capability but Egypt and Syria attacked anyway. Other cases would be Argentina invading the British Falkland Islands in 1982 and the Iraqi attack on Israel in the 1991 Persian Gulf War. But the goal was never to overthrow the regime in the United Kingdom or in Israel. It was only to regain territory. See Berry et al., "Delegitimizing Nuclear Weapons," 26–27; Paul, *The Tradition of Non-Use of Nuclear Weapons,* 145. It is tempting to mention the 1967 war as a precedent given that Israel had assembled a crude nuclear device in the run-up to the war (Avner Cohen, "Crossing the Threshold: The Untold Nuclear Dimension of the 1967 Arab-Israeli War and Its Contemporary Lessons," *Arms Control Today* 37, June 2007) and that the goal of the Arab coalition might have been to overthrow the regime in Israel. The rhetoric on the Egyptian radio on the eve of the conflict was challenging the Israeli leader Levi Eshkol and suggesting that opening fire would lead to the "death and annihilation of Israel." See Pierre Hazan, 1967, *la guerre des six jours: la victoire empoisonnée* (1967, the six-day war: the poisoned victory) (Paris: Complexe, 2001), 18. However, the Egyptian leadership at the time was not aware of the Israeli capability. See Avner Cohen, *Israel and the Bomb* (New York: Columbia University Press, 1998), 259–276.

Noting that dictators can change their minds and calculations about the utility of nuclear weapons even after pursuing these weapons for decades[112] is important but not sufficient, since we only have a few cases of renunciation of an existing arsenal. It is worth focusing on the supposed worst-case scenario of a dictator keeping nuclear weapons while other states have disarmed. To reassess this scenario, I will make two points: first, nuclear weapons do not protect against coups and popular uprisings; and second, the incentives to denuclearize would be enormous because of the combined pressures of global norms, big-power opposition, economic sanctions, and powerful conventional forces arrayed against the holdout.

---

112. Moammar Gadhafi was the case in point. It is true that the Libyan regime did not achieve much in terms of nuclear technology. However, the focus on technological failure does not account for the timing of Gadhafi's decision to disarm. Given that he started a nuclear-weapon program as soon as he took power in 1969 and did not make significant progress, why suddenly give up in 2003? Sanctions tell only part of the story: they had asphyxiated the country since the 1970s and, most importantly, sanctions imposed by the UN Security Council since 1992 (UNSC Res 731, 748, 883) were removed before 1999, that is, several years before the decision to give up weapons of mass destruction. Sanctions from the European Union had also been softened since the late 1990s. The explanation based on the threat of regime change after the United States invaded Iraq is dubious, too, for two reasons: (1) The 1986 bombings intended to kill Gadhafi did not lead him to give up the WMD programs, so why should a more remote threat produce a stronger effect? (2) In the 1990s, during the secret negotiations with the United States and the United Kingdom, the Libyan regime offered to give up its weapons of mass destruction after the threat of regime change was removed, not because of it. So technological failures, sanctions, and regime change policy in Iraq might have played a role in the decision to give up WMDs, but they neglect the fact that the Gadhafi regime had lost its original rationale for building the weapons and, since the early 1990s, its foreign policy and security perspective were shifting from pan-Arabism to pan-Africanism, a context in which the value of nuclear weapons was definitely lower. A fuller analysis of the Libyan case can be read in Pelopidas, *Renoncer à l'arme nucléaire*.

Nuclear weapons do not protect against coups, popular uprisings, and destabilization campaigns by non-state actors

Nuclear weapons may deter the United States from invading countries to change their regimes. However, they are powerless against coups, popular uprisings, or destabilization campaigns by non-state actors. As George Shultz, William Perry, Henry Kissinger, and Sam Nunn note, "In the case of the Soviet Union, nuclear weapons did not prevent collapse or regime change"[113] in 1990. In that respect, the lesson learned from the Libyan story assumes that the popular uprising alone would not have been enough to overthrow the regime. This might be true even if we remember that external support was not decisive in the success of the Egyptian uprising against Hosni Mubarak.[114] But does it mean that the United States and foreign powers would not have increased their support for the protesters in indirect ways? It is reasonable to assume that the allies would have welcomed opportunities to overthrow the regime by other means, too. If so, the defeat of the opponents of Gadhafi, had he kept his weapons program, becomes even more uncertain. The popular uprisings in the Arab world tell another story. Even if they study popular uprisings and try to learn how to defeat them, dictators should fear their own populations. Nuclear weapons cannot protect them against popular uprisings.

Nuclear weapons cannot deter destabilization campaigns by secessionist organizations and other non-state actors either. This was true during the Cold War and remains true today. Lebanese and Palestinian militant groups have launched offensives against Israel since the 1970s. In the 1980s, the Tamil Tigers attacked a presumably nuclear-armed India, and Chechen rebel groups have struggled against Russia since 1994.[115] Even if the purpose of these attacks was not to change the regime, it

---

113. George P. Shultz, William J. Perry, Henry A. Kissinger, and Sam Nunn, "Deterrence in the Age of Nuclear Proliferation," *Wall Street Journal*, March 7, 2011.

114. Erica Chenoweth and Maria J. Stephan, *Why Civil Resistance Works: The Strategic Logic of Nonviolent Conflict* (New York, Columbia University Press, 2011), 230.

115. Paul, *The Tradition of Non-Use of Nuclear Weapons*, 145.

is also worth recalling the Pakistani-supported terrorist attacks in India even after New Delhi officially became a nuclear-weapon possessor in 1998, the terrorist attacks against US interests supported by Libya in the 1980s, and the attacks of Al Qaeda against the United States, United Kingdom, and Russia.

This should not be read as an incentive to support violent insurrections in nuclear-weapon states since chaos would increase the risk of theft of nuclear material and possibly of nuclear use. If this analysis is correct, the United States should shift from a threat-based strategy—of which deterrence is one type—to a reassurance strategy, which credibly rejects regime change and emphasizes the increased vulnerabilities associated with nuclear-weapons possession.[116] Awareness of this last point and of other limits of nuclear safety and security appears as a first step to make a dictator more amenable to giving up his weapons.

Could a dictator keep nuclear weapons indefinitely?

The dictatorship we are discussing is easy to identify: North Korea. If the problem is framed in terms of rogue states or states of concern, one should then include Iran if it acquires nuclear weapons and, possibly, Pakistan. The assumption is that because we think these leaders will never give up their nuclear arsenals, we should give up the goal of getting to zero. So would a world without nuclear weapons except for one dictatorship be more dangerous than the world we live in? To answer that question, one can then build two scenarios: either the dictator is non-deterrable and wants to create the maximum of damage or he is deterrable. In the first scenario, keeping nuclear weapons or not will not change the outcome, unless a credible missile defense is built[117] and no accidental launch

---

116. For example, John Steinbruner suggested a form of cooperative or consensual security that would subordinate the practice of deterrence to that of reassurance in "Consensual Security," *Bulletin of the Atomic Scientists* 64, no. 1 (March–April 2008).

117. This would require specifying the detection systems because even if a credible missile-defense system were built, which is unlikely, the nuclear dictatorship could

happens: once the undeterrable dictator is in power and possesses a nuclear-weapon capability as well as delivery vehicles, millions will die. In the second scenario, the question becomes: can conventional capabilities deter a nuclear attack?

Opponents of the goal of a world without nuclear weapons have not decoupled deterrence and nuclear weapons. "If such states cannot be disarmed," argue Josef Joffe and James Davis, "they must be deterred. But how can nuclear weapons be deterred unless with nuclear weapons?"[118] The argument is misguided in multiple ways.

First, it misses the fact that nuclear disarmament is a long-term process and that the North Korean case will be reconsidered when we reach a lower level of nuclear arsenals in the world. By then, the situation will probably have changed in ways we cannot fully grasp today. For instance, in a world approaching zero nuclear weapons, stringent prohibitions on nuclear testing would be in place and efforts to detect cheaters would increase considerably, so the number of hidden weapons would be limited and they would probably not be tested. Given this uncertainty, renouncing a policy goal because of our expectations about the future behavior of a dictatorship grants the ruler of this state much more power and leverage than is deserved.

More fundamentally, the deterrent value of conventional capabilities will have increased considerably and, in any case, these conventional capabilities will remain sufficient to inflict unacceptable damage to a nuclear dictatorship. I realize that precision-guided munitions have been emphasized several times since the 1970s to re-legitimize conventional deterrence, with only limited success.[119] However, the recent

---

send decoys to defeat it and launch its nuclear warheads only once the anti-ballistic missile defense had been defeated.

118. Josef Joffe and James W. Davis, "Less than Zero: Bursting the New Disarmament Bubble," *Foreign Affairs,* January–February 2011: 8.

119. The classical critique of conventional deterrence in general, and of this argument in particular, remains John Mearsheimer, *Conventional Deterrence* (Ithaca, NY: Cornell University Press, 1983).

developments of drone technology and the project of prompt global strike capabilities should lead us to consider that these weapons may credibly be used to destroy key assets of a nuclear dictatorship. If so, their deterrent potential would be at least as good as that of nuclear weapons. In other words, US possession of a military advantage and destructive capability is one reason to believe in the efficacy of a conventional deterrent in these circumstances. Robert Jervis convincingly argues that it is overwhelming and that small nuclear arsenals are not enough to compensate.[120] Even if this superiority declined, the broad coalition of countries that would unite against the threat of a nuclear-armed state in a world with only a few of them could create a convincing deterrent capability.[121] A few analysts even argue that progress in conventional capabilities and the so-called revolution in military affairs make the prospect of a decapitating first strike against a weak nuclear-armed state "more than just a theoretical possibility, although a state contemplating such a strike could be deterred by the remote possibility of nuclear retaliation."[122] The late ambassador-at-large Paul Nitze had already made this argument in his last op-ed for the *New York Times* on October 28, 1999.[123]

---

120. Robert Jervis, "Deterrence, Rogue States and the U.S. Policy," in *Complex Deterrence,* 134.

121. Dennis Gormley convincingly argues that US conventional superiority is an obstacle to the ultimate goal of a world without nuclear weapons in "American Conventional Superiority: the Balancing Act," in *Getting to Zero.* David Holloway and Edward Ifft rightfully observe that the enforcement problem would be harder if the cheater were a great power. See Edward Ifft, "Practical Considerations Related to Verification," in *Deterrence: Its Past and Future,* 331; and David Holloway, "Deterrence and Enforcement in a World Free of Nuclear Weapons," 343.

122. Michel Fortmann and Stéfanie von Hlatky, "The Revolution in Military Affairs: Impact of Emerging Technologies on Deterrence," in *Complex Deterrence,* 317.

123. Paul H. Nitze, "A Threat Mostly to Ourselves," *New York Times,* October 28, 1999. Hypothesizing that there could be such a thing as unambiguous intelligence, he wrote: "As for the so-called rogue states that are not inhibited in their actions by the consensus of world opinion the United States would be wise to eliminate their nuclear capabilities with the preemptive use of our conventional weapons—when

Regarding the threat of theft of nuclear material and proliferation, the available quantity would be much smaller than it is now and all the former nuclear-weapon states would have a common incentive to enforce nonproliferation. As Pavel Podvig writes, "A world with North Korea as the only nuclear power would be a rather uncomfortable place, but the world in which it is the *ninth* nuclear weapons state is even more uncomfortable."[124]

These two scenarios would require further elaboration about my assumptions in terms of latency, availability of other weapons, intentions, crisis stability, and interstate relations in the world I describe. In this chapter, I just want to show that apparently obvious objections to the goal of a world without nuclear weapons become much weaker as soon as you decouple the notion of deterrence and nuclear weapons and keep in mind our current level of nuclear threat.

Conclusion: Beyond the "Nuclear Straitjacket"

Earlier in the chapter, I asked whether seventy years is a high enough standard of evidence for us to surrender our fate to nuclear weapons forever. In brief, we don't know what caused the lack of war between great powers. Several answers compete. So far, we have decided to trust one answer that would cost millions of lives if it were proven wrong because there is no foreseeable protection against a nuclear strike.[125] We will never reach

---

necessary, and when we have unambiguous indication of these countries' intent to use their nuclear capability for purposes of aggrandizement. The same principle should apply to any threat emanating from unstable states with nuclear arsenals."

124. Pavel Podvig, "What if North Korea Were the Only Nuclear Weapon State?," *Bulletin of the Atomic Scientists,* May 27, 2009.

125. This has been true at least since nuclear-tipped ballistic missiles could be launched underwater from a submarine which is impossible to detect. As a consequence, destroying the missile before it is launched became impossible. It is well established that civil defense programs make promises that are impossible to keep. See Lee Clarke, *Mission Improbable: Using Fantasy Documents to Tame Disaster* (Chicago:

a level of certainty that makes this policy choice as obvious as some claim it to be.[126] The critique of the goal of a world without nuclear weapons raising the specter of the return of great-power war has to face this uncertainty. It must also face the mixed record of nuclear weapons as peacemakers.

Not only is the reliance on nuclear deterrence a bet portrayed as a certainty in practice if not in words, but this bet considerably overestimates the peace-keeping capacities of this strategy. Nuclear deterrence has, at times, favored more risk-prone behavior in a series of cases, does not avoid organizational and command-and-control problems, and has not been sufficient to keep the peace in a series of critical situations.

The idea that reaching a world without nuclear weapons will "unleash the dogs of war" is unconvincing.

We cannot and will not know for sure what kept peace in the last seven decades. Looking for certainties and silver bullets is what makes the nuclear peace hypothesis so appealing. What we know is that the long peace was limited in time and space, that luck played a significant role that cannot be replaced by deterrence, that we might not yet know the full extent of its role due to persisting secrecy about nuclear-weapons-related accidents and that nuclear deterrence as a strategy created more

---

University of Chicago Press, 1999), 30–40, 90–97; Dee Garrison, *Bracing for Armageddon: Why Civil Defense Never Worked* (Oxford: Oxford University Press, 2006). Even if the current missile-defense project could be made credible, it is not intended as a complete protection against a nuclear strike, for two reasons. First, it focuses on threats from regional powers only. Second, it is a US system and there is little prospect of sharing it.

126. This is quite a recent development. As Daniel Deudney aptly notes: "Early proponents emphasized the tentative, second-best, and temporary character of [deterrence statism, i.e., the idea that nuclear weapons make war prohibitively costly], but many of its contemporary proponents are confident that this solution is highly enduring and close to the best of all solutions," *Bounding Power,* 247. James Goodby and Steven Pifer develop this point in the last section of their chapter in this volume. On the role and risk of overstated certainties in the nuclear discourse and the shift from one to another, see Benoît Pelopidas, "Critical Thinking about Nuclear Weapons," *Nonproliferation Review* 17, no. 1 (2010): 191–193.

risk-prone behavior on the part of the nuclear possessors and did not ultimately prevent nuclear-armed states from fighting a war.

So the only question worth asking is whether a war among great powers would be more or less likely than it is now. The trend toward a decline
in inter-state wars seems to be robust and suggests that such wars might
be less likely. In any case, war in a world without nuclear weapons would
not run the risk of nuclear escalation, provided that the absence of such
weapons is properly enforced.

To sum up, nuclear proliferation risks are not likely to increase if the
United States decreases the size of its nuclear arsenal. A closer look at
nuclear history demonstrates that, contrary to the accepted wisdom, a
positive nuclear security guarantee has not been a silver bullet for nonproliferation even if it played a role in a couple of nuclear choices.
Current policy discussions overestimate the appeal of nuclear weapons
and wrongly assume that states are seeking to organize their national
security around the alternative between an independent nuclear deterrent and a "nuclear umbrella." They neglect the most recent studies that
underplay the threat of massive proliferation of nuclear weapons by states
in the next decades as well as the challenges associated with successful
proliferation. More importantly, they underestimate the enormous credibility problem of extended nuclear deterrence and the facts that it might
make the protégé feel more insecure or, on the contrary, might not alter
his plans for a national nuclear-weapons capability. These key problems
of extended nuclear deterrence are going to remain for the foreseeable
future. Finally, extended nuclear deterrence is not well-equipped to deter
terrorists from acquiring nuclear weapons. Because of these problems,
a more cooperative and tailored policy of security guarantees could
be elaborated that would not rely so explicitly on nuclear weapons.
Conventional threats would be much more credible and would not invite
nuclear retaliation.[127] This shift, which would require close consultations

---

127. This borrows and modifies Scott Sagan's argument in "The Commitment
     Trap: Why the United States Should Not Use Nuclear Threats to Deter

with allies who understand the nuclear umbrella as the ultimate sign of US protection, would free the United States from a possible reputation cost of not keeping its promises if an ally is attacked. It might also address the concerns of allies who consider that having US nuclear weapons on their soil makes them more vulnerable.

The idea that dictators will never give up their nuclear arsenal is not entirely convincing. It might seem to be early to consider this case, but opponents of the goal of a world without nuclear weapons intend to use it to delegitimize the goal and stop the conversation. So it is worth rebutting the argument right now. To do so, one should emphasize that nuclear weapons do not protect against coups, popular uprisings, or destabilization campaigns by non-state actors and that the incentives for a nuclear-armed dictator to disarm would be enormous.

In the remainder of this chapter, I will suggest three ways in which opponents to nuclear status quo or endless modernization can move the conversation beyond the nuclear straitjacket.

Address the contradiction between nuclear deterrence and nonproliferation

The perceived value of nuclear weapons and the scope of their mission have evolved. Historically, their scope has been shrinking. The period starting in the 1990s—reaffirming that nuclear weapons can also deter chemical and biological attacks—appears anomalous. Therefore, decoupling "nuclear" from "deterrence" in order to reassess the added deterrent value of nuclear weapons and the effectiveness of deterrence as a strategy remains promising. This endeavor might highlight the contradiction between absolute faith in nuclear deterrence and unconditional rejection of nuclear proliferation. Indeed, a strong faith in nuclear deterrence as an exceptional strategy for great-power peace and nonproliferation would actually contradict US efforts toward nonproliferation: logically,

---

Biological and Chemical Weapon Attacks," *International Security* 24, no. 4 (Spring 2000).

if nuclear weapons are peacemakers provided that they spread slowly and in a managed way, one should welcome their spread.[128] On a policy level, it would overstate the otherwise declining utility of these weapons for security and regime survival instead of emphasizing our common vulnerability to the nuclear danger. As a consequence, pretending that the "atomic magic" is intact would encourage proliferation[129] and, because of the tendency of dictators attracted to the bomb to overstate their potential achievements as I outlined above, would jeopardize the main rationale for these leaders to give up their nuclear ambitions. Therefore, shifting toward a "no-first-use policy" seems to be the next step, for three main reasons. First, it would decrease reliance on nuclear weapons by reducing the scope of their mission. Second, it would avoid a "commitment trap"[130] leading the United States to lose credibility if it does not respond to a WMD attack with nuclear weapons. Third, since the expected casualties on the US side after this type of strike are much more limited, it might "bolster conventional deterrence"[131] by increasing the reputation for resolve of the United States.

---

128. Kenneth Waltz is consistent in that respect. See "Why Iran Should Get the Bomb: Nuclear Balancing Would Mean Stability," *Foreign Affairs,* July–August 2012. French theorist Pierre-Marie Gallois made the same argument.

129. This is why the choice we are facing for the future is often characterized as either nuclear proliferation or global nuclear disarmament. George P. Shultz, William J. Perry, Henry A. Kissinger, and Sam Nunn wrote that "continued reliance on nuclear weapons as the principal element for deterrence is encouraging, or at least excusing, the spread of these weapons," in "Deterrence in the Age of Nuclear Proliferation," *Wall Street Journal,* March 7, 2011. See also Holloway, "Deterrence and Enforcement in a World Free of Nuclear Weapons," 363; and Sagan, "The Great Debate," 88.

130. See Sagan, "The Commitment Trap"; and Scott Sagan, "The Case for No First Use," *Survival* 51, no. 3 (June–July 2009), 171.

131. Michael Gerson, "No First Use: The Next Step for U.S. Nuclear Policy," *International Security* 35, no. 2 (Fall 2010): 47; and Fortmann and von Hlatky, "The Revolution in Military Affairs," 309–310.

Engage the expected veto player

The amount of opposition to the goal might be overestimated. Cold War history offers several examples of high-level US and Soviet officials who understood that the current course of nuclear policy in their country was flawed but did not speak up because they thought a third party would be reluctant to change and powerful enough to block any change.[132]

For example, the US secretaries of defense under the Ford and Carter administrations kept referring to an external audience that was supposed to believe that the balance of nuclear forces was a relevant measurement of American power. This supposed belief about other international actors seems to have been a central driver of nuclear policies. In the report to Congress for fiscal year 1975, President Ford's secretary of defense, James Schlesinger, recognized that the Soviet Union was in no position to launch a disarming first strike against the United States or even hope to do so, but nonetheless called for immediate measures to counter the increase in size of their nuclear arsenal. "There must be essential equivalence between the strategic forces of the US and the Soviet Union— an equivalence perceived not only by ourselves, but by the Soviet Union *and third audiences as well.*"[133] This expected perception by a third party is decisive in his reasoning. He therefore concludes that "to the degree that we wish to influence the perception of others, we must take appropriate steps (*by their lights*) in the design of the strategic forces."[134] In other words, the supposed perception of the US arsenal by other actors

---

132. At the end of a historical investigation of the support for the goal of a world without nuclear weapons in the United States, Jonathan Pearl concluded that "when the barriers to disarmament seemed lowest, political and popular enthusiasm for this goal largely dissipated." Jonathan Pearl, "Forecasting Zero: U.S. nuclear history and the low probability of disarmament," Strategic Studies Institute, US Army War College, November 2011: 40–41.

133. Steven Kull, "Nuclear Nonsense," *Foreign Policy* 58 (Spring 1985): 32. Author's italics.

134. Ibid., 32–33.

was a major driver in designing the force beyond the requirements of deterrence.[135] These "third parties" might have been more amenable to change than had been supposed. In other words, some change was achievable if they had not anticipated that the opponents to change were impossible to convince or defeat. Engaging them and revealing those past missed opportunities is a first step.

The number of opponents to the goal might diminish in another way. Historically, a few genuine opponents to nuclear disarmament and arms control turned out to be involuntary supporters: they crafted proposals that were so ambitious or so demanding that the Soviets would not accept them. As in the cases described above, they were wrong about the "expected veto player" in a way that ended up promoting nuclear disarmament. A case in point would be Richard Perle's support of the "zero option" in the early 1980s. In other words, the United States would forgo the deployment of Pershing 2 and ground-launched cruise missiles in Europe if the Soviets gave up their intermediate range forces. It has been most often interpreted as an option designed to be unacceptable by the Soviets[136] . . . but five and a half years later, General Secretary Gorbachev accepted it within the Intermediate Nuclear Forces treaty framework.[137]

These instances suggest that proponents of change might be more numerous than we think but that convincing them is not enough. They

---

135.   Ibid. The entire article is a convincing case for this. Other good examples are the report to Congress by Secretary of Defense Harold Brown in 1979, and Secretary of Defense Robert McNamara asking for more weapons after he learned that the missile gap was in the United States' favor.

136.   William E. Pemberton, *Exit with Honor: The Life and Presidency of Ronald Reagan* (New York: M.E. Sharpe, 1998), 167; and Thomas Risse-Kappen, "Did 'Peace Through Strength' End the Cold War? Lessons from INF," *International Security* 16, no. 1 (Summer 1991): 170.

137.   Thomas Risse-Kappen, *The Zero Option: INF, West Germany and Arms Control* (New York: Westview, 1988), 82.

also have to come to believe that coming out as a proponent of change is safe for them and effective.[138] Tactical mistakes will do the rest.

Think about possible futures, beyond proliferation

Things that never happened before happen often. This is also true in the nuclear arena even if analysts and policymakers in this field tend to see the unprecedented only as bad news. For example, unprecedented cases of nuclear disarmament in South Africa, Ukraine, Belarus, and Kazakhstan were not anticipated by academic analysts and intelligence agencies alike.[139] They were unprecedented and unexpected: before they happened, all the observers would have said that they were impossible. Similarly, in 1986, who would have expected that the global nuclear stockpile would have been reduced by two-thirds in the next twenty-five years?[140] This worst-case assumption is still there today, with the degradation of the recent climate taken by the opponents to the goal of zero as revealing the truth of its impossibility. This pessimistic view of the world assumes that the latest wave of support for disarmament will be the last one, carrying a definitive verdict about the possibility of future nuclear arms levels. Contrary to this myopic view of the world, past failures of worst-case scenarios suggest that a disarmament initiative might happen in the future, too, in spite of the fact that we do not anticipate it now.[141]

---

138. This argument is fully developed in my "Innovation in Nuclear Thinking: Incompetent, Dangerous or Futile," under review by *Ethics & International Affairs*.

139. Benoît Pelopidas, "The Oracles of Proliferation"; Jeffrey Richelson, *Spying on the Bomb: American Nuclear Intelligence from Nazi Germany to Iran and North Korea* (New York: W.W. Norton, 2006), 373–400.

140. Hans Kristensen and Robert Norris, "Global Nuclear Weapons Inventories: 1945–2010," *Bulletin of the Atomic Scientists* 66, no. 4 (July–August 2010): 81–82. Based on their most conservative estimates for 2010, the global nuclear stockpile has been reduced by 67.6 percent between 1986 and 2010.

141. Benoît Pelopidas, "La couleur du cygne sud-africain, Le rôle des surprises dans l'histoire nucléaire et les effets d'une amnésie partielle" (The Color of the South African Swan: The Role of Surprises in Nuclear History and the Effects of a Partial Amnesia), *French Yearbook of International Relations*, 2010 (in French), http://www.afri-ct.org/IMG/pdf/Pelopidas.pdf.

CHAPTER 2 **The Nuclear Dilemma:**
Constants and Variables
in American Strategic Policies

James E. Goodby

Introduction

Plenty of changes have appeared in the nuclear arena in the past seven
decades. Numbers of nuclear weapons have risen sharply and have just as
sharply declined. The perceived utility of nuclear weapons, once thought
to be ideal for the conduct of coercive diplomacy, has shrunk to the point
where deterrence against their use is almost their sole purpose. The technology of the nuclear components of the weapons advanced spectac-
ularly for many years but has now leveled off. The types of weapons
perceived to be needed for deterrence have changed from "city-busting"
multi-megaton weapons to lower-yield weapons.

There have been constants, too, in the nuclear arena, primarily on
the political-psychological side of the equation. One of them is that
progress toward ending reliance on nuclear weapons for defense purposes has depended on factors other than a cost-benefit analysis of the
weapons themselves. These factors include national leadership attitudes
and the state of the relationships between nuclear-armed nations. One
of the basic nuclear constants has been public confidence in the ability of nuclear weapons to preserve peace and to protect the safety of the

homeland. British Prime Minister Winston Churchill's dictum of 1955 is still broadly accepted: ". . . safety will be the sturdy child of terror, and survival the twin brother of annihilation." Churchill described the practice of nuclear deterrence as a "sublime irony." So it must have seemed. But Churchill envisaged an end to reliance on nuclear deterrence, that it would someday "reap its final reward," enabling "tormented generations to march forth serene and triumphant from the hideous epoch in which we have to dwell."

The dilemma that "tormented generations" face now is how to judge that nuclear deterrence has reaped its final reward, how to decide that whatever utility it had as an immediately usable instrument of unprecedented destruction to the planet has ended. The task of resolving this dilemma requires a review of the experiences of successive American presidents as they sought to control the dangers of nuclear weaponry. This review will help us understand why the trajectory of constantly growing stockpiles took a sharp turn in the late 1980s. Some of the assumptions made about nuclear deterrence need serious reconsideration. We ought to understand why.

Nuclear deterrence, in the form of an assured ability to inflict massive damage on an enemy's homeland even after absorbing an initial nuclear attack by that enemy, has been a constant in American strategic doctrine almost since the beginning of the US-Soviet nuclear competition. Nuclear deterrence has been assumed to "work" under different levels of nuclear forces and very different doctrines for employment of nuclear weapons. What the threat of a nuclear strike actually deterred was always a matter of conjecture and had to remain so. Nuclear weapons have never been used after 1945 and never at all in a two-sided nuclear war. All the certitudes about the effectiveness of nuclear deterrence are based on theory, not on practice.

Another constant—the upward trajectory in the numbers of nuclear weapons held by the United States and the Soviet Union—endured for about a quarter of a century. That trajectory then made a sharp transition to a downward trend. Today the world's nuclear arsenals contain only about one-third of the numbers they held in 1986. Why did this happen?

What Causes Basic Change?

In their foreword for a 1997 publication of Stanford University, George Shultz and William Perry wrote:

> History has shown that Reykjavik was a true turning point. Three major treaties between the United States and the Soviet Union were negotiated by the end of 1992; they resulted in substantially reduced levels of nuclear weapons. That happened as the Cold War was ending and, as the Russians say, it was no coincidence. A dramatic change in the relationship between the Soviet Union and the United States made it possible. A readiness, both in Washington and in Moscow, to open a new chapter in their relationship prepared the way.

So the answer as to why the nuclear trajectory reversed course, quite simply, is that eliminating nuclear weapons is not achievable through a process that focuses exclusively on nuclear weapons, whether that process be a pragmatic step-by-step approach or through a comprehensive blueprint. "Creating the conditions for a world without nuclear weapons," as the UN Security Council has put it, is clearly the right way to think about it.

Validating the Theory of Change

The validity of this proposition can be found in the experiences of American presidents who sought to control the nuclear threat. Their successes undoubtedly made the world safer. But so long as ingrained antagonistic attitudes prevailed in the US-Soviet relationship, deep reductions in nuclear warheads were impossible to achieve. President Harry S. Truman was the first American president to seek to negotiate controls over nuclear weapons. The result, had the effort been successful, would have changed the course of the nuclear age. He introduced a radical plan for the international control of nuclear weapons (the so-called Baruch Plan adapted from the Acheson-Lilienthal Report). But Josef Stalin's government, not surprisingly, had determined that there must be Soviet nuclear bombs. *In 1952, Truman's last year in office, the United States had about one thousand nuclear bombs and warheads and the Soviet Union had fifty.*[1] The Truman disarmament proposals, through essentially dead, remained on the books for nearly a decade.

After Stalin's death in 1953, President Dwight D. Eisenhower opened a new chapter in arms control. In a speech before the UN General Assembly on December 8, 1953, Eisenhower called for negotiations to "begin to diminish the potential destructive power of the world's atomic stockpiles." He pledged that the United States would "devote its entire heart and mind to find the way by which the miraculous inventiveness of man shall not be dedicated to his death, but consecrated to his life." In the last two years of his first term, he adopted partial measures, that is, separable steps on the way to general disarmament. A nuclear test ban was one such step. In his last full year in office, 1960, Eisenhower came close to succeeding in his quest for a test ban treaty. *But at the end of his administration, the United States had twenty thousand nuclear bombs and warheads and the Soviet Union had one thousand six hundred.*

A surge in the nuclear arsenals of the United States and the Soviet Union began in the Kennedy administration, which was influenced by fear that vulnerable US weapons systems could be destroyed in a Soviet surprise attack. The US buildup prompted Soviet leader Nikita Khrushchev to deploy nuclear weapons in Cuba. President John F. Kennedy's June 10, 1963, speech at American University was a landmark in terms of an

1. This and other estimates of US and Soviet/Russian numbers of nuclear weapons were published by the Natural Resources Defense Council. See "Table of Global Nuclear Weapons Stockpiles, 1945–2002," www.nrdc.org/nuclear/nudb/datab19.asp.

appeal for peace. Yet, at his death later that year, Kennedy had authorized building more nuclear bombs and warheads so that *US numbers came to nearly thirty thousand. The Soviet Union had around four thousand.*

The first treaty to affect US and Soviet nuclear operations, the Limited Test Ban Treaty, entered into force in 1963. However, spurred on by an ignominious retreat from their nuclear deployments in Cuba, the Soviet leaders ousted Khrushchev and began a massive buildup of nuclear weapons, which peaked in 1986.

Kennedy's successor, President Lyndon B. Johnson, negotiated the nuclear Non-Proliferation Treaty (NPT), one of the foundation stones of the arms control edifice. He also succeeded in engaging the Soviet leadership on what became the SALT negotiations, the Strategic Arms Limitation Talks. But in 1964 China tested a nuclear weapon and became the fifth nuclear weapon state. *The US nuclear stockpile peaked at 31,175 weapons in 1967 and had declined to about 29,000 by the time Johnson left office in 1969. The Soviet nuclear weapon stockpile at that time had grown to over nine thousand.*

President Richard Nixon and his national security adviser and later secretary of state, Henry Kissinger, called for an era of negotiations. They succeeded in negotiating the first limitations on strategic offensive forces and the Anti-Ballistic Missile Treaty (ABM), which limited ballistic missile defense testing and deployments on both sides. They sought and, to a large degree, obtained a period of détente in the US-Soviet relationship, based on what they hoped was a shared interest in the status quo. They saw this as a rational American foreign policy in a period of retrenchment leading up to the US withdrawal from Vietnam.

President Gerald Ford, who took office after Nixon's resignation, essentially ended the official policy of seeking détente with Moscow but tried to preserve its nuclear elements. A strategic arms limitation framework was negotiated by Ford and Soviet General Secretary Leonid Brezhnev in Vladivostok in 1974. Under Ford's administration, defense spending received new public and congressional support in response to the continuing nuclear arms buildup by the Soviet Union. *When Ford left office in 1977, the United States had nearly twenty-six thousand nuclear weapons and the Soviet Union had over seventeen thousand.*

President Jimmy Carter entered office in 1977 determined to re-emphasize nuclear arms negotiations with the Soviet Union. His first effort was a seriously intentioned nuclear arms control proposal unveiled in Moscow by Secretary of State Cyrus Vance. Brezhnev bluntly rejected the proposals, which significantly altered the contours of the Vladivostok accords. Carter did finally succeed in negotiating SALT II, a treaty that built on the Vladivostok accords. That treaty was withdrawn from the Senate in 1979 when the Soviet Union invaded Afghanistan.

By the time Carter left office, the Soviets had caught up with the Americans. The total number of nuclear weapons stood as follows: Soviet Union—thirty thousand; United States—twenty-four thousand. As one of his last major decisions, Carter approved a strategic doctrine predicated on preparations for "protracted nuclear war."

President Ronald Reagan came to office in January 1981, determined to reverse what had become known as "a decade of neglect" in US defense efforts. He significantly changed US defense priorities but *the total numbers of US nuclear weapons remained fairly constant during his eight years in office, at about twenty-three thousand. Soviet holdings peaked at about forty thousand in 1986 and thereafter began to decline.*

The Turning Point

Reagan also saw nuclear weapons reductions as part of an effort to make a decisive turn in US-Soviet political relations and in the Cold War itself. Reagan thought that the status quo was not something in which the United States should acquiesce. It included the division of Europe and of Germany into Communist and non-Communist parts. It included wholesale violations of human rights. Status-quo thinking had failed to move US policy beyond a containment strategy based on mutual assured destruction, although historian George Kennan had predicted from the very beginning that change in the Soviet method of governance was inevitable.

Reagan rejected the doctrine of mutual assured destruction and its corollary, a steady increase in nuclear arsenals. He called for nuclear reductions, not just a controlled buildup. His appeal for elimination of nuclear weapons reversed two decades of arms control theory. Although 1983 was seen in Moscow as one of the most dangerous periods in the history of the US-Soviet relationship, by 1984 Reagan was calling for constructive engagement with the Soviet Union. By 1985, a new Soviet leader, Mikhail Gorbachev, as revolutionary in his way as Ronald Reagan, had become general secretary.

On November 19 and 20, 1985, Reagan and Gorbachev met in Geneva. They issued a joint statement which said the two sides "have agreed that a nuclear war cannot be won and must never be fought." Two years later, they signed a treaty eliminating a whole class of nuclear delivery systems through the treaty on intermediate-range nuclear forces (INF).

When Reagan left office in January 1989, the Cold War was on its way out. Young Germans began to demolish the Berlin Wall during the night of November 9, 1989. Germany was reunited by October 1990. Boris Yeltsin proclaimed the independence of Russia. Gorbachev resigned as president of the Soviet Union and the Union of Soviet Socialist Republics dissolved on December 25, 1991.

Change and Continuity after Reagan

President George H.W. Bush carried forward the nuclear reductions begun by Reagan. START I, the Strategic Arms Reduction Treaty, was signed on July 31, 1991, and entered into force on December 5, 1994. The treaty required the United States and the Soviet Union, later Russia, to *reduce their deployed strategic arsenals to one thousand six hundred delivery vehicles carrying no more than six thousand warheads* as defined in the treaty's counting rules.[2] A START II treaty was signed by Bush near

---

2. As cited by the Arms Control Association (www.armscontrol.org).

the end of his term but it never entered into force. *In 1992, the United States had nearly fourteen thousand nuclear bombs and warheads, while Russia had about twenty-five thousand.*

An innovation introduced by President Bush in 1991 showed that nuclear constraints could proceed without lengthy negotiations leading to a treaty. In parallel with similar actions taken by Gorbachev, and later by Russian President Yeltsin, Bush took some nuclear weapons off full alert and removed other short-range nuclear weapons from forward deployment.

The administrations of Bill Clinton and George W. Bush focused on the consequences of the breakup of the USSR, a nuclear-armed super-power. "Loose nukes" preoccupied President Clinton. No long-term transformational changes in the basic US-Russian relationship occurred despite much discussion about it and despite a period of enhanced US-Russian cooperation.

President George W. Bush sought to revise the relationship between Russia and the United States but tried to do so on terms that Russia's leadership—President Vladimir Putin, especially—found offensive. This approach included US abrogation of Nixon's 1972 ABM treaty. The two presidents succeeded in concluding a treaty that provided for *reductions over a ten-year period of deployed nuclear warheads on each side to between one thousand seven hundred and two thousand two hundred.* That treaty entered into force in June 2003 and was superseded by President Barack Obama's New START treaty in 2011.

Obama declared in a major speech in Prague on April 5, 2009, that "the existence of thousands of nuclear weapons is the most dangerous legacy of the Cold War." He spoke of "America's commitment to seek the peace and security of a world without nuclear weapons." On February 5, 2011, a US-Russian nuclear reductions treaty—New START—entered into force. *It called for a ceiling on strategic nuclear warheads of one thousand five hundred fifty for each side.* On June 19, 2013, Obama announced in Berlin that the United States' "deployed strategic nuclear weapons" could be reduced by up to one-third. This would bring that category of nuclear weapons to about one thousand warheads. Reductions to that level would be a major accomplishment. But the process has become frozen and shows little sign of thawing any time soon. Why has this happened?

What Inhibits Basic Change?

More than any other lethal device available to the world's militaries, nuclear weapons have the power to influence fundamentally the perceptions that nations have of their own security and the threats they face. Efforts to reduce dependence on nuclear deterrence cannot move beyond the overall state of relations between adversaries. How can one get off the tiger's back? As suggested above, the answer appears to be that only a broad-based effort to improve the basic state of relations between two nuclear-armed rivals will allow the nuclear competition to be safely ended.

A false corollary of this conclusion is the familiar gibe that "arms control becomes possible only when it is not needed." It is false because a basic improvement in the relationship is not likely to be achieved while two nations remain nuclear-armed strategic rivals. This situation has contributed to the stalemate in which the United States and Russia now find themselves. The two processes have to proceed hand-in-hand, as Reagan and his secretary of state, George Shultz, demonstrated.

Just as Reagan was right to use nuclear reductions to effect basic change in the US-Soviet relationship and to end the Cold War structure of the international system, so would the contemporary American leadership be right to set a goal of creating a new global security commons, with a core element being a commitment to creating the conditions for a world without nuclear weapons. Challenging the global status quo is essential to dramatic reductions in nuclear arsenals, just as reductions in nuclear arsenals are necessary to lubricate the gears of the international system as it makes the transition to a very different set of relationships.

The Constant of Nuclear Deterrence vs. New Threats

On September 21, 2014, the *New York Times* reported in some detail what it called "a nationwide wave of atomic revitalization that includes plans for a new generation of weapon carriers. A recent federal study put the collective price tag, over the next three decades, at up to a trillion dollars." The article cited a view among disappointed advisers to the administration that "the modernization of nuclear capabilities has become an end unto itself."[3]

A major factor inhibiting change is that "nuclear deterrence" has become an intellectual crutch, often making it harder to deal with the real problems in the world today. "Deterrence" has become so associated with nuclear weapons that deterrence by other means is hardly thought of as the same concept. But deterrence in any form is not necessarily the best intellectual construct for addressing twenty-first-century problems.

A new form of medievalism threatens all responsible governments and the international order itself. The availability of deadly force on a large scale is no longer the monopoly of governments. An order based on the preservation of nation-states is no longer the goal of some extremist groups. This threat is not one that can be deterred by the threat of crushing retaliation with nuclear weapons. It may not be influenced by any form of deterrence.

Insurrections and civil wars rage in Africa and the Middle East. Deterrence in any form lacks the credibility to stop them. Russia was not deterred by the opinion of other nations when it annexed Crimea and nuclear retaliation was never considered by other nations. Today's threats

---

3. William J. Broad and David Sanger, "US Ramping Up Major Renewal in Nuclear Arms," *New York Times*, September 21, 2014.

require the integration of all elements of national power to serve US national interests. The point is not to take force off the table but to elevate other factors to more prominence in the US approach to international relations.

The Changing Utility of Nuclear Deterrence

Deterrence as a tool of statecraft is here to stay. *Nuclear* deterrence, especially as it was practiced during the Cold War, is not. Moral arguments have been part of the conversation about nuclear weapons since the 1940s. They have not swayed national leaders, with very few exceptions—Ronald Reagan being one. But arguments about nuclear deterrence and nuclear weapons reductions based on the *disutility* of nuclear weapons have gradually been having an effect on how nuclear weapons are viewed by political leaders and military planners, at least in the United States. In a documentary called *The Nuclear Tipping Point,* General Colin Powell said, "And the one thing I convinced myself of, after all these years of exposure to the use of nuclear weapons, is that they were useless. They could not be used." But, perceptions derived from the Cold War still dominate most of the public debate. The following assertions, coupled with challenges to them in each case, illustrate the contours of a public debate that has yet to occur. These issues will be discussed in more detail in subsequent sections of this chapter.

- *Nuclear deterrence can cope with whatever weapon nations happen to choose to threaten others.* In fact, international peace and security are threatened by new modes of altering the status quo, while new technologies have emerged that render nuclear deterrence moot.
- *Nuclear forces must be maintained continuously on high alert in order to be ready for a surprise attack.* But reliance on a responsive nuclear infrastructure has become more essential than an instantly usable standing force.

- *Small nations like North Korea will always yield to the logic of superior nuclear forces held by larger nations.* In fact, many of the world's confrontations pit small nations against larger ones where the smaller nations have much more at stake than the larger nations that would like to deter or coerce them, thus creating an asymmetric situation in which nuclear coercion is not effective.
- *China, Russia, and the United States operate within a framework of mutual nuclear deterrence that restrains their behavior toward each other.* In fact, nuclear deterrence is largely irrelevant to relations among the five recognized nuclear weapons states.
- *Nuclear deterrence theory and strategic stability theory can be extrapolated from Cold War experience and practiced in much the same way.* But in a world with multiple nuclear-armed states, nuclear deterrence and strategic stability must operate differently than they did in the bipolar structure of the Cold War, because nuclear operations cannot be decoupled from the calculations of other nuclear-armed nations.
- *The fear of nuclear retaliation is the most effective basis for deterrence.* In fact, deterrence achieved through the clear ability to deny an adversary his objectives through military or other means is a safer and surer method than deterrence based on the threat of nuclear retaliation.
- *The US "nuclear umbrella" is essential to prevent allies from acquiring nuclear weapons.* The historical evidence does not validate this thesis, whether in terms of allies that acquired nuclear weapons or of those that refrained from doing so. The anticipation that nuclear weapons will always be a part of the world's armed forces is a more fundamental long-term driver of proliferation within alliance systems.
- *Nuclear weapons are necessary to stabilize regional disputes.* Almost the opposite is true. Wherever nuclear weapons have been introduced into conflict situations, they have been the cause of more tension and conflict.

Technology Has Moved beyond Nuclear Deterrence

Technology has been one of the major drivers of evolving theories of deterrence. Future concepts of deterrence are likely to be shaped by technologies only now emerging as potential game-changers in warfare. A discussion of only a few of them will illustrate the difficulties of projecting nuclear-based Cold War theories of nuclear deterrence into the future.

Cyberwarfare

Relatively benign attacks on a nation's ability to conduct business already have occurred. One was in Estonia in 2007; another was in Georgia in 2008. Both incidents shut down those governments' ability to use their official websites for a few days. More recent cyberattacks on the United States reportedly originated in China, Iran, and North Korea. Stuxnet, the virus reportedly used by a US-Israeli cyberwarfare program called Operation Olympic Games, seems to have been highly effective in delaying Iran's centrifuge-based uranium enrichment program. The attack on SONY, thought to be from North Korea, was effective and very costly to that company.

Command, control, and communications are key to military operations. Sabotaging those systems by rendering communication nodes incapable of functioning can give an attacker a decided advantage, provided he can prevent his victim from also rendering his own communications useless.

Can deterrence of such attacks be found in a declaratory policy that says nuclear weapons will be the response? Not very likely. It is very difficult to find the correct return address for cyberattacks in a timely and actionable way. Rules of the road may become possible. But deterrence, especially with nuclear weapons, will be very hard to establish and to sustain.

Synthetic Biology

In this field, science has been making rapid progress in a direction highly beneficial to humankind. This technology also could be misused to create biological weapons. Major nations already have access to biological weapons technology. The new technologies will not advance them significantly beyond the capabilities they now have.

But this technology and the weapons it could produce may become interesting to terrorist groups. So, once again, the question is whether terrorists can be deterred. In this case, the terrorists would be equipped with biological weapons that ultimately could do damage to human life on the scale of nuclear weapons. The answer almost certainly is that nuclear deterrence as understood in the Cold War will not be available. What can be done is essentially the same as what is being done to contain the threat of nuclear weapons: improve intelligence, develop forensics, organize internationally to prevent the threat from getting out of control, and help publics everywhere understand better how to manage the risks. Cooperation, rather than threat-based policies, will be essential.

Space Attacks

Several countries are already capable of wreaking havoc in space. China has dramatically demonstrated its anti-satellite capabilities. With much of the world dependent now on space-based instruments for surveillance and communications, it may be just a matter of time before some nation works out its grievances against another by destroying a vital communications satellite. That could be seen as the precursor to a major attack.

This capability is not yet available to most nations or to terrorists. It is somewhat analogous to cyberwarfare: in many applications it is nonlethal to humans, provocative, but not a *casus belli* unless it is perceived to be the beginning of a "decapitating" first nuclear strike. In such a case, the destruction of critical command and control modes at a crucial moment in a limited conflict could be a serious setback to a defender.

In the space warfare case, the same principle that deterred the onset of major war between the Soviet Union and the United States in Europe during the Cold War is relevant. Each was too vested in the status quo to want to make war against each other, especially with nuclear weapons. Deterrence worked because both sides wanted it to. Its scope of relevance was carefully delimited. Much the same can be said of satellites in space. All parties that have the capabilities to launch and destroy satellites prefer the status quo to the alternatives.

Will this situation prevail at times of high tension or even limited conflict? Will it prevail in a world of multiple nuclear-armed states? It may not, but cooperation is the strategy most likely to prevent space wars, not the threat of nuclear retaliation. Unless one party has determined that a major war is inevitable, mutual deterrence based on satisfaction with the status quo is likely to prevail.

Drones

The use of force through unmanned drones or special-forces operations has become commonplace. The Obama administration has developed guidelines for the use of drones in responding to terrorist threats. Ultimately these kinds of guidelines will become doctrines and declared policies more broadly among technologically advanced nations.

Nearly all the literature on nuclear deterrence quite naturally is based on the assumption that the threat of punishment applies to an entire nation. Much more theoretical work is needed to develop deterrence concepts that apply to more discriminating types of deterrence/coercion. The threat of using nuclear weapons is clearly not a plausible deterrent against the use of drones—unless that use were to be perceived as the beginning of an attack on a nation's national command authority.

Are Missiles Ready for Instant Launch the Key to Deterrence?

Obama's June 2013 nuclear guidance called for reducing US capabilities for rapid launch of armed missiles. Nuclear deterrence is not dependent on that kind of capability. In fact, nuclear-based deterrence would not disappear for many years to come even if these weapons were eliminated, as the late author Jonathan Schell pointed out many years ago. It would be manifested in a new form: the ability to reconstitute small nuclear arsenals from a "responsive nuclear infrastructure." A responsive nuclear infrastructure means functioning nuclear laboratories and some capacity to produce nuclear weapons, if needed, in a timely way. The US Stockpile Stewardship Program even today is a model for what nuclear deterrence will look like as zero is achieved and for a while thereafter.

Big vs. Small: The Case of North Korea

Despite some nuclear near misses, war between the Soviet Union and the United States was avoided because each side believed that its goals could be met in ways that did not require an all-out challenge to the other. That is not often the case where a relatively weak country is challenging a stronger power. North Korea is a case in point.

Nuclear coercion cannot be applied successfully by the United States or other countries to roll back the North Korean nuclear weapons program because the current status quo, while minimally acceptable to the United States, is not acceptable to the Kim Jong-un regime. The survival of the United States is not an issue in this relationship, whereas the survival of North Korea is very much an issue to the North Korean government.

Short of regime change or major war, a rollback of North Korea's nuclear weapons program cannot be achieved unless the government of that nation concludes that a new method of assuring the survival of the regime and the nation is in place. Very little sustained effort has ever gone into considering that side of the equation, partly because North Korea's negotiating partners have consistently miscalculated the odds that that nation will survive over the long term.

Are Nuclear Deterrence Considerations Key to Relations between the United States, Russia, and China?

Britain, France, and the United States have long since entered into a relationship that can be described as a *stable* peace: that is, for them war is not a conceivable policy option. But it is fair to say that peace is still *conditional* as between the United States, Russia, and China. The use of force in their mutual relationship is a very remote possibility but it is not entirely excluded. Unfortunately, military force, whether nuclear or conventional, still figures in calculations about the relationships, whether measured in numbers of nuclear weapons or in deployments of naval, air, and ground forces. Presidents Bush and Putin mutually declared that the hostility that characterized their relations in the Cold War had ended. But each still paid serious attention to the other's force planning. At the same time, overt cooperation between the two countries in security, economic, and political matters has been until recently a significant part of the relationship. Both face similar transnational threats from terrorists, criminal groups, and climate change. Ukraine has become a serious issue between Russia and the West, but there is no sign that nuclear weapons use by anyone is seen as a rational response. The situation, of course, has the potential to become yet another driver of nuclear proliferation.

As regards the salience of a nuclear deterrent in Russia-China relations or US-China relations, the situation is not very different. China has maintained a relatively small nuclear force, apparently calculating that it is sufficient to make other countries more cautious in their dealings with China. China naturally is sensitive to US ballistic missile defense planning and to US academic writings that claim the United States has a first-disarming-strike capability against China. But nuclear deterrence has not become a major factor in the US-China or Russia-China relationship despite China's growing interest in laying claim to waters and islands in its vicinity and its concerns about US ballistic missile defense programs.

Can Cold War Nuclear Deterrence Theory Be Applied in a Multipolar Nuclear Environment?

During the Cold War, nuclear deterrence was essentially a US-Soviet calculation. After the Cold War, China began to loom larger in US planning, but the premise that deterrence was essentially a bilateral interaction remained. In the future, situations that are not demonstrably bilateral may become the norm. Even now, but especially in the event global nonpro-liferation efforts fail to meet current challenges, the nuclear deterrence calculations of the United States and other states armed with nuclear weapons will have to be based on a much more complex set of global and regional dynamics.

In such a system, if nuclear weapons were used or even if their use were threatened, there would be an action-and-reaction effect that might involve several nations, not just two as in the Cold War paradigm. For example, the alert status of nuclear delivery systems probably would be changed to a higher level of readiness by several nations. There might be movements of air and naval forces equipped with nuclear weapons. A great deal of ambiguity can be expected in the event of a nuclear explosion as to which nation had detonated a nuclear weapon. Once nuclear weapons attacks occurred, terminating the war could be difficult. Conceivably, three or four nuclear-armed states could become engaged in hostilities that might have originated with just one nation initiating a nuclear attack. The dynamics of nuclear conflict in the Middle East, South Asia, or Northeast Asia would require qualitatively different deterrent cal-culations from those the five Non-Proliferation Treaty nuclear weapons states have been accustomed to making.

"Catalytic" nuclear war was one of the worries of the Kennedy and Johnson administrations. It meant that the United States could become engaged in a nuclear war because a nuclear-armed US ally had used a nuclear weapon and their common adversary, the Soviet Union, had decided to use nuclear weapons in response. Those worries would also figure in a complex world of perhaps fifteen or so nuclear-armed states, which would also include the unknown capabilities of terrorist groups and the likelihood that cyber-mischief would accompany any nuclear attack. How does one measure strategic stability in such a situation?

Cold War thinking is not useful in many areas of international rela-tions. One of them is how to think about "strategic stability." Still, the basic thinking about strategic stability is one of the constants that per-sist up to the present day. In its present incarnation, strategic stability was discussed, though not explicitly defined or re-defined, in the Obama administration's first Nuclear Posture Review Report. The report assumed that everyone understood what strategic stability is and that US officials know how to make it work for the United States.

The challenge of how the United States and the Soviet Union could use "strategic stability" as a commonly understood metric or standard by which to gauge the appropriateness of defense actions was never resolved during the Cold War. Each side tended to see what it was doing as "stabilizing" and what the other side was doing as "destabilizing." The simple idea of a secure second strike eventually morphed into the concept of "protracted nuclear war," a capability of retaining a retaliatory blow even after several waves of US-Soviet nuclear attacks on each other.

The agenda for successful strategic stability talks in a multipolar nuclear universe cannot be a laundry list of things each nation wants to do, in its own way, and with little regard for how others see such actions. Strategic stability has everything to do with the broad context in which the nations are operating and little to do with first and second strikes as between, say, the United States and North Korea or between India and China. A process of close consultation and accommodation where possible is more likely to yield a measure of strategic stability, both in the US-Russian context and in the US-Chinese context, than an exclusive focus on military hardware and doctrine. It would be appropriate for consultations among other sets of nations possessing nuclear weapons, as well.

Is the Threat of Nuclear Retaliation the Key to Extended Deterrence?

A major question today is how to think about extended deterrence and whether a requirement for extended deterrence is incompatible with a policy of trying to create the conditions for a world without nuclear weapons. "Extended deterrence" amounts to a US threat to use nuclear weapons if an ally is attacked. Today, for all practical purposes, the US nuclear deterrent exists to deter the use of nuclear weapons by other nations or to respond to their use by an adversary. Therefore, the US nuclear umbrella serves the purpose of deterring an enemy's use of nuclear weapons, so long as such weapons exist.

The US nuclear umbrella would not be available to deter a conventional attack in a world without nuclear weapons. Does that mean that the ability to deny an enemy his aggressive goals through means other than nuclear retaliation would not exist? Of course not. American allies and the United States itself would be in a safer place if deterrence could be achieved by the patently obvious capability of the United States and its allies to deny an aggressor the ability to achieve his goals without resort to nuclear weapons. If that condition existed in regions where the United States has vital interests, a policy of seeking a world without nuclear weapons would clearly be the prudent policy to adopt.

Deterrence by denial is far and away the most relevant means of exercising deterrence of today's most plausible contingencies in the real world. Wherever one looks, deterrence by denial seems to be a practical and credible means both to persuade an adversary that an attack would be futile and to maintain or restore peace and security.

Does the US Nuclear Umbrella Prevent Nuclear Proliferation?

It can be taken as a given that so long as nuclear weapons exist, US nuclear weapons will also exist to deter the use of nuclear weapons by adversaries of the United States or of its allies. It also can be assumed that deterrence—even nuclear deterrence—will still exist in a world without nuclear weapons. But nuclear weapons are not synonymous with deterrence, despite the unfortunate habit of conflating the two. In fact, the use of nuclear weapons in some cases is so unlikely that the idea of deterrence can be undermined by thinking solely in terms of the "nuclear umbrella."

Will allies of the United States conclude that they must have nuclear weapons if the world's nuclear stockpiles are shrinking? Not very likely. The incentives for nuclear proliferation have increased in recent years. But that is because national expectations are that nuclear weapons are here to stay and are being acquired by nations that might actually use them, certainly not on the theory that nuclear weapons are disappearing.

Do Nuclear Weapons Help Stabilize Regional Conflicts?

The persistence of nuclear deterrence thinking in regional disputes is undeniable. This points to the special factors that influence regional confrontations, such as asymmetries of one sort or another that drive nuclear weapons decisions. It is in these areas that the danger of nuclear weapons use is now the highest and where security asymmetries must be addressed with some sense of urgency. Persuading leaders in those regions that their nations' security can be safeguarded by other means than threats of nuclear devastation must be a part of this diplomatic campaign.

Many nations, especially those trapped in regional conflicts, believe that deterrence by denial cannot be achieved and so nuclear deterrence is their only choice. If that conclusion stands in the way of a search for political settlements, it is dangerous and self-defeating. This is the situation in Northeast Asia and is largely the case in South Asia, too. The Iranian standoff shows how nuclear weapons complicate the search for a political settlement.

During the Cold War, the practice of nuclear deterrence carried with it the vast risk of annihilation on a global scale. But Moscow and Washington each believed that its side would ultimately prevail, largely through peaceful means, and that preventive war was unnecessary. Moreover, the United States and the Soviet Union had no territorial claims against the other. They were insulated by thousands of miles from the daily frictions that arise when adversaries live side by side. Given these circumstances, the Soviet Union and the United States had the luxury of time to develop rules, tacit and otherwise, to tilt the scales against the use of nuclear weapons. These circumstances do not exist in the Middle East, Northeast Asia, or South Asia. To assume that nuclear deterrence will always and forever work successfully, even in very different conditions, is an exercise in wishful thinking.

Conlusions

Build a Coalition of the Willing

Great political leaders have always understood that rallying the people in support of great causes requires inspiration more than managerial skills. Inspiration is supplied by projecting a big idea. The threats that the United States and the world face today require that kind of inspiration. How can the vision of a world free of nuclear weapons become the foundation for a program designed to achieve a new global commons?

Russia and the United States have succeeded in the post-Cold War era in striking agreements that have reduced their nuclear arsenals. They still possess about 90 percent of the world's nuclear warheads. A global program of nuclear constraints forged in part by the United States and Russia could be a core element in a new global commons. No global security commons could be created without full Russian participation.

Nations of Asia must also become engaged in measures of nuclear constraint. This does not require the United States to turn away from negotiations with Russia. But it does mean that a more proactive role in order-building diplomacy must be played by Japan, North and South Korea, China, India, and Pakistan. It means a greater emphasis on multilateral measures that will bring all of the nuclear-armed states, and others, into common agreements.

Two agreements that meet this requirement are the Comprehensive Nuclear-Test-Ban Treaty and the proposed Fissile Material Cutoff Treaty. Progress in bringing these two agreements into force would both reduce proliferation dangers in Asia and bring Asian nations into the mainstream of arms control.

A third, more sweeping proposal would be to negotiate a joint enterprise: a coalition of nations committed to working together to create the conditions for a world without nuclear weapons. This would include both political and a security components. Success in putting such a program into force would be far more important than a modest reduction in numbers of warheads held by the United States and Russia.

Challenge the Status Quo

The post-World War II effort to build a new global commons was remarkably successful. The victorious Allies, led by a relatively new global power, the United States, created new institutions that they hoped would prevent the crises that had brought on two world wars and a great depression. China and Russia participated in this institution-building to a limited degree.

In Washington, great hopes were placed in the United Nations, which was intended to be a global organization for security and cooperation. These hopes were dashed on the rocks of the Cold War global confrontation between the United States and the Soviet Union. In Europe, the Western allies created the North Atlantic Treaty Organization, designed to defend and sustain the people of Western Europe against the multifaceted threat posed by Moscow. The European Union, originally the European Community, was created to help prevent the kinds of internecine conflicts within Europe that led to both World War I and World War II. The World Bank and the International Monetary Fund were created to support global trade and economic development. The General Agreement on Tariffs and Trade was later established to ease barriers to trade. In the Asia-Pacific region, disputes over Taiwan and the Korean peninsula led to a confrontation between the United States and China and to a security framework based on alliances between the United States and Japan and the United States and South Korea. The Vietnam War consolidated that system.

Although the Cold War ended a quarter of a century ago, nothing like the international security organizations created at the beginning of the Cold War have been created to reflect new realities, especially in Asia. The rise of China and India means that Asian concerns and outlooks will have to be incorporated more completely into what must become a revamped global security commons. This will require an intensive and probably protracted period of order-building diplomacy. Hopes that

Russia would be able to play a major role in a Euro-Atlantic security community after the Cold War have not been met for various reasons, some internal to Russia, others because of international developments. But a global security commons will require Russian participation in building it.

The goal of seeking a world without nuclear weapons as a core element in a new global security commons would deal with the most devastating weapon humanity has ever devised. Striving to create the conditions for a world without nuclear weapons has the added virtue of highlighting issues that need to be resolved if nuclear weapons are ever to be eliminated, thus setting an agenda for global and regional security.

CHAPTER 3 **A Realist's Rationale for a World without Nuclear Weapons**

Steven Pifer

Introduction

Speaking in Prague on April 5, 2009, President Barack Obama declared "America's commitment to seek the peace and security of a world without nuclear weapons." The president attached important qualifiers to his objective. "This goal will not be reached quickly—perhaps not in my lifetime," he said, and also, "As long as these weapons exist, the United States will maintain a safe, secure and effective arsenal to deter any adversary. . . ."[1] Many, however, ignored the measured language and immediately dismissed the president's goal as unattainable, idealistic, and even naïve.

Sometimes it takes a great goal to inspire great achievement, even if reaching that goal, or planning to do so, will be difficult. President John F. Kennedy in 1961 set the objective of putting a man on the moon by the end of the decade, even though the United States at the time had taken just baby steps in space. When he delivered his May 25 speech calling for

---

1. The White House, Office of the Press Secretary, "Remarks by President Barack Obama, Hradcany Square, Prague, Czech Republic," April 5, 2009.

"longer strides," only one American, Alan Shepard, had been in space—and just on a suborbital flight. Eight years later, Neil Armstrong and Buzz Aldrin stood on the moon.

Obama's goal may seem idealistic to some. But acknowledged realists also have called for a world without nuclear weapons. Writing in the *Wall Street Journal* in January 2007, four senior American statesmen—George Shultz, Bill Perry, Henry Kissinger, and Sam Nunn—noted the growing risks posed by nuclear weapons and endorsed "setting the goal of a world free of nuclear weapons and working energetically on the actions required to achieve that goal."[2] The authors developed that theme in subsequent *Wall Street Journal* opinion pieces, proposing a "joint enterprise" to move toward the objective. The goal of a world free of nuclear weapons has been endorsed by other senior statesmen who are considered realists, including many associated with the Global Zero movement.

When Americans consider the goal of a world without nuclear weapons, two main questions arise. First, is the objective desirable from the point of view of US security interests? Second, is it feasible to achieve that goal safely?

This chapter makes a realist's argument for why a world without nuclear weapons is a desirable objective. In particular, it argues why such a world would be less risky and in the national security interest of the United States. The chapter closes with some brief comments on the feasibility of achieving that goal.

As we approach the seventieth anniversaries of the first detonation of a nuclear weapon at Alamogordo, New Mexico, and of the destruction of Hiroshima and Nagasaki in Japan, nuclear deterrence remains the fundamental underpinning of US security, as it has since the 1950s. Nuclear weapons and nuclear deterrence protected the United States and its allies during their Cold War with the Soviet Union. By all appearances,

---

2. George P. Shultz, William J. Perry, Henry A. Kissinger, and Sam Nunn, "A World Free of Nuclear Weapons," *Wall Street Journal,* January 4, 2007.

nuclear deterrence worked . . . but with one important qualifier: in several instances, we were lucky. Events quite plausibly could have played out in another way, with disastrous consequences for the United States and the world.

Will the United States and others stay lucky in a nuclear world, one in which not all nuclear-armed states inspire confidence in their ability to responsibly and safely manage their destructive arsenals and in which the number of nuclear-weapons states might increase? The growing risk that a nuclear weapon could be used provided a major motivating factor behind the Shultz/Perry/Kissinger/Nunn articles.

A world without nuclear weapons should be of interest to Americans. It would eliminate the risk that nuclear arms might be used against the United States—either intentionally or by miscalculation or accident. Moreover, blessed with a favorable geographic position, a global network of allies, and the world's most powerful and technologically advanced conventional military, the United States would be in a strong position to ensure its security and that of its allies in a nuclear weapons-free world.

Deterrence would not vanish in such a world; it would merely change in character. Conventional US military forces would still have the capability to threaten risks and impose costs that would outweigh the benefits an adversary might hope to achieve from conventional aggression and would thereby deter the aggression in the first place. Some adjustments would be needed, to be sure. The United States would have to devote adequate resources to its conventional forces, and allies would likely have to contribute something more toward their own defense. But the safety of a world without nuclear arms compares favorably to the risks the United States and the world will run if nuclear weapons remain.

Of course, ridding the world of nuclear arms, or even achieving the conditions for a world without nuclear arms, poses a daunting task. In the end, it might not be achievable. There is nevertheless a realist's argument for the objective.

Nuclear Deterrence

Nuclear deterrence has provided the bedrock of US security policy since the early 1950s. Deterrence seeks to create a situation in which the risks and costs of aggression far outweigh any gains or benefits that the aggressor might hope to achieve. Successful deterrence requires getting into the mind of a potential adversary, understanding his motives, and then being able to hold the things he values at risk. It requires creating in the adversary's mind a credible prospect of a potentially devastating response.

Nuclear weapons, with their immense destructive capabilities, proved ideally suited for deterrence. Their potential retaliatory use confronts a possible adversary with unimaginably huge consequences for aggression. What potential gains might entice an opponent to use military force to pursue those gains if that raised a credible risk of nuclear retaliation, including the destruction of much of his military, industrial base, and population—indeed, the possible end of his country's existence as a functioning society?

In the short-lived period of overwhelming American nuclear dominance, Washington adopted a policy of massive retaliation. By the early 1960s, the United States was well on its way to building a robust strategic triad—consisting of long-range heavy bombers, intercontinental ballistic missiles (ICBMs), and submarine-launched ballistic missiles (SLBMs)—augmented by nonstrategic nuclear weapons, many of which were deployed forward in Europe and the western Pacific. These gave the US military the capability to impose tremendous damage on any possible opponent.

By the mid-1960s, the Soviet Union had begun building a strategic triad of its own and Washington had moved away from massive retaliation to a policy of flexible response. As both Washington and Moscow acquired sufficiently capable, survivable, and diverse strategic forces that could inflict massive destruction on the other, even after absorbing a first strike, a state of mutual nuclear deterrence evolved. This balance, often referred to as mutual assured destruction, was one of the defining characteristics of the face-off between the United States and the Soviet Union during the Cold War.

The United States and the Soviet Union piled on nuclear arms in the 1950s, 1960s, and 1970s. In 1967, the US nuclear arsenal topped out at 31,255 weapons.[3] The total number declined thereafter, though the number of American ICBM and SLBM warheads and strategic bomber weapons climbed into the late 1980s, peaking at more than ten thousand attributable weapons when the 1991 Strategic Arms Reduction Treaty was signed. The Soviet arsenal may have reached as many as forty-five thousand weapons in the 1980s.[4] The large numbers were driven in part by strategies that went way beyond mere deterrence to include doctrines of counterforce (to target and destroy an adversary's nuclear and other military forces), damage limitation (to destroy as much of an adversary's nuclear capability as possible in order to reduce damage to one's own country), and follow-up strikes (to try to achieve a dominant position following a nuclear exchange).

By all appearances, nuclear deterrence worked. The United States and Soviet Union opposed each other politically, militarily, economically, and ideologically. They engaged freely in proxy wars around the globe. But, despite tensions and hundreds of thousands of American and Soviet soldiers facing off for decades in Central Europe, the two countries avoided direct conflict. Finding historical examples in which two states found themselves in such intractable opposition and yet did not go to war is no easy task. Nuclear weapons appear to be a major reason why the US-Soviet rivalry did not go the way of other great-power confrontations and lead to war. Nuclear deterrence seems to have worked.

---

3. Department of Defense, "Fact Sheet: Transparency in the U.S. Nuclear Weapons Stockpile," April 29, 2014.

4. Nuclear Threat Initiative, "Country Profile: Russia—Overview," http://www.nti.org /country-profiles/russia.

The Risks of Nuclear Deterrence

At several points, however, there were very close calls, and the United States was lucky. Over the past sixty years, there have been numerous cases where a miscalculation in a time of crisis, a computer or mechanical error, a human mistake, or some combination could have produced unprecedented disaster.

First of all, the United States and Soviet Union were fortunate to avoid a direct conflict. Given NATO's conventional inferiority in the 1960s, 1970s, and 1980s, US and North Atlantic Treaty Organization policy envisaged rapid escalation to use of nuclear weapons if conventional direct defense failed. NATO military and civil-military exercises regularly included nuclear consultations and nuclear use procedures. And it was discovered after the end of the Cold War that, despite Moscow's declared policy of "no first use" of nuclear weapons, Soviet and Warsaw Pact doctrine envisaged early use of nuclear arms, even if NATO did not go nuclear first.

Other cases illustrate how fortunate the United States was during the Cold War. Take the 1962 Cuban missile crisis. The Soviet deployment to Cuba of nuclear-tipped SS-4 and SS-5 intermediate-range ballistic missiles that could reach much of the United States sparked the most dangerous crisis of the Cold War. President Kennedy applied a naval quarantine—a blockade—of the Caribbean island while conducting a quiet exchange of letters with Soviet leader Nikita Khrushchev. Kennedy's wise leadership and effort not to box in Khrushchev ultimately defused the crisis and resulted in withdrawal of the Soviet missiles and nuclear warheads.

But the standoff could have turned out very differently. When the president opted for a naval quarantine of Cuba, he set aside the policy course favored by many of his advisers, including all members of the Joint Chiefs of Staff: conventional air strikes on Cuba followed shortly by a ground invasion. This would have been a major military operation. The first wave of air strikes envisaged a thousand combat sorties, and the Pentagon planned to land as many as one hundred eighty thousand troops on the island.[5] The forces had massed in southeastern US ports and were prepared to launch an airborne assault on five days' notice, with an amphibious element to follow three days later.[6] Many Soviet soldiers (and a lot of Cubans) would have died.

What Kennedy, the US military, and the Central Intelligence Agency did not know in 1962 was the control procedures for Soviet nuclear weapons in Cuba. And, while well aware of the presence of Soviet intermediate-range missiles and their nuclear warheads, Washington had no idea that Moscow had also deployed shorter-range tactical nuclear weapons to Cuba. At a 2002 conference on the crisis, a retired Soviet military officer said that, although General Issa Pliyev, the commander of Soviet forces on the island, needed an explicit order from Moscow in order to launch missiles against the United States, he had been given release authority for use of tactical nuclear weapons in the event of a US attack.[7]

Indeed, Khrushchev had personally notified Pliyev that, if the United States attacked Cuba and he was unable to contact Moscow for instructions, he would be permitted to decide whether to use nuclear-armed short-range missiles or Il-28 nuclear-armed bombers to attack the American invasion force. Soviet Minister of Defense Rodion Malinovsky ordered that this exceptional guidance not be confirmed in writing, but a draft message dated September 8, 1962, confirmed that twelve Luna nuclear-armed

5. Robert S. McNamara, James G. Blight, Robert K. Brigham, Thomas J. Biersteker, and Herbert Y. Schandler, *Argument Without End: In Search of Answers to the Vietnam Tragedy* (New York: Public Affairs, 1999), 10.

6. Office of the Historian, US Department of State, "Foreign Relations of the United States, 1961–1963, Volume X, Cuba, January 1961–September 1962, Document 439," https://history.state.gov/historicaldocuments/frus1961-63v10/d439.

7. Robert S. Norris, "The Cuban Missile Crisis: A Nuclear Order of Battle, October/ November 1962," presentation at the Woodrow Wilson Center, October 24, 2012, http://www.wilsoncenter.org/sites/default/files/2012_10_24_Norris_Cuban_Missile _Crisis_Nuclear_Order_of_Battle.pdf.

missiles and six Il-28 bombers armed with nuclear bombs were being shipped to Cuba.[8] The message reiterated that the weapons were to be used for "destruction of the enemy on land and along the coast" at the instruction of the Soviet Ministry of Defense, or at Pliyev's discretion if communications between Cuba and Moscow were lost.

Alternative history is more art than science. But consider what might have happened if Kennedy had approved the recommendation for conventional air strikes and landings on Cuba, and the Soviet commander had responded with nuclear strikes against the US naval base at Guantánamo Bay and the American beachhead. Thousands of US servicemen would have died. The president would have faced tremendous pressure, probably irresistible pressure, to launch a retaliatory nuclear strike against Soviet forces in Cuba.

Could the nuclear exchanges have been confined to Cuba? No one can say "yes" with any degree of confidence. One of the big fears confronting Kennedy was that US action in Cuba might trigger a Soviet move against West Berlin, where numerous Soviet and East German divisions far outnumbered the US Berlin Brigade and its British and French counterparts. That could have easily led to a broader clash in Central Europe and escalated to use of nuclear weapons there. The Cuba scenario or Cuba-plus-Berlin scenario would also have raised a significant likelihood of US and Soviet strategic nuclear attacks on the other's homeland; the Strategic Air Command's plans at the time leaned heavily toward early and massive use of nuclear weapons.

We were lucky.

A second episode from the Cuban missile crisis again shows how close things came to getting out of hand. As part of the naval quarantine, the US Navy pursued an aggressive antisubmarine warfare effort, using active sonars and small depth charges (sometimes just hand grenades, designed to annoy but not sink submarines). US destroyers sought to force Soviet

---

8. Anatoli I. Gribkov, William Y. Smith, and Alfred Friendly, *Operation Anadyr: U.S. and Soviet Generals Recount the Cuban Missile Crisis* (Chicago: Edition Q, 1993), 5–6.

submarines to surface and turn away from Cuba. The Soviets had four Foxtrot-class diesel attack submarines approaching the island. One of the submarines was the B59, which among its armaments carried a nuclear-tipped torpedo.

With US destroyers continuously harassing the submerged B59, its electric batteries running low, and no communications with Moscow, the submarine's commander ordered preparations to launch the nuclear-armed torpedo.[9] One of three officers required to authorize a launch, Vasiliy Arkhipoy, objected and averted the torpedo launch. The B59 instead surfaced and turned back toward the Soviet Union.[10]

What would have happened had Arkhipoy gone along with his commander, and the B59 launched its nuclear torpedo? The use of a nuclear weapon at sea likely would have had less momentous consequences than the use of nuclear weapons against US forces in Cuba. It nevertheless could still have triggered unforeseen effects, including US use of nuclear weapons against Soviet submarines and perhaps a broader nuclear exchange.

Again, we were lucky.

Other close calls involved the North American Aerospace Defense Command (NORAD, formerly the North American Air Defense Command), which maintains a constant watch for missile and aircraft threats to the United States and Canada. In 1979 and 1980, its main watch center, buried under Cheyenne Mountain outside of Colorado Springs, Colorado,

---

9. Report prepared by USSR Northern Fleet Headquarters, "About participation of submarines 'B-4,' 'B-36,' 'B-59,' 'B-130' of the 69th submarine brigade of the Northern Fleet in the Operation 'Anadyr' during the period of October–December, 1962," trans. Svetlana Savranskaya, *National Security Archive,* George Washington University, http://www2.gwu.edu/~nsarchiv/NSAEBB/NSAEBB399/docs/Report%20of%20the%20submarine%20mission.pdf.

10. Leon Watson and Mark Duell, "The Man Who Saved the World: The Soviet submariner who single-handedly averted WWIII at height of the Cuban Missile Crisis," *Mail Online,* September 25, 2012, http://www.dailymail.co.uk/news/article-2208342/Soviet-submariner-single-handedly-averted-WWIII-height-Cuban-Missile-Crisis.html.

accidentally and falsely reported that the United States was under ballistic missile attack:

> On November 9, 1979: "For about three minutes, a test scenario of a missile attack on North America was inadvertently transmitted to the operational side of the 427M system in the Cheyenne Mountain Complex Operations Center. The test data was processed as real information, displayed on missile warning consoles in the command post, and transmitted to national command centers. About eight minutes elapsed between the time the test data appeared and NORAD assessed confidence that no strategic attack was underway."[11]

> On June 3, 1980: "Failure of a computer chip within a line multiplexer (Nova 840 computer) of the NORAD Control System caused false missile warning data to be transmitted to Strategic Air Command, the National Command Center, and the National Alternate Command Center."[12] . . . "Displays showed a seemingly random number of attacking missiles. The displays would show that two missiles had been launched, then zero missiles, and then 200 missiles. Furthermore, the numbers of attacking missiles displayed in the different command posts did not always agree."[13]

Things happened during those eight minutes in November 1979. NORAD officers woke people in Washington to pass the alert and immediately convened a threat assessment conference involving commanders at Cheyenne Mountain, the Pentagon, and the Alternate National Military Command Center at Fort Ritchie, Maryland. Launch control centers for

---

11. North American Aerospace Defense Command, Office of History, "A Brief History of NORAD," December 31, 2013: 23.

12. Ibid.

13. Geoffrey Forden, "False Alarms in the Nuclear Age," *NOVA*, PBS, November 6, 2001, http://www.pbs.org/wgbh/nova/military/nuclear-false-alarms.html.

the US Minuteman ICBM force received preliminary warning of a possible attack. NORAD also alerted the Strategic Air Command (SAC), which began sending the alarm to alert bombers—B-52s at various airbases around the country with nuclear weapons on board and ready to take off within minutes in hopes of being able to get away from the airbases before the Soviet ICBM warheads arrived. The entire continental air defense interceptor force was also put on alert, and at least ten aircraft took off. Even the National Emergency Airborne Command Post, the president's "doomsday plane," took off, albeit without the president on board.[14]

Happily, both cases turned out to be false alarms. What might have happened had it taken longer for the NORAD watch center to conclude that a test scenario or a faulty computer chip rather than a real attack had triggered the alert? How might the Soviets have reacted had they suddenly seen a spike in SAC's alert level and radio traffic and the hurried launch of some US bombers and their accompanying tanker aircraft? The Soviet military could have activated its own alert which, when detected by US sensors, might have been interpreted to reaffirm the mistaken initial reports of a missile attack.

Again, we were lucky.

Moscow also had its false alarms. On September 26, 1983, just weeks after a Soviet fighter plane shot down a Korean Air Lines Boeing 747 with sixty-two Americans on board, triggering a major crisis between Washington and Moscow, the Soviet early warning system reported ballistic missile launches from the United States. The duty officer at the time, Stanislav Petrov, believed the warning to be a false alarm. He ignored the protocol—to immediately alert his chain of command so that a retaliatory strike could be considered—and instead reported "a system malfunction." It turned out that Petrov was right; there was no US ICBM attack.[15]

---

14. Ibid.

15. Pavel Aksenov, "Stanislav Petrov: The Man Who May Have Saved the World," BBC Russian Service, September 26, 2013.

On January 25, 1995, a joint Norwegian-American research rocket took off from northern Norway. The Russian early warning system detected the rocket as it climbed higher into the atmosphere and incorrectly categorized it as a US Trident II SLBM launch, perhaps a precursor to a more massive nuclear strike. The alert reportedly went all the way to Russian President Boris Yeltsin. His nuclear suitcase (the equivalent of the nuclear "football" that is never far from the US president) was activated as he consulted with his defense leadership. Fortunately, this came at a time when there was no crisis—instead, relatively positive US-Russian relations— and Yeltsin took no action.[16]

What might have happened had Petrov followed procedure and sounded the alarm? US-Soviet relations in September 1983 were extremely tense because of the KAL shoot-down and the looming deployment of US intermediate-range nuclear missiles to Europe. Would the Soviet protocol have held back a nuclear strike on the United States? If the Soviet military instead just increased its alert levels, how would that have been interpreted by American intelligence and military watch officers? As for the January 1995 incident, that is the only reported instance when a Russian leader was personally alerted of a potential nuclear threat.

In both of these cases, we were lucky.

One last example of our good fortune: in 1961, a US B-52 bomber broke up over Goldsboro, North Carolina, releasing both of the Mark 39 nuclear bombs that it carried on board. Each of the weapons had a yield of three to four megatons.[17] One bomb plunged into a bog and broke apart, requiring a good amount of digging to find most of the pieces. The second was more easily recovered. The good news: its parachute had deployed, allowing the weapon to land intact (the parachute was

16. David Hoffman, "Shattered Shield: Cold-War Doctrines Refuse to Die," *Washington Post,* March 15, 1998.

17. Strategic Air Command, "Chart of Strategic Nuclear Bombs," http://www.strategic-air -command.com/weapons/nuclear_bomb_chart.htm.

designed to slow the bomb's descent in order to give the B-52 time to get away before the bomb detonated). The bad news: its parachute had deployed, which was one of the six steps in the bomb's arming sequence. When technicians recovered the bomb, they found that five of the six arming steps had triggered. One more, and North Carolina would have suffered a nuclear explosion between two hundred and two hundred seventy times larger than the yield of the bomb that destroyed Hiroshima.[18]

To be sure, an accidental detonation of a US nuclear weapon is an extremely low-probability event. The US military, Department of Energy, and nuclear establishment take extraordinary care to build safe nuclear weapons that will detonate only on an explicit and authorized command. There has never been an accidental detonation of a US nuclear weapon that produced a nuclear yield. But these are extraordinarily complex pieces of machinery. For example, each B61 nuclear gravity bomb contains more than six thousand parts in more than one thousand eight hundred sub-assemblies manufactured by five hundred seventy suppliers and nine primary contractors.[19] The United States maintains about four thousand five hundred nuclear weapons of various types in its arsenal (not counting several thousand more that have been retired and await dismantlement). Moreover, can we be confident that other countries, including states such as North Korea, take equal care with regard to the safety of their nuclear arms?

Maintaining nuclear weapons means continuing to live with a degree of risk—the risk of miscalculation in a crisis, the risk of misreading of errant data, the risk of accidents. And there is the risk that nuclear weapons might be used intentionally.

---

18. Eric Schlosser, *Command and Control: Nuclear Weapons, the Damascus Accident, and the Illusion of Safety* (New York: Penguin, 2013), 245–249.

19. Jeffrey Lewis, "After the Reliable Replacement Warhead: What's Next for the U.S. Nuclear Arsenal?" *Arms Control Today,* https://www.armscontrol.org/act/2008_12/Lewis.

The sum total of these risks poses one of the paradoxes of the modern nuclear age. During the Cold War, there was a possibility—small but certainly not zero—of a US-Soviet nuclear exchange that would have brought an end to both countries, to say nothing about effects on other states. Today, the chances of that kind of conflict between the United States and Russia are almost infinitesimally small. Yet the odds of a nuclear weapon being used in anger are greater than they were during the Cold War, in part because more states have acquired nuclear weapons since the Cold War ended.

North Korea, whose leadership can be described most charitably as erratic, has a small nuclear arsenal. Pakistan, which is unable to fully wrest control of its own territory from Islamist extremist groups, maintains some one hundred nuclear weapons, is increasing its stocks of nuclear material, and faces a growing nuclear competition with India.

Many analysts worry about the South Asian situation. It is not clear that the US-Soviet experience easily translates to the India-Pakistan relationship. Those two countries have gone to war three times in the past seventy years, not counting the 1999 conflict along the Line of Control in Kashmir. India and Pakistan border one another; they are not separated by an ocean (or at least the Bering Strait). They do not have the developed command-and-control systems that Washington and Moscow had. And Pakistan's recent interest in developing tactical nuclear weapons raises troubling questions about the security of the weapons and their impact on crisis stability.

As China continues its strategic rise, Washington and Beijing face the challenge of managing their relationship in a manner that steers it away from dangerous confrontation. A confrontational Sino-American relationship could introduce a greater nuclear risk than has been the case in the western Pacific for the past sixty years.

With the exception of a few crisis periods during the Cold War, the risk of a nuclear weapon detonating by intent, miscalculation, or accident is greater today than at any time since the dawn of the nuclear age. That risk will grow if the number of nuclear-weapons states increases. Many analysts fear, for example, that if Iran acquires a nuclear weapon, that will greatly increase the pressure on countries such as Saudi Arabia and Turkey to follow suit.

The risk of use of nuclear weapons may be small, but the consequences would be catastrophic. We will have to live with that risk, and nuclear deterrence will remain a key part of US security policy as long as nuclear weapons exist. Are we prepared, however, to live with that risk indefinitely?

The Advantages of a Non-Nuclear World

Set against the risks of a nuclear world, a world without nuclear weapons—and a world in which the United States has the most powerful conventional forces—could offer certain security advantages to the United States. The following discussion assumes—and this is a key assumption—that a mechanism could be developed and agreed upon, by which all nuclear weapons were reliably and verifiably eliminated.

In such a non-nuclear world, deterrence would continue to apply and continue to serve as a major element of US security policy. It would just work without nuclear weapons. Deterrence is a complex concept. As noted earlier, creating potential costs that will deter a potential adversary requires getting into that adversary's mind and understanding his motivations and what he values. Those things can then be held at risk.

Conventional weapons will not be able to replicate the effects of nuclear arms. Some thus argue, correctly, that conventional forces cannot have the deterrent value of nuclear forces. But that does not mean that conventional deterrence cannot be effective in posing significant risks and costs to a potential adversary.

US advances in intelligence, surveillance, and reconnaissance, plus the advent of extremely accurate conventional weapons, open the possibility of using conventional means to hold at risk and destroy targets that previously could only be threatened by nuclear weapons. In a non-nuclear world, the United States would not be able to hold entire cities at risk of nuclear attack. But the US military has powerful conventional forces capable of striking deep into the territory of any adversary. What if the US Air Force directed ten B-2 bombers, each armed with fifteen two thousand-pound precision-guided conventional bombs, to attack one hundred fifty key buildings in an adversary's capital? The effects would not be nuclear, but they could well prove devastating. The threat of such a strike would certainly affect an opponent's calculation of the risks and potential costs of conflict (above and beyond the fear that the leadership itself could be specifically and directly targeted for attack).

Alternatively, one Trident guided-missile submarine could unleash up to one hundred fifty-four conventionally armed land-attack cruise missiles against an adversary's city; the effects would be smaller than the postulated B-2 attack, because the cruise missile warheads would not be as large as two-thousand-pound bombs. The threat nevertheless would get an adversary's attention and affect how an opponent weighed the advantages and disadvantages of going to war with the United States.

The above discussion focuses on deterrence by punishment or retaliation, i.e., imposing high costs on an aggressor. But deterrence can also work by denial—denying an adversary the gains he might hope to achieve by aggression. US conventional military forces have capabilities that, in most scenarios, could deny an adversary his desired potential gains by directly defeating the attack.

Several factors would benefit US security in a non-nuclear world. The first is the United States' favorable geography. Despite the problem of illegal immigration, America enjoys peaceful borders with Canada and Mexico. Canada is an ally and fellow NATO member, and the three countries' economies are tightly interwoven by the North American Free Trade Agreement. It is virtually inconceivable that Canada or Mexico would present a military threat to the United States.

To the east and west, the broad expanses of the Atlantic and Pacific oceans protect America, meaning that potential adversaries would have to cross thousands of miles of open sea to invade or attack the United States. Neither Russia nor China—the two peer competitors that most closely rival American military power—have the sea-lift capabilities to deploy a sizable ground force invasion across an ocean, and they would have to fight their way through the world's most powerful conventional navy.

Beyond geography, a second major factor would benefit US security in a non-nuclear world: the sheer power and technological superiority of American conventional forces. The United States currently spends $640 billion per year on defense. By comparison, estimates are that China and Russia spend $188 billion and $88 billion per year, respectively. The United States accounts for over 36 percent of the global total defense expenditure of $1.75 trillion.[20]

A non-nuclear world, moreover, would free up substantial resources that the United States would otherwise have to devote to modernizing and maintaining nuclear forces, including the nuclear enterprise that supports the nuclear weapons themselves. For example, estimates project the cost of US nuclear forces running as high as $1 trillion over the next thirty years. Some of those costs would be necessary in a non-nuclear world (e.g., for long-range bombers, dismantlement of retired nuclear weapons, and perhaps for some reconstitution capability as a hedge against cheating). But a non-nuclear world would allow significant defense funding to be shifted to support conventional force requirements.

The US conventional advantage is particularly stark when it comes to power projection. Consider three elements: heavy bombers, aircraft carriers, and conventionally armed cruise missiles.

The US Air Force currently maintains twenty B-2, seventy-four B-52, and sixty B-1 bombers. The plan is to draw the B-52 force down to forty aircraft, which will leave a total of one hundred twenty long-range heavy

---

20. Sam Perlo-Freeman and Carina Solmirano, "Trends in World Military Expenditure, 2013," fact sheet, Stockholm International Peace Research Institute, April 2014, http://books.sipri.org/product_info?c_product_id=476.

bombers. The B-2, with the smallest payload of the three, can neverthe-less carry fifty thousand pounds of ordnance. All three bomber types can be refueled in midair, which gives them the capability to fly anywhere in the world. (In the first Gulf War in 1991, B-52 bombers flew missions from Barksdale Air Force Base in Louisiana against targets in Iraq.) The Pentagon plans to purchase from eighty to one hundred Long-Range Strike Bombers, beginning in the 2020s, to replace older aircraft.

Only one other country in the world has comparable airplanes. Russia flies about seventy Tu-95 Bear-H and Tu-160 Blackjack bombers. The per-formance characteristics of the Bear and Blackjack do not match those of the B-52 and B-1, and Russia has nothing comparable to the B-2 stealth bomber.[21] US bomber crews, moreover, on average fly more than their Russian counterparts.

The United States Navy maintains ten nuclear-powered aircraft carri-ers, with an eleventh to be commissioned in 2016. At one hundred thou-sand tons displacement each, these are the largest naval vessels in the world, capable of carrying from seventy-five to ninety fixed-wing strike, fighter, and support aircraft and helicopters. US carriers operate globally, and four, five, or more may be at sea at any one time—the navy's normal operating tempo. The carriers can project power far inshore; they have aircraft that can refuel other planes in flight to extend their range and reach. Thus, US Navy F-18 fighter aircraft and other planes for more than a decade have regularly flown off of carriers in the north Arabian Sea to carry out missions over Afghanistan.

In addition to the ten large aircraft carriers, the US Navy has nine amphibious assault ships, which most other navies would categorize as aircraft carriers. These mostly carry helicopters for ferrying Marines ashore, but many also carry Harrier fighter aircraft and will be able to carry and operate the F-35B fighter, once that plane enters service. The

---

21. Military Factory, "Compare Aircraft Results," http://www.militaryfactory.com/aircraft /compare-aircraft-resultsasp?form=form&aircraft1=27&aircraft2=289&Submit =Compare+Aircraft.

new America-class amphibious assault ships are expected to be able to house twenty F-35Bs in addition to helicopters.

By contrast, the rest of the world's navies combined possess twenty fixed-wing or helicopter carriers. China and Russia each have one true aircraft carrier. Both are about two-thirds the size of US aircraft carriers and can carry a complement of only about fifty aircraft and helicopters. Furthermore, China and Russia lack a proven capability to conduct carrier-based air-to-air refueling, which limits the range of their aircraft.

Another key element of US power projection is its long-range conventionally armed cruise missiles, delivered by bombers and naval vessels. The US Navy has an inventory of about three thousand six hundred conventionally armed Tomahawk land-attack cruise missiles, which are deployed on surface ships, attack submarines, and four former ballistic-missile submarines that have been refitted so that each can carry one hundred fifty-four cruise missiles.[22] These missiles can reach far inshore, having ranges in excess of one thousand two hundred kilometers (about seven hundred forty-six miles). The navy used these weapons extensively in both Iraq conflicts, against Libya in 2011, and against Islamic State targets in 2014.

The US Air Force possesses a limited number of AGM-86 air-launched subsonic cruise missiles, which it deploys on its B-52 bombers. Each B-52 can carry up to twenty AGM-86 missiles.[23] The air force has said that the AGM-86 will remain in service until 2030, at which point the Pentagon hopes to replace it with a new air-launched cruise missile to be fitted to the planned Long-Range Strike Bomber.[24]

---

22. Jeffrey Lewis, "When the Navy Declassifies . . ." *Arms Control Wonk* (blog), July 12, 2012, citing Department of the Navy Operations and Maintenance budget accounts' figures for FY2013.

23. US Air Force fact sheet, "AGM-86B/C/D Missiles," May 24, 2010, http://www.af.mil /AboutUs/FactSheets/Display/tabid/224/Article/104612/agm-86bcd-missiles.aspx.

24. Tom Z. Collina, "No More Nuclear-Tipped Cruise Missiles," *Defense One*, October 31, 2013, http://www.defenseone.com/management/2013/10 /no-more-nuclear-tipped-cruise-missiles/73010/.

A third factor that benefits US security is its extensive alliance system. NATO brings together the United States, Canada, and twenty-six European states. Washington has bilateral alliances with Japan, South Korea, Australia, New Zealand, the Philippines, Thailand, and states in Central and South America providing for collective defense.[25] These allies, plus other friendly states such as Singapore and Bahrain, provide basing facilities that allow the US military to deploy much of its conventional power forward in Europe, the Persian Gulf, and the western Pacific.

US allies also have significant military power of their own. Of the ten countries with the largest defense budgets in the world, six—Saudi Arabia, France, Great Britain, Germany, Japan, and South Korea—are American allies. Just those six allies plus the United States account for 54 percent of global defense spending.[26] Of the eleven non-US commissioned aircraft carriers—not including amphibious assault ships or helicopter carriers—six are operated by US allies.[27]

These are just some of the conventional advantages that the US military enjoys today and that it could maintain in a world without nuclear weapons. Geography is not going to change. In a world free of nuclear weapons, Washington would need to take care to maintain appropriate levels of defense spending, ensure cutting-edge research and development to sustain its technological advantages, and keep robust alliance relationships. With proper attention, in a nuclear-free world the United States should readily be able to ensure its security based on conventional forces alone.

---

25. US Department of State, "U.S. Collective Defense Arrangements," http://www.state.gov/s/l/treaty/collectivedefense.

26. Perlo-Freeman and Solmirano, "Trends in World Military Expenditure, 2013."

27. Walter Hickey and Robert Johnson, "These are the 20 Aircraft Carriers in Service Today," *Business Insider,* August 9, 2012, http://www.businessinsider.com/the-20-in-service-aircraft-carriers-patrolling-the-world-today-2012-8?op=1.

The Risks of a Non-Nuclear World

A number of challenges have been voiced regarding the risks of such a non-nuclear world. The first centers on the fact that US military forces currently provide security to allies through extended deterrence, i.e., US nuclear weapons provide a nuclear umbrella over American allies. As the 2012 NATO "Deterrence and Defence Posture Review" put it, "The supreme guarantee of the security of the Allies is provided by the strategic nuclear forces of the Alliance, particularly those of the United States. . . ."[28] US nonstrategic nuclear weapons deployed in Europe also contribute to the extended deterrent, as does the capability to forward-deploy nonstrategic nuclear weapons into the western Pacific region if needed.

Would the United States still be able to provide extended deterrence to allies without nuclear weapons? Several points should be made. First, as noted earlier, even without nuclear arms, the US military would still have the capability to inflict severe punishment on an adversary, sufficiently severe that the adversary would see high risks and potential costs to aggression. US conventional forces, moreover, could contribute in major ways—in some cases, in decisive ways—to deterrence by denial and, if necessary, to actually winning a defensive battle against an attacker.

Second, the real threats facing American allies should be considered. Given Russia's 2014 aggression against Ukraine, NATO is reassessing how much effort it needs to devote to collective defense in accordance with Article 5 of the Washington Treaty (which provides that an attack against one will be considered an attack against all). Russia is modernizing its conventional forces, many of which are outdated. It could nevertheless muster superior conventional forces in certain subregions, such as opposite the Baltic members of NATO.

---

28. NATO, press release, "Deterrence and Defence Posture Review," May 20, 2012.

NATO's European members have a combined economy seven times the size of Russia's economy, so there is no reason why they should not be able to finance a military structure that could deter and, if necessary, defeat a Russian conventional attack—particularly since they would have the assistance of the US military. Some European members of the Alliance should, and may have to, increase their defense spending. But those increases would be relatively modest. NATO's European members should also spend their defense dollars more wisely and look for cost efficiencies so that they can purchase more conventional bang for the buck (or euro).

Many analysts see Asia as posing more difficult challenges, given the robust nature of the Chinese economy and its growing military, plus the unpredictable threat posed by North Korea. But four of the five American allies in the western Pacific region—Japan, Australia, New Zealand, and the Philippines—are island nations, which bestows a degree of protection. South Korea, which faces North Korea across a demilitarized zone, does not enjoy the same geographic advantage but has built a strong conventional military capable of defeating a conventional North Korean attack (with the help of US forces there). Taiwan poses a special case, lacking a formal US defense commitment but nevertheless of great interest to Washington, which supports peaceful, not forceful, reunification with the mainland. Being an island confers certain defensive advantages, particularly as long as China lacks major amphibious assault capabilities.

Some might argue that a US extended deterrent based solely on conventional forces could mean that American allies would face a greater degree of risk. Perhaps. But offsetting that would be the elimination of the risk of a nuclear conflict, with all of its catastrophic consequences for the United States and its allies.

Moreover, extended deterrence with nuclear weapons has been a difficult proposition ever since the concept was introduced. No potential aggressor could doubt that his nuclear attack on the United States would lead to a US nuclear response. Extended deterrence, however, poses a more daunting question: would an American president use nuclear weapons to defend an ally if that raised the risk of a nuclear attack on the United States? As it was often phrased during the Cold War, would the president use nuclear weapons to defend West Germany and thus risk Chicago for Bonn?

US leaders, diplomats, and senior military officers have spent countless hours seeking to assure their allied counterparts that the answer to that question is an unequivocal yes. Furthermore, the US military has deployed nuclear weapons to forward locations, introduced "nuclear sharing" with NATO allies, and developed Alliance doctrine—all intended to support that answer. Some two hundred American nuclear bombs reportedly remain deployed in Europe precisely to make that point. Yet, despite the time, effort, and expense devoted to signaling potential adversaries and assuring allies that Washington would use nuclear weapons in the defense of allies, doubts have always lingered.

The nuclear element of extended deterrence has never been as solid as theorists or practitioners would like. In a non-nuclear world, however, allied leaders could have far greater confidence in an American president's commitment to use conventional forces in their defense and to punish the aggressor. Such use would not raise the risk of a nuclear attack on the US homeland; the threat to use conventional forces to defend an ally and punish an aggressor thus would carry greater credibility, with both the ally and the potential adversary.

A second serious challenge to a non-nuclear world is the following question: would the elimination of nuclear arms make the world "safe" for large-scale conventional war, such as the world wars of the twentieth century? In World War II, the atomic bombs dropped on Hiroshima and Nagasaki killed some two hundred thousand people; conventional bombs, tanks, artillery, rifles, bayonets, and other means killed more than fifty million. Without the deterrence generated by the fear of use of nuclear weapons, could such a conventional conflict again engulf the world?

A non-nuclear world might pose some risk. But two points should be made.

First, the world has changed considerably since the mid-twentieth century, with major powers becoming far more interconnected. If the countries of the world could negotiate a verifiable plan to reliably eliminate all nuclear weapons—a big if, which gets to the point of the feasibility of a non-nuclear world—that would presuppose a degree of progress in interstate relations. That might not end the risk of major conventional conflict, but it would certainly reduce it.

Second, the risk of a major conventional war in a non-nuclear world would have to be weighed against the risk of a catastrophic use of nuclear weapons that the world will continue to face with the continuing existence of nuclear arms. Where one comes out on this question depends on one's judgment of the balance of risks between a nuclear and a non-nuclear world, and reasonable people can come to different conclusions.

My own conclusion is that the growing risks of a nuclear world and the advantages of a non-nuclear world for the United States, given its geographic position, conventional forces, and alliance systems, combine to argue that a world without nuclear weapons would be in the security interest of the United States and its allies. It is thus in the US interest to seek to create the conditions for a world without nuclear arms.

Getting There Safely

The above arguments make the case for the desirability of a world without nuclear weapons. A related but separate question is the feasibility of the objective, i.e., whether nation-states, with their varied and often competing interests, could ever agree on a path to achieve a non-nuclear world. Reaching such an agreement would require resolving numerous hard questions, including the following:

- Ultimately, all nuclear-armed states would have to commit to reduce and eventually eliminate their nuclear arsenals. Many nuclear-weapons states have endorsed the objective—and the

United States, Great Britain, China, France, and Russia committed to the goal of nuclear disarmament in the Non-Proliferation Treaty—but actions suggest their endorsement is, at best, half-hearted. Moreover, not only the five UN Security Council permanent members, but all other nuclear-weapons states, including countries such as Pakistan and North Korea, would have to be prepared to eliminate their nuclear stockpiles.

- New and more intrusive monitoring measures would have to be devised as part of a verification regime that could give all parties confidence that any cheating would be quickly and unambiguously detected. Such verification steps would have to go far beyond those included in current agreements, such as the 2010 New Strategic Arms Reduction Treaty between the United States and Russia. The US government now uses a standard of "effective verification," that is, the ability to detect a militarily significant violation in time to take countermeasures so that US security would not be adversely affected. In an agreement limiting each side to one thousand five hundred fifty deployed strategic warheads, a bit of cheating by one side would not matter much to the overall strategic balance (though it would matter greatly in terms of the other side's confidence in the treaty). But in a world of zero nuclear arms, where a covert stockpile of ten weapons could prove a game-changer, a far more stringent verification standard would have to apply.

- Any arrangement that eliminated nuclear weapons would require a robust, almost automatic, enforcement mechanism to dissuade states from cheating by posing a rapid response with severe punishment for the cheating state. This could not be a threat to refer the offending party to the United Nations Security Council. The enforcement mechanism would need to impose swift and painful consequences. (An additional disincentive to cheating would be the possibility that states might reconstitute a nuclear weapons capability.)

- Finally, the world's nations could not move to eliminate all nuclear weapons without resolving or easing key territorial and other interstate disputes—or at least reaching a point where states conclude that nuclear weapons no longer provide a critical means for defending their key national interests.

These questions pose stiff challenges to the creation of a world without nuclear arms or even to the creation of the conditions for a world without nuclear arms. It might turn out that these challenges could not be overcome, in part because different states will make different calculations about their security interests. A non-nuclear world should look very attractive to the United States. Such a world may look different to Russia, which borders on NATO and a rising China, faces a difficult demographic situation, lags behind the West in high-tech conventional weaponry, and looks to face increasing difficulties in competing in the modern global economy.

All that said, the feasibility of the objective of a world without nuclear weapons is a different question than the desirability of such a world for the United States.

Conclusion

The United States and the world have lived with nuclear weapons for almost seventy years. Those weapons have been used in conflict only twice, at the dawn of the nuclear age. Nuclear deterrence was a key feature of the Cold War standoff between the United States and the Soviet Union and contributed to preventing a direct conflict between the two. Though the Cold War is over, nuclear weapons continue to play an important role in deterrence and an important, if somewhat declining, role in US national security.

While nuclear deterrence has apparently worked, it has to be said that the record is not wholly reassuring. At several points over the past seven decades, miscalculation in a crisis, human error and/or computer or mechanical failure could have plunged the United States, the Soviet Union/Russia, and much of the rest of the world into a horror unlike anything seen in human history.

While the risk of a nuclear clash between Washington and Moscow has diminished to almost zero, the risk of the use of a nuclear weapon today is greater than it was during the Cold War. That risk will continue as long as nuclear weapons exist, and it will grow should the number of nuclear-weapons states increase further.

Compared to this world, a world without nuclear weapons offers definite security advantages for the United States. Blessed by a unique geographic setting, having built an unrivaled alliance system, and maintaining the world's most powerful and technologically advanced conventional forces, the United States is well-suited to defend itself and its allies in a non-nuclear world. Such a world would pose some risks, to be sure, but those risks would be outweighed by the lifting of the risks posed by nuclear arms.

Many see the goal of creating the conditions for a world without nuclear weapons as idealistic. Realists, however, can also see the advantages of such an objective. Creating the conditions for a nuclear-free world would require Herculean efforts, unprecedented international cooperation, and significant changes in the current international system. In the end, the objective might prove unattainable. But even if it were possible to move only partway toward that goal, a well-designed nuclear arms reductions plan would leave the United States and the world in a more secure position than at present. The difficulty of the objective should not mean that it is not worth an attempt.

Introduction to Part Two

Continuing the theme of "Deterrence in the Age of Nuclear Proliferation,"[1] Part Two examines nuclear deterrence from the vantage points of nations in Europe, the Middle East, and Asia, with all of whom there is some form of security relationship with the United States, cooperative or competitive. Opinions about nuclear weapons vary considerably. That *Wall Street Journal* article recognized that

> . . . for some nations, nuclear weapons may continue to appear relevant to their immediate security. There are certain undeniable dynamics in play—for example, the emergence of a nuclear armed neighbor, or the perception of inferiority in conventional forces—that if not addressed could lead to the further proliferation of nuclear weapons and an increased risk they will be used. Thus, while the four of us believe that reliance on nuclear weapons for deterrence is becoming increasingly hazardous and decreasingly effective, some nations will hesitate to draw or act on the same conclusion unless regional confrontations and conflicts are addressed. We must therefore redouble our efforts to resolve these issues.

---

1. George P. Shultz, William J. Perry, Henry A. Kissinger, and Sam Nunn, *Wall Street Journal,* March 7, 2011.

The article concludes that

> . . . non-nuclear means of deterrence to effectively prevent conflict and increase stability in troubled regions is a vital issue. Changes to extended deterrence must be developed over time by the U.S. and allies working closely together. Reconciling national perspectives on nuclear deterrence is a challenging problem, and comprehensive solutions must be developed. *A world without nuclear weapons will not simply be today's world minus nuclear weapons.* (Emphasis added.)

The following essays address contemporary nuclear issues, seventy years after the world's first nuclear weapons leveled Hiroshima and Nagasaki. One of the most striking themes struck in this series of essays is the spotlight placed on global versus regional diplomacy and institution-building. From an American perspective, globalization looms very large and solutions to security problems include potential cooperation within a global framework. For those nations locked in regional conflicts, regional solutions seem more urgent, if not necessarily more achievable.

This prompts the editors to add the following thoughts about the balance to be struck between nationalism, regionalism, and globalization, drawing on a paper co-written by one of the editors.[2]

The international system of nation-states is evolving into something more complex and indeterminate. One important development has been the creation of regional communities. If these are to thrive in their own distinctive ways, national governments, including the United States, will need to support creative policies that harmonize interests, not only within such communities but also among them. Policy planners, therefore, must think globally and act regionally.

---

2. James Goodby and Kenneth Weisbrode, "Redirecting U.S. Diplomacy," *Parameters* 43, no. 4 (Winter 2013–14): 1–7.

The Westphalian system has given way to one in which the dominance of nation-states is challenged by global and regional entities, as well as subnational ones. National governments no longer have a monopoly over the use of force on a large scale and, hence, over decisions concerning war or peace. Their power is seeping away.

This development does not mean that nation-states are going away or that their powers are permanently lost. In fact, one of the striking things about the history of nation-states is not merely how enduring they have been, but also how successful most have been in adapting to new geopolitical and economic conditions.

So long as nation-states exist, so will nationalism. The transition of a system based on one form of national behavior into another is bound to generate conflict, particularly of the old-fashioned nationalist variety. How best can national governments mitigate it? For Americans in particular, the rule of law, backed by global institutions like the United Nations, was the stock answer.

For many nations, it still is the correct answer. And yet global institutions have had limited success in dealing with regional conflicts. For those conflicts, which are the main threats to global peace today, a region-based approach is essential. Indeed, regionalism has emerged as the preferred way in which the middle powers of the world have elected to pool their sovereignty.

Good governance will demand that regional communities not act as blocs, shutting out one another's members or allowing others to fall through the cracks. Regional communities will only work over the long term if they consistently promote both intra- and inter-regional cohesion.

American interests and policies loom large in every regional setting. This is true closest to home. It is seldom mentioned how potentially powerful North America has become. In an article that appeared in the *Wall Street Journal* on July 11, 2013, one of the editors, George

Shultz, remarked on the integration of the economies of the United States, Canada, and Mexico:

> The three countries constitute around one-fourth of global GDP, and they have become each other's largest trading partners. A 2010 NBER study shows that 24.7% of imports from Canada were U.S. value-added, and 39.8% of U.S. imports from Mexico were U.S. value-added. (By contrast, the U.S. value-added in imports from China was only 4.2%.) This phenomenon of tight integration of trade stands apart from other major trading blocks including the European Union or East Asian economies.[3]

A cohesive North America thus can exert a strong influence on global trade and the strengthening of liberal institutions, foreshadowing a world of regions where armed frontiers are transformed into prosperous borderlands and where economic power and political influence go hand in hand.

Preventing conflict appears to be more the task of regional interaction than of globalization per se. It has taken too long for it to sink in that while globalization by definition has spread around the world, it affects different places very differently and, in some, strengthens rather than diminishes the draw of nationalism. For the United States, still the world's most powerful nation-state, this reality calls out for recognition and action. Aside from embedding US regional diplomacy in a unified coherent strategy for peace, a better approach calls for finding and exploiting near-term regional opportunities.

The basic principle of regional self-help, rather than external tutelage, has the potential to construct more peaceful and prosperous neighborhoods. The realization that even long-established rivals sitting side by side

---

3. George P. Shultz, "The North American Global Powerhouse," *Wall Street Journal,* July 11, 2013.

can transform their enmities into patterns of cooperation need not mean sacrificing every national source of power and influence in the process. But it does require a demonstrable sharing of power among nations and regions. It takes continuous and difficult negotiation, and, most of all, public understanding and support.

Of course, global institutions are essential in terms of pointing the way to a universal system of norms and obligations to support peace with justice. But for the rest of this century, an active regional diplomacy will be the best way to manage the fundamental transformation in the global system now under way.

CHAPTER 4 **The Debate Over Disarmament within NATO**

Isabelle Williams and Steven P. Andreasen

A US government study recently concluded that a 10-kiloton nuclear bomb detonated by terrorists a few blocks north of the White House would kill 45,000 people and leave 323,000 wounded.[1] That bomb would be less powerful than most tactical nuclear weapons (TNW) now sitting in European storage bunkers. What is even more alarming: TNW are smaller and more portable, making them inviting targets for terrorists.

TNW were originally deployed by NATO and Russia during the Cold War to reduce risks—in this case, a war on the European continent. There has never been much transparency or regulation associated with these deployments. Neither NATO nor Russia provides information on their number or location throughout Europe. So NATO and Russian publics have little information with which to assess the risks or benefits associated with their continued deployment.

---

1. Brooke Buddemeier, John Valentine, Kyle Millage, and L. D. Brandt, "Key Response Planning Factors for the Aftermath of Nuclear Terrorism," Lawrence Livermore National Laboratory, November 2011, http://www.fas.org/irp/agency /dhs/fema/ncr.pdf.

Before the current crisis in Euro-Atlantic security centered in and around Ukraine, a discussion had been building—both inside and outside of NATO—as to whether maintaining current deployments of TNW in Europe was still in NATO's interest, two decades after the collapse of the Soviet Union.

In April 2010, General James E. Cartwright, who at the time was vice chairman of the US Joint Chiefs of Staff, made clear his view that these weapons do not serve a military function not already addressed by allied strategic and conventional forces.[2] And if TNW have virtually no military utility, it is hard to argue they have any real value as a deterrent or political symbol of North Atlantic Alliance resolve. Taking note of Cartwright's view, former senator Sam Nunn wrote in 2011 that, given new threats to global security, TNW are more of a security risk than an asset to both NATO and Russia. They are dangerously corroding the system they were initially designed to strengthen.[3]

Even before the collapse of the government in Kiev in February 2014 and Russia's intervention in Ukraine, the debate among NATO members on the future of these weapons demonstrated how difficult it is to find consensus on issues relating to nuclear policy, nonproliferation, and disarmament within the Alliance. At the 2010 Lisbon and 2012 Chicago summits, NATO members were unable to develop a clear strategy to change the status quo on NATO nuclear policy—or to synchronize that policy with NATO's policy toward Russia and the Alliance's commitment to create conditions for a world without nuclear weapons. Despite several years of debate among NATO members and discussions with Russia, policymakers in Washington, Brussels, and Moscow failed to develop a clear strategy or process for reducing the systemic risks associated with TNW

---

2. Federal News Service, "Council on Foreign Relations meeting," April 8, 2010, http://www.defense.gov/npr/docs/council_on_foreign_relation.pdf.

3. Sam Nunn, "The Race Between Cooperation and Catastrophe," in *Reducing Nuclear Risk in Europe: A Framework for Action,* ed. Steve Andreasen and Isabelle Williams, 2011, http://www.nti.org/media/pdfs/NTI_Senator_Nunn_essay.pdf?_=1322694397.

in European security and for seriously evaluating the costs and benefits associated with maintaining the status quo.

Today, the debate about NATO nuclear policy and posture has been subsumed and made more difficult by the crisis in Ukraine and the resulting rupture in relations between Russia, on the one hand, and the United States, NATO, and the European Union, on the other. Washington's recent determination that Russia has violated the Intermediate-Range Nuclear Forces (INF) Treaty underscores what was already a grim outlook for security policy and arms control in Europe. An increased effort by the United States and NATO to reassure[4] its Allies, strengthen its defense capabilities, and deter Russian political, economic, or military aggression against NATO member states is now underway. This effort is likely to require substantially more in the way of resources from Washington and its Allies.

However, NATO still has security and budgetary incentives to implement reassurance and defense policies in ways that seek to preserve existing areas of cooperation with Russia and leave open pathways for rebuilding trust. New NATO requirements relating to conventional reassurance and defense could be the catalyst to a change in NATO's nuclear posture over the next few years so that it is more credible, safer, and more affordable. A substantial portion of the savings could be devoted to sustaining and expanding NATO's reassurance initiatives.

NATO Nuclear Policy

Since the end of the Cold War, the role of nuclear weapons in NATO security policy has steadily been reduced, both operationally and politically. NATO's strategy, while remaining one of war prevention, is no longer dominated by the possibility of escalation involving nuclear weapons, as was

---

4. "Reassurance" in NATO parlance relates to commitments, programs, and activities that reconfirm the bond between NATO nations to defend one another under Article V of the North Atlantic Treaty.

the case during much of the Cold War when there were thousands of these weapons deployed by both sides in Europe. Moreover, today the US forward-deployed TNW in Europe are no longer targeted against any country and readiness is now described in terms of months, versus hours or days.

While NATO as an international organization does not possess nuclear weapons, its claim to be a nuclear alliance is based on the willingness of its nuclear-armed members to make their own weapons available to NATO for deterrence and defense. All of the United Kingdom's submarine-based nuclear weapons are formally assigned to NATO, except where the UK may decide that its supreme national interests are at stake. France's nuclear weapons, while not assigned to NATO, "contribute to the overall deterrence and security of the Allies."[5] (France is not a member of NATO's nuclear structure.) While there is no formal consensus on the extent to which US nuclear forces are assigned to NATO, America's TNW are often assumed to be; they have remained deployed in Europe under nuclear sharing arrangements with NATO members for decades.[6]

The number of US weapons in Europe has declined significantly since a peak of approximately eight thousand during the Cold War, reflecting the elimination of a large-scale conventional threat to NATO and the reshaping of the European security environment in the late 1980s and 1990s. Data from various non-governmental sources indicate that the United States currently deploys somewhere between 150 and 240 air-delivered nuclear weapons (B61 gravity bombs) that are deliverable by NATO aircraft (F-15s, F-16s, and Tornados) at six air force bases in five countries.[7] Through a series of Presidential Nuclear Initiatives, the

---

5. NATO, "Strategic Concept for the Defence and Security of the Members of the North Atlantic Treaty Organisation," November 2010, paragraph 18.

6. Malcolm Chalmers, "Words that Matter? NATO Declaratory Policy and the DDPR," in *Reducing Nuclear Risks in Europe*, ed. Steve Andreasen and Isabelle Williams, 2011, 56, http://www.nuclearsecurityproject.org/uploads/File/NTI_Framework_full _report.pdf.

7. Malcolm Chalmers and Simon Lunn, "NATO's Tactical Nuclear Dilemma," occasional paper, Royal United Services Institute, March 2010, 1–2.

United States and Russia retired or destroyed thousands of TNW designed for European missions. That said, Russia still retains a significant number of TNW in its inventory, with estimates ranging somewhere around two thousand weapons in its active stockpile.[8]

The current nuclear weapons-sharing arrangements within NATO consist of sets of US B61 nuclear gravity bombs housed in sites within NATO host countries. These weapons are "dual key" systems which require the authorization of both the United States and the host country in order to be used. The gravity bombs are kept under US military control, but the "dual-capable aircraft" (DCA) used to deliver them are purchased, maintained, and flown by each host country's air force as part of the burden-sharing arrangement.

Historically, "nuclear sharing" has played a key role in reassurance of NATO allies—a highly visible manifestation of the US commitment to the defense of NATO. During much of the Cold War, the United States deployed thousands of TNW on the territory of its European NATO allies. The purpose of these deployments, under the broad rubric of extended deterrence, was to underscore the political link between the United States and Europe and provide a military capability to deter and, if necessary, defeat numerically superior Soviet and Warsaw Pact tank armies poised to invade NATO through Germany. NATO's first Strategic Concept of 1949 called for insuring "the ability to carry out strategic bombing including the prompt delivery of the atomic bomb."[9] The United States provided the same nuclear protection to its principal Asian allies, assuring these nations of the US commitment to their security.

The United States and NATO continue to maintain a "neither confirm nor deny" policy on the presence or absence of nuclear weapons at any NATO installation or in any specific country. Moreover, NATO continues

8. Stockholm International Peace Research Institute, *SIPRI Yearbook 2010* (Oxford, UK: Oxford University Press, 2010), 344.

9. NATO, "The Strategic Concept for the Defense of the North Atlantic Area," November 19, 1949, http://www.nato.int/docu/stratdoc/eng/a491119a.pdf.

to underscore the principle of nuclear burden-sharing, both through the deployment of US nuclear weapons in a number of NATO states and by agreement that, in the event of war, some of these weapons would be transferred to allied forces and delivered by allied aircraft. NATO members have also reaffirmed its nuclear declaratory policy of not ruling out the first use of nuclear weapons.

Security context for NATO

Over the past two decades since the collapse of the Soviet Union, there has been an uneasy partnership between NATO and Russia. The geographical expansion of NATO and incidents of instability along NATO's eastern periphery complicated NATO's relationship and the security context with Russia. The unique security concerns held by many of the newer NATO member states were also a driving factor in the trust deficit between NATO and Russia and in a renewed focus on NATO's core commitment of collective defense to shield member states from armed aggression. Simply stated, doubts persisted between NATO and Russia about the intentions and policies of the other.

Those doubts have risen to new highs as the crisis in Ukraine has unfolded over the past several months. Russia today looks much more like a potential adversary to NATO, in particular to those countries that share borders with Russia and have heard clearly President Vladimir Putin's statements regarding the protection of ethnic Russians outside of Russia. Senior Alliance officials and some NATO member states' leaders believe that NATO's assumptions about the nature of its relationship with Russia need to be reassessed in light of Russia's complete disregard for democratic principles and Ukrainian sovereignty, independence, and territorial integrity. In particular, they wish to spotlight the unilateral commitments that were made in the context of the 1997 NATO-Russia Founding Act, especially those relating to not putting substantial conventional forces in new NATO member states.

As a result, NATO is now grappling with how to respond to the current crisis with Russia amid a more complex set of security considerations, including instability and conflict both along and beyond NATO's borders; cyberattacks; energy dependency; and environmental and resource constraints. Meanwhile, some security concerns appear to have been moved to the back burner, behind Russia. Those include threats posed by the proliferation of nuclear weapons and other weapons of mass destruction (most urgently in a conflict-prone Middle East and North Africa), their means of delivery, and terrorism Nevertheless, these concerns are still a central driver with respect to other related issues, including missile defense, and are a central aspect of US and NATO relations with a number of states, including Iran, Syria, Saudi Arabia, Pakistan, Egypt, Libya, and Israel.

NATO Nuclear Policy—The 2010 Strategic Concept and 2012 Deterrence and Defense Posture Review (DDPR)

At the 2009 NATO Strasbourg-Kehl Summit, NATO leaders endorsed a call for the drafting of a new Strategic Concept—the document that sets out the fundamental purpose, tasks, and strategy of NATO. (The previous Concept had been agreed upon in 1999.) The updating of NATO's Strategic Concept opened the door for discussions among member states on possible revisions to NATO's nuclear policy and NATO's role in nonproliferation and disarmament. Of specific concern were: whether NATO's declaratory policy could be modified to reduce the role of its nuclear weapons; whether further changes should be made to deployment of the remaining US TNW forward-based in Europe; and creation of a new arms control committee. The revision process for this new Concept was completed for approval by member states at the Lisbon Summit in November 2010.

2010 Strategic Concept. In the lead-up to the Lisbon Summit, the complexities of the nuclear issues and the many different positions represented within the Alliance made it difficult for NATO members to agree on several fundamental issues relating to NATO nuclear policy. The Strategic Concept therefore made few changes to NATO's nuclear policy. It did, however, embrace two core principles: that NATO was committed to the goal of creating the conditions for a world without nuclear weapons according to the goals of the Nuclear Non-Proliferation Treaty; and that for as long as there are nuclear weapons, NATO would remain a nuclear alliance. In this context, the 2010 Strategic Concept also contained the following key language on nuclear policy-related issues, which at least left the door open for further discussions among members.

- The Concept repeats language from the 1999 Strategic Concept asserting that the "supreme guarantee of the security of the allies is provided by the strategic nuclear forces of the Alliance, particularly those of the U.S." and that "the independent nuclear forces of the United Kingdom and France, which have a deterrent role of their own, contribute to the overall deterrence and security of the Allies."
- The Concept states that members will "seek to create the conditions for further reductions (of nuclear weapons stationed in Europe) in the future . . ." and that "In any future reductions, our aim should be to seek Russian agreement to increase transparency on its nuclear weapons in Europe and relocate these weapons away from the territory of NATO members. Any further steps must take into account the disparity with the greater Russian stockpiles of short-range nuclear weapons."
- NATO members also reaffirmed the importance of burden-sharing among allies, stating they would "ensure the broadest possible participation of Allies in collective defence planning on nuclear roles, in peacetime basing of nuclear forces, and in command, control and consultation arrangements."
- NATO members did not agree on a declaratory policy that clearly outlined the policy for the use of nuclear weapons, although the Concept noted, "The circumstances in which any use of nuclear weapons might have to be contemplated are extremely remote."

2012 Deterrence and Defense Posture Review. To further advance the dialogue on NATO nuclear policy both in design and practice beyond these basic principles, the North Atlantic Council was tasked at Lisbon with conducting a Deterrence and Defense Posture Review (DDPR). This was intended to review NATO's overall nuclear and conventional posture in deterring and defending against a full range of threats, including "NATO's nuclear posture, and missile defense and other means of strategic deterrence and defense."

The DDPR provided a vehicle for members to further discuss issues that had been difficult to find consensus on during deliberations over the 2010 Strategic Concept. Of particular concern were: the role of nuclear weapons, including declaratory policy, in deterrence and defense; the role NATO intends to play in future arms control efforts, primarily with Russia; the willingness and ability of members to sustain the current nuclear mission, as well as alternatives to NATO's existing nuclear arrangements; and the future direction of relations with Russia. The review also importantly provided an opportunity for members to assess whether the Alliance has the appropriate mix of nuclear and conventional capabilities to address current and emerging threats and to ensure that the various components of NATO strategy relate to each other in a coherent way.

The final DDPR document was announced at the Chicago NATO Summit in May 2012. Despite the fact that internal discussions within NATO on nuclear policy had been initiated four years earlier, NATO members remained unable to find consensus on any significant changes in either declaratory policy or nuclear force posture.

Why did this occur? Two factors seem most relevant. First, NATO had been focused on other priorities the previous four years, most obviously the war in Afghanistan—the central issue addressed at the Chicago summit. This was particularly true for the United States, whose leadership would be required for any change to the nuclear status quo within NATO. Second, there clearly were member states that believed the status quo remained in their interest, or at least they had not been convinced they had anything to gain from a change in the status quo. Finally, there were perhaps some NATO members who feared that any change in NATO nuclear policy or posture—or, rather, the open discussion and debate that would precede it within the Alliance—might reopen the public debates over nuclear deployments in NATO member states of the INF deployment years in the early 1980s and the resulting fissures within the Alliance.

With respect to declaratory policy, the Alliance could not come to agreement on a clear statement of NATO nuclear use policy. Instead, the DDPR restates the Lisbon formula (i.e., "the circumstances in which any use of nuclear weapons might have to be contemplated are extremely remote") and simply takes note of the individual negative security assurances (and the separate conditions attached) of the United States, United Kingdom, and France. The DDPR also makes clear that US and UK weapons assigned to NATO are covered by the US/UK national assurances.

With respect to force posture, the DDPR states, "the Alliance's nuclear force posture currently meets the criteria for an effective deterrence and defense posture." However, with respect to future changes, the DDPR laid out more goals and tasks for further work but little if anything in the way of a strategy for achieving these goals.

- *Nuclear sharing.* The DDPR stated the North Atlantic Council will "task the appropriate Committees to develop concepts for how to ensure the broadest possible participation of Allies concerned [i.e., those allies in the Nuclear Planning Group, not France] in their nuclear sharing arrangements, including in case NATO were to decide to reduce its reliance on non-strategic nuclear weapons based in Europe." Unlike the 2010 Strategic Concept, the DDPR has no explicit reference to ensuring the broadest possible participation "in peacetime basing of nuclear forces," recognizing that nuclear sharing need not be dependent on the peacetime basing of forces.
- *Transparency and confidence-building measures.* The DDPR states the Alliance will be "continuing to develop and exchange transparency and confidence building ideas with the Russian

Federation in the NATO-Russia Council, with the goal of developing detailed proposals on and increasing mutual understanding of NATO's and Russia's NSNF [non-strategic nuclear forces] postures in Europe." This discussion on transparency was clearly a priority for NATO members.

- *Further reductions.* Very similar to the Strategic Concept's formula linking reductions to reciprocity from Russia, the DDPR states, "NATO is prepared to consider further reducing its requirement for non-strategic nuclear weapons assigned to the Alliance in the context of reciprocal steps by Russia, taking into account the greater Russian stockpiles of non-strategic nuclear weapons stationed in the Euro-Atlantic area."

- *Reciprocity.* The DDPR does not endorse any specific formula for reciprocity, which was perhaps good news for some member states in that a restrictive formula was avoided. But it states that the North Atlantic Council "will task the appropriate committees to further consider, in the context of the broader security environment, what NATO would expect to see in the way of reciprocal Russian actions to allow for significant reductions in forward-based non-strategic nuclear weapons assigned to NATO."

During the DDPR debate, NATO members also continued a serious discussion on the Alliance's role in arms control and disarmament. Although such a role would be limited by the fact that NATO itself is not a party to arms control agreements,[10] several members urged that NATO play a more active role in arms control and disarmament, noting in particular the increased interest in curbing proliferation through reducing and eliminating nuclear weapons.

---

10. In negotiations where NATO's interests are directly involved, the role of NATO has been to provide the framework within which to coordinate an Alliance position.

Following the Lisbon 2010 NATO Summit, a new committee on control and disarmament of weapons of mass destruction was created to act as an institutional center for NATO members to exchange views on disarmament issues and to function as the forum for the United States to consult with Allies on the prospect of negotiations on TNW. However, during discussions on the DDPR it was decided that this committee was to be replaced. In February 2013, members agreed on the mandate of a new arms control body intended to help prepare a dialogue on confidence-building and transparency measures on TNW with Russia. The difficult discussions over this new body reflected the concern of a few countries, including France, about NATO assuming a greater role in disarmament and arms control.

The 2010 Strategic Concept and the 2012 DDPR that followed opened the door for all members to begin a dialogue and process within NATO to develop a more coherent and focused strategy for adapting defense priorities to reflect the rapidly evolving security context—including further reducing the role of nuclear weapons in NATO security policy and significant changes in NATO nuclear force posture.

In June 2013 in Berlin, President Obama said, "We'll work with our NATO allies to seek bold reductions in US and Russian tactical weapons in Europe," indicating that changing the status quo could become a priority in his second term.

However, even under the best of circumstances, progress was going to be difficult, requiring the sustained engagement of NATO political leaders and a commitment by NATO to address issues surrounding alternatives for nuclear sharing, reassurance of allies, and the successful engagement of Russia. The circumstances as they have evolved in 2014 have further complicated any chance to make progress. Achieving a true strategic partnership between NATO and Russia is now less likely than at any time since the early 1990s. As a result, the Alliance is refocusing on its core mission—the defense of NATO member states—and, in particular, reassurance to new NATO member states that border Russia, an implicit rejection of any notion that NATO does not face an adversary to its east.

2014 Wales Summit. In the Wales Summit Declaration adopted September 5, 2014, by NATO Heads of State and Government, members did not make any changes to the framework for nuclear policy set out in the 2010 Strategic Concept and 2012 DDPR. In brief, NATO reaffirmed language from the Strategic Concept and the DDPR relating to NATO maintaining the full range of capabilities and the appropriate mix of forces—as well as NATO remaining a nuclear alliance. The strategic forces of the Alliance were reaffirmed as the supreme guarantee of the security of the Allies and the declaration restates NATO's commitment to seek to create the conditions for a world without nuclear weapons. The only specific reference to TNW is in the context of aspiring to confidence-building measures and transparency with Russia.

Different Perspectives on Nuclear Policy, Disarmament, and Nonproliferation

Within NATO's twenty-eight member states there are many perspectives on the role of nuclear weapons in NATO security policy, nonproliferation, and disarmament. These represent a number of factors, including: varying levels of involvement by countries in the internal debates on nuclear policy; national public support for disarmament that has traditionally been strong in certain countries; and threat perspectives and security concerns which are now heightened in certain members due to the current situation. The fundamentals underlying these different perspectives persist—though they are perhaps less visible under the dark shadow cast by the current crisis in Euro-Atlantic security.

Any discussions within NATO on nuclear policy are also subject to the nature and workings of the Alliance and the commitment to collective defense. This commitment emphasizes cohesion and solidarity and results in states each bringing to the table their own specific national interests and concerns. The discussions over the Strategic Concept and DDPR as well as the response to the Ukraine crisis adopted at the Wales Summit demonstrated this approach and the constraints it can have on adopting new policies.

The geographical expansion of NATO to Central and Eastern European states that began in the 1990s fundamentally changed the internal debate on the role of nuclear weapons in both deterrence and assurance within NATO. In the deliberations leading up to the Strategic Concept and the DDPR, most NATO countries recognized there was no military purpose for the Alliance's TNW, though many of these newer members placed a renewed emphasis on the role of the remaining US weapons as political instruments of deterrence.

In particular, countries in Central and Eastern Europe voiced their concerns about the commitment of the United States to assurance of its European allies—especially given the US pivot to the Asia-Pacific region and the prospect of further US and European defense cuts. These states generally supported NATO placing an increasing emphasis on its tradi-tional role as the guarantor of the borders and territory of its European members. Their concerns played an important role in shaping the final language of both the Lisbon and Chicago summit documents which reaf-firmed Article 5 collective defense as NATO's core mission and identified reassurance measures as priorities for NATO.[11]

While France is not a member of NATO's Nuclear Planning Group, it has also been very wary of any changes to the existing status quo—with respect to NATO declaratory policy in particular, but also with respect to NATO's nuclear force posture—that could be perceived as a weakening of nuclear deterrence or that could put French nuclear forces under a spotlight. Accordingly, France played a key role in the debate over NATO declaratory policy leading to the Chicago summit, resisting any outcome that could have been perceived as a change in France's national policy (a position that has likely hardened over the past year). And while French officials maintain that what the United States does with its TNW stockpile

11. Jamie Shea, "Keeping NATO Relevant," Carnegie Endowment for International Peace, April 19, 2012.

based in Europe is a matter for the United States and the basing countries, they are widely perceived as being resistant to any change in the existing arrangements—or to being isolated as the only NATO member state with nuclear weapons based on the European continent.

In general, NATO basing countries have tended to accept their missions, albeit with varying degrees of enthusiasm, including between various ministries. Some officials believe the stationing of US nuclear weapons provides their countries with additional status and leverage—both with the United States and within the Alliance. However, others convey a sense of concern about the resources necessary to maintain the arrangements and believe they are political and security liabilities, both in terms of domestic politics over possible modernization of US TNW (and allied DCA) and what they believe should be NATO's broader diplomatic goals relating to nonproliferation and disarmament.

At least since President Obama's Prague speech in April 2009, these perspectives have been shared by non-basing countries, such as Norway, that believe that twenty years after the Cold War ended, the nuclear deterrence mission—including assurance of NATO allies—can be accomplished without the presence of US TNW on European soil. Before the crisis in Ukraine, Germany and Norway had been the most active NATO member states in promoting a change to the Alliance status quo.[12] Indeed, Germany appeared unlikely to provide a DCA capability once the Tornado aircraft reach the end of their service lives (though just when that might be is an open issue). The possibility of closing certain bases over the next decade relating to nuclear storage in Germany has reportedly been a topic of discussion between the government and the Bundestag.[13]

---

12. In the aftermath of President Obama's Prague speech in April 2009 proclaiming support for the vision of a world free of nuclear weapons, five European states (Germany, the Netherlands, Belgium, Luxembourg, and Norway) called for a discussion on how NATO can reduce the role of nuclear weapons and move closer to the objective of a world free of nuclear weapons.

13. Oliver Meier, "Germany pushes for changes in NATO's nuclear posture," posted by Tim Farnsworth in *Arms Control Now* (blog), Arms Control Association, March 14,

Turkey is sometimes cited as the one NATO member state that might actually reconsider its status as a non-nuclear-weapon state if the US nuclear umbrella over NATO were perceived by Ankara to be eroding— perhaps through the complete withdrawal of US TNW from Europe. This concern is often underlined by noting Turkey's unique strategic position within the Alliance and fears that Ankara may seek to match an Iranian nuclear weapons capability with one of its own.

That said, Turkish decision-making on this issue would inevitably be more complex than a simple one-dimensional assessment vis-à-vis Iran and the potential shift in regional power dynamics that a nuclear-armed Iran could precipitate. Most important, Ankara would take into account the strength of its bilateral security relationship with Washington (which the current crisis in Syria has put under great strain) and would want to be consulted before any decision that might lead to the withdrawal of US TNW from Europe.[14] Other factors, beyond NATO's conventional deterrent, would include steps that could be taken by NATO to strengthen nuclear sharing arrangements and to reassure allies, embedded within a broad commitment in both the Strategic Concept and DDPR that as long as there are nuclear weapons, NATO will remain a nuclear alliance. Thus, to the extent there is a discussion within NATO today regarding the US nuclear umbrella and incentives for proliferation, it is not being driven by Alliance-wide perceptions relating to the goal of zero nuclear weapons—at least, not yet.

Can the Status Quo Be Sustained?

NATO nuclear policy today has its roots in the Cold War, when NATO faced a fundamentally different set of security challenges. Dramatic

---

2012, http://armscontrolnow.org/2012/03/14/germany-pushes-for-changes-in-natos
-nuclear-posture/.

14. Sinan Ülgen, "Turkey and the Bomb," *The Carnegie Papers*, February 2012.

political, security, and economic developments have occurred since then: the collapse of the Soviet Union and the Warsaw Pact; the Balkans war; the addition of new NATO member states; terrorist attacks in the United States and Europe; the wars in Iraq and Afghanistan; the global financial crisis and the ongoing debt crisis in Europe and the United States; the NATO intervention in Libya; and, now, the crisis in Ukraine and the Euro-Atlantic region.

To remain relevant, NATO needs to continuously assess its evolving security context and existing and emerging threats and take these developments into consideration for its deterrence and defense posture. Maintaining the status quo, with its attendant costs and risks, can undermine rather than strengthen NATO security.

Both the 2010 Strategic Concept and the 2012 DDPR endorsed further reductions of TNW. There has also been an increasing recognition that the status quo within NATO is not sustainable given the financial and political pressures over the next ten years on both sides of the Atlantic. However, NATO members have failed to develop a clear long-term strategy on TNW that takes these factors into consideration and that assesses the costs and benefits of either maintaining the status quo or implementing changes that reflect financial and political realities while strengthening Alliance security.

A change in the nuclear status quo would also make strategic sense in light of the Ukraine crisis. NATO's serious conventional capability gaps and resource constraints for likely contingencies strongly suggest that, over the long term, NATO should not sustain a program that spends scarce defense resources on TNW capabilities that are no longer militarily useful. To continue doing so is not smart—and it is not defense.

Financial Considerations.   Discussions of NATO nuclear policy have been held against the backdrop of a significant decline in the defense spending of NATO European members. Even with some increases in spending by Allies in response to the Ukraine crisis, members will need to assess all capabilities and resources based on emerging threats and what may still be declining budgets in many countries. Financial considerations will therefore likely continue to have a significant effect on how members view the role of nuclear weapons.

NATO members hosting US TNW will need to consider the financial cost of maintaining the status quo, including the cost of maintaining DCA, either by extending the life of existing aircraft or by providing funding for nuclear-capable replacement aircraft—in particular, the joint strike fighter (F-35), a key issue for Belgium and the Netherlands. Financially, it is also hard to imagine a scenario whereby the sequester that is still looming in Washington does not lead to cuts in defense spending over the next ten years, which would affect US nuclear programs—including those relating to TNW.

The current B61 life extension program would consolidate both the strategic and non-strategic variants of the B61 into one weapon (the B61-12), with the first production unit available in fiscal year 2019. Approximately four hundred B61-12s would be produced by the end of FY 2023; roughly half of those weapons would be deployed in Europe. In a January 2014 report, the Center for Nonproliferation Analysis estimated that the B61-12 is now projected to cost $13 billion through 2038.[15]

NATO DCA are also reaching the end of their original service lives. Estimates regarding the financial costs of either extending the life of existing aircraft or providing funds for nuclear-capable replacement aircraft, in particular the F-35, are not as precise as those for the B61 life extension program. That said, giving the F-35 the capability to deliver the B61 will add hundreds of millions of dollars (or euros) to the price of that aircraft ($350 million in the United States alone)—with hundreds of millions of dollars or euros more to upgrade nuclear storage facilities in Europe.[16]

---

15. Jon B. Wolfsthal, Jeffrey Lewis, and Marc Quint, *Trillion Dollar Nuclear Triad: US Strategic Modernization over the Next Thirty Years,* James Martin Center for Nonproliferation Studies, Monterey, CA, January 2014, http://cns.miis.edu/opapers /pdfs/140107_trillion_dollar_nuclear_triad.pdf.

16. Barry Blechman and Russell Rumbaugh, "Bombs Away: The Case for Phasing Out U.S. Tactical Nukes in Europe," *Foreign Affairs,* July/August 2014,

Political and Security Considerations. Beyond the substantial financial costs, maintaining NATO's current nuclear posture over the next decade will incur political and security costs.

With respect to political costs, NATO members hosting US tactical nuclear weapons and deploying DCA will need to consider whether they are willing to invest the political capital necessary to achieve parliamentary approval for any new nuclear-related investments which could be viewed by their publics as "nuclear modernization" or even "nuclear rearmament." Before the Ukraine crisis, a clear path for achieving parliamentary approval for any necessary nuclear investments was not apparent in most basing countries. Even with the most serious security crisis on the continent in two decades, it is not clear that this calculation has changed.

With respect to security costs, one key risk is that of a terrorist attack on a European base with US forward-deployed weapons. As Sam Nunn has written, "No matter what degree NATO assesses the risk of a terrorist attack against a European NATO nuclear base—and I am convinced there is a significant risk—the political and security consequences of such an attack would shake the Alliance, even if the attack failed."[17] Here, too, the Ukraine crisis does not fundamentally alter this assessment.

Nuclear Sharing Arrangements. The DDPR directed the North Atlantic Council in May 2012 to "task the appropriate Committees to develop concepts for how to ensure the broadest possible participation of Allies concerned in their nuclear sharing arrangements, *including in case NATO were to decide to reduce its reliance on non-strategic nuclear weapons based in Europe*" (emphasis added). However, even before the crisis in Ukraine, certain NATO members could not envision NATO nuclear policy without the current nuclear arrangements, including NATO DCA and US TNW deployed in Europe. To some, an end to the current arrangements

---

http://www.foreignaffairs.com/articles/141484/barry-blechman-and-russell-rumbaugh/bombs-away.

17. Nunn, "The Race Between Cooperation and Catastrophe."

would mean non-nuclear allies are no longer directly involved in the Alliance's nuclear deterrence posture.

That said, there has been a growing recognition within NATO—including those states that currently operate NATO DCA—that there are alternatives to the current arrangements that would maintain nuclear sharing even without US forward-based TNW and that could provide a more credible and sustainable posture for NATO.

Assessments of these alternatives should continue, even if the timing for any implementation has been affected by the current crisis. If current arrangements are indeed not sustainable in the long term, NATO must begin a serious dialogue on how these alternatives might be developed and implemented by consensus in ways that strengthen the Alliance. The focus should then be on options relating to four dimensions: nuclear information sharing, nuclear consultations, common planning, and common execution.

NATO Relations with Russia and NATO Reassurance. All NATO members recognize the importance of the relationship with Russia. They understand that no country stands to benefit if the relationship further deteriorates down a path to a new Cold War. The reality is that US/NATO/Russian cooperation is required to reduce nuclear threats in the Euro-Atlantic region.

The Ukraine crisis underscores the deep mistrust and suspicion in the Euro-Atlantic region that undermine attempts at cooperation between NATO and Russia. Breaking down these persistent barriers to cooperation will require political will from the highest levels in Washington, Brussels, and Moscow.

Is it reasonable to expect American, European, and Russian political leaders to grapple with the broad contours of Euro-Atlantic security while the Ukraine crisis continues to unnerve Europe?

Many would say "no"—in both the West and in Russia. Within NATO, many countries, in particular new NATO member states, believe the only appropriate goal in the wake of the crisis in Ukraine is to strengthen NATO to deter future Russian aggression, a narrative grounded in their own historical experiences with Moscow. And it is clear that there are those in Russia—possibly including Putin—who have also given up on any dialogue with the West, which from their perspective has ignored Russian security interests for years.

That said, NATO has an interest in at least attempting to ensure that steps to reassure allies are taken in ways that *minimize the incentives for a Russian response* that would further inflame Euro-Atlantic security or foreclose a more cooperative approach to security on the continent. Ideally, these steps would also *reduce the longer-term costs of reassurance*.

Moreover, the West's emerging response to Russian policy may help highlight for the leaders in the Kremlin Moscow's near-term interest in minimizing the costs of its Ukraine policy and long-term interest in taking a more cooperative approach to Euro-Atlantic security. True, there are those in Moscow today who apparently think otherwise (or think that NATO and the European Union simply will not follow through with their "threats"). But the reality of billions of dollars of capital already fleeing Russia and the prospect of a NATO defense force that becomes more focused and capable on its eastern border have the potential to be important factors in Russian decision-making.

Looking Ahead

The Alliance has committed itself to remaining a nuclear alliance and to creating the conditions to move toward a world free of nuclear weapons. Even before the Ukraine crisis, tensions persisted within the Alliance and the United States as to whether these two points were mutually exclusive or mutually reinforcing—in particular, whether NATO can remain a nuclear alliance in the absence of US TNW deployed in Europe. NATO members have adopted President Obama's Prague goals, but have also agreed that any move to alter the status quo with respect to NATO's TNW posture cannot be unilateral and must be supported by all members. Before Ukraine, this had resulted in an effective stalemate as to how to move forward. In the wake of Ukraine, that stalemate appears even more robust.

All members nevertheless have a continuing responsibility to demonstrate that NATO's nuclear posture and policies reflect their nonproliferation and disarmament commitments and are tailored in the most effective way to ensure that they strengthen Alliance security; address the complexity of threats, both old and new, now facing the Alliance; and take into consideration NATO's broader role and mission, including cooperation and partnerships with key global states.

The Desirability and Feasibility of Reducing the Profile of Nuclear Deterrence in NATO.   Deterring threats will always be a core component of NATO. However, questions remain: What is the appropriate mix of tools for this task? Can the role of nuclear weapons in deterrence be reduced? These questions are, if anything, more pertinent than ever in light of recent developments in Euro-Atlantic security and new requirements for conventional and other reassurance.

Reading the Strategic Concept and DDPR as policy prescriptions, NATO was pointed in the direction of identifying a safer, more stable form of deterrence which would of necessity require an increased role for cooperative security in the Euro-Atlantic region and improved relations with Russia. Before the Ukraine crisis, there was little in the way of a strategy—and very little urgency or energy—to fill this prescription. Today, there is even less so. Yet the debate is unavoidable as NATO members, including the United States, grapple with decreasing budgets and an increasingly complex set of threats and security priorities, including a more assertive Russia.

It is now even more urgent that NATO's nuclear policies and posture—including the future of US TNW deployed in Europe—be cast in a larger Euro-Atlantic security framework than would be permitted by a debate purely over the future of NATO's nuclear posture. Such a framework should be built on an updated set of understandings and arrangements within NATO to strengthen the trans-Atlantic security guarantee in the absence of US nuclear weapons on the ground in Europe. The framework should also facilitate a new set of understandings between all nations in the Euro-Atlantic region—including Russia—about European security.

Building Mutual Security in the Euro-Atlantic Region. Security policies in the Euro-Atlantic region continue to remain largely on Cold War autopilot—a posture now reinforced by the crisis in Ukraine. Large strategic nuclear forces remain ready to be launched in minutes; thousands of tactical nuclear weapons remain in Europe; a decades-old missile defense debate remains stuck in neutral; and new security challenges associated with prompt strike forces, cybersecurity, and space remain contentious and inadequately addressed.

Nunn, former Russian foreign minister Igor Ivanov, former German deputy foreign minister Wolfgang Ischinger, and former British defense secretary Des Browne co-chaired a group of senior political, military, and security experts from the Euro-Atlantic region to address just this challenge. In March 2013, several months before the Ukraine crisis exploded in Europe, they published a new report recommending a fresh approach—one that could be developed jointly by all nations in the Euro-Atlantic region—tailored so that governments can reduce risk, reduce costs, and build trust in a dynamic and sustainable way.[18] They also warned of the risks of inaction and a sustained status quo approach.

The group recommended that a new, continuing process of *comprehensive security dialogue* should be mandated at the highest political levels. Once begun, the dialogue could proceed in both concept and practice on existing or new tracks. The group also recommended that *practical steps* be agreed upon for a broad range of security issues, including nuclear weapons, missile defense, prompt strike forces, conventional forces, cybersecurity, and space.

Such a dialogue could support specific steps that would not require new, legally binding treaties but could help facilitate treaties where

---

18.   Des Browne, Wolfgang Ischinger, Igor Ivanov, and Sam Nunn, *Building Mutual Security in the Euro-Atlantic Region* (Washington, DC: Nuclear Threat Initiative, 2013), http://www.buildingmutualsecurity.org.

necessary. This could create a positive dynamic for discussions and further boost and deepen cooperation. Within this flexible framework for dialogue, priorities could be established and progress implemented in phases, with issues relating to nuclear weapons and missile defense receiving the highest priority. A premium would be placed on the early implementation of options that would increase transparency, confidence, and trust.

Advocates of this approach believed that, if implemented by governments, it could move Europe, Russia, the United States, and, ultimately, other regions toward a safer and more stable form of security with decreasing risks of conflict and greater cooperation, transparency, defense, and stability worldwide.

The question now is whether the political will exists in key capitals to even envision the creation of such a process. The potential gains are clear: pulling both sides back from an increasingly costly conflict. However, is it possible to envision practical steps consistent with the vision of building mutual security in today's Europe? And could those steps lead to a change in the nuclear status quo within NATO?

Role for arms control and disarmament involving NATO

In 2010 and 2012, the Strategic Concept and the DDPR both committed the Alliance to further reductions in TNW, albeit in the context of reciprocal measures with Russia (though Allies continued to grapple with what would constitute reciprocal measures).

Today, even if Russian policy were to shift dramatically toward working with Kiev and the West on a political settlement and the long-term stabilization of Ukraine, the flames of distrust that have been fanned over the past year may take many years to burn themselves out in many Western capitals. The damage has been done, and that damage may well have a lasting impact on security policy and arms control in the Euro-Atlantic region.

It now seems even less likely that any new, legally binding arms control agreements are in the cards for the next few years. Even before the

Ukraine crisis, Moscow was cold to US offers to negotiate further bilateral reductions in nuclear forces. Efforts to revive the Conventional Armed Forces in Europe Treaty were making little headway. Added to this now is a heightened level of mistrust between the West and Russia that will be difficult to surmount—in terms of both negotiating any new legally binding agreements and achieving any necessary approval by legislatures, including the US Senate. More likely than not, in Washington, any work in this area will be left to the next administration.

The current crisis in Euro-Atlantic security may ultimately be the catalyst for a change in NATO's nuclear posture. Despite renewed calls by some for the Alliance to delay any changes to NATO's nuclear posture (and to incur the substantial financial and political costs necessary to maintain the status quo), important decisions relating to that posture will need to be taken over the next few years. These will overlap with decisions related to funding and the future direction of any reassurance activities.

For many, the crisis in Ukraine underlines the fact that reassuring NATO Allies must be strongly correlated with visible steps that fill serious conventional capability gaps and that address new unconventional, non-nuclear threats, rather than steps relating to tactical nuclear weapons capabilities that few, if any, believe are militarily useful. If US TNW in Europe have virtually no military utility, it is hard to argue they have any concrete value as a real deterrent in today's—or tomorrow's—Euro-Atlantic security space, in particular when the strategic forces of the United States, United Kingdom, and France remain visible and credible in any NATO context.

There is, however, a strong case to be made for a continuing reassurance requirement beyond two years (what is now budgeted in the United States), given the severity of the tear in the fabric of European security and with the strong possibility that Putin will remain president of Russia for another ten years. New resources from Washington and Europe will be needed to pay for increasing the American military presence in Europe, providing more exercises and training, and building partner capacity. Where will the resources come from?

One sensible part of the answer is for Washington and its NATO allies, over the next few years, to reduce the staggering costs associated with a planned $13 billion modernization of the US B61 nuclear bomb now stored in European bunkers and associated NATO DCA; to decisively alter the nuclear component of NATO's defense posture; and to use these savings to capitalize various reassurance initiatives over at least the next five years.

Under this scenario, NATO would take three specific steps.

First, it would restate that as long as nuclear weapons exist, NATO will remain a nuclear alliance.

Second, it would commit to restructuring NATO's nuclear deterrent so that it is more credible, safer, and more affordable. This will include:

- Maintaining the supreme guarantee provided by the strategic nuclear forces of the Alliance, particularly those of the United States, and providing a more visible demonstration of this guarantee to European Allies (e.g., visits of US strategic bombers to European bases).
- Modifying NATO nuclear sharing arrangements to enhance information sharing, consultations, common planning, and common execution.
- Phasing in a consolidation of US tactical nuclear weapons (now dispersed at bases in Europe) to the United States and scaling back the US B61 modernization program and associated DCA modernization.

Third, it would commit to devoting a substantial portion of the savings from restructuring NATO's nuclear deterrent to sustaining and expanding reassurance over the next five years. This would include contributions from both the United States and European Allies. This could provide an additional $1.5 billion to $3 billion for reassurance (roughly double what is now in the budget). This is a reasonable figure in light of estimated savings from scaling back the B61 modernization (perhaps as much as

$8 billion), plans to make the F-35 nuclear-capable (hundreds of millions of dollars), and recent commitments by a number of Allies to increase their defense spending.

There remain NATO Allies who value the political symbolism of US nuclear forces stationed in Europe—even more so given recent Russian actions in Ukraine. Even if these Allies can be convinced that maintaining the nuclear status quo within NATO is unnecessary, or even counterproductive, a political and diplomatic strategy would be necessary to ensure that governments and publics understand that a change in the nuclear status quo does not signal a reduced US commitment to the Alliance—nor does it affect NATO's capacity to remain a nuclear alliance.

In the months ahead, there are important incentives for NATO to, at a minimum, do what it can to leave open pathways that could help define the contours of a new security strategy for the Euro-Atlantic region, one that includes—but looks beyond—reassuring NATO. Indeed, that very effort may be the essential prerequisite to resolving the crisis in Ukraine in the years ahead. Leaders from the West should continue to offer to discuss with Russia pathways out of the current crisis. Without new diplomacy during this difficult period, efforts to reassure NATO risk contributing to another generation of East-West conflict.

CHAPTER 5 **Russia, Strategic Stability, and Nuclear Weapons**

Pavel Podvig

Russia's views of the role of nuclear weapons and deterrence in its national security strategy have been largely shaped by the legacy of the Cold War and by the presence of the large Soviet nuclear arsenal and the institutions that created and maintained the nuclear complex. When Russia emerged as an independent state from the breakup of the Soviet Union, it inherited not only the legal status of its predecessor, but also the basic conceptual national security framework that existed in the Soviet Union.

At the critical moment of transformation of the national security agenda in the early 1990s, the very existence of a nuclear arsenal dictated a certain approach to security that relied on the deterrence capability provided by the nuclear forces. Even as the ideological component that defined the Cold War confrontation had disappeared, other elements of the security environment appeared to have remained in place: Russia's relative isolation from the West and the presence of a US nuclear arsenal that was sized to deter Russia. The economic and political upheaval of the first post-Soviet years also added a sense of vulnerability as Russia saw the deterioration of its conventional military forces. The combination of these factors caused Russian leaders to perceive the nuclear option as the only choice that was realistically available to Russia at the time.

Nuclear deterrence nominally remains one of the central elements of Russia's national security strategy, even though its views on the role of nuclear weapons, while still deeply rooted in the past, have been gradually changing in response to the changing nature of the security threats that Russia is facing today. As many of these threats, ranging from local and regional conflicts to terrorism, are distinctly different from the Cold War confrontation that shaped its nuclear arsenal in the past, Russia has been trying to reconcile its traditional reliance on nuclear weapons with the diminishing utility of these weapons in directly addressing new security challenges. This process produced an extremely cautious approach to nuclear disarmament—while Russia has been reducing the size of its strategic arsenal, the idea of complete nuclear disarmament has not yet received visible support among its political and military leadership or among the public. Even advocates of nuclear disarmament stress that it should be predicated on "a serious overhaul of the international system" that would maintain international security and stability.[1] Others believe that deep nuclear disarmament is not attainable and, indeed, would undermine international security.[2]

Most of the arguments in this discussion reflect the key objections against nuclear disarmament outlined in the opening chapter of this book. Specifically, nuclear weapons are credited with preventing large-scale wars between nuclear weapon states, deterring the use of force as

---

1. Yevgeny Primakov, Igor Ivanov, Yevgeny Velikhov, and Mikhail Moiseev, "From Nuclear Deterrence to Universal Security," *Izvestia,* October 15, 2010. English translation is available at http://rbth.co.uk/articles/2010/10/28/from_nuclear _deterrence_universal_security05073.html.

2. See, for example, Sergey Karaganov, "Global Zero and Common Sense: Nuclear Weapons in the Modern World," *Russia in Global Affairs,* July 7, 2010, http://eng.globalaffairs.ru/number/Global_Zero_and_Common_Sense-14889.

an instrument of international relations, and moderating the arms race in other, non-nuclear, areas. Even though Russian experts generally accept that nuclear disarmament strengthens the efforts to prevent proliferation of nuclear weapons, this analysis does not necessarily extend to a world free of nuclear weapons.[3] Most importantly, Russia's attitude toward complete nuclear disarmament is apparently shaped by concerns about a potential rise in the role of non-nuclear military force, which would seriously undermine its status in the existing system of international relations or even create a direct military threat to the state.[4] This seems to confirm the widespread perception, in Russia as well as outside, of the key role that nuclear weapons play in Russia's national security policy. These weapons are believed to compensate for the inferiority of its conventional forces, the technological gap in the capabilities of advanced weapon systems (such as high-precision global strike, missile defense, or military space) between Russia and the West, and the difficulty of providing adequate protection of Russia's large territory. The combination of these factors would definitely make Russia an extremely reluctant participant in the movement toward nuclear zero. This perception, however, stems from assumptions about the nature of security threats and potential military conflicts that reflect the legacy of the Cold War rather than the actual military utility of nuclear weapons. And while this legacy remains a potent force in shaping Russia's national security agenda, it is also possible to see a path toward a smaller role for nuclear weapons and eventually to their complete elimination.

---

3. Alexei Arbatov, "The Dialectics of Nuclear Disarmament and Nonproliferation," in *Nuclear Reset: Arms Reduction and Nonproliferation,* ed. Alexei Arbatov, Vladimir Dvorkin, and Natalia Bubnova (Moscow: Carnegie Moscow Center, 2012), 349–362.

4. Primakov et al., "From Nuclear Deterrence to Universal Security"; Karaganov, "Global Zero and Common Sense."

Strategic stability and national security

One of the most important elements of Soviet nuclear policy was a focus on confrontation with the United States that dominated the development of nuclear forces from the early days of the Soviet program. This focus helped shape the structure of the nuclear force as the Soviet Union first strove to achieve the capability to hold the territory of the United States at risk and then invested a substantial amount of effort in obtaining quantitative and qualitative parity with the United States. These policies later gave rise to a rather elaborate notion of strategic stability that the Soviet Union defined not only as a balance of the capabilities of military forces, but also as a status of relationships that guaranteed that neither side could gain a decisive advantage over its adversary in the long term. This definition of strategic stability provided an extremely flexible framework for development of strategic nuclear forces. It was used to justify a wide range of military programs, from achieving numerical parity with the United States to improving missile accuracy and investing in missile defense.

As it relied on the concept of strategic stability, the Soviet Union never developed an elaborate concept of nuclear deterrence. The foundation of its nuclear strategy was the capability to deliver a retaliatory strike against the United States. Although the United States believed that the Soviet Union worked to obtain the capability to attack US strategic forces and wage a protracted nuclear war, the documentary evidence suggests that the Soviet nuclear forces never approached this capability and that it was never considered a viable option.[5] The Soviet Union did invest considerable efforts into survivability of its nuclear force, since it believed that effective and credible deterrence required a demonstrated capability to inflict a certain amount of damage in a retaliatory strike. However, the amount of damage that would be required for deterrence to work was never determined with any degree of precision. The capability to ensure

---

5. Pavel Podvig, "The Window of Vulnerability That Wasn't: Soviet Military Buildup in the 1970s—A Research Note," *International Security* 33, no. 1 (Summer 2008): 118–138.

retaliation was apparently more important than the size of a retaliatory strike as long as the damage was reasonably large. For example, an internal Soviet assessment made in the 1980s estimated that, after withstanding a first strike, the Soviet ICBMs, which carried more than six thousand warheads at the time, could destroy about eighty targets on US territory and that the Soviet Union would need the capability to destroy about two hundred US targets to provide effective deterrence.[6] These numbers appear to be quite arbitrary as they reflect the existing and projected retaliatory potential of strategic forces rather than any specific targeting strategy. For the most part, the size and structure of the strategic nuclear forces were determined by the requirements of the broadly understood policy of strategic stability—specifically, as an approximate quantitative and qualitative parity with the United States.

This general approach toward the role of nuclear weapons in national security strategy remained largely intact during the transition from the Soviet Union to Russia. After the breakup of the Soviet Union, Russia undertook an effort to formalize its nuclear policy in a military doctrine. It was a relatively new development, as the Soviet Union had never produced a formal document that would openly declare the principles of a possible use of nuclear weapons. While the actual structure of strategic forces did not necessarily reflect any specific doctrinal concept, these documents and the discussions that accompanied their preparation and release provide an important insight into the process that determined the role of nuclear weapons and nuclear deterrence in the overall architecture of national security.

The first Russian military doctrine, developed in 1993, was meant to be a transitional document. Indeed, it was released under the title, "The Basic Provisions of the Military Doctrine of the Russian Federation."[7] One of

---

6. Pavel Podvig, "The myth of strategic stability," *Bulletin of the Atomic Scientists,* October 31, 2012, http://thebulletin.org/myth-strategic-stability.

7. "Basic Provisions of the Military Doctrine of the Russian Federation," approved by Executive Order No. 1833 of the President of the Russian Federation, November 2,

the most important elements of the first Russian military doctrine was the reversal of the principle of "no first use" of nuclear weapons that was formally declared by the Soviet Union in 1982.[8] The use of nuclear weapons, however, was reserved to situations in which the sovereignty and the very survival of the state were at stake—the threat that the doctrine admitted was almost entirely eliminated. The doctrine saw the main danger to stability and peace in local wars and conflicts, although it allowed for a possibility of these conflicts escalating into a large-scale war.

The 1993 doctrine explicitly stated that the main mission of nuclear weapons is to deter a potential nuclear war:

> The aim of the Russian Federation's policy in the sphere of nuclear weapons is to eliminate the danger of nuclear war by deterring the launching of aggression against the Russian Federation and its allies.

While this provision would directly apply only to scenarios involving aggression against Russia or its allies, the doctrine appears to suggest a somewhat broader role of the deterrent potential of the Russian nuclear force. First, one of the key missions assigned to the Russian armed forces was "the maintenance of the composition and status of the strategic nuclear forces at a level ensuring guaranteed intended damage to the aggressor." Also, the doctrine listed a threat to strategic stability among the main sources of military dangers to Russia. These provisions were largely in line with the traditional role that strategic stability played in the Soviet concept of national security; maintaining the deterrent potential of the strategic forces was not only a tool of preventing nuclear war, but also

---

1993. Only a summary of the document was released to the public. For an English translation, see "The Basic Provisions of the Military Doctrine of the Russian Federation," Federation of American Scientists, http://www.fas.org/nuke/guide/russia /doctrine/russia-mil-doc.html.

8. Nikolai Sokov, "Russia's Nuclear Doctrine," Nuclear Threat Initiative, August 1, 2004, http://www.nti.org/analysis/articles/russias-nuclear-doctrine.

part of a strategy that would "ensure the deterrence of potential aggressors from unleashing any wars" against Russia's interests.

This understanding of the role of nuclear weapons appears to be distinct from the readiness to use them in situations threatening the survival of the state. The role of the strategic nuclear forces, which are explicitly mentioned in this context, would be to provide what could probably be called strategic deterrence by preventing local wars and countering other military threats that would normally fall below the threshold of nuclear use. This concept has never been explicitly articulated or critically examined, but it was generally consistent with an approach to national security that emphasized strategic stability and the balance of forces.

Preserving the strategic balance between Russia and the United States indeed became the primary goal of Russia's nuclear policy in the 1990s. In the nuclear area, Russia saw the threat to strategic stability coming from two directions: the disparity of offensive potentials and missile defense. The START II arms control treaty, signed in 1993, created conditions for numerical disparity between US and Russian strategic arsenals as it required Russia to eliminate most of its multiple-warhead ballistic missiles. To compensate for this, Russia would have to produce a significant number of new ICBMs, something that it could not afford given the state of the economy in the 1990s. Characteristically, the discussion of the START II treaty in Russia never seriously considered a possibility that it may not need to maintain numerical parity with the United States. Rather, the parity was taken to be a necessary and sufficient condition of an effective deterrence posture.

If Russia believed that strategic parity with the United States would help it protect a broad range of national security interests, its experience during the 1990s provided a mixed record. While Russia's concerns certainly influenced US debate on arms control, missile defense, and other security issues, they rarely affected the outcome of the debate or the decisions that were made. Even though Russia was able to reach an understanding with the United States on the parameters of nuclear arms reductions that accommodated some of Russia's concerns about the START II treaty, the key parameters of that treaty remained intact. On missile defense, Russia was unsuccessful in changing the course of the US program or preventing US withdrawal from the Anti-Ballistic Missile Treaty (ABM).

Another foreign policy setback that Russia believed had important security implications was its inability to prevent the enlargement of NATO that expanded the alliance to the territory of former Soviet allies in Eastern Europe. The 1993 doctrine explicitly listed the possibility of a development of this kind among military dangers. But as it turned out, Russia had little leverage over this decision. At the same time, Russia's opposition to enlargement wasn't completely ignored—as part of the decision to admit new members, NATO agreed to set up the NATO-Russia Council and to accept certain limits on deployment of forces on the territories of new members.

NATO's intervention in Kosovo in 1999 was the most serious test of Russia's assumption that maintaining strategic stability could help deter others from "unleashing any wars which threaten the interests of the Russian Federation." Russia strongly opposed the intervention, which it saw as an act of aggression and a model for possible future local wars and conflicts at its periphery.[9] The NATO operation in Kosovo demonstrated to Russia that its capability to protect its own interests in conflicts of this kind is quite limited—nuclear forces simply couldn't offer a credible deterrence strategy in this case. While Russia clearly never contemplated using a nuclear threat to stop the NATO intervention (and such a threat would not be considered credible anyway), it seemed to believe that its status as a nuclear power would afford it a greater role in the situation. Indeed, one outcome of Russia's experience with the NATO operation in Kosovo was a demonstration of its willingness to use nuclear weapons to terminate an intervention of this kind if it were directed against Russia, which it could not rule out completely. This capability was demonstrated during the Zapad-99 military exercise staged shortly after the NATO

---

9. Oksana Antonenko, "Russia, NATO, and European Security after Kosovo," *Survival: Global Politics and Strategy* 41, no. 4 (Winter 1999–2000): 132.

operation was over. In the exercise, Russia used strategic bombers to simulate nuclear strikes that were supposed to de-escalate the conflict after all conventional defense options were exhausted.[10]

Although de-escalation strategies apparently came to occupy a prominent place in Russian military thinking, they do not necessarily provide an alternative to strategic deterrence.[11] At the very least, credible options that involve a limited nuclear strike, whether conducted for de-escalation or in response to an overwhelming conventional attack, would require a capable nuclear force that could provide deterrence at the strategic level. This means that if Russia were to rely on de-escalation it would still have to be concerned about its ability to maintain strategic balance with the United States.

However simple and attractive the concept of strategic stability appears to be, Russia's experience during the 1990s strongly suggested that it could no longer provide a foundation for effective national security policy. Despite the economic and political upheavals of that decade, Russia largely maintained the capability to deliver a strategic nuclear strike to the United States (or any other country). The fact that it has difficulty converting this potential into effective national security policies indicates that the political role of nuclear weapons has dramatically shrunk, even if it did not entirely disappear. Russia, however, appeared to have reached a different conclusion. The policy setbacks of the 1990s were attributed to the erosion of strategic stability that resulted from Russia's inability to demonstrate credible commitment to maintaining its strategic nuclear arsenal at the level that would balance US strategic potential. From Russia's point of view, this could undermine strategic stability even further and eventually leave Russia with few options to protect its national security interests.

---

10.   Sokov, "Russia's Nuclear Doctrine."

11.   On de-escalation, see Nikolai Sokov, "Nuclear Weapons in Russian National Security Strategy," in *Russian Nuclear Weapons: Past, Present, and Future,* ed. Stephen J. Blank, Strategic Studies Institute, November 2011.

One problem that Russia was facing at the time was economic constraints that limited its capability to support a strategic nuclear arsenal on a par with the United States. Nevertheless, the decisions taken in the immediate aftermath of the Kosovo crisis included measures that would strengthen the strategic forces, primarily by extending the service life of some older missiles and submarines. The Russian government also reportedly made a commitment to modernization of its tactical nuclear arsenal. But later developments suggested that it was a decision to extend the range of scenarios for potential use of nuclear weapons to regional conflicts rather than an investment into new, nonstrategic weapon systems.

The new military doctrine that was accepted in 2000 was deeply influenced by the NATO intervention in Kosovo and reflected a shift toward expanding the role of nuclear weapons.[12] While key provisions of the new doctrine repeated the statements made in the 1993 document, some of them were made more explicit. In an almost direct reference to the Kosovo scenario, the doctrine included "humanitarian interventions" and "operations conducted without UN mandate" to the list of destabilizing factors. Most importantly, Russia reserved the right to use nuclear weapons in case of an attack against it with nuclear weapons or other weapons of mass destruction or in response to a large-scale conventional aggression "in situations critical for national security of the Russian Federation." The doctrine apparently intended to lower the nuclear threshold, as it no longer set a threat to sovereignty and the survival of the state as conditions for nuclear weapons use. One notable statement that warned about the high probability of nuclear escalation in a large-scale conventional war was

---

12. "Voyennaya doktrina Rossiiskoy Federatsii [The military doctrine of the Russian Federation]," approved by Executive Order No. 706 of the President of the Russian Federation, April 21, 2000, *Nezavisimaya gazeta,* April 22, 2000, http://www.ng.ru /politics/2000-04-22/5_doktrina.html. For an English translation, see "Russia's Military Doctrine," *Arms Control Today* 5 (2000), http://www.armscontrol.org /act/2000_05/dc3ma00.

clearly directed at preventing the possibility of an attack against Russian strategic forces by conventional, most likely high-precision, weapons.

Despite changes that reflected the political developments of the moment, the overall thrust of the new doctrine remained largely intact: Russia stated that it "maintains its status of a nuclear power to deter (prevent) an aggression against it or its allies." The link between status and the nuclear arsenal was made even more explicit. The list of external threats to Russia's national security included "attempts to ignore interests of the Russian Federation in addressing problems of international security and to prevent [Russia] from strengthening its position as one of the centers of the multi-polar world."

Shortly after the new doctrine was approved, the Russian military establishment became involved in an intense debate that directly questioned the key premise of the strategic stability approach to national security. A series of proposals that emerged from the General Staff suggested significant unilateral reductions of the strategic nuclear force, mostly at the expense of intercontinental ballistic missiles that traditionally constituted the core of the Russian force, with redirection of most of the resources toward conventional forces. These proposals generated a great deal of controversy and, after a period of discussion and bureaucratic infighting, were largely rejected at the August 2000 session of the Russian Security Council. That decision involved a series of compromises, but overall it clearly signaled that the Russian military and political leadership was not ready to abandon reliance on the strength of its strategic forces as the key element of national security policy.

Indeed, the notion of importance of strategic deterrence has taken a greater hold of Russia's security policy during the 2000s, as Russia gradually emerged from the economic slump of the 1990s and directed an increasing share of its resources to the modernization of its military forces. One of the program documents that set the parameters of the military reform, the White Book released by the Ministry of Defense in 2003, placed "deterrence of military and political-military threats to security and interests of the Russian Federation" at the top of the list of tasks assigned to the Russian armed forces.[13] It also directly stated that "preservation of the potential of the strategic deterrence forces" should be the first priority of the military modernization program. The White Book reiterated the position of the earlier doctrinal documents that, in order to achieve effective deterrence, Russia should maintain the composition of its strategic nuclear forces that would guarantee inflicting a "predetermined level of damage" to an aggressor.

The role of the strategic nuclear forces outlined in the White Book was fairly broad. It asserted that maintaining modern and capable armed forces is one of the conditions of "a successful and seamless integration [of Russia] in the emerging system of international relations." Furthermore, the document set a very ambitious, if unrealistic, goal—Russia's military power was supposed to prevent "irreversible disintegration of the system of international relations based on the principles of international law" and provide a foundation for "global stability in the broad sense of this term." The strategic nuclear forces were clearly expected to play the central role in this undertaking.

The extent to which the Russian political leaders believed in the importance of strategic stability for national security was most vividly demonstrated in the aftermath of a terrorist attack in Beslan, North Ossetia, in September 2004, in which separatists took hundreds of schoolchildren hostage, many of whom died in the resulting fighting between the terrorists and Russian security forces. In his address to the nation after the crisis was violently resolved, President Putin linked the attack to attempts by unspecified forces to take advantage of Russia's weakness:

We showed weakness, and the weak are trampled upon. Some want to cut off a juicy morsel from us while others are helping them. They are helping because they believe that, as one of the world's major

---

13. "Actualnyye zadachi razvitiya vooruzhennykh sil Rossiyskoy Federatsii [Immediate Tasks of Development of the Armed Forces of the Russian Federation]," *Krasnaya Zvezda*, October 11, 2003.

nuclear powers, Russia is still posing a threat to someone, and therefore this threat must be removed.[14]

This reaction to a terrorist attack draws an almost direct link between
Russia's strength and its ability to deter and counter threats to its national
security, including the threat of terrorist attacks. Mentioning Russia's status as a major nuclear power also suggested that the strength was understood primarily, if not exclusively, in terms of the potential of the Russian
nuclear forces.

Responding to its vision of the role of strategic nuclear forces and
largely free from the economic constraints of the 1990s, the Russian government embarked upon a modernization program that included substantial investment in the traditional nuclear triad. The program included
extending the service life of existing intercontinental ballistic missiles and
developing a multiple-warhead version of the new Topol-M missile. Russia
also invested in acceleration of a number of strategic fleet programs—
constructing new submarines and overhauling older subs, developing the
Bulava submarine-launched missile, and modernizing older missiles—
and initiated modernization of its strategic bomber fleet. Taken together,
these programs were designed to allow Russia to prevent the decline
in size of its strategic arsenal that would result from retirement of old
delivery systems deployed in the 1980s. The United States would still be
able to retain a substantial quantitative (and qualitative) advantage over
Russian strategic forces, but Russia would largely secure its status as a
"major nuclear power."

From the point of view of the Russian leadership, this strategy has
generally paid off, although it was closely interlinked with the improvement of Russia's economic position that gave it a considerable degree of
freedom in conducting more assertive foreign policy, especially toward
the countries of the former Soviet Union. In its strategic relationship with

---

14. "Address by President Vladimir Putin," Kremlin, Moscow, September 4, 2004,
http://archive.kremlin.ru/eng/speeches/2004/09/04/1958_type82912_76332.shtml.

the United States, Russia negotiated a new arms control treaty, New START, which was more equitable than previous post-START agreements. New START gave Russia a significant degree of freedom in carrying out its strategic modernization program and addressed some of its concerns about the US missile defense program and conventional strategic delivery systems. It is difficult to say to what extent Russia's effort to strengthen its strategic nuclear forces was a factor in these developments, but Russia definitely saw it as playing an important role.

In February 2010 Russia released its new military doctrine.[15] This document didn't contain significant changes in the analysis of military threats and dangers facing Russia—NATO's expanding role and its encroachment on Russian borders were still at the top of the list of military dangers. Strategic stability also figured quite prominently; attempts to undermine stability and the deployment of missile defenses that could "upset the existing missile-nuclear balance" were also listed among the main military dangers. Tasks assigned to the armed forces included protection of sovereignty of the state and "strategic deterrence, including prevention of military conflicts." Since the definition of a military conflict in the document includes all kinds of armed confrontations—from small armed conflicts and local wars to regional and large-scale wars—strategic deterrence was probably meant to be a factor that should deter military actions at all levels.

The most prominent change in the doctrine was the more limited role of nuclear weapons in response to a conventional aggression. If the 2000 document allowed for the use of nuclear weapons "in situations critical for national security" of the state, the new doctrine stated that nuclear weapons could be used only if "the very existence of the state" is in

---

15. "Voyennaya doktrina Rossiiskoy Federatsii [Military doctrine of the Russian Federation]," approved by the president of the Russian Federation on February 5, 2010, http://news.kremlin.ru/ref_notes/461 [in Russian]. For an English translation, see "Text of Newly-Approved Russian Military Doctrine," Carnegie Endowment for International Peace, February 5, 2010, http://carnegieendowment.org/2010/02/05 /text-of-newly-approved-russian-military-doctrine.

danger. It is unclear, though, if this statement translated into a real change of the nuclear use policy—the 2010 doctrine was accompanied by a document that described the principles of nuclear deterrence but which has not been made public, leaving some room for uncertainty.[16] However, it appears that strategic deterrence retained its central role in national security policy. Indeed, the fact that Russia limited the range of situations in which it could resort to nuclear weapons might reflect growing confidence in the capability of its strategic nuclear forces.

Threats to strategic stability

Given the central role of strategic stability in its national security strategy, it is not surprising that Russia paid close attention to US programs that it believed had the potential to undermine strategic balance and restrain Russia's capability to exercise strategic deterrence. Russia traditionally considered US efforts to build missile defense as one of the most serious threats to its deterrence potential, although in recent years it has also expressed serious reservations about advances in US capability to deliver high-precision conventional strikes and its move toward deployment of conventionally armed strategic launchers.[17] Russia has invested a significant amount of effort and political capital in addressing its concerns about these developments and protecting what it called "the existing missile-nuclear balance." This experience also reinforced Russia's view of

---

16. "Principles of State Nuclear Deterrence Policy to 2020." See "Dmitry Medvedev signed the Military Doctrine and the Principles of State Nuclear Deterrence Policy to 2020," February 5, 2010, http://archive.kremlin.ru/eng/text/news/2010/02 /224154.shtml.

17. Eugene Miasnikov, "Precision Guided Weapons and Strategic Balance," Center for Arms Control, Energy, and Environmental Studies at the Moscow Institute of Physics and Technology, November 2000; Eugene Miasnikov, "The Air-Space Threat to Russia," in *Missile Defense: Confrontation and Cooperation,* ed. Alexei Arbatov and Vladimir Dvorkin (Moscow: Carnegie Moscow Center, 2013), 121–146.

strategic stability as an essential factor in its security policy. The Russian leadership must have concluded that unless it maintains strategic balance it could not prevent the United States from undermining strategic stability, which would in turn lead to even greater erosion of strategic balance.

Russia's concerns about missile defense could be traced back to the disagreement between the United States and the Soviet Union about the Strategic Defense Initiative program (often called Star Wars in the United States) and its impact on strategic stability and disarmament. Even though in the 1990s the US program was substantially scaled down and concentrated on countering medium- and short-range ballistic missiles, Russia insisted on its opposition to US attempts to deploy a missile defense system and invested a considerable amount of political capital in protecting the ABM treaty, which it invariably referred to as a "cornerstone of strategic stability." Russia explicitly linked the treaty to nuclear disarmament and non-proliferation and warned about adverse consequences that could be triggered by US withdrawal from the treaty.[18] That effort, however, ultimately proved unsuccessful and the United States formally withdrew from the treaty in 2002.

The US withdrawal from the ABM treaty was a significant setback for Russia. Its military doctrine directly mentioned the threat to strategic stability that could result from violations of international arms control agreements among the key military dangers. Now Russia saw that danger materialize. From its perspective, the end of the ABM treaty would allow development of missile defenses with potentially serious consequences for Russia's deterrence. The facts that the United States insisted that its missile defense was not directed against Russia and the system's clear lack of capability to counter Russian ballistic missiles were usually not taken

---

18. Igor S. Ivanov, minister for foreign affairs, Russian Federation, "Statement at the Non-proliferation Treaty Review Conference," New York, April 25, 2000, http://www.mid.ru/bdomp/dip_vest.nsf/99b2ddc4f717c733c32567370042ee43 /25de7700e9ba953ec32568ef0027c951!OpenDocument [in Russian].

into account. Russia concentrated on the open-ended nature of the program, arguing that the lack of constraints would allow the United States to move toward deployment of a more capable system that would pose a threat to Russia's retaliatory potential.[19]

As with other developments of the time, the Russian leadership probably viewed the US withdrawal from the ABM treaty as a result of Russia's inability to support its opposition to missile defense by credible measures that would counter the program. Russia's reaction to the US decision was quite muted, especially compared with the rhetoric of the previous years that declared the ABM treaty "the cornerstone of strategic stability." In reality, it is quite unlikely that a stronger Russian response would have changed the political calculation in the United States and affected the decision to abandon the treaty—the US program was driven primarily by concerns about missile threats from other countries. But Russia invariably saw the US decision through the prism of US-Russian relations and made its conclusions accordingly.

The demise of the ABM treaty was not the only threat to strategic stability that Russia saw as emerging from US policies. Another important development was the steady advance in US capability to project conventional power with high accuracy, which in theory could allow the United States to hold at risk a broad range of targets. As this capability improved, Russia became concerned about the vulnerability of its strategic forces to a conventional first strike and a scenario in which the United States could deny Russia a retaliatory capability without crossing the nuclear threshold. This prospect was especially worrying in the absence of limits on conventional delivery systems and their capability.[20]

---

19. Vladimir Putin, president of Russia, "Speech and the Following Discussion at the Munich Conference on Security Policy," Munich, February 10, 2007, http://archive.kremlin.ru/eng/speeches/2007/02/10/0138 _type82912type82914type82917type84779_118123.shtml.

20. Miasnikov, "The Air-Space Threat to Russia."

The results of the US Nuclear Posture Review that was released in 2001 only reinforced Russia's concerns. The review introduced the concept of a "new triad" that combined all offensive strike systems, nuclear and non-nuclear, in one of its legs and elevated defense to the status of a separate component of the triad.[21] Although the document emphasized departure from the planning practices of the Cold War and their focus on Russia, the role that the review assigned to conventional strike systems and missile defense clearly caused alarm in Russia, which saw the new concept as a confirmation of US intent to develop new capabilities that would upset the existing strategic balance.

From the technical standpoint, neither missile defense nor conventional strike capability was able to pose a serious threat to Russian strategic nuclear forces and their deterrence capability. But for Russia the problem was not necessarily the actual or even projected capability of these systems. Rather, it was a matter of its political commitment to protect the principle of strategic stability and to secure a similar commitment from the United States.

Russia has made it clear in the past that it wants to preserve the formal nuclear arms control process with its implicit assumption of an equal status of US and Russian strategic nuclear arsenals and to create a mechanism that would give it some influence over the direction of the US missile defense program. But it has also demonstrated that it values political aspects of this process, such as the legally binding nature of agreements, more highly than specific technical details that these agreements may include. This leaves plenty of room for compromise on any of these issues, if compromise does not affect the central principles of Russia's concept of strategic stability.

---

21. "Nuclear Posture Review Report," US Department of Defense, January 9, 2002, http://www.defense.gov/news/Jan2002/d20020109npr.pdf.

Nonstrategic nuclear weapons

While Russian doctrinal documents discuss the role of strategic deterrence in great length, they are largely silent on the role of nonstrategic nuclear weapons. This seems to contradict the widespread notion that Russia has been increasing its reliance on tactical nuclear weapons to offset its conventional inferiority to NATO and possibly China. This apparent contradiction could be explained, at least partially, by the focus on strategic stability and strategic deterrence that is so prominent in Russia's national security strategy.

Russia is believed to maintain a sizable arsenal of nonstrategic nuclear weapons, although it has never disclosed the number or composition of this component of its nuclear force. Estimates suggest that Russia has from one thousand to two thousand nonstrategic nuclear weapons in its active arsenal and up to three thousand weapons in reserve or awaiting dismantlement.[22] The active weapons could be assigned to a range of nonstrategic delivery systems: medium- and short-range bombers, air-defense systems, torpedoes, submarine-launched cruise missiles, and short-range ballistic missiles.[23] The operational status and role of these weapons, however, is not clear. The Russian government has repeatedly stated that all its tactical nuclear weapons are consolidated in centralized storage facilities, so they are not operationally deployed on a day-to-day basis.[24]

---

22. Hans M. Kristensen and Robert S. Norris, "Russian nuclear forces, 2012," *Bulletin of the Atomic Scientists* 68, no. 2: 87–97; Igor Sutyagin, "Atomic Accounting: A New Estimate of Russia's Non-Strategic Nuclear Forces," Royal United Service Institute, occasional paper, November 2012: 3.

23. Hans M. Kristensen, *Non-Strategic Nuclear Weapons,* Federation of American Scientists, special report no. 3 (May 2012): 53.

24. See, for example, a series of interviews with directors of the 12th Main Directorate that operates nuclear storage facilities. "Poryadok v yadernykh chastyakh [Order in nuclear units]," *Krasnaya zvezda,* September 5, 2006, http://old.redstar.ru/2006 /09/05_09/1_02.html [in Russian]; "Dezhurstvo u yadernoy knopki [On duty at the

Even though this does not rule out the possibility that Russia is planning to redeploy nonstrategic weapons in a crisis, it strongly suggests that they have a limited role in military planning.

Doctrinal documents and the pattern of military exercises indicate that while Russia allows for the possibility of using nuclear weapons in conflicts that fall short of a large-scale war, it does not consider them battlefield weapons that would be used to achieve specific military goals in the theater of operations. Rather, the use of nuclear weapons is seen as a political measure designed to de-escalate the conflict by signaling that the stakes of the conflict are extremely high and that Russia is willing to use measures of last resort to protect its national interests. This mission normally would not require nonstrategic delivery systems since some strategic systems, heavy bombers in particular, might be the best suited for delivery of this kind of message.

Indeed, in a series of exercises, Russia invariably simulates use of its long-range and medium-range bombers to deliver nuclear strikes against military bases or forces that are used to stage an attack.[25] In recent years, Russia appears to have extended the range of delivery systems that could be involved in this kind of demonstration strike. It thus maintains ambiguity about the nuclear capability of the short-range ballistic missiles that were also used in some exercises to deliver what appeared to be nuclear strikes.[26] Targets of these strikes could include air bases and military facilities in European NATO countries, military targets in the United States, and aircraft carrier groups. Scenarios of the exercises suggest that nuclear weapons would be used at a relatively late stage of a conflict,

nuclear button]," *Rossiyskaya gazeta,* September 4, 2007, http://www.rg.ru/2007/09/04/orujie.html [in Russian]; "Garanty yadernogo shchita [Guarantors of the nuclear shield]," *Krasnaya zvezda,* September 3, 2012, http://www.redstar.ru/index.php/component/k2/item/4428-garantyi-yadernogo-schita.

25. For an overview of military exercises, see Sokov, "Russia's nuclear doctrine."

26. "NATO-Russia: NAC Discusses Russian Military Exercises," *Aftenposten,* February 13, 2011, http://www.aftenposten.no/spesial/wikileaksdokumenter/23112009-NATO-RUSSIA-NAC-DISCUSSES-RUSSIAN-MILITARY-EXERCISES-6276946.html.

apparently at the point when it becomes clear that all other means of repelling aggression have been exhausted. The number of weapons used in these simulated strikes was rather limited—normally no more than ten. This pattern is consistent with the de-escalation strategy—a limited strike against military targets that are directly linked to the attack could deal with the immediate threat and at the same time send a dual signal about a possible nuclear exchange. On the one hand, a limited strike suggests an intention to keep the exchange from escalating, but at the same time a nuclear strike demonstrates readiness to escalate the conflict to the strategic level, where Russia presumably maintains a reliable strategic deterrence potential.

It appears that Russia has been considering options that would give nonstrategic nuclear weapons a somewhat more prominent role in its military strategy. For example, during the deliberations that led to the adoption of the 2010 military doctrine, the Russian Security Council, which was responsible for the development of the document, suggested expanding the mission of nuclear weapons to allow their use in local wars and contemplated including the possibility of preventive nuclear strikes in situations critical for national security.[27] Also, several statements by the Russian military commanders seem to suggest that they see a role for tactical nuclear weapons in military operations. However, none of these options were reflected in the 2010 doctrine. As discussed earlier, the doctrine instead limited the range of scenarios that could include the use of nuclear weapons and reiterated a commitment to strategic deterrence as a primary instrument of national security policy.

The emphasis on de-escalation that implies reliance on strategic deterrence potential does not necessarily mean that nonstrategic nuclear weapons have no role in this strategy. This role, however, might be different from directly balancing out the conventional inferiority that Russia

---

27.   V. Mamontov, "Menyaetsya Rossiya, menyaetsya i ee voyennaya doktrina (Russia is changing, its nuclear doctrine is changing too)," *Izvestia,* October 14, 2009, http://izvestia.ru/news/354178 [in Russian].

clearly has in Europe. Rather, nonstrategic weapons bring an uncertainty to scenarios of potential conflict and therefore could be seen as strengthening Russia's deterrence. In fact, Russia has been almost deliberately introducing additional ambiguity to the situation by refraining from clarifying the nuclear status of some of its nonstrategic systems, such as short-range ballistic missiles and submarine-launched cruise missiles. It also emphasizes its capability to use high-precision strikes as a means of deterrence. Since in most cases the systems that could deliver such strikes are nuclear-capable, this adds to the ambiguity and, at least in Russia's view, could work toward deterring potential military conflicts.

The China factor

The focus of the Russian security policy on strategic balance with the United States and NATO leaves open the question about the role of deterrence in its relationships with other nuclear weapon states. China is the most important case, as its rising economic and military strength could potentially change the traditional bipolar picture of strategic stability that Russia has long regarded as a given in its national security calculations.

Russia has always acknowledged that China has an important role in the international security system and has apparently accepted that it would play a role as one of the centers of the multi-polar world. However, as far as the military aspects of national security are concerned, Russia has been reluctant to consider scenarios that would assume that China could be a source of military threat to Russia. None of the Russian doctrinal documents directly mention scenarios that would involve military confrontation with China; these scenarios are also virtually absent from discussions of national security issues.

To a considerable degree, Russia's reluctance to openly discuss the military threat that could be posed by China can be explained by the fact that relationships between the two countries are officially described as a "strategic partnership." Indeed, Russia and China are in agreement on a wide range of international security issues and have no unresolved territorial disputes between them. The two countries have been involved in close military cooperation that includes regular, although infrequent, joint exercises. Another factor that could play a role is that in many respects China is a distant and unfamiliar threat, especially if compared with the United States and NATO.

In those cases when China's military power enters the Russian national security debate, it does so almost invariably in the context of the implications that development of the relationship between China and the United States could have for Russia. One of the primary concerns is that China would undertake an effort to achieve parity with the United States by quickly building up its nuclear arsenal. This, of course, would bring the Chinese strategic nuclear forces, at least in terms of numbers, to a level comparable to that of Russia and change the balance among the three countries, not least by triggering a response from the United States.

Russian analysts have already expressed concerns about China's lack of transparency about its current nuclear arsenal and its military modernization plans. According to some estimates that are increasingly gaining acceptance in Russia, China already has an arsenal of up to nine hundred nuclear warheads in its stockpile and has the potential to increase the number of deployed weapons.[28] Although most of these weapons are presumably assigned to nonstrategic systems, this number already places China within reach of the level of one thousand five hundred fifty deployed strategic warheads achieved by Russia and the United States in their bilateral nuclear disarmament process. Should China choose to undertake a buildup program, Russia would lose its status as one of the two "nuclear superpowers" and would have to enter into a complex relationship with the United States and China in which it is unlikely to play a leading role. China is therefore a very important factor in Russia's efforts to maintain its traditional strategic stability, which it understands

---

28. Alexei Arbatov and Vladimir Dvorkin, *The Great Strategic Triangle* (Moscow: Carnegie Moscow Center, 2013), 10.

primarily in terms of a strategic balance between Russia and the United States. Russia's objections against a range of US programs, from missile defense to the Prompt Global Strike, are motivated in part by the potential effect these programs could have on China's decision to expand its nuclear arsenal.

Another factor in the security relationship between China and Russia is the clear disparity between the conventional forces of the two countries in the Far East. This seems to suggest that Russia might need to rely on nonstrategic nuclear weapons to compensate for its conventional inferiority. There is virtually no information that would indicate that Russia is indeed preserving this option. As discussed earlier, the doctrinal documents do not seem to assign nonstrategic nuclear weapons a direct role in potential military confrontations. Rather, they are intended to be used as a de-escalation tool that would eventually rely on the deterrence potential of strategic forces to terminate the conflict. The same logic could apply to China, especially taking into account that Russia enjoys clear strategic superiority over Chinese nuclear forces. Assuming that this situation does not change, Russia should be able to rely on strategic deterrence as its primary means of ensuring its security in the East.

While the China factor and the uncertainty associated with potential strategic competition between China and the United States could seriously complicate Russia's national security calculations, the emphasis on maintaining a strategic balance with the United States most likely provides Russia with the most viable strategy for dealing with these factors. Even as Russia has no control over China's strategic modernization effort or US policies regarding China, its general goal of preserving strategic stability is generally in line with the interests of all parties. By strongly opposing US missile defense and conventional Prompt Global Strike programs, Russia in effect helps China to make its case for constraining these developments. On the other hand, Russia and the United States have a common interest in making the Chinese nuclear arsenal and policies more transparent and preventing any significant increase in the number of weapons in China's nuclear arsenal.

Russia's interest in maintaining stability in the region also leads it to invest serious effort in containing the threat of nuclear proliferation related to North Korean nuclear and ballistic missile programs. Russia is unlikely to be directly affected by any adverse developments in the region. But heightened tensions, not to mention an open military confrontation, would seriously change the balance of forces close to the Russian borders and undermine the status quo. It is not clear if Russia believes that North Korea's nuclear program could trigger a proliferation chain reaction among its neighbors. But this prospect, even if considered distant, also creates incentives for Russia to actively participate in restricting North Korea's nuclear and missile activities.

Russia's contribution to nuclear disarmament

Russia has long regarded its nuclear arsenal not only as one of the fundamental elements of its national security strategy, but also as part of the identity of the Russian state. Most recently this view was expressed by then prime minister Putin during his 2012 presidential campaign:[29]

> [O]ur national task—not just our national task even, but our responsibility to humankind—is to preserve the balance of strategic forces and capabilities. . . . [T]he balance of strategic forces has allowed us to avoid large, global conflicts, and therefore our task is to preserve this balance. In view of our partners' missile defense plans, we must make the necessary efforts to maintain this balance as an element of global stability.

---

29. "Prime Minister Vladimir Putin meets with experts in Sarov to discuss global threats to national security," transcript of a meeting in Sarov, Russia, February 24, 2012, http://archive.premier.gov.ru/eng/events/news/18248.

Discussion of national security issues in Russia has rarely questioned the main premise of this policy; political and military leadership, the expert community, and the society in general appear to accept the notion that nuclear weapons serve as the ultimate guarantor of the sovereignty and independence of the state. Even when the discussion turns to contemporary threats, associated with the proliferation of weapons of mass destruction, terrorism, or the conflicts that could threaten the integrity of the state (all of which are represented in the most recent military doctrine), these tend to be understood and interpreted in a way that points at the strategic stability and deterrence potential of strategic nuclear forces as essential elements in dealing with these threats.

Whether this strategy could provide an effective answer to Russia's security concerns is very much an open question. To some extent the answer depends on how Russia would define its national security. Nuclear weapons and strategic deterrence could be effective in deterring certain kinds of threats, such as direct military intervention, but they are much less useful for dealing with others that in the end could prove to be much more dangerous. The Soviet experience showed quite clearly that a strong strategic deterrence, which the Soviet Union definitely had, is not a guarantee of the survival of a state or the security of its population. However, the circumstances of the Soviet Union's demise apparently led many Russians to believe that it was caused by the weakness of the country rather than the gross mismatch between the narrow focus on military aspects of national security and the actual security, understood in broad terms, that the state could provide to its citizens.[30]

The central role of nuclear weapons in Russia's understanding of its own security would definitely complicate the effort to engage Russia in an effort to reduce the role of nuclear arsenals and move toward comprehensive nuclear disarmament. At the same time, by all indicators, Russia does

---

30. See, for example, Alexei Arbatov, "Russia's Own Imperial Road," in *20 Years Without the Berlin Wall: A Breakthrough to Freedom,* ed. Natalia Bubnova (Moscow: Carnegie Moscow Center, 2011), 29–58.

not necessarily consider nuclear deterrence an indispensable element of its security strategy. Rather, it sees its nuclear forces in particular as a necessary condition of "a successful and seamless integration in the emerging system of international relations," in the words of the 2003 White Book. This is probably true today, but this does not preclude a change in Russia's attitude toward nuclear weapons if the international security environment evolves to de-emphasize the role of military forces, and nuclear weapons in particular.

This change, however, could only happen if the international community could launch a process that would help Russia as well as other states to build a new security framework, or a joint enterprise, with the express purpose of eliminating nuclear weapons. Russia, as a state with one of the largest nuclear arsenals, would have to be an active player in this effort, as its position on a range of issues, especially those related to nuclear weapons, will be crucial for this transformation. This position, in turn, will depend on whether Russia sees that transformation as a way to preserve its role as one of the key players in international affairs, a role that it apparently believes is an essential element of the existing strategic balance.

Russia has already been involved in a number of important initiatives that positively contribute to the goal of the joint enterprise, from bilateral US-Russian nuclear reductions and verification to nuclear security. Recent developments in nuclear disarmament show that once its status is protected, Russia is willing to get constructively involved in the nuclear disarmament effort.

For example, the Russian leadership apparently considers the US-Russian nuclear disarmament process as a very important component of the strategic balance. Throughout the 1990s and 2000s it invested considerable effort in maintaining this element of the bilateral relationship, even though the terms of formal agreements were often not favorable to Russia. For example, the Moscow treaty of 2002 (on strategic offensive reductions) was largely a political commitment that did not even define the subject of the treaty. However, Russia insisted on giving this agreement a formal treaty status as it helped preserve the continuity of the arms control process. Similarly, in order to secure success of the New START treaty, signed in 2010, Russia had to make some substantial concessions. It dropped, albeit temporarily, its insistence on limiting the US missile defense program and changed its position on US reserve nuclear warheads, which could allow the United States to quickly increase the number of deployed strategic weapons. It is true that during the negotiations the United States had to make a number of concessions as well and that the resulting treaty is a fairly balanced agreement that benefits the security of both countries. However, it was clear that for Russia the fact of having a legally binding arms control treaty with the United States was at least as important as the substance of the treaty.

Further progress in bilateral nuclear arms reductions could prove more complicated. Russia left unanswered the US proposal to begin negotiations of a New START follow-on agreement that would reduce strategic nuclear arsenals to about one thousand deployed warheads. It has also resisted calls to include nonstrategic nuclear weapons in negotiations. This, however, does not mean that another round of bilateral reductions, which would be vital to build a foundation for a move toward multilateral negotiations, is impossible. Most of Russia's concerns about its balance with the United States are focused on non-nuclear capabilities, such as missile defense, precision-guided munitions (the Prompt Global Strike program in particular), and space weapons. Once Russia and the United States find a way to address these issues, reductions of offensive nuclear arsenals would become possible.

Missile defense is probably the most contentious issue in US-Russian relations. For Russia, missile defense is an important part of its position in the existing balance of power. After US withdrawal from the ABM treaty in 2002, Russia lost its most significant instrument for influencing developments in this area. As the US missile defense program evolved, Russia returned to its demand that the United States should provide a legally binding guarantee that this program will not threaten the potential of its strategic forces. Since a guarantee of this kind is highly unlikely, the problem may appear intractable. However, a limit on the capabilities of a specific missile defense system may not be the main goal of Russia's policy. Rather, Russia would like to defend, or indeed to bring back, its right to influence the US program. Whether Russia would actually need to exercise this right is, in fact, a secondary issue—the principle appears to be much more important in this case. Also, Russia's approach to missile defense is fairly flexible. For example, it apparently considers cooperation on missile defense as one of the ways to protect its interests in this area. This position has been supported by the political and military leadership and the expert community (even though it is often affected by the politics of the moment). This means that an appropriate combination of politically and legally binding obligations, transparency, confidence-building measures, and cooperation could result in an arrangement that would resolve the current controversy over missile defense.

Some elements of a joint enterprise could greatly benefit from Russia's contribution. Chief among them is verification. Together with the United States, Russia has more than twenty-five years of experience in verifying nuclear disarmament treaties, such as the INF Treaty, START, and New START. This experience includes regular data exchanges, site inspections, and notifications, as well as other verification activities. As a first step, Russia and the United States could urge other nuclear weapon states to join them in the verification activities and could share their extensive experience in this area.[31] Other existing arrangements, such as ballistic missile launch notification agreements with the United States and China, could also be important building blocks of the future multilateral cooperation framework.

---

31. Tamara Patton, Pavel Podvig, and Phillip Schell, "A New START Model for Transparency in Nuclear Disarmament," United Nations Institute for Disarmament Research, Geneva, Switzerland, 2013, http://unidir.org/files/publications /pdfs/a-new-start-model-for-transparency-in-nuclear-disarmament-en-409.pdf.

Nuclear security is another area where Russia's contribution could be particularly strong. In the decades following the end of the Cold War, Russia has made substantial investment in securing its nuclear materials and facilities. Since most of this work has been done with outside assistance, this program could provide a useful model for a broader multinational effort to secure vulnerable nuclear materials. In addition, Russia and the United States have worked cooperatively and unilaterally on reducing their fissile material stocks. As part of the Megatons to Megawatts program, Russia has eliminated five hundred tons of its highly enriched uranium from dismantled weapons. It discontinued production of fissile materials for weapons purposes and agreed to submit a substantial amount of weapon-grade plutonium—about eighteen tons—under monitoring to ensure that it will not be used for weapon purposes. In a bilateral US-Russia agreement, it made a commitment to eliminate thirty-four tons of weapon-grade plutonium. As part of the Trilateral Initiative, Russia and the United States worked with the International Atomic Energy Agency (IAEA) to develop methods that would allow verified disposition of fissile materials extracted from dismantled nuclear weapons. This experience will be invaluable as states begin to develop comprehensive verification measures that would support deep reductions of nuclear arsenals and fissile material stocks.

These examples show that Russia could be brought into the future joint enterprise at very early stages. Indeed, in some areas its participation would be indispensable. At the same time, the long-term prospects of its participation in building a nuclear weapon-free world would depend on whether this effort creates conditions for a substantive change in the way Russian society perceives its national security interests. While in today's environment it may be difficult to see that Russia would fully support complete elimination of nuclear weapons, it is not impossible to imagine a scenario that would make it possible.

First and foremost, there is no reason why strategic stability, which is so central to Russia's understanding of its security, has to rely on nuclear

weapons or their deterrence potential.[32] Already there is a growing realization of the declining political and military utility of nuclear weapons.
While nuclear forces remain an instrument of strategic deterrence, the
range of scenarios in which this mission would provide a useful capability is steadily shrinking. This process, indeed, has been already reflected
in the evolution of Russia's military doctrines. As described earlier in
this chapter, even though these documents still place nuclear forces at
the center of the national security strategy, their military role is highly
uncertain and their use is reserved for contingencies, such as a large-scale
intervention endangering the very existence of the state, that hardly represent a realistic threat for Russia today. As for the political role of nuclear
weapons and their status value, several experts in Russia have already
pointed out that nuclear weapons are increasingly becoming a "weapon
of the poor," associated with countries that have no other instruments of
influence in international affairs.[33]

Second, although the opposition to nuclear disarmament in Russia
is fairly strong, it should not be overestimated. Most of this opposition
reflects the structure of the internal political debate, which is often framed
in terms that exaggerate confrontation with the United States and the West.
This debate is also characterized by a traditionally strong influence of the
defense industry and the military and the near-absence of independent
critical views. At the same time, there is room for discussion even within
these constraints. Indeed, there has been some criticism of the current
level of military spending, which incudes substantial investment in the
modernization of strategic forces. As experience shows, when confronted
with difficult choices, the Russian political and military leadership could

---

32. On this point, see David Holloway, "Deterrence and Enforcement in a World Free of
Nuclear Weapons," in *Deterrence: Its Past and Future,* ed. George P. Shultz, Sidney
D. Drell, and James E. Goodby (Stanford: Hoover Institution Press, 2011), 335–372.

33. Alexei Arbatov, "Real and Imaginary Threats: Military Power in World Politics in the
21st Century," *Russia in Global Affairs,* April 15, 2013, http://eng.globalaffairs.ru
/number/Real-and-Imaginary-Threats-15925.

consider a wide range of options regarding military strategy. Since Russia has been able to allocate significant resources to its military modernization in the past decade, it hasn't seen the need to make these choices yet. But that does not mean that investment in nuclear forces will remain unquestioned in the future.

Finally, while nuclear weapons have been a strong factor shaping the Soviet and then Russian national security agenda for more than sixty years, this does not necessarily mean that they will play that role indefinitely. There have been dramatic changes in seemingly intractable positions in this area in the past. For example, the agreement to eliminate all intermediate-range nuclear missiles was believed to be impossible only two years before it was reached. The recent steps of the Russian leadership have definitely brought confrontation into the relationship between Russia and the West. However, they are as likely to precipitate a crisis that will eventually lead to a fundamental change of the political circumstances in Russia and the much needed rethinking of its national security. While it may still take a long time before Russia fully embraces the cause of elimination of nuclear weapons, there is little doubt that cooperative security arrangements and active participation in a joint nuclear disarmament enterprise are the only viable options for a long-term national security strategy.

CHAPTER 6 **Comparing German and Polish Post-Cold War Nuclear Policies: A Convergence of European Attitudes on Nuclear Disarmament and Deterrence?**

Katarzyna Kubiak and Oliver Meier

Europe plays a key role in efforts to reduce the role of nuclear weapons in international security. The European Union, which has two nuclear-weapon states (France and the United Kingdom) among its twenty-eight members, aspires to a greater role in international security, even though its Common and Foreign Security Policy does not have a nuclear dimension. In addition, the EU is increasingly an important actor in multilateral disarmament and nonproliferation fora, such as the nuclear Non-Proliferation Treaty (NPT). NATO also wants to play a greater role in arms control, nonproliferation, and disarmament and has declared in its 2010 Strategic Concept that it is "resolved to seek a safer world for all and to create the conditions for a world without nuclear weapons in accordance with the goals of the Nuclear Non-Proliferation Treaty, in a way that promotes international stability, and is based on the principle of undiminished security for all."[1] NATO policies have a decisive influence on the international nuclear debate, if only because three of the five NPT

---

1. "Active Engagement, Modern Defence: Strategic Concept for the Defence and Security of the Members of the North Atlantic Treaty Organisation, adopted by Heads of State and Government in Lisbon," November 19, 2010, paragraph 26.

nuclear-weapon states and eight of the fourteen states with nuclear weapons on their territory are members.

The effectiveness of European efforts to make progress toward a world free of nuclear weapons hinges on the ability of Europeans to overcome differences among themselves on nuclear disarmament and on efforts to reduce the role of nuclear weapons in European security. Germany and Poland are two key actors in this regard. After the Cold War, Berlin and Warsaw became representatives of two groups of states within the Alliance which held divergent views on the role of nuclear weapons in European security.[2] In 2009, Germany promised to work toward a withdrawal of US nuclear weapons from Europe, while Poland opposed the German initiative, partly because it was unhappy with the way Berlin had pursued it. Subsequently, Berlin and Warsaw were opinion leaders of the respective camps in the debate about a reform of NATO's nuclear policies and a future nuclear arms control approach toward Russia.

While they differ on nuclear policies, the foreign policy styles of both countries are similar. Germany and Poland shy away from radical positions and try to build coalitions to support their own positions and strategies. Berlin and Warsaw are committed to approaching NATO nuclear policies and arms control on the basis of NATO agreement and EU consensus, ruling out unilateral approaches. During the recent debate over NATO's 2010 Strategic Concept and its 2012 Deterrence and Defence Posture Review (DDPR) report, both countries actively searched for partners within Europe and beyond and wanted to occupy the middle ground within the Alliance on how to make progress on nuclear disarmament.

Given the importance of both players in the nuclear debate in Europe, their divergent positions, and their similar policy styles, we argue that Europe's role in nuclear disarmament would be strengthened if and when Poland and Germany worked together on nuclear policies. And vice versa: as long as Berlin and Warsaw disagree on the next steps to reduce the role

---

2. See Oliver Meier, "NATO, Arms Control and Nonproliferation: An Alliance Divided?" *Arms Control Today*, April 2009: 29–35.

of nuclear weapons, it is difficult to conceive a more ambitious European agenda. In a nutshell, we argue that Polish and German convergence on nuclear deterrence and nuclear arms control is a necessary (though certainly not sufficient) condition for Europeans to take a proactive stance on reducing the role of nuclear weapons in Europe and beyond.

This chapter therefore compares German and Polish policies, debates, and attitudes toward nuclear weapons and nuclear arms control in order to draw out options for a broader European engagement on nuclear disarmament. It focuses on discussions in NATO, rather than the EU, because discussions under the Common and Foreign Security Policy heading have rarely touched on nuclear disarmament and deterrence. Discussions on nuclear deterrence and defense postures are generally still perceived to be the prerogative of NATO.[3]

First, we briefly describe Germany's and Poland's Cold War nuclear policies in order to identify the roots of their post-1990 approaches to deterrence and disarmament. We then compare post-Cold War policies by briefly sketching the interests of key domestic actors and describing relevant policies on nuclear deterrence and disarmament. We conclude by identifying issues which may be particularly suitable for future cooperation between the two countries.

Officials from Berlin and Warsaw dealing with nuclear weapons, arms control, and disarmament meet regularly in various formats and contexts. Apart from regular interactions in NATO and the EU, Germany and Poland are both members of the Non-Proliferation and Disarmament Initiative (NPDI), which was set up in 2010 and brings together twelve countries from different global regions to coordinate approaches on nonproliferation and disarmament.[4] Germany and Poland, together with

---

3. Discussions among EU members in the context of the NPT are an exception to this rule. These do involve a debate on issues such as disarmament commitments or security assurances. Often, however, EU common positions are little more than descriptions of the lowest common denominator among EU members.

4. The NPDI members are Australia, Canada, Chile, Germany, Japan, Mexico, the Netherlands, Nigeria, the Philippines, Poland, Turkey, and the United Arab Emirates.

France, form the so-called Weimar Triangle, which provides a platform for regular consultations on foreign and security policy issues. From 2011 to 2014, representatives from both governments have also met with their Russian counterparts in the so-called Kaliningrad Trialogue to discuss current issues, including problems of arms control.[5]

(West) German and Polish Cold War nuclear policies

During the Cold War, Germany and Poland were front-line states which played different roles in their respective alliances. At the peak of the Cold War, the Federal Republic of Germany (West Germany) and the German Democratic Republic (East Germany) hosted thousands of short-range and intermediate-range nuclear weapons on their territory. Germany became the country with the biggest concentration of nuclear weapons on its territory worldwide. Within NATO, West Germany was a key actor in nuclear issues while East Germany was never an independent political player on nuclear policies in the Warsaw Treaty Organization and had to follow the Soviet Union's lead.

After West Germany's accession to NATO in 1955, Bonn's nuclear policies were dominated by two competing goals. On the one hand, West German politicians wanted to prevent a military conflict between East and West, which could have turned Central Europe into a nuclear battlefield. At the same time, there was a constant concern that NATO-Europe could be "de-coupled" from the US strategic deterrent. Thus, Bonn was interested in linking European security to the United States, while also maintaining its influence on nuclear decision-making of the nuclear allies.

---

5. See for example Alexander Rahr, "The Russia–Germany–Poland Trialogue Continues," *The Valdai Discussion Club,* April 3, 2012, http://valdaiclub.com/europe/40740.html; "Deutsch-russisch-polnischer Trialog," Auswärtiges Amt, June 10, 2014; http://www.auswaertiges-amt.de/DE/Aussenpolitik/Laender/Aktuelle_Artikel/RussischeFoederation/140610_Trialog_St_Petersburg.html.

Two instruments were key to achieving these competing goals of conflict prevention and strategic coupling. The first was nuclear sharing. It provided for information and consultation by the NATO nuclear-weapon states (with the exception of France, which has never put any element of the Force de Frappe at the disposal of the Alliance) with non-nuclear Alliance members. The Nuclear Planning Group and associated committees provided a forum in which the Alliance members were supposed to decide jointly on nuclear policy guidelines and possible nuclear weapons use in the European theater of conflict. On that ground, nuclear sharing meant that some US nuclear weapons deployed in Germany (and other nuclear host nations) would be delivered to their targets by European delivery systems. This political and military integration of nuclear policy within the Alliance was designed to ensure that the United States would not abandon Europe, and thus it strengthened the credibility of deterrence.

Arms control was the complementary instrument favored by Bonn to prevent an unchecked nuclear arms race. In the context of the 1967 Harmel report (Report of the Council on the Future Tasks of the Alliance), NATO stated that it was a political as well as a military alliance. Members agreed that they wanted to simultaneously pursue the twin objectives of deterrence/defense and détente vis-à-vis the Warsaw Pact. The report paved the way for the Alliance's role on arms control and thus was in line with Bonn's *Ostpolitik* of engaging East Germany and its partners. The key elements of this approach—involvement through nuclear sharing and engagement on the basis of arms control—continued to be the bedrock of German nuclear policies in NATO after the Cold War.

Poland's nuclear policies during the Cold War were heavily influenced by its World War II experience. After the war, being part of the Warsaw Pact, its main security interests were easing tensions between the Cold War blocs, diminishing military threats, and searching for a margin of political discretion on the international level. The Polish government's position reflected socialist and humanitarian principles and the desire for peaceful coexistence. Warsaw consistently promoted disarmament, general elimination, and a ban on nuclear weapons. It found nuclear weapons did not fit into the ethical frame of a modern civilization and could be used as an instrument of international politics and blackmail. Given the lack of progress in curbing nuclear weapons on a global level, the remilitarization of West Germany, including plans for a NATO Multilateral Force, and horizontal proliferation of nuclear weapons, Warsaw looked for regional approaches to address nuclear arms control. Several Polish initiatives aimed at the establishment of a nuclear weapons-free zone in Central and Eastern Europe: the Rapacki Plan (1957), Gomulka Plan (1963), and Jaruzelski Plan (1987).

At the same time, Poland remained a staging ground for some of the Soviet Union's nuclear weapons, though Moscow never disclosed how many nuclear warheads it kept in Poland. Polish pilots were trained to fly nuclear-capable aircraft in order to deliver tactical nuclear weapons to NATO's Northern Flank during war.[6] Nuclear sharing arrangements were highly classified. Poland's involvement in nuclear sharing was revealed publicly on April 7, 1991. The next day the Red Army began its withdrawal from Poland and the dismantling of the nuclear weapons infrastructure, though it is believed that Moscow had already withdrawn some nuclear warheads in the late 1980s. In 2006, Radosław Sikorski, then minister of defense, declassified the Warsaw Pact's archives for exclusive insight by the Institute of National Remembrance. Because these documents also revealed Polish participation in the Warsaw Pact's nuclear deterrence arrangements, he was criticized for infringing on diplomatic customs and harming Poland's image as an ally.[7]

---

6. "Tajemnice Układu Warszawskiego bron atomowa w PRL," OTVP, 2006, http://www.youtube.com/watch?v=ckZVXl8JaCk.

7. "Polacy o ujawnieniu planów byłego Układu Warszawskiego," CBOS BS/3/2006, Warsaw, January 2006, http://www.cbos.pl/SPISKOM.POL/2006/K_003_06 .PDF; "Odtajnienie akt to operacja medialna," WP, http://wiadomosci.wp .pl/kat,1342,title,Odtajnienie-akt-to-operacja-medialna,wid,8103679,wiadomosc .html?ticaid=113ee4&_ticrsn=3.

A comparison of German and Polish
post-Cold War nuclear attitudes and policies

With the end of the Cold War, the foreign and security policies of Germany and Poland converged. In 1990, Germany regained its full sovereignty with the conclusion of the 2+4 Treaty; yet its foreign and security policy remained integrated in the EU and NATO. After the collapse of the Warsaw Pact in July 1991, Poland reoriented its foreign policy toward the West and joined NATO in 1999 and the EU in 2004.

Yet, even when Germany and Poland began working together in the EU and NATO, their different histories were still shaping their respective policies on nuclear weapons and nuclear disarmament. In addition, different domestic environments and divergent outlooks on the role of NATO, deterrence, and arms control continue to hinder joint German-Polish initiatives on arms control.

Domestic politics

The post-Cold War nuclear debate in Germany was formulated against the background of a broad and deep anti-nuclear sentiment in German society. The German political elite is divided among those who want to pursue nuclear disarmament and those who view NATO's nuclear sharing arrangements as an instrument to increase Germany's influence in the Alliance.

Germany is one of five NATO members that still host US nuclear weapons on their territory. The government neither confirms nor denies the presence of those weapons but it is believed that about twenty B61 free-fall bombs are deployed at Büchel Air Base for delivery by German Tornado fighter-bomber aircraft.[8]

The German Federal Foreign Office (and its arms control section), which leads policy on all issues related to arms control, disarmament,

8. See, for example, Hans M. Kristensen, "Non-Strategic Nuclear Weapons," *Federation of American Scientists,* Special Report 3, May 2012.

and nonproliferation,[9] has repeatedly explored ways to reduce the role of nuclear weapons. Since the end of the Cold War, three German foreign ministers from three different parties have taken their own initiatives on nuclear disarmament. Thus, Klaus Kinkel (1992–1998, Liberal Party) promoted the idea of nuclear transparency and pushed for a nuclear weapons register. Joschka Fischer (1998–2005, Green Party) tried to initiate a discussion within NATO on a nuclear no-first-use policy.[10] During his first term (2005–2009), Frank-Walter Steinmeier (Social Democratic Party) also attempted to trigger a discussion on a reform of NATO's nuclear sharing practices.[11] All of these ideas and initiatives were popular domestically but received no visible support from major allies and particularly the three NATO nuclear-weapon states: France, the United Kingdom, and the United States.

Often, the German Federal Ministry of Defense was the Foreign Ministry's counterpart in discussions on arms control. That ministry is in charge of Germany's policy in the context of NATO, including the Alliance's nuclear sharing arrangements. A key motivation for the Ministry of Defense is to preserve Germany's direct involvement in NATO discussions on nuclear sharing through the Nuclear Planning Group. All NATO members are eligible for participation in the Nuclear Planning Group but many acknowledge that nations hosting US nuclear weapons on their territory and providing dual-capable aircraft for their delivery have a special say in nuclear policies. Thomas Kossendey, then German assistant secretary for defense, argued in a 2008 parliamentary debate that Germany's continued involvement in nuclear sharing is essential for national security

9. Responsibility for nuclear export controls rests with the Federal Ministry for Economic Affairs and Energy.

10. See, for example, Oliver Meier, "A Civilian Power caught between the lines: Germany and nuclear non-proliferation," in *Germany as a Civilian Power? The foreign policy of the Berlin republic,* ed. Sebastian Harnisch and Hanns W. Maull (Manchester, UK: Manchester University Press, 2001), 68–87.

11. Oliver Meier, "Steinmeier Calls for U.S. to Withdraw Nukes," *Arms Control Today,* May 2009, http://www.armscontrol.org/act/2009_5/Steinmeier.

because it gives Berlin "the possibility to influence a decision about the use of nuclear weapons within NATO."[12]

The Chancellery has traditionally supported this stance. Chancellor Gerhard Schröder is reported to have rejected proposals for a German initiative toward withdrawal of US nuclear weapons from Europe in 2006, saying that "because of these twenty things in Büchel, I won't quarrel with the Americans."[13] In one of the few direct comments by Chancellor Angela Merkel on nuclear sharing, she also emphasized in a 2009 parliamentary debate the importance of staying involved in nuclear sharing in order to influence the policies of NATO nuclear-weapon states.[14]

There is broad parliamentary support for reducing the role of nuclear weapons in NATO's security policy. Yet, the powers of the Bundestag to shape foreign policy are limited. Parliament can use resolutions to support or criticize the government or urge it to take certain actions. But its resolutions on foreign policy are not binding for the executive. At the end of the day, parliament can only use its budgetary powers to steer foreign and security policy.[15]

A key place for parliamentary discussions on nuclear policies is the subcommittee on disarmament, arms control, and nonproliferation, a joint body of the foreign and defense committees. In 2010, ahead of the NPT Review Conference, the subcommittee was the birthplace of a rare cross-party initiative of ruling and opposition parties when the Bundestag passed a resolution supporting the government's goal of advocating

---

12. Cited in Oliver Meier, "NATO Mulls Nuke Modernization, Security," *Arms Control Today,* September 2008: 37–39, http://www.armscontrol.org/act/2008_09/NATO.

13. Cited in Eric Chauvistré, "Feige vor dem Freund," *taz,* June 9, 2005, http://www.taz .de/1/archiv/?dig=2005/06/09/a0089 (translation by Oliver Meier).

14. "Plenarprotokoll 16/214," Deutscher Bundestag, March 26, 2009: 23124, http://dip21.bundestag.de/dip21/btp/16/16214.pdf.

15. The exception here is the power of parliament to mandate all major out-of-area deployments of German armed forces.

withdrawal of US nuclear weapons from Germany and supporting nuclear disarmament.[16]

This unity among the parties in the Bundestag has been somewhat reduced after the 2013 elections. Under conditions of a "grand coalition" where the two largest parties—the conservative CDU (Christian Democratic Union) and the Social Democrats of the SPD—rule together, the (small) opposition has few reasons to cooperate. And Steinmeier, since he began his second term as foreign minister in 2013, has not spoken publicly on the issue of reducing tactical nuclear weapons.

The size and influence of the German movement for disarmament are small compared to the early 1980s, when millions protested in Bonn and elsewhere against the deployment of US intermediate-range nuclear systems. Yet, the movement can count on a general anti-nuclear sentiment in the population that can be activated quickly. When asked about the presence of US nuclear weapons, about two-thirds of the population consistently support withdrawal.[17]

In contrast to Germany, nuclear weapons policy and nuclear arms control are not priority issues for the Polish government. It is indicative that the Polish foreign ministry, unlike its German counterpart, does not have a separate arms control division and no federal commissioner for disarmament.

Poland does not operationally participate in the NATO nuclear mission but is an active member in the Support of Nuclear Operations with Conventional Air Tactics mission (SNOWCAT), which in case of a nuclear weapons attack mission provides non-nuclear support in the form of air

---

16. "Deutschland muss deutliche Zeichen für eine Welt frei von Atomwaffen setzen," Antrag der Fraktionen der CDU/CSU, SPD, FDP, Bündnis 90/ Die Grünen, Deutscher Bundestag (Drs. 17/1159), March 24, 2010. The Socialists were not invited to join the resolution but also support withdrawal of US nuclear weapons.

17. But less than half of those interviewed in 2006 were aware of the presence of nuclear weapons. See Stratcom, "Nuclear Weapons in Europe: Survey Results in Six European Countries," study coordinated by Strategic Communications for Greenpeace International, May 25, 2006.

refueling or search-and-rescue operations.[18] In the 1997 NATO-Russia Founding Act, the Allies stated that they had "no intention, no plan, and no reason to deploy nuclear weapons on the territory of new members, nor any need to change any aspect of NATO's nuclear posture or nuclear policy—and do not foresee any future need to do so."[19] As a consequence, NATO has ruled out the possibility of deploying nuclear weapons on the territory of any of the new member states.

At the time, this policy was in line with the expectations of society. Polls conducted in 1997 and 1999, preceding the Polish accession to NATO, suggested that 83 percent and 81 percent of respondents, respectively, did not support the idea of deploying nuclear weapons on Polish territory.[20]

In the parliament, there is virtually no debate on nuclear arms control and little support for nuclear disarmament efforts. No member of parliament has supported public calls for the removal of tactical nuclear weapons from Europe.[21] For example, none of the Sejm (lower house)

---

18. According to Hans Kristensen of the Federation of American Scientists, Poland in 2014 sent for the first time two F-16s to NATO's Steadfast Noon Exercise. This annual maneuver is used to test NATO's nuclear sharing arrangements. See Hans M. Kristensen, "Polish F-16s In NATO Nuclear Exercise In Italy," Federation of American Scientists, *Strategic Security* (blog), October 27, 2014, http://fas.org/blogs /security/2014/10/steadfastnoon/.

19. NATO, "Founding Act on Mutual Relations, Cooperation and Security between NATO and the Russian Federation," May 27, 1997, http://www.nato.int/cps/en /natolive/official_texts_25468.htm. On SNOWCAT, see Karl-Heinz Kamp and Robertus C.N. Remkes, "Options for NATO Nuclear Sharing Arrangements," in *Reducing Nuclear Risks in Europe,* ed. Steve Andreasen and Isabelle Williams (Washington, DC: Nuclear Threat Initiative, 2011), 76-95, http://www.nti.org /analysis/articles/options-nato-nuclear-sharing-arrangements.

20. "Polska w NATO," Centrum Badania Opinii Społecznej, Komunikat BS/40/99, Warsaw, March 1999, http://www.cbos.pl/SPISKOM.POL/1999/K_040_99.PDF.

21. See, for example, "Sign-on letter for Members of the European Parliament Re: Tell Obama to take nuclear weapons out of Europe," April 2013, http://archive.pnnd .org/archives/MEP_Obama.html; "Letter to Congress", May 6, 2014, http://fcnl.org /issues/nuclear/B61_NATO_Sign_On_Letter_to_Congress.pdf.

parliamentarians is a member of the Parliamentarians for Nuclear Non-proliferation and Disarmament.[22]

There is a broad political and public consensus in support of Polish membership in NATO and the presence of US tactical nuclear weapons in Europe. The 2013 White Book on National Security of the Republic of Poland, a collective effort of more than two hundred experts representing independent think tanks, academia, and governmental structures, states that "[i]t is in Poland's interest to have the American arsenal of tactical nuclear weapons kept in Europe."[23] There are literally no grass-roots disarmament organizations in Poland. International movements like Global Zero, International Campaign to Abolish Nuclear Weapons, Pugwash Conferences on Science and World Affairs, or Mayors for Peace have either no interest or have great difficulties enlisting Polish support.[24]

Threat assessments and the role of deterrence

With the end of the Cold War, Germany, for the first time in its history, was completely surrounded by friends and allies. This has a marked influence on the threat perception of Germans and their views on nuclear deterrence. In stark contrast to the 1980s, when the role of nuclear weapons in European security was an important and contentious topic of political and public debate, deterrence discussions have become less frequent and intense. Mostly, these issues are now debated among experts and policymakers but rarely among the public.

---

22. Parliamentarians for Nuclear Non-proliferation and Disarmament (PNND) has members in nineteen of the twenty-eight NATO member states. No members of parliaments in Albania, Bulgaria, Croatia, Latvia, Lithuania, Poland, Portugal, Romania, or Slovenia have joined PNND.

23. "White Book on National Security of the Republic of Poland," National Security Bureau, 2013: 162, www.spbn.gov.pl/english.

24. Only eight Polish city mayors signed the Mayors for Peace pledge. By comparison, in Germany, 412 mayors have joined the initiative. See "Mayors for Peace," 2015: 16, http://www.mayorsforpeace.org/data/pdf/01_monthly_updating/01_document_pack _en.pdf.

In line with the 2003 EU Security Strategy, Germany sees security challenges and threats stemming primarily from diffuse risks associated with terrorism, proliferation, regional conflicts, organized crime, and state failure. Rather than deterrence of—and defense against—specific threats, Germany in its 2006 Defense White Book promoted a concept of "comprehensive security" that aims also to tackle the root causes of conflict.[25] The White Book states that NATO's deterrence posture "for the foreseeable future" will require a mix of conventional and nuclear capabilities. It describes nuclear sharing arrangements as a necessary part of Alliance solidarity and burden-sharing, rather than as an element of that deterrence mix.[26]

Germany's *Ostpolitik* has continued in the post-Cold War period. Until recently, Russia was seen as a difficult partner but not as a threat. That perception has changed as a result of Russia's aggression against Ukraine, although it is too early to tell how far and how deep that shift has gone in Germany's political elite.

This outlook on Russia's role in European security has separated Berlin from Warsaw. Poland's post-Cold War security perspective has been—and continues to be—dominated by the perceived threat of Russia's confrontational policy. Moscow is seen as striving to regain its superpower status at the expense of its neighbors.[27] Russian aggression against Georgia (2008) and Ukraine (2014) as well as Russian activities in Belarus, such as the Zapad and Ladoga exercises in 2009–13, are seen as examples of Moscow's regional military power projection. Polish authorities carefully monitor Russian military potential at the Alliance's borders, most notably in the Kaliningrad Oblast and Belarus. The lack of transparency of Russian military capabilities deployed in the Kaliningrad region has

---

25. "Weißbuchzur Sicherheitspolitik Deutschlands und zur Zukunft der Bundeswehr," Bundesministerium der Verteidigung, 2006, www.weissbuch.de.

26. Ibid, 32 (translation by Oliver Meier).

27. "National Security Strategy of the Republic of Poland," 2014, 22, http://www.bbn .gov.pl/ftp/dok/NSS_RP.pdf.

been frequently cited in parliamentary debates as a specific threat.[28] The government in Warsaw is also concerned because of rhetorical threats that Russian decision-makers have directed against Poland in response to plans to build a land-based missile-defense interceptor site in Rędzikowo as part of NATO's European Phased Adaptive Approach. Russia systematically intimidates Poland with the (threat of) deployment of nuclear-capable short-range Iskander missiles and/or nuclear warheads in Kaliningrad.[29] Then foreign minister Radosław Sikorski stated in 2011 that "the experience from the last three hundred years taught [Poles] to take seriously any threats announced by Russia."[30]

Alliance politics

Germany sees NATO as a military and a political alliance. For Berlin, NATO should not only provide for collective defense but also play a stronger role in arms control, disarmament, and nonproliferation. Thus, Germany wanted to use the opportunities offered by President Obama's April 5, 2009, Prague speech to promote nuclear disarmament by, for example, working toward withdrawal of US nuclear weapons from

---

28. See, for example, "Biuletyn z Posiedzenia Komisji Spraw Zagranicznych (nr 59)," September 17, 2008, http://orka.sejm.gov.pl/Biuletyn.nsf/0 /8D84BD112B396ECFC12574DE002EFAB6/$file/0114006.pdf; "Biuletyn z posiedzenia Komisji Spraw Zagranicznych, nr 109; Komisji Obrony Narodowej, nr 188," October 27, 2010, http://orka.sejm.gov.pl/Biuletyn.nsf/wgskrnr6/SZA-188; "Biuletyn z posiedzenia Komisji Obrony Narodowej nr 127; Komisji Spraw Zagranicznych, nr 207," February 24, 2011: 8, http://orka.sejm.gov.pl/Biuletyn .nsf/0/76DCC1CEB291A22BC1257853004FE6EA/$file/0473306.pdf.

29. Jacek Durkalec, "The Future of NATO's Defence and Deterrence Posture: V4 Perspectives," in *The Future of NATO's Deterrence and Defence Posture: Views from Central Europe,* ed. Łukasz Kulesa (Warsaw: The Polish Institute of International Affairs, December 2012). See also Dmitry Medvedev, "Address to the Federal Assembly of the Russian Federation," November 5, 2008, http://archive.kremlin.ru /eng/speeches/2008/11/05/2144_type70029type82917type127286_208836.shtml.

30. "Интервью," *ExoMoskvy,* December 14, 2011, http://echo.msk.ru/programs /beseda/839184-echo/ (translation by Katarzyna Kubiak).

Germany and Europe. In October 2009, the newly elected conservative-liberal government vowed to work toward a change in NATO's nuclear posture and promised to "advocate within the Alliance and with our American allies the removal of the remaining nuclear weapons from Germany."[31] This initiative was framed in terms of supporting global disarmament and nonproliferation efforts, specifically Obama's Global Zero speech and the NPT Review Conference, which was going to take place in the spring of 2010.

The government's initiative was the most ambitious, most public, and clearest commitment by any German government to work toward withdrawal of US nuclear weapons deployed under nuclear sharing arrangements. Berlin wanted NATO to lead on nuclear disarmament and was able to find support for its goal of an open-ended debate about NATO's nuclear posture among some of its allies in Western Europe (but not among new Alliance members).[32] In February 2010, the foreign ministers of Belgium, Germany, Luxembourg, the Netherlands, and Norway wrote a joint letter to NATO Secretary General Anders Fogh Rasmussen urging him to make NATO's nuclear posture an issue of discussions at the April 22–23, 2010, foreign ministers' meeting in Tallinn, Estonia. In a September 6, 2010, speech to Germany's ambassadors, then German foreign minister Guido Westerwelle argued that the joint letter had the purpose of ensuring "that disarmament and arms control will remain a

---

31. "Growth. Education. Unity. The coalition agreement between the CDU, CSU and FDP for the 17th legislative period," 2009: 170.

32. According to a Wikileaks report, during the drafting of the coalition agreement, designated Foreign Minister Westerwelle "underlined that President Obama is moving forward toward a 'nuclear-free world' and that he wants Germany to be in the lead." Chancellor Merkel reportedly argued that "Germany is not that important in this regard." Wikileaks, "US Embassy Berlin: Westerwelle Firm On Removal Of Nuclear Weapons From Germany In Coalition Negotiations," www.wikileaks.ch /cable/2009/10/09BERLIN1271.html.

key issue, also within NATO's new Strategic Concept that is to be adopted at the Lisbon Summit in November."[33]

Once it became clear that there would be no consensus among allies on a change of NATO's nuclear posture at the Lisbon summit, Germany shifted its attention to the creation of a new high-level arms control body within the Alliance. Berlin wanted such a committee to have a permanent mandate to review NATO's nuclear posture and thus ensure a political debate beyond the Lisbon summit.[34] Germany also successfully pressed NATO to include a specific section on arms control, nonproliferation, and disarmament in the Strategic Concept's section on "promoting international security through cooperation."

Poland sees NATO's solidarity between Allies as a guarantee of the "fulfillment of its core mission—collective defense."[35] Poland joined NATO hoping for a univocal interpretation of Article 5 of the North Atlantic Treaty on collective defense. The "old NATO" was meant to provide security guarantees. Since then, Poland has continuously called for more visible assurances including the development of NATO infrastructure on its territory and exercises to improve conventional readiness.[36] The updat-

---

33. "Speech by Guido Westerwelle, Federal Minister for Foreign Affairs, at the Opening of the Ambassadors Conference at the Federal Foreign Office," Berlin, September 6, 2010, www.auswaertiges-amt.de/diplo/en/Infoservice/Presse/Reden/2010/100906 -BM-BokoEroeffnung.html.

34. "Antwort der Bundesregierung auf die Kleine Anfrage der Abgeordneten Uta Zapf, Dr. Rolf Mützenich, Rainer Arnold, weiterer Abgeordneter und der Fraktion der SPD 'Bisherige Fortschritte in Richtung auf einen Abzug der in Deutschland stationierten US-Atomwaffen und Einflussnahme der Bundesregierung auf die Reduzierung der Rolle von Nuklearwaffen im neuen Strategischen Konzept der NATO,'" Deutscher Bundestag, Drucksache 17/2639, July 20, 2010, answer to question 9, dipbt.bundestag.de/dip21/btd/17/026/1702639.pdf.

35. "National Security Strategy of the Republic of Poland," 20.

36. See, for example, "Biuletyn Z posiedzenia Komisji Spraw Zagranicznych, nr 109; Komisji Obrony Narodowej, nr 188," October 27, 2010: 8, http://orka.sejm.gov.pl /Biuletyn.nsf/wgskrnr6/SZA-188; Marcin Bosacki, "NATO's mission—a Polish perspective," National Post, August 26, 2014, http://fullcomment.nationalpost

ing of NATO contingency plans that provide for the collective defense of Polish territory is a constant concern that Warsaw has repeatedly raised domestically and in NATO fora.

Poland has also been interested in securing the permanent presence of Allied troops on Polish soil. Warsaw sees such a deployment as linking Poland to NATO and particularly the United States. Yet, the NATO-Russia Founding Act's promise not to permanently deploy substantial combat forces on the territory of new NATO members restricts Allies' options. Warsaw thus views the deployment of missile defenses as one way to ensure a presence of US "boots on the ground." Through such pledges, Warsaw tries to ensure that the implementation of Article 5 of the North Atlantic Treaty will gain credibility and that it will be triggered automatically in case of an attack on Poland.[37] NATO exercises are another instrument to validate NATO's security guarantees. Thus, in 2010, Bogdan Klich, then Poland's minister of defense, stated before parliament that "from the point of view of visible assurances, most important are exercises in the military training area due to their high visibility."[38]

.com/2014/08/26/marcin-bosacki-natosmission-a-polish-perspective/?__federated=1; "Biuletyn z Posiedzenia Komisji Obrony Narodowej (Nr 52) i Komisji Spraw Zagranicznych (Nr 105)," May 6, 2009, http://orka.sejm.gov.pl/Biuletyn.nsf/0 /F6AD58F9140D793EC12575B500366CB3?OpenDocument; Stanisław Koziej, "Polska Polityka Bezpieczeństwa i Prezydencja w Radzie UE. Wykład Wygłoszony w Instytucie Wyższych Studiów Obrony Narodowej - IHEDN (Institut Des Hautes Etudes De Defense Nationale)," May 16, 2011, www.bbn.gov.pl/download .php?s=1&id=7051.

37. See, for example, "Biuletyn Z posiedzenia Komisji Obrony Narodowej, nr 49," October 27, 2010, http://orka.sejm.gov.pl/Biuletyn.nsf/0 /FD8286919264ACEDC125759E00446BB3/$file/0210406.pdf; "Biuletyn Z posiedzenia Komisji Spraw Zagranicznych, nr 109; Komisji Obrony Narodowej, nr 188," October 27, 2010: 8, http://orka.sejm.gov.pl/Biuletyn.nsf/wgskrnr6/SZA-188.

38. See for example "Biuletyn Z posiedzenia Komisji Spraw Zagranicznych, nr 109; Komisji Obrony Narodowej, nr 188" Nr 4325/VI, Kancelaria Sejmu, Biuro Komisji Sejmowych, October 27, 2010, 8, http://orka.sejm.gov.pl/Biuletyn.nsf/wgskrnr6/SZA -188; see also Marcin Bosacki, "NATO's mission—a Polish perspective," *National Post*, August 26, 2014, http://fullcomment.nationalpost.com/2014/08/26/marcin

The German decision in 2009 to publicly advocate withdrawal of US nuclear weapons from Europe took Warsaw (and other Allies) by surprise. But the Polish government initially did not openly declare its opposition. Instead, Warsaw preferred consultations behind closed doors at NATO headquarters in Brussels to avoid the impression of public interference in German domestic policy. Warsaw stalled, waiting to see how the other NATO members, particularly host states and the United States, would position themselves. Its position evolved from a quiet status-quo defender,[39] through a supporter of a bilateral Russia-United States arms control regime,[40] to an advocate of a multilateral NATO-Russian reciprocity-based step-by-step solution aimed at the reduction of tactical nuclear weapons in Europe.[41]

When NATO agreed on a new Strategic Concept in November 2010, Allies tasked the North Atlantic Council with undertaking a comprehensive review on "NATO's overall posture in deterring and defending against the full range of threats to the Alliance." Essential elements were to "include the range of NATO's strategic capabilities required, including NATO's nuclear posture, and missile defence and other means of strategic

---

-bosacki-natos-mission-a-polish-perspective/?__federated=1 (translation by Katarzyna Kubiak).

39. Łukasz Kulesa, "Polish and Central European Priorities on NATO's Future Nuclear Policy," Arms Control Association, British American Security Information Council, and Institute for Peace Research and Security Policy at the University of Hamburg, November 2010, http://ifsh.de/file-IFAR/tacticalnuclearweapons/Nuclear_Policy_Paper_No2.pdf.

40. Carl Bildt and Radek Sikorski, "Next, the Tactical Nukes," New York Times, February 2, 2010, http://www.nytimes.com/2010/02/02/opinion/02iht-edbildt.html.

41. See Jonas Gahr Store and Radosław Sikorski, "Joint Statement by Foreign Ministers of Norway and Poland," April 9, 2010, http://www.msz.gov.pl/resource/21ffcb7a-16dc -4680-a3b0-4e6b56a18200; Jonas Gahr Store and Radowsław Sikorski, "NATO, Russia and Tactical Nuclear Arms," New York Times, May 14, 2012, http://www .nytimes.com/2012/05/15/opinion/nato-russia-and-tactical-nuclear-arms.html.

deterrence and defence."[42] In the context of this and the DDPR, Allies also agreed on a new arms control committee. Thus, German Foreign Minister Westerwelle in a 2011 parliamentary debate hailed this step as a success of German foreign and security policy: "Never before has there been so much disarmament in NATO!"[43]

Berlin saw the DDPR as an opportunity to continue to support a reduction of the role of nuclear weapons in European security. Again, Germany framed the issue of nuclear sharing in a political, rather than military, context. Rolf Nikel, then commissioner for arms control, disarmament, and nonproliferation, argued that "[g]iven the small remaining numbers," the debate about the future of US tactical nuclear weapons in Europe was "more about their political value for Alliance cohesion and solidarity than about their real deterrence value."[44]

Yet, Berlin's position on the other two elements of NATO's deterrence mix—conventional weapons and missile defenses—remained ambiguous. Germany has never been an enthusiastic supporter of US missile defense plans. During the George W. Bush administration, many in Berlin resented the way in which Washington sidelined NATO by pursuing bilateral agreements on the basing of missile defense installations with the Czech Republic and Poland.

---

42. NATO, "Lisbon Summit Declaration: Issued by the Heads of State and Government participating in the meeting of the North Atlantic Council in Lisbon," November 20, 2010, paragraph 30, http://www.nato.int/cps/en/natolive/official_texts_68828.htm.

43. Cited in Oliver Meier, "France and Germany agree on truce over nuclear arms control committee as NATO works on Deterrence and Defense Posture Review," *Arms Control Now* (blog), Arms Control Association, October 3, 2011, http://armscontrolnow.org/2011/10/03/france-and-germany-agree-on-truce-over -nuclear-arms-control-committee-as-nato-works-on-deterrence-and-defense -posture-review.

44. Rolf Nikel, "The Future of NATO's Nuclear Weapons," Arms Control Association, British American Security Information Council, and Institute for Peace Research and Security Policy at the University of Hamburg, Nuclear Policy Paper 9: 2, http://ifsh .de/file-IFAR/tacticalnuclearweapons/Nuclear_Policy_Paper_No9.pdf.

Germany changed its stance on NATO missile defense ahead of the 2010 Lisbon summit, after the Obama administration in 2009 cancelled the Bush administration's plans for a "third site" of US missile defenses in Europe. Westerwelle gave two reasons for this shift. First, NATO missile defense, he argued, had "completely changed direction" because the Obama administration had made this a joint project of all NATO allies by announcing the European Phased Adaptive Approach. And, second, Russia's willingness to consider a dialogue on missile defense was a "historic development" and the "peace dividend" of decades-long efforts to turn the project into a cooperative undertaking.[45] Thus, missile defenses were perceived as a potentially positive game-changer in NATO-Russian relations.

After the change of government after the 2013 parliamentary elections, Berlin continued to argue that nuclear sharing was a means to influence the policies of NATO. The new government's program argued that "[a]s long as nuclear weapons play a role as instruments of deterrence in NATO's Strategic Concept, Germany has an interest in participating in strategic discussions and planning processes."[46] Yet, this emphasis on nuclear sharing as a political mechanism to influence the nuclear weapons policies of the nuclear-armed allies is at odds with Germany's reluctance to enter into a substantive debate about the deterrence implications of NATO's nuclear weapon modernization efforts. When Washington announced plans to replace the existing B61 nuclear weapons with newer weapons which are more reliable and safer, but also more accurate, the government reacted by saying that the B61-12 "life extension program" is a national decision by the United States which does not need to be debated in NATO.

---

45. Guido Westerwelle, "Rede von Außenminister Westerwelle im Deutschen Bundestag zum Strategischen Konzept der NATO," Auswärtiges Amt, November 11, 2010, http://www.auswaertiges-amt.de/DE/Infoservice/Presse/Reden/2010/101111-BM-BT-Nato-Rede.html.

46. "Deutschlands Zukunft gestalten: Koalitionsvertrag zwischen CDU, CSU und SPD," December 16, 2013: 170 (translation by Oliver Meier).

The Polish government's position on tactical nuclear weapons covers several goals, including supporting disarmament, striving for NATO unanimity and cohesion, and aiming to build up trust and confidence in relations with Russia. Former foreign minister Radosław Sikorski stated in 2010 that tactical nuclear weapons have no role in resolving current security challenges and called them "dangerous remnants of a dangerous past."[47] Witold Sobków, permanent representative of Poland to the United Nations, mentioned at the 2010 NPT Review Conference that "[l]arge arsenals of sub-strategic nuclear weapons seem anachronistic in the post–Cold War world and increase the risk of proliferation by non-state actors. Instead of enhancing our security they make it more volatile."[48]

Poland, however, values nuclear deterrence as a fundamental guarantee for its security.[49] For the Polish government, the current mix of credible NATO deterrence capabilities supported by political security commitments is indispensable. Polish governmental officials see the number of US nuclear weapons deployed in Europe as adequate.[50] As such, they support the Chicago Summit notion that NATO will remain a nuclear alliance as long as there are nuclear weapons in the world. Some representatives of the Ministry of Defense also fear that a withdrawal of US nuclear weapons from Europe would mean the end of nuclear consultations in NATO.[51] In case NATO were to consider alternative deterrence postures, Poland would insist that remaining nuclear capabilities would

---

47. Bildt and Sikorski, "Next, the Tactical Nukes."

48. "Statement by H. E. Witold Sobków, Permanent Representative of the Republic of Poland to the UN Head of the Polish Delegation," May 5, 2010, http://www.un.org/en/conf/npt/2010/statements/pdf/poland_en.pdf.

49. See, for example, "Oświadczenie MSZ ws. informacji o nieprzestrzeganiu przez Rosję Traktatu INF," July 30, 2014, http://www.msz.gov.pl/pl/aktualnosci/dla_mediow/oswiadczenia/oswiadczenie_msz_ws__informacji_o_nieprzestrzeganiu_przez_rosje_traktatu_inf.

50. Interview by Katarzyna Kubiak in the Ministry of Foreign Affairs, October 17, 2013.

51. Interviews in the Ministry of Defence by Katarzyna Kubiak, October 17, 2013, and October 25, 2013.

be sufficient to ensure NATO integrity and solidarity. In practical terms, from the Polish perspective this implies a requirement for NATO to maintain its nuclear deterrence credibility with a simultaneous requirement to engage in new forms of cooperation with Russia on global nuclear security issues, including on tactical nuclear weapons.

Nuclear arms control and disarmament

The DDPR report, published at NATO's 2012 Chicago summit, did not substantially alter the nuclear status quo or NATO's position on arms control.[52] The Allies repeated that "NATO is prepared to consider further reducing its requirement for non-strategic nuclear weapons assigned to the Alliance in the context of reciprocal steps by Russia, taking into account the greater Russian stockpiles of non-strategic nuclear weapons stationed in the Euro-Atlantic area."[53] NATO Allies also supported and encouraged Russia and the United States "to continue their mutual efforts to promote strategic stability, enhance transparency, and further reduce their nuclear weapons."[54]

The DDPR did extend the mandate of the arms control committee, which was later to become the Special Advisory and Consultation Committee on Arms Control, Disarmament, and Non-Proliferation.[55] Germany's push to strengthen NATO's role in arms control, nonproliferation, and

---

52. The DDPR draft was approved at the April 18–19, 2012, defense ministers' meeting in Brussels. See Paul Ingram and Oliver Meier, "NATO's DDPR: What to Expect and What Needs to Be Done After the Chicago Summit," *Arms Control Now* (blog), Arms Control Association, May 3, 2012, armscontrolnow.org/2012/05/03/natos-ddpr-what-to-expect-and-what-needs-to-be-done-after-the-chicago-summit/#more-2907.

53. NATO, "Deterrence and Defence Posture Review," May 20, 2012, paragraph 26, www.nato.int/cps/en/SID-D2530093-661337FA/natolive/official_texts_87597.htm?mode=pressrelease.

54. Ibid., paragraph 28.

55. Oliver Meier, "NATO agrees on new arms control body," *Arms Control Now* (blog), Arms Control Association, February 26, 2013, http://armscontrolnow.org/2013/02/26/nato-agrees-on-new-arms-control-body.

disarmament seemed to have been successful. Yet, this achievement had no immediate impact on NATO's nuclear posture. The new committee began evaluating a list of possible confidence- and security-building measures that NATO might want to discuss with Russia, but never got very far. It stopped meeting in February 2014, at the outset of the Ukraine crisis. At the time of writing it was unclear when it might reconvene.[56]

Warsaw is generally skeptical of unilateral nuclear disarmament and was more reserved than Germany on proposals to strengthen NATO's role in arms control, nonproliferation, and disarmament. According to a 2012 report by the Royal United Service Institute, many in Poland perceive nuclear disarmament as "a project of left-leaning apologists for communism" rather than as a mainstream position.[57]

Poland looks for pragmatic, manageable, and feasible solutions. The Polish government reacted with limited enthusiasm to Obama's vision of a world free of nuclear weapons.[58] Warsaw sees a world free of nuclear weapons as a very distant goal and disarmament as an evolutionary process. Thus, in March 2012, the Council of Ministers adopted the "Polish Foreign Policy Priorities 2012–2016," which states that "it is necessary to include tactical nuclear weapons into an arms control regime and discussing the issue on a multilateral basis."[59] Like Germany, it believes that this goal can best be achieved step by step. Reflecting his work in the NATO Group of Experts, which had been charged with discussing NATO's new Strategic Concept ahead of the Lisbon summit, former Polish Foreign Minister Adam Rotfeld wrote in 2012 that as long as nuclear weapons

---

56. See Oliver Meier and Simon Lunn, "Trapped: NATO, Russia, and the Problem of Tactical Nuclear Weapons," *Arms Control Today,* January/February 2014: 18–24.

57. Andrew Somerville, Ian Kearns, and Malcolm Chalmers, "Poland, NATO and Non-Strategic Nuclear Weapons in Europe," RUSI Occasional Paper, February 2012: 10, https://www.rusi.org/downloads/assets/Poland-NATO-and-NSNW-120217.pdf.

58. Kulesa, "Polish and Central European Priorities on NATO's Future Nuclear Policy."

59. "Priorytety Polskie Polityki Zagranicznej 2012–2016," March 2012: 14, http://www.msz.gov.pl/resource/aa1c4aec-a52f-45a7-96e5-06658e73bb4e:JCR (translation by Katarzyna Kubiak).

exist, the politics of Western states need to "take into account realities and not wishful thinking."[60] Warsaw sees disarmament efforts as an instrument of making nuclear weapons less attractive to nuclear proliferators. Like Germany, it believes that disarmament and non-proliferation are mutually reinforcing.

Poland argues that US nuclear weapons should only be withdrawn from Europe on the basis of a legally binding, verifiable arms control treaty and NATO consensus. Early in the debate, in 2009, Aleksander Kwaśniewski, Tadeusz Mazowiecki, and Lech Wałęsa, prominent statesmen formerly governing Poland, called on Russia and the United States to take responsibility for nuclear disarmament efforts.[61] In 2012, Przemysław Grudziński, Poland's ambassador to the United Nations in Vienna, summarized the Polish approach to tackling the problem of tactical nuclear weapons this way:

> We hope that nuclear weapons states will build on the positive experience of the New START Treaty and include the category of tactical nuclear weapons in their future reduction talks. Before we reach this stage, it is important to lay the foundations for any future reductions by enhancing the transparency of existing nuclear arsenals and increasing mutual confidence.[62]

As a new and relatively poor member, but eager to contribute to the Alliance, Warsaw focused on the development of transparency and

---

60. Adam Daniel Rotfeld, *Myśli o Rosji . . . i nie tylko* (Warsaw: Świat Książki, 2012), 142.

61. Aleksander Kwaśniewski, Tadeusz Mazowiecki, and Lech Wałęsa "The Unthinkable Becomes Thinkable: Towards Elimination of Nuclear Weapons," *Gazeta Wyborcza,* April 6, 2009, http://www.abolitionforum.org/site/the-unthinkable-becomes-thinkable -towards-elimination-of-nuclear-weapons.

62. "Statement by H.E Przemysław Grudziński to the Preparatory Committee to the 2015 NPT Review Conference," April 30, 2012, http://www.un.org/disarmament/WMD /Nuclear/NPT2015/PrepCom2012/statements/20120430/Poland.pdf.

confidence-building measures. Together with Germany, it was one of the leading parties to develop the NATO North Atlantic Council 2000 Report on Options for Confidence and Security Building Measures, Verification, Non-Proliferation, Arms Control and Disarmament, which described a range of options for engaging Russia.[63]

The Polish government expects that any reductions of tactical nuclear weapons in Europe would be preceded by an agreement with Moscow on transparency and confidence-building measures, including on the withdrawal of such weapons from the Kaliningrad region and the Kola Peninsula and the destruction of their storage facilities. At a hearing of the Foreign Affairs Committee in June 2013, Bogusław Winid, then undersecretary of state in the Ministry of Foreign Affairs, indicated that "Russian tactical weapons in Europe are in the focus of our considerations. We hope [they are] not stationed in the vicinity of our border. We strive for transparency, predictability, exchange of information as a starter for an American-Russian dialogue on this issue."[64] As a consequence, Poland is actively engaged in creating proposals for transparency- and confidence-building measures within both the NATO arms control committee and the NPDI. Together with Germany, Norway, and the Netherlands, Poland co-sponsored a 4+6 paper to the April 2011 NATO foreign ministers' meeting in Berlin on increasing transparency and confidence with regard to tactical nuclear weapons in Europe.[65]

---

63. NATO, "Report on Options for Confidence and Security Building Measures (CSBMs), Verification, Non-Proliferation, Arms Control and Disarmament," Press Communiqué M-NAC-2(2000)121, December 14, 2000.

64. "Pełny zapis przebiegu posiedzenia Komisji Spraw Zagranicznych," no. 82, June 12, 2013, http://orka.sejm.gov.pl/zapisy7.nsf/0 /D252AC1F5D43CF0EC1257B90003C7A4C/%24File/0191407.pdf (translation by Katarzyna Kubiak).

65. "Non-paper Submitted by Poland, Norway, Germany and the Netherlands on Increasing Transparency and Confidence with Regard to Tactical Nuclear Weapons in Europe. Proposal on Increasing Transparency and Promoting Confidence with

The way forward: a convergence of attitudes?

A review of German and Polish nuclear weapons and arms control policies provides part of the explanation why Europe has so far not played a larger role on nuclear disarmament. Serious differences remain among Europeans on the role of nuclear weapons, even between two moderate non-nuclear-weapon states like Germany and Poland.

Berlin and Warsaw continue to see nuclear weapons through different lenses. Berlin generally views nuclear weapons as an obstacle to more security, while Warsaw believes that nuclear weapons are useful instruments to achieve greater security. Different visions for European security and NATO's role also continue to complicate joint German-Polish undertakings on nuclear arms control in the context of the Alliance. Poland believes that NATO should recommit to collective defense as its primary mission. Berlin recognizes that collective defense has become more important but continues to maintain that NATO could and should play a greater political role, including on arms control, nonproliferation, and disarmament. Germany has more options to influence nuclear politics, not only because it is a host nation but also because it is a member of the so-called Quad. This informal group consists of the three NATO nuclear-weapon states and Germany. Several key compromises during debates on the 2010 Strategic Concept and the 2012 DDPR were agreed upon in the Quad.

While such disagreements and inequalities are important factors influencing the potential of both countries in cooperating on nuclear weapons-related issues, it should also be noted that Berlin and Warsaw share fundamental assumptions about nuclear arms control and disarmament. Both countries believe in a step-by-step approach to nuclear disarmament and would like to see more progress toward a reduction of the role of nuclear weapons. As a first step, Germany and Poland would like to see a

---

Regard to Tactical Nuclear Weapons in Europe," April 15, 2011, http://www.fas.org/programs/ssp/nukes/nuclearweapons/nato-nonpaper041411.pdf.

dialogue with Russia on confidence-building measures. Both also believe that Moscow and Washington together should undertake the next nuclear arms control step and that a future bilateral legal agreement should cover tactical nuclear weapons, including those in Europe.

Two current trends may bring German and Polish positions on nuclear disarmament even closer. First, Russia's annexation of Crimea and its aggression against Ukraine are likely to facilitate convergence of Polish and German arms control policies. In effect, Germany is in the process of revising its engagement policy vis-à-vis Russia. Before the Ukraine crisis broke out, Germany had already altered its stance on whether NATO should change its nuclear posture only on the basis of reciprocal Russian actions. Previously, Westerwelle had never clearly ruled out the option that NATO could and should reduce nuclear weapons independently of Russian actions.[66] The new German government, however, stated in its 2013 program that "[s]uccessful disarmament talks create the pre-condition for a withdrawal of the tactical nuclear weapons deployed in Germany and in Europe."[67] This statement builds on the 2010 NATO Strategic Concept. Thus, Poland need no longer be suspicious of Germany pursuing unilateral initiatives on nuclear weapons deployed in Europe. In any case, such a push by Germany or any other NATO members would be doomed to fail under the current climate of distrust toward Russia.

The initiative on the humanitarian impact of nuclear weapons may also push Germany and Poland closer together. Berlin, like Warsaw, views that initiative with some skepticism.[68] Some of its supporters promote

---

66. He did, however, rule out the possibility of German unilateral actions.

67. "Deutschlands Zukunft gestalten. Koalitionsvertrag zwischen CDU, CSU und SPD. 18. Legislaturperiode," 170, https://www.cdu.de/sites/default/files/media/dokumente/koalitionsvertrag.pdf (translation by Oliver Meier).

68. Poland for the first time officially expressed its position on that initiative at the 2014 Vienna Conference on the Humanitarian Impact of Nuclear Weapons, "Statement of Poland," http://www.bmeia.gv.at/fileadmin/user_upload/Zentrale/Aussenpolitik/Abruestung/HINW14/Statements/HINW14_Statement_Poland.pdf.

negotiations on a Nuclear Weapons Convention, which would aim to ban all nuclear weapons, as an alternative to the step-by-step approach to nuclear disarmament that continues to remain at the core of Germany's and Poland's arms control policies. At the 2015 UN First Committee meeting, Berlin and Warsaw supported the statement of twenty nations sponsored by Australia.[69] One important reason why the two states did not go along with the 155 states that supported the alternative statement was that Berlin and Warsaw were unwilling to state that the use of nuclear weapons "under any circumstances" would be illegitimate.[70] Disagreements on the humanitarian impact initiative have already complicated agreement on a common position by the European Union for the 2015 NPT Review Conference. This must be a shared concern for Germany and Poland, too, as is the fact that NPDI members hold different views on the humanitarian impact initiative.

In the future, German and Polish nuclear arms control policies are therefore likely to be more pragmatic and guided by the primary goal of preventing a further erosion of existing arms control instruments. What does this mean for the different contexts in which Berlin and Warsaw might jointly pursue a further reduction of the role of nuclear weapons?

---

69. "Joint Statement on the humanitarian consequences of nuclear weapons delivered by Ambassador John Quinn, Australian Permanent Representative to the United Nations, Geneva and Ambassador for Disarmament," United Nations General Assembly First Committee, October 20, 2014, http://australia-unsc.gov.au/2014/10/humanitarian-consequences-of-nuclear-weapons. Apart from Germany and Poland, NATO members Belgium, Bulgaria, Canada, Croatia, Czech Republic, Estonia, Greece, Hungary, Italy, Lithuania, Luxembourg, the Netherlands, Poland, Portugal, Slovakia, and Spain supported the statement. Thus, seventeen of the twenty signatories were NATO member states.

70. "Joint Statement on the Humanitarian Consequences of Nuclear Weapons," delivered by Ambassador Dell Higgie of New Zealand, United Nations General Assembly First Committee, October 20, 2014, http://reachingcriticalwill.org/images/documents/Disarmament-fora/1com/1com14/statements/20Oct_NewZealand.pdf.

Revisiting arms control priorities

Against the background of the crisis in Ukraine, expectations of a stronger role for NATO in nuclear arms control in Europe are unrealistic, at least in the near term. NATO, as a military alliance, probably has never been the best framework for promoting nuclear arms control and disarmament in Europe. It is probably less so now, with military tensions growing. The vision of Russia becoming a strategic partner of the Alliance, which was still part of NATO's 2010 Strategic Concept, can no longer be a short-term guiding principle for NATO's arms control policies. Clearly, NATO's arms control policy must now be aimed at creating more stability, just as it was during the Cold War, ever since the Harmel report. The idea of engaging Russia in a cooperative endeavor to reduce nuclear weapons can only be a long-term goal.

Strengthening existing mechanisms for crisis prevention and creating new instruments to prevent unintended escalation of the current conflict in Europe should be priorities. Russia's attempt to nuclearize the Ukraine conflict already has had negative consequences for European security and arms control. It demonstrates the need for additional crisis prevention and confidence-building measures.[71] Poland and Germany may be in a good position to promote better channels of communications and regular exchanges with Russia to avoid incidents. This would be in line with the outcome of NATO's September 2014 Wales summit, where Allies declared that they:

> continue to aspire to a cooperative, constructive relationship with Russia, including reciprocal confidence building and transparency measures and increased mutual understanding of NATO's and Russia's non-strategic nuclear force postures in Europe, based on our common security concerns and interests, in a Europe where each country freely

---

71. Oliver Meier, "Die nukleare Dimension der Ukraine-Krise," Berlin, Stiftung Wissenschaft und Politik, Oktober 2014, http://www.swp-berlin.org/fileadmin /contents/products/aktuell/2014A66_mro.pdf.

chooses its future. We regret that the conditions for that relationship do not currently exist.[72]

In this context, NATO may want to revisit its decision of early April 2014 to reduce the size of Russia's mission at NATO headquarters.[73] And Russia should rethink its decision of late 2013 to cancel all direct discussion of nuclear issues with the Alliance. Such offers could help to pave the way for a dialogue to reduce the risk of inadvertent escalation and increase the likelihood for a dialogue aimed at conflict prevention.

A crisis management mechanism could then be the basis on which both sides could attempt to reinitiate a dialogue on transparency and confidence-building measures related to nuclear weapons deployed in Europe. Such a dialogue seems even more relevant than it was before the Ukraine crisis and could serve to rebuild relations with Russia. Exchanges on nuclear doctrines as well as nuclear accidents and incidents may be good starting points. On both issues, NATO and Russia have been engaged in fruitful discussions and joint undertakings in the past.[74] If and when progress is made, the Kaliningrad Trialogue may be revived.[75]

---

72. "Wales Summit Declaration: Issued by the Heads of State and Government participating in the meeting of the North Atlantic Council in Wales," September 5, 2014, paragraph 22, http://www.nato.int/cps/en/natohq/official_texts_112964.htm.

73. NATO, "Measures following NATO Ministers' decision to suspend all practical cooperation with Russia," April 7, 2104, http://www.nato.int/cps/en/natolive /news_108902.htm?selectedLocale=en.

74. See Katarzyna Kubiak, "NATO and Russia Experiences with Nuclear Transparency and Confidence-Building Measures," Stiftung Wissenschaft und Politik, Working Paper FG03-WP No 02, March 2014, http://www.swp-berlin.org/fileadmin/contents /products/arbeitspapiere/wp_kubiak_April2014.pdf.

75. In 2013, Germany initiated the first trilateral meeting of the German, Polish, and Russian directors of foreign ministries arms control sections. At the Berlin meeting, problems associated with tactical nuclear weapons were discussed, among other issues. See "Bericht der Bundesregierung zum Stand der Bemühungen um Rüstungskontrolle, Abrüstung und Nichtverbreitung sowie über die Entwicklung

A second area where Germany and Poland might intensify collaboration is the discussion among Alliance members on next steps in arms control. Both countries share an interest in advancing NATO unity on this issue. This includes a clarification of the future role of NATO's arms control committee. One specific mission for that committee may be a further discussion of the requirements for nuclear secrecy. When NATO in 2013 elaborated a possible list of topics to be discussed with Russia to build confidence and security, it became clear that arcane secrecy rules stand in the way of even modest transparency measures. Such a discussion would also lend greater credibility to calls by the NPDI for more openness by the nuclear-weapon states and would increase the accountability and, thus, the legitimacy of the Alliance's nuclear policies.[76]

Security assurances are a third area where Germany and Poland might jointly initiate a debate within the Alliance. Against the background of Russia's violation of the 1994 Budapest Memorandum and the negative security assurance contained in the document, NATO must make it clear that it honors its security pledges. Otherwise, there is a real danger that the other nuclear-weapon states will be perceived to be "guilty by association."[77] This is a loaded topic which has been discussed in the context of the adoption of the Strategic Concept and also the DDPR, but it may be well worth revisiting now. A NATO commitment to a no-first-use policy would not affect its relationship with Russia but would be an important measure to strengthen nonproliferation commitments and the NPT. These issues could be placed on NATO's agenda ahead of the next summit, scheduled in Warsaw in 2016.

Germany and Poland should also continue to push for a stronger role of the EU in nuclear nonproliferation. Here, their policies are similar.

---

der Streitkräftepotenziale 2013," http://www.auswaertiges-amt.de/cae/servlet/contentblob/679566/publicationFile/193991/ABRBericht2013.pdf.

76.   Meier and Lunn, "Trapped."

77.   Mark Fitzpatrick, "The Ukraine Crisis and Nuclear Order," *Survival* 56, no. 4: 81–90.

They could attempt to strengthen a pragmatic position of the EU, mediating between the nuclear-weapon states France and the United Kingdom, on the one hand, and states like Austria and Ireland, which lean toward a normative approach toward nuclear disarmament and nuclear deterrence.

Clearly, there is room for the NPDI to pursue a more ambitious nuclear disarmament agenda. The diversity of views and perspectives in that group is its main strength but has also at times hindered the development of a progressive disarmament agenda. NPDI states have, with limited success, tried to make progress on improved transparency and also tactical nuclear weapons. Both issues rank high on Berlin's and Warsaw's arms control agendas, too.

Finally, Germany and Poland may think about other formats that may be suited to pursue nuclear arms control and disarmament. The Kaliningrad and Weimar triangles are unsuitable because they include Russia and France. Both nuclear-weapon states are currently uninterested in reducing the role of their nuclear weapons. However, Berlin and Warsaw may choose other partners. The collaboration on the April 2011 4+6 paper on increasing transparency and confidence with regard to tactical nuclear weapons in Europe may serve as one model for initiating a new group to discuss how the role of nuclear weapons in European security might be reduced. Smaller coalitions may also be a viable option. Thus, in late 2013 both countries teamed up with Denmark to revitalize conventional arms control in Europe.[78] Such a format is interesting because the possibility for regional measures in the Baltic Sea region is one specific area where both countries could engage.[79]

78.　"Statement of foreign ministers of Poland, Germany and Denmark on conventional arms control in Europe," September 27, 2013, http://www.msz.gov.pl/en/news /statement_of_foreign_ministers_of_poland__germany_and_denmark_on _conventional_arms_control_in_europe.

79.　For an ambitious approach see, for example, Fredrik Lindvall, John Rydqvist, Fredrik Westerlund, and Mike Winnerstig, "The Baltic Approach: A next step? Prospects for an Arms Control Regime for Sub-strategic Nuclear Weapons in Europe," Swedish Defense Research Agency, Stockholm 2011.

Whether such initiatives are successful will ultimately depend on the willingness of Russia and the NATO nuclear-weapon states to engage in transparency, confidence-building, and arms control. Joint German and Polish initiatives, possibly with other states, would be difficult to ignore because both countries have a great deal of credibility in seeking out the middle ground on realistic next steps. Berlin and Warsaw should invest that political capital to further a debate within NATO and with Russia on how to reduce the role of nuclear weapons in Europe.

CHAPTER 7 **Utility of Nuclear Deterrence
in the Middle East**

Shlomo Brom

Introduction

The purpose of this chapter is to examine the utility of nuclear deterrence in the Middle East as well as regional perceptions of its utility there. Perceptions are important because policy decisions are often determined by perceptions rather than by realities, even assuming that these realities can be identified and described accurately. This examination is useful in understanding the motivations for nuclear proliferation in the Middle East as well as for a credible assessment of the obstacles to establishment of a nuclear weapons-free zone there on the way to a world free of nuclear weapons.

So far, the Middle East (defined for the purposes of this chapter as the nations of the Arab League plus Iran, Turkey, and Israel) seems to be lagging behind other regions in establishing regional security arrangements. It is bereft of any cooperative security regime, and attempts to establish such collective security regimes have been mostly unsuccessful. Nevertheless, the idea of establishing an area free of weapons of mass destruction (WMD) in the Middle East has been a part of the region's discourse from as early as 1990, when Egypt introduced such a proposal.

This was preceded by the idea of establishing a nuclear weapons-free zone, following the example of other regions. Establishment of a nuclear weapons-free zone in the Middle East was first called for by Iran in 1974, a call which was endorsed by the UN General Assembly in December 1974.[1] The move from the idea of a nuclear weapons-free zone to the idea of a WMD-free zone took place because Israel insisted that although it supports in principle the idea of establishing a nuclear weapons-free zone in the Middle East, the implementation of this idea cannot be delinked from also dealing with other categories of WMD that Middle Eastern states hold and even use. Egypt, the driving force behind discussion of the establishment of a WMD-free zone, was hoping that broadening the scope of the zone would take care of the issue. However, regional discussions on the establishment of this zone have never started. All that is strongly connected to the perceptions of the utility of nuclear deterrence in the Middle East. Israel is playing a major role in these perceptions as being the only Middle Eastern state that is considered a de facto nuclear power by most of the players in the international, as well as the regional, arena.

The exceptionalism of the Middle East

Where nuclear proliferation and nuclear deterrence are concerned, the Middle East is exceptional in comparison to other regions. And within the Middle East, Israel is exceptional compared to other nuclear states. On one hand, all states of the Middle East—with the exception of Israel— have acceded to the Non-Proliferation Treaty (NPT) as non-weapon states. On the other hand, most cases of nuclear proliferation in recent years have taken place in the Middle East. It is a region with one perceived and recognized (de facto) nuclear-weapon state, Israel, and a number

---

1. Arms Control Association, "WMD-Free Middle East Proposal at a Glance," Fact Sheets & Briefs, http://www.armscontrol.org/factsheets/mewmdfz.

of nuclear proliferators that are NPT members but which violate the treaty.

Israel is exceptional among recognized nuclear-weapon states as the only one that has never admitted it is a nuclear-weapon state. It adopted a policy of nuclear opacity based on a statement that includes two elements. The first is: "Israel will not be the first to introduce nuclear weapons to the Middle East." The second is: "But Israel will not be the second to introduce this weapon."[2] This policy was also enshrined in an understanding with the White House that as long as Israel does not declare that it has nuclear weapons and does not perform a nuclear test, it adheres to this commitment. This understanding was first established in 1969 in a meeting between President Richard Nixon and Prime Minister Golda Meir and has been reaffirmed since then with every new US administration.[3]

Because Israel has a nuclear program, it is often accused of being the reason for proliferation of nuclear weapons in other Middle Eastern states. However, the Middle East has been characterized for decades by the proliferation of political, religious, and ideological conflicts that often turn into armed conflicts. Thus, when other proliferators in the Middle East are examined on a case-by-case basis, it is usually found that they are driven by a number of reasons. Israel's perceived possession of nuclear weapons is only one of those reasons. These Middle Eastern proliferators are using the weaknesses of the monitoring regime based on the International Atomic Energy Agency (IAEA) safeguards agreements and IAEA monitoring to engage in military nuclear programs violating the NPT without formally withdrawing from the NPT. They hope in this way to continue

---

2. This implies that if another Middle Eastern state introduces nuclear weapons, Israel will be ready with its own nuclear weapons.

3. The National Security Archive, "Israel Crosses the Threshold," National Security Archive Electronic Briefing Book no. 189, http://www2.gwu.edu/~nsarchiv /NSAEBB/NSAEBB189/index.htm; Avner Cohen and William Burr, "Israel Crosses the Threshold," *Bulletin of the Atomic Scientists* 62, no. 3 (May/June 2006), http://thebulletin.org/2006/may/israel-crosses-threshold.

enjoying the benefits of NPT membership and avoiding the consequences of a formal withdrawal from the treaty.

The case of Israel

Israel started its nuclear program a short time after its inception due to its threat perception. Since its establishment, the State of Israel has had to face a hostile environment comprised of the Arab states unwilling to accept its existence. The Arab states were adamant in considering the 1948–1949 War, Israel's Independence War, only as the first round in a longer war that would eventually bring about the demise of the newly born state. Consequently, Israel had to prepare for the next round. But there was another important element to this predicament. There were vast asymmetries between Israel and its enemies. The first asymmetry was, and still is, in the size of the population, which meant its enemies had a larger manpower pool to draw from for building large military forces. The second asymmetry was in the size of the territory, which meant that Israel lacked strategic depth while its rivals enjoyed ample strategic depth. The third asymmetry was in wealth. The Arab world had at that time much more economic resources than the tiny Israeli state, which meant better abilities to build up well-equipped militaries. The fourth asymmetry was in political power. The isolated State of Israel was facing all the states of the Arab League that were enjoying the support of the other Muslim states as well as of the Non-Alignment Movement, which meant that Israel alone, with no allies, was facing a huge block of hostile states in all international forums.

Israel's civilian and military leaders devised different means to deal with its predicament and create a more favorable balance of power. This was done by augmenting potential force multipliers, such as developing a qualitative edge as an offset to its quantitative inferiority; building a relationship with at least one superpower, which might turn into a stronger alliance; and devising a national defense doctrine that built on its strengths and neutralized its weaknesses. However, they were painfully aware of the fragility of these remedies for the basic asymmetries. All this thinking was taking place against the background of the most terrible disaster the Jewish people had ever endured: the Holocaust, in which six million Jews were murdered by the Nazi killing machine during World War II. There was a strong sense that Israel, the "safe refuge" of the Jewish people, needed a better insurance policy. After World War II, nuclear weapons seemed the ultimate insurance policy for the survival of the newly born Jewish state. Thus, the Israeli nuclear option was intended from its inception to deal with existential threats to the State of Israel and not any other necessity.

The nature of the existential threats Israel faced during the 1950s was completely different from the threats Israel is facing nowadays. Following the experience of the War of Independence in which all the members of the Arab League declared war on Israel and invaded its territory right after the declaration of its independence, the main scenario of concern was one in which a broad Arab coalition attacked simultaneously. This scenario envisioned a surprise attack taking advantage of the small size of Israel's standing army and its complete dependence on the mobilization of its larger reserve forces, with the attackers seeking to put an end to Israel's existence. For years, the main operational plan of the Israel Defense Forces (IDF), called "the case of all" ("*mikre hakol*"in Hebrew),[4] was intended to deal with this scenario. Many were concerned that the success of these operational plans was based on a series of problematic assumptions, and a failure of one of them meant the collapse of the whole plan. This doomsday scenario was realized once fully, in the 1948–1949 war, and once partially in 1973, when the Arab coalition that started a war against Israel included only two Arab states, Egypt and Syria, with limited expeditionary forces from a number of other Arab states. There was a substantial difference between the two wars. The first was indeed

---

4. Brig. Gen. (ret.) Dov Tamari, "We won. What now?," *Walla 1967* (blog), May 23 2007, http://1967.walla.co.il/?w=/2065/1107316 (in Hebrew).

a total war in which the stated objective was the elimination of the infant state. The second was a limited war aimed at gaining back the territories occupied by Israel in 1967 by achieving limited territorial gains and exerting a significant cost on the IDF. Some scholars in Israel concluded that one of the main reasons for Egypt's and Syria's limited objectives in the 1973 war was their recognition of Israel's nuclear option. This is cited often as proof of the validity of Israel's nuclear strategy,[5] albeit there were other reasons for the limited scope of the Arab attack in 1973, which may provide a better explanation.

The Israeli defense doctrine designed to deal with this predicament was based on a conception developed during the 1920s by Zeev Jabotinsky, a Zionist political leader who led the opposition to the elected leadership of the movement. Called "the iron wall conception," it was later adopted by Jabotinsky's bitter political adversary, David Ben-Gurion, who became the first prime minister of Israel. According to this conception, the Jewish state would have to build an iron wall on which the recurrent attacks of the hostile Arab neighbors would shatter. Eventually, after a long series of defeats, the Arab states would have to reconcile with the existence of a Jewish state in the midst of the Arab Middle East.[6] From the Israeli point of view, this conception was vindicated when Egypt concluded a peace treaty with Israel in 1979 followed by the conclusion of a peace treaty with Jordan in 1995 and peace negotiations with Syria and the Palestinians.

During the first years of the buildup of Israel's nuclear option, two paradigms ruled the debate. The first supported the idea that the nuclear

---

5. See, for example, Ariel E. Levite and Emily Landau, *Israel's Nuclear Image: Arab Perceptions of Israel's Nuclear Posture* (Tel Aviv: Tel Aviv University Papyrus Press, 1994), 43 (in Hebrew); or, summarized in English, "Arab Perceptions of Israel's Nuclear Posture, 1960–1967," *Israel Studies* 1, no. 1 (Spring 1996), http://mtw160-198.ippl.jhu.edu/login?auth=0&type=summary&url=/journals/israel_studies/v001/1.1levite.pdf.

6. Avi Shlaim, *The Iron Wall: Israel and the Arab World Since 1948* (New York: W.W. Norton & Company, 1999).

option should be the principal mainstay of Israel's deterrence posture, even at the expense of Israel's conventional forces, because of the higher credibility of nuclear deterrence and as a way to avoid the huge defense expenditures needed to build a large conventional force that could deter the much larger Arab conventional forces. This paradigm also had supporters in Israeli academia.[7] The second paradigm considered the nuclear option an instrument of last resort, an insurance policy that, ideally, would never be used. Supporters of this paradigm argued that Israel should build up its conventional military power and manage its wars as if the nuclear option did not exist. Eventually, the second paradigm gained dominance in the Israeli strategic community. What Israel's prime minister, Levi Eshkol, referred to as "the Samson Option" became the basic Israeli strategic concept: the nuclear option as, they hoped, a never-used national insurance policy.[8]

Since then the nature of military threats Israel is facing has changed tremendously. The incidence of state-to-state wars went down substantially. In the Arab world today, state structures are constantly threatened by non-state actors. The Middle East's Arab states are weak and cannot really threaten Israel. Also, the politics of the Arab world are fragmented and the probability of several Arab states forming a war coalition against Israel is somewhere between extremely low and nonexistent. The more frequent threat to Israel is by the kind of non-state actors that threaten the Arab states and also choose to engage in asymmetric war against Israel. Sometimes these actors serve as proxies of states. Hezbollah in Lebanon, for example, has its own agenda but also serves as a proxy for Iran and Syria. From the point of view of Israel, these kinds of wars are not existential in nature.

---

7.   Shai Feldman, *Israeli Nuclear Deterrence: A Strategy for the 1980s* (New York: Columbia University Press, 1983).

8.   Avner Cohen, *Israel and the Bomb* (New York: Columbia University Press, 1998), 235–9.

That, of course, raises the question: is nuclear deterrence still relevant for Israel? The answers to this question are based on rational calculations mixed with some psychological factors. When Israelis ask this question they have first to ask themselves whether nuclear deterrence was useful in the past. There is a broad consensus in Israel that it was useful. Israelis believe that although the nuclear option was not a tool that was actually used by Israel to repel Arab attacks on "the iron wall," the perception of Israel's nuclear option was a very useful tool.

First, the nuclear option prevented the Arab parties from posing existential threats to Israel even when they decided to wage war, as was the case in 1973. Another relevant question is: why didn't any Arab parties use weapons of mass destruction in their wars with Israel even when these parties faced humiliating defeats? Since the 1960s, Arab states have possessed chemical weapons and, later, biological weapons. They didn't hesitate to use chemical weapons against other targets. Egypt used chemical weapons in Yemen to support the regime during the sixties and Iraq used chemical weapons during the Iran-Iraq war (1980–1988). But Egypt did not use chemical weapons when it was defeated by Israel in 1967, nor did it use these weapons when Israeli forces crossed the Suez Canal in 1973 and only limited Egyptian forces separated the IDF and Cairo. Similarly, Syria did not use chemical weapons in 1973 when Israeli forces overcame the Syrian defenses and advanced toward Damascus. It makes sense that the Arab states were deterred by perceived Israeli nuclear capabilities.

Second, many Israelis believe the nuclear option played a major role in the Arabs' understanding that they have to reconcile with the existence of the Jewish state because they cannot really threaten its existence without paying an unacceptable price.[9] It is of course not possible to get a confirmation from the Arab parties of this thesis. They will never

---

9. This theme is presented in Max Fisher, "Why is the U.S. OK with Israel having nuclear weapons but not Iran?" *Washington Post,* December 2, 2013.

state: "We decided to have peace with Israel because we were afraid of its nuclear weapons." But if this thesis is accepted, one can argue that the 2002 Arab Peace Initiative (API), in which all the Arab states accepted the existence of Israel, represents the culmination of the success of the Israeli nuclear option as a deterrent.

The next question Israelis should ask themselves is whether the nuclear option is still needed as a deterrent, taking into account the enormous changes in Israel's environment and the regional balance of force. The answers to this question are more complicated. It is true that no Arab state or combination of Arab states is currently posing an existential threat to Israel. They are both unwilling and incapable of doing so. However, Israel must take into account three important new developments.

First is the rise of the non-Arab states in the Middle East and the change in the balance of force between them and the Arab states. The two significant actors are Iran and Turkey. Both states have two relevant characteristics: they are ruled by Islamists and they are hostile to Israel, although with different intensities. Iran is extremely hostile to Israel. It defines itself as an Islamic republic, which means it is a religious autocracy, and its hostility stems directly from its Islamist ideology, although it also has utilitarian reasons. Iranian leaders apparently believe that hostility to Israel is very useful as a way of winning the hearts and minds of the Arab masses and thus acquiring influence in the Arab Middle East. Turkey is a different case because the regime is basically democratic. But it is ruled by an Islamic party, which enjoys a clear majority among the Turkish public and is probably going to continue to enjoy this majority support for many years. President Recep Tayyip Erdogan, the leader of the Islamic AKP party, is also showing increasingly autocratic inclinations, causing concerns that Turkish democracy is gradually eroding. Erdogan's world outlook is strongly affected by his religion and he has adopted strong anti-Israeli positions. Iran and Turkey have also succeeded in maintaining cohesion and building up their military forces, in contrast with the Arab states. That has changed completely the balance of force in the Middle

East and has changed basic Israeli calculations. In the 1950s and '60s, Israel adopted the idea of the "alliance of the periphery"[10] and considered these two states as potential allies against the Arab states. But now Israel considers Iran its number one enemy state, with Turkey on its way to becoming an enemy state. Israelis are especially concerned about the combination of enmity to Israel with religious fanaticism, which makes it more probable that the enmity will be translated to direct existential threats.

The second important development is the proliferation of weapons of mass destruction in the Middle East. In the past, the common phenomenon was the spread of chemical and biological weapons, the poor man's nuclear weapons. Since the 1980s, the main problem has become proliferation of nuclear weapons, while the threat of chemical and biological weapons has abated. Iraq and Libya have been disarmed of chemical and biological weapons, and Syria was recently disarmed of its chemical weapons. Only Egypt still has chemical and biological weapons, but it is no longer considered an enemy of Israel and it is not clear how much of Egypt's obsolete weapons are operational. Israel's main concern is Iran's nuclear program. Iran is already a threshold nuclear state. Its breakout time to a military nuclear capability is short. Israel is also concerned that once Iran acquires military nuclear capabilities, other states in the Middle East will follow.

The third significant development in Israeli eyes was the rise of the non-state actors. These are independent actors with their own well-equipped militias. Sometimes these militias develop military capabilities that are better than the military capabilities of the states that host them. A typical case is Hezbollah. It practically rules southern Lebanon and other pieces of Lebanese territory. Another case is the Islamic State, which as of this writing controls vast areas in Syria and Iraq. In many cases, these non-state

---

10. Leon T. Hadar, "The Collapse of Israel's 'Periphery Doctrine': Popping Pipe(s) Turkey Dreams," *The World Post,* May 25, 2011, http://www.huffingtonpost.com/leon-t -hadar/the-collapse-of-israels-p_b_617694.html.

actors wish to become states, but for now are hybrid combinations of state and non-state actors. A classic case is the Hamas organization that became the actual government in the Gaza Strip while at the same time retaining characteristics of a non-state actor. Sometimes these non-state actors also serve as proxies of state actors. Iran is particularly proficient in the use of proxies based on religious identity. Thus its proxy in Lebanon, Hezbollah, represents to Israel a combination of the threat of a hostile, powerful non-Arab Middle Eastern state with a hostile, non-state actor that dwells on its borders.

There are two competing paradigms as to the role of nuclear weapons in preserving peace or enabling states that acquired these weapons to deter threats other than nuclear threats. On one end stands Kenneth N. Waltz,[11] who argued that nuclear weapons put an end to war among states. On the other end stand those who doubt the value of nuclear weapons in preventing wars among states and argue that the long period of avoidance of war among the great powers after the Second World War stemmed from other reasons. These scholars are quoted extensively in Benoit Pelopidas's essay in this book.[12] Proponents of the second approach like to cite the example of the Kargil incident (1999), in which Pakistan invaded Indian-held territory and initiated a border clash with India, although the two states had demonstrated that they had operational nuclear weapons in a series of nuclear tests a short time before this incident. The people in this camp argue that the Kargil incident disproves the theory that a nuclear-armed state cannot be attacked. Proponents of the first approach can look at the other side of the coin and argue that before India and Pakistan became nuclear powers, they were engaged in two major wars, in 1965 and 1971, which could be considered existential wars, at least for Pakistan. The two wars started with Pakistani provocations similar to the Kargil incident.

---

11. Kenneth N. Waltz, *The Spread of Nuclear Weapons: More May Be Better,* Adelphi Papers, Book 171 (London: International Institute for Strategic Studies, 1981).

12. For example, Steven P. Lee, *Morality, Prudence, and Nuclear Weapons* (Cambridge, UK: Cambridge University Press, 1993).

In contrast to these wars, Kargil and later Pakistani provocations didn't escalate to major wars, probably because of mutual nuclear deterrence.

The Israeli take on this debate is to call for a more nuanced and sophisticated analysis to gauge the utility of nuclear deterrence in preventing war. One has to look at the nature of the actors involved in each case and at the differing contexts, whether the Cold War or today's regional conflicts. One major issue concerns the difference between status quo powers and powers that challenge the status quo. One can argue that during the Cold War the two opposing sides were basically status quo powers. But in the Pakistan-India case, Pakistan is a classical anti-status quo power. It wishes to put an end to what it perceives as India's occupation of Kashmir-Jammu. That explains the recurrent incidences between Pakistan and India. But the fact that they did not turn into major wars indicates that even when one of the parties involved is an anti-status quo power, it is deterred from posing an existential threat to a nuclear- armed state. A variation on this theme is the proposition—quite common in Israel—that acquisition of nuclear capabilities by a power that challenges the status quo actually encourages it to pose low-level challenges to the status quo power since it knows such a challenge will not turn into a major armed conflict due to its nuclear deterrence. Thus, Israelis who want to justify the Israeli position—which claims that Iran should never be allowed to acquire nuclear weapons, and should be stopped by any means—argue that once Iran has nuclear weapons, it will use its extended deterrence to push its proxies deployed on the Israeli borders, such as Hezbollah, to provoke Israel more frequently and more intensively.[13]

---

13. For a typical quotation in an Israeli daily newspaper, see Reuters and *Israel Hayom* staff, "Hamas, Hezbollah would run riot under Iranian nuclear umbrella, general warns," *Israel Hayom,* January 18, 2012: "The major-general [Amir Eshel] made it clear that Israel—widely reputed to have the region's only atomic arsenal—is worried that Syria, Lebanon's Hezbollah militia and the Palestinian Hamas Islamists who rule Gaza could one day find reassurance in an Iranian bomb. . . . "They will be more aggressive. They will dare to do things that right now they would not dare to do." http://www.israelhayom.com/site/newsletter_article.php?id=2724.

The Israeli position can be summed up as follows: Israel is a responsible status quo power with a history of restraint concerning its nuclear option and the use of nuclear threats. Consequently, it should be allowed to retain its nuclear option because this option has only one objective: preventing the realization of existential threats to the State of Israel. Other parties in the Middle East should not be allowed to develop nuclear capabilities because they do not face existential threats and they are powers that challenge the status quo and are motivated by radical religious beliefs. Nevertheless, if the worst case scenario of these states becoming nuclear powers materializes sometime in the future, Israel can through its nuclear deterrence prevent these actors from threatening its survival, because for nuclear deterrence to be credible the threat it should aim to deter should be existential.

In any case, Israeli nuclear weapons cannot play a role in deterring non-state actors. Those actors are not posing a threat to the existence of the Jewish state and threats of nuclear retaliation for their actions against Israel will not be credible. The question that troubles Israel is whether the rise of these non-state actors represents a permanent feature of the new Middle East or only a transition to a new Middle East that will be even more threatening to Israel. In the 1990s, when peace treaties were already concluded with Egypt and Jordan and peace negotiations were taking place with other Arab parties parallel to regional security talks with a large group of Arab states, it looked as if the new Middle East would be more accepting of Israel, leading to a reduction of existential threats to Israel and a diminishing role for the Israeli nuclear option. That led Israeli foreign minister (and later prime minister) Shimon Peres to make a speech in 1993 at the signing ceremony of the Chemical Weapons Convention in Paris, which was interpreted as an Israeli commitment that after the conclusion of comprehensive peace treaties with the Arab world, Israel would be willing to enter concrete negotiations on the establishment of a WMD-free zone in the Middle East.[14]

---

14. Foreign Minister Peres said: ". . . Accordingly, we have formulated our policy on regional security and arms control, once peace has been attained. . . . In the spirit

But those rosy days passed away and optimism as to the nature of Israel's relations with the Arab world gave way to pessimism. Israel is concerned that eventually the upheaval in the Arab world will lead to changes of regimes, and that hostile regimes will come to power in the states that concluded peace treaties with Israel—regimes that will abrogate those treaties. When the Muslim Brotherhood came to power in Egypt and Mohammed Morsi was elected president, it seemed that this negative scenario was about to be realized. However, Morsi did not abrogate the peace treaty and eventually he was toppled by a combination of popular protest and a military coup d'état. Nevertheless, Israeli concerns are still strong. Today they are focused on Jordan. There is a strong concern that the Islamic State will spread to Jordan and that Israel will have to face a hostile eastern front. As a result, there is now more reluctance in Israel to take concrete steps toward a Middle Eastern WMD-free zone.

In the NPT review conference of 2010, the final document included a decision on convening a Middle Eastern WMD-free zone conference in 2012. Israel's initial reaction to this decision was negative because it was adopted by a forum in which Israel is not a member. Israel also rejected the association of the idea of a Middle Eastern WMD-free zone with the NPT, which implied singling out nuclear weapons and singling out Israel, although a WMD-free zone is supposed to deal with all categories of WMD. Nevertheless, Israel was willing to start discussions with the other Middle Eastern parties through the Finnish facilitator on terms of reference that would enable Israeli participation in the conference. Agreement was not concluded on these terms of reference and the conference hasn't

---

of the global pursuit of general and complete disarmament, and the establishment of regional and global arms control regimes, Israel suggests to all the countries of the region that a mutually verifiable zone, free of surface-to-surface missiles and of chemical, biological and nuclear weapons be constructed. . . .", Address by Foreign Minister Peres at the Signing Ceremony of the Chemical Weapons Convention Treaty, Paris, January 13, 1993, http://mfa.gov.il/MFA/ForeignPolicy/MFADocuments /Yearbook9/Pages/51%20Address%20by%20Foreign%20Minister%20Peres%20at %20the%20Signin.aspx.

yet convened. This reflects, to a great extent, Israeli reluctance to begin concrete talks on establishment of a Middle Eastern WMD-free zone, including its nuclear component.

Other nuclear programs in the Middle East and their implications

The Middle East is a region in which states that are formally adherents to the NPT tend not to comply with the treaty but rather develop secret programs aimed at developing nuclear weapons. Best known are Iraq and Libya for trying to produce nuclear weapons based on the assistance of Pakistani scientist A. Q. Khan. Syria started to build a plutonium production reactor with the help of North Korea. Iran is suspected of having a nuclear program with military objectives and is currently the main subject of concern for Israel in the nuclear domain. Naturally, Israelis have to be engaged with questions pertaining to the best way Israel should deal with this threat. The approach adopted by Israel is a counter-proliferation approach, sometimes called the Begin Doctrine (after Prime Minister Menachem Begin's decision to bomb the Iraqi nuclear reactor). It is based on efforts to foil these nuclear programs by diplomatic pressure and by covert and military operations. Nevertheless, Israel has to take into account that eventually this doctrine will fail and Israel will have to deal with Muslim/Arab nuclear states in the Middle East.

A nuclear-armed Iran will have far-reaching implications, not only because of the direct threat to Israel of nuclear weapons held by Iran and the way they will influence Iran's behavior, but also because of the wider implications on the global nuclear nonproliferation regime and on further nuclear proliferation in the region.

Three alternative responses will have to be considered: moving to an open nuclear posture, continuing with the nuclear opacity policy, or embarking on a disarmament path, with consideration of concrete steps for the establishment of a Middle Eastern WMD-free zone.

The first alternative is based on belief in the credibility of nuclear deterrence vis-à-vis other nuclear powers. Many Israelis believe the model of mutually assured destruction that proved successful during the Cold War is relevant also for the Middle East. However, there are lingering doubts. An Iranian leadership guided by radical Islamic ideology might be willing to make sacrifices and pay higher costs to achieve a religious goal such as eradicating the heretical Zionist implant in the Muslim Middle East. Further nuclear proliferation might take place in the Middle East following Iran's acquisition of nuclear weapons. A balance of deterrence in a multi-nuclear environment is inherently less credible and more unstable because of the high probability of miscalculations and mistakes. Also, efforts to retain credible mutual deterrence might lead to an unrestrained arms race which the Middle East can ill afford. It would be difficult for a state like Israel with a very small territory (sometimes called a one-bomb state) to adopt a doctrine based on minimal sufficiency of its nuclear arsenal. Worst-case scenario considerations might lead to a wish to have a large and versatile arsenal.

Israelis are beginning to debate whether Israel will have to consider moving to an open nuclear posture and give up its nuclear opacity policy when Iran becomes a nuclear power.[15] Students of nuclear deterrence theory argue that for a credible nuclear deterrence the party that should be deterred should be convinced that the other party has a credible nuclear deterrent. Therefore, the state that wants to have credible deterrence should expose is nuclear capability. That will not be possible as long as Israel continues with its nuclear opacity. However, the Israeli experience to some extent disproves this proposition. In spite of Israel's nuclear opacity so far, nobody in the Middle East or elsewhere seems to doubt the credibility of Israel's nuclear deterrence. This debate may soon become moot. Once Iran or another Middle Eastern party acquires nuclear capabilities, Israel will have to demonstrate its second-strike capability. The

---

15. Ephraim Kam, "A Nuclear Iran: Analysis and Implications," Memorandum no. 87 (Tel Aviv: Institute for National Security Studies, 2007), 70 (in Hebrew).

Israeli decision will depend to some extent on Iran's choice of nuclear policies. Iran may choose to emulate Israel and adopt its own version of nuclear opacity, hoping that will help it deal with the repercussions of its breakout to a nuclear posture. In that case, Israel might also choose to stay with nuclear opacity. However, this could increase the risks of miscalculation because it will be more difficult to establish credible communication channels between two nations that deny they have nuclear capabilities.

Embarking on the path of disarmament and establishment of a WMD-free zone in the Middle East may seem a way of responding to all these problems. However, Israelis see a number of roadblocks to adoption of this option. The first one pertains to the validity of the basic assumptions on which this idea is based. One assumption is that the regional parties perceive existential threats originating only from the other regional parties; therefore, when this zone is established, they can assume no existential threats will be posed to them. That may be true for Israel. But reality in most of the Middle East is different. Iran, for example, perceives the United States as its main existential threat, and the US threat is one of its main motivations for acquiring nuclear capabilities. The Iranians have watched the West's attempts at regime change by force, first in Iraq by a Western coalition invasion in 2003 and then in Libya by a NATO military intervention in 2012. It's no surprise that the leaders of the Islamic regime in Iran believe they need nuclear weapons to deter the United States, and the West in general. The Libyan case is especially significant. A few years earlier, Moammar Gadhafi had concluded an agreement with the United States and the United Kingdom calling for Libya to rid itself of its WMD and its nuclear program, in return for guarantees for the survival of the regime. But that only made Gadhafi easy prey when the West sensed an opportunity for a regime change in Libya. The West's claims that intervention was motivated only by humanitarian considerations are falling on deaf ears in the Middle East. Iranians and others there are also looking at the difference between the world's, and specifically the West's, approach to Iraq and Libya, on the one hand, and to North Korea on the other. The obvious conclusion is that the main reason for the different approach is the concern that North Korea might use its nuclear weapons if the regime faced an existential threat.

The other problematic assumption is that the only motivation for building nuclear capabilities is the perception of threat. In the Middle East, prestige and the ability to acquire influence by projection of power also play major roles. Those may be additional motivations for the Iranian nuclear program. These doubts are leading Israel to suspect that even if Israel disarmed, parties such as Iran might not give up their nuclear programs. These parties also have a record of noncompliance with agreements they have signed, so what would be the guarantee that these states would not also cheat on the WMD-free-zone agreement? It is also much easier for these states to cheat because of the nature of their regimes and because their large territories offer more possibilities for concealing their programs. It would be much easier to monitor the small territory of Israel.

As mentioned earlier, Israel's original motivation for building a nuclear option was to deal with existential threats posed by Arab conventional forces and WMD. Therefore, Israel sees a strong connection between the general security layout of the Middle East and the feasibility of establishing a WMD-free zone. The two most important elements are the nature of the political environment and the availability of cooperative security arrangements. Israel believes that only when comprehensive peace is established in the Middle East and Israel is accepted as a legitimate state, recognized by all, will it be possible to consider the WMD-free zone. Israel also thinks that the WMD-free zone should be one element of a more comprehensive cooperative security regime that will also deal with other threats. The feasibility of the WMD-free zone is dependent also on the ability to establish this kind of security regime. It does not seem that Israel will be willing to start discussions of the WMD-free zone separately from the wider discussion of comprehensive peace and a regional security regime. Israel also believes that discussions and resolution of these matters should precede, and be a condition for, a useful and concrete discussion of a WMD-free zone.

The last attempt to have this kind of discussion took place during the 1990s when the Arms Control and Regional Security group established in the framework of the Madrid Process negotiated arms control in parallel with regional security arrangements. The talks stalled when it became evident that the Arab parties, led by Egypt, were not willing to consider regional security arrangements as long as Israel wasn't committed to adhering to the NPT. Further attempts were made to develop these concepts in unofficial Track II initiatives organized by different groups, but none of them matured to become a policy supported by governments in the Middle East.

Conclusions

The path to nuclear disarmament in the Middle East is long and filled with an abundance of obstacles. States in the Middle East believe in the utility of nuclear deterrence as a tool that can safeguard national survival, whether the survival of the nation-state (the Israeli case) or the survival of the regime (the Iranian case). Regimes in the Middle East tend often not to distinguish between the survival of the nation-state and the survival of the regime. From their point of view, the state and the regime are one. The issue is becoming more complicated because states tend to attribute additional uses to nuclear weapons beyond deterrence. In their perception it is an instrument of prestige and influence.

There was a window of opportunity in the 1990s for discussion of nuclear disarmament in the Middle East in the context of a wider discussion of WMD disarmament and cooperative security arrangements. But this window of opportunity closed—first, because of the collapse of the Israeli-Arab peace process, and later, in recent years, because of growing instability and disarray in the Middle East. In many cases it is difficult even to determine who is representing these Middle Eastern states. States focused on domestic conflicts and chaos find it difficult to allocate attention to arms control arrangements that seem more like pie in the sky than like something useful and relevant to their major concerns. That explains why developments that in the past were considered improbable—like Syria's disarmament of chemical weapons—are received with general apathy, rather than being seen as a first step that might enable a wider discussion of WMD disarmament in the Middle East.

Israel, the only perceived nuclear power in the region, also has difficulties in giving any attention to the subject of nuclear disarmament when it is facing an unstable, continuously changing environment. The international community did not succeed in developing sufficient incentives for Israel to pay more attention to this subject, perhaps because other important actors in the international community do not think that it is so important and so urgent in the current environment. Until the international attitude changes, it's unlikely that the Middle East, with all its troubles, will play a pioneering role in this area. The opposite is to be expected.

Israel would probably support the idea of establishing a joint enterprise process to create the conditions for a world without nuclear weapons, which means working on a new security environment for all. However, from Israel's point of view, more thinking should be invested on the construction of the forum that should engage in this process, namely the states that should be participating in this enterprise. Israel would probably not like a situation in which all the onus for creating the new security environment is put on the nuclear states while other states, including states with nuclear ambitions that play a major role in regional security environments, do not play any role. That is the main issue for Israel. States like Israel are less concerned about the global security environment and more concerned about their regional security environment. So it will be necessary to develop within this enterprise process a framework that combines this global joint enterprise process with parallel regional processes, if Israel's participation is sought.

In the meantime, the best action seems to be a focus on expanding the intellectual and political community in the Middle East that is familiar with this subject, thereby developing an infrastructure that will facilitate progress in the future when the political environment improves.

CHAPTER 8 **Proliferation and Deterrence beyond the Nuclear Tipping Point in the Middle East**

Karim Haggag

At first glance, the Middle East does not seem to present a formidable obstacle toward global nuclear disarmament. The region's sole nuclear power, Israel, does not face a peer competitor that would engender the kind of nuclear competition that is evident in, for example, South Asia between India and Pakistan. Nor does the Middle East figure in the context of the global nuclear competition between the United States and Russia, or the global nuclear balance between the five recognized nuclear-weapon states. The nuclear question in the Middle East seems to play out solely within a regional context.

Moreover, nuclear weapons have not figured prominently in the defense policies or military strategy of the major powers vis-à-vis the region, including the United States, which has only intermittently resorted to nuclear threats to deter its adversaries. Similarly, the United States does not depend on its nuclear arsenal to underpin its long-standing alliance

Karim Haggag is a career Egyptian diplomat. The views contained in this chapter are his own and do not represent the position of the Egyptian Foreign Ministry or the Government of Egypt.

commitments in the region, relying instead on a robust conventional deterrent capability through its extensive military deployments in the Mediterranean and the Persian Gulf.

Thus, whatever obstacles the region presents in the context of global nuclear disarmament, they apparently pale in comparison to the complexities entailed in reaching the end state of a world without nuclear weapons. These complexities include negotiating phased mutual nuclear drawdowns between the United States and Russia, bringing the middle nuclear powers (France, Britain, and China) into this process, and calibrating the military balance at the conventional level in various regional settings commensurate with the security requirements of those countries that will give up their nuclear arsenals.

In short, the nuclear question in the Middle East operates in a much less complex regional setting. This reality would seemingly present a less challenging set of circumstances to overcome in order to realize the vision of global nuclear disarmament enunciated by George Shultz, William Perry, Henry Kissinger, and Sam Nunn.[1] The "joint enterprise" they propose includes a series of "agreed and urgent steps that would lay the groundwork for a world free of nuclear weapons." Much of the steps envisioned in this agenda are understandably focused on the global level of nuclear disarmament: enhancing and accelerating the US-Russia nuclear disarmament process; relaxing the alert status of nuclear weapons; bolstering the global nuclear security regime; discarding the strategy of Mutual Assured Destruction (MAD) while lessening the reliance on nuclear deterrence as a basis for security; and bringing into force the Comprehensive Test Ban Treaty (CTBT).

Elements of this agenda can be developed and adapted to various regional settings by strengthening the Nuclear Nonproliferation Treaty (NPT); devising a system of international control for the nuclear

---

1. This vision was articulated in a series of essays published in the *Wall Street Journal*. These are made available by the Nuclear Threat Initiative at http://www.nti.org/media /pdfs/NSP_op-eds_final_.pdf?_=1360883065.

fuel cycle; creating a system for the management of spent nuclear fuel; and ameliorating regional conflicts in order to foster a more benign security environment and the creation of nuclear-weapon-free zones.

Tailored to the Middle East context, this agenda can be utilized to institute an interim regime of nuclear control to govern all aspects of the nuclear fuel cycle for all states that possess nuclear facilities. An emphasis on nuclear transparency can eventually develop into an effort to decrease and eventually eliminate regional stocks of fissile material. Similarly, a renewed focus on strengthening the NPT can be coupled with a drive toward realizing its universality, along with an effort to encourage Middle East states to join or ratify the other major international treaty regimes: the CTBT, Chemical Weapons Convention (CWC) and Biological and Toxin Weapons Convention (BTWC). These measures could underpin a regional process that would realize the long-standing objective of creating a nuclear-weapon-free zone in the Middle East and the more ambitious aim of a zone free of weapons of mass destruction.

However, a closer look at the nuclear issue in the Middle East reveals that the region is likely to present serious challenges to this vision. The Middle East stands apart as one of the few regions not to have benefited from a viable disarmament or arms control process at the conventional or unconventional level. In the absence of such a negotiated process, the Middle East has witnessed a creeping proliferation of weapons of mass destruction that is beginning to alter the nuclear status quo in the region. As a result, the nuclear order in the Middle East is now in flux, approaching what Shultz, Kissinger, Perry, and Nunn referred to as the tipping point where nuclear proliferation will contribute to bringing about "a new nuclear era that will be more precarious, psychologically disorienting, and economically even more costly than was Cold War deterrence." Unless this trend is checked and ultimately reversed, the ramifications are likely to be profound, affecting the context that has governed the operation of nuclear deterrence in the region and possibly presenting an insurmountable obstacle to the objective of a world without nuclear weapons.

The Nuclear Question in the Middle East

At the heart of the nuclear question in the Middle East is Israel. As the region's sole nuclear-weapon state, Israel presents a truly unique case in the annals of nuclear proliferation in terms of its pathway to nuclear weapons acquisition, its posture of nuclear opacity, and its highly conditional approach to nuclear arms control and disarmament.

Unlike Pakistan, which pursued a nuclear capability through incremental steps largely in response to India's nuclear development, Israel's drive toward nuclear weapons acquisition exhibited a sustained effort from the very inception of its nuclear program dating back to the first decade after its independence, during which it did not face any nuclear adversary. Similarly, whereas India set out to develop an extensive nuclear infrastructure that was designed to support its ambitious plans for civil nuclear power and eventually a military nuclear capability, Israel's nuclear program was narrow in focus, dedicated solely to the purpose of providing a military nuclear deterrent.[2]

The contrast becomes even more apparent when considering how each state chose to incorporate nuclear weapons into its national military capability. Unlike India and Pakistan, which integrated nuclear weapons into their military force structures, Israel followed a distinctly different model regarding the role of nuclear weapons within its overall military strategy. As far as can be discerned, a decision on the part of Israel's leadership to separate nuclear weapons from its military force structure meant that the Israel Defense Force (IDF) would operate solely as a conventional military force. Despite the fact that Israel did indeed weaponize its nuclear capability after 1967, the IDF was not assigned a nuclear mission, and consequently did not elevate its military doctrine to the nuclear level.[3]

---

2. Avner Cohen, *The Worst-Kept Secret: Israel's Bargain with the Bomb* (New York: Columbia University Press, 2012), 250.

3. Ibid., 67.

Important as these differences are, the feature that truly sets Israel apart in terms of its nuclear approach is its doctrine of nuclear opacity. This posture rests on the twin pillars of official non-acknowledgment of nuclear weapons possession, while at the same time conveying the perception, now universally accepted, that Israel is indeed a nuclear-weapon state.[4] Adopting such a posture required Israel to refrain from conducting nuclear tests as a means of declaring its nuclear capability, as did the other nuclear-weapon states. It also required ensuring that the nuclear program would remain shrouded in layers of secrecy both at the official level and in the realm of public debate. While the issue of nuclear weapons is subjected to various levels of oversight and public scrutiny in all of the other nuclear-weapon states (with the exception of North Korea, given the nature of the regime), in Israel it remains insulated from any form of public discussion.

Opacity emerged as an ad hoc response to deal with the competing pressures facing Israel as it embarked on the path toward acquiring a nuclear weapons capability. Under pressure from the Kennedy and Johnson administrations to submit to inspections of its nuclear facility at Dimona, and forced to respond to the emerging NPT regime just as its nuclear program was approaching the threshold of nuclear weapons acquisition, Israel opted for a posture of ambiguity entailing neither confirmation nor denial of its nuclear capability. This position was subsequently articulated in the form of a formal pledge not to be the first to introduce nuclear weapons in the Middle East, a pledge that stands to this day. Yet the posture of opacity was not simply intended as a means of diplomatic obfuscation to deflect external pressure. In essence, opacity was Israel's response to the strategic dilemma posed by nuclear weapon possession. While seeking to demonstrate resolve in developing a nuclear weapons capability, Israel's leadership was also cognizant that this would entail the risk of triggering reactions from regional states to develop a similar

---

4. Avner Cohen, *Israel and the Bomb* (New York: Columbia University Press, 1998), 1–2.

capability. Should Israel's reliance on an overt nuclear weapons capability result in a regional nuclear arms race, the prospect of a nuclearized Middle East would confront it with precisely the type of existential threat that its nuclear capability was intended to avert. Opacity thus enabled Israel to avoid this predicament, or at the very least forestall its consequences, by maintaining what Israeli historian Avner Cohen describes as a "nearly impossible and uniquely creative response to its nuclear dilemma."[5]

Israeli analysts generally characterize Israel's nuclear policy as an unqualified strategic success. Proponents of this view claim that its nuclear deterrent has not only shielded Israel from threats to its existence over the course of the last half century, but has also exerted a discernible political effect on its adversaries by limiting Arab war aims against Israel and eventually drawing key Arab states into relationships of peace after abandoning the long-held strategic goal of bringing about Israel's destruction. Furthermore, Israel's posture of nuclear opacity has met with similar success. It has enabled the United States to provide diplomatic cover for Israel's nuclear program while shielding it from international pressure to join the global nuclear non-proliferation regime. Similarly, the concern that Israel's nuclear capability would trigger a regional nuclear arms race has thus far not been realized.

However, the benefits accrued to Israel from its possession of nuclear weapons are highly questionable. Israel's nuclear arsenal has not afforded it the measure of strategic deterrence that it was intended to provide. Furthermore, its policy of opacity has lead Israel to adopt a highly obstructive policy toward global and regional arms control. As a consequence, the Middle East remains one of the few regions without the benefit of any form of arms control process, a reality that leaves the region vulnerable to further proliferation and the possible emergence of a nuclear competitor, thus prompting the very strategic threat to Israel's security that its nuclear weapons were designed to forestall. More importantly, nuclear weapons

---

5.   Cohen, *Worst-Kept Secret,* xxxiii.

have proven to be irrelevant with respect to the cumulative threats Israel faces resulting from the absence of an overall settlement of the Arab-Israeli conflict and a viable two-state solution to the Palestinian question.

The Superfluous Quality of Nuclear Deterrence in the Middle East

The Middle East has a poor record of weapons of mass destruction providing deterrence for their possessors, despite the proliferation of every class of WMD in the region over the course of the last half-century. Iraq's possession of chemical and biological weapons (CBW) did not deter Iranian incursions during the eight-year Iran-Iraq war, the US-led coalition against Iraq in 1991, or the US invasion and overthrow of the Iraqi regime in 2003. Similarly, Syria's arsenal of chemical weapons, believed to be the world's largest,[6] failed to prevent the near complete destruction of the Syrian air force by Israel during the 1982 Lebanon war or to deter the Israeli air strike against its suspected nuclear site in 2007, or to prevent the threat of military force by the Obama administration in the summer of 2013 in response to the reported use of chemical weapons by the Syrian regime against the Syrian opposition.

Yet Israel stands out as the clearest example in this regard with the failure of its nuclear deterrent. There is little to substantiate the argument that credits Israel's nuclear weapons with deterring a full-scale military attack by a pan-Arab war coalition. Similarly, the assumption that attributes the diminished scope of Arab war aims to Israel's nuclear deterrence also rests on dubious evidence. Such claims gain a semblance of credibility only when made at a level of generality that is divorced from a close examination of the available evidence regarding the context of decision-making on both the Arab and Israeli side during times of crisis. In fact, an objective assessment of the relevance of Israel's nuclear capability

---

6. Following US and Russian destruction of their chemical weapons stockpiles in accordance with their obligations under the Chemical Weapons Convention, Syria's chemical weapons arsenal was believed to have been the largest in the world.

in those conflicts in which nuclear deterrence was supposedly a factor presents a picture that is at best mixed.

The 1967 war provides the first case of deterrence failure. It was during the May–June crisis of 1967 that led to the outbreak of war that Israel supposedly crossed the nuclear threshold by producing at least two crude nuclear devices.[7] There is no information to indicate whether Israel decided to communicate such a capability to Egypt's leadership on the eve of the war.[8] However, it is safe to assume that the Arab side was aware of the fact that Israel possessed some sort of nuclear capability given that the existence of the Dimona reactor was by then well-known. Whatever the state of knowledge regarding Israel's nuclear capability on the Arab side at the time, there can be little doubt that Egypt was not deterred from violating Israel's declared casus belli by closing the Straits of Tiran and expelling the United Nations Emergency Force from the Sinai. Israel's nascent nuclear capability thus failed to deter what Israel's political and military leadership clearly perceived to be an existential military threat.[9]

The 1973 war constituted the most severe test for Israel's nuclear deterrence. Proponents of Israel's nuclear policy refer to the limited scope of Egypt's war aims as a clear example of the efficacy of Israel's nuclear deterrent, which prompted Egypt's leadership to opt for a military plan to recapture a portion of the Israeli-occupied Sinai Peninsula rather than a full-scale assault on Israel proper. However, there is no evidence to

---

7. Cohen states that "by May of 1967, Israel was a nuclear weapon state." *Israel and the Bomb*, 275.

8. Zeev Maoz states, "It seems implausible that Israel's decision to arm its nuclear weapons during the crisis would not have been accompanied by a—possibly secret— threat to Nasser that an all-out Egyptian attack might provoke nuclear retaliation. Otherwise, arming nuclear weapons would have been meaningless." Zeev Maoz, "The Mixed Blessing of Israel's Nuclear Policy," *International Security* 28, no. 2 (Fall 2003): 53.

9. Ibid., 54. See also Yair Evron, *Israel's Nuclear Dilemma* (Ithaca, NY: Cornell University Press, 1994), 49–52; and Shlomo Aronson, "Israel's Nuclear Programme, the Six Day War and its Ramifications," *Israel Affairs* 63, no. 3–4 (2000): 83–95.

indicate that Israel's nuclear capability was factored into either Egyptian or Syrian military planning or decision-making before or during the war. That the military objectives of the Arab parties were limited in nature was not due to any discernible effect of Israel's nuclear capability. Neither the memoirs of Egypt's political and military leaders at the time, nor the leading biography of the late Syrian leader Hafez al-Assad, nor the minutes of meetings of Egypt's National Security Council before the war, make any mention (or even implicit reference) to Israel's nuclear weapons as a factor in decision-making during the war.[10] Rather, the Arab military strategy was derived from the specific political goals of the war which, at least from the Egyptian side, focused on breaking the military stalemate in order to initiate a diplomatic process to regain those territories occupied by Israel during 1967.

More importantly, the assertion that Egypt's limited war aims reflect the success of Israel's nuclear policy, rather than the actual·failure of its nuclear deterrence, also clearly belies the assessment of Israel's senior leadership at the time. That the war was perceived in existential terms

---

10. All of the major Egyptian military leaders of the October 1973 war have written their memoirs, including Chief of Military Operations Field Marshal Mohamed Abdel Ghani El-Gamasy, Minister of Defense Field Marshal Ahmad Ismail, and Chief of Staff of the Egyptian Armed Forces Lt. Gen. Saad el-Din el Shazly. None of them remotely make reference to Israel's nuclear capability anywhere in their memoirs. See *Musheer Al-Nasr* (Field Marshal of Victory, Memoirs of Ahmed Ismail), introduction by Magdy El-Gallad (Cairo: Nahdet Misr Publishing, 2013) (in Arabic); Lt. General Saad el Shazly, *The Crossing of the Suez* (San Francisco: American Mideast Research, 1980); Mohamed Abdel Ghani El-Gamasy, *The October War: Memoirs of Field Marshal El-Gamasy of Egypt* (Cairo: American University in Cairo Press, 1993). In his book on the October war, Muhammad Hasanayn Haykal has compiled the major documents relating to Egypt's military planning for the war, including the minutes of the meetings of the Egyptian National Security Council, diplomatic cables, and correspondence between President Anwar Sadat and Syrian President Hafez Assad, none of which reveal any mention of Israel's nuclear weapons. See Muhammad Hasanayn Haykal, *October 73: al-Silah wa al-Siyassah* (Arms and Politics) (Cairo: al-Ahram Foundation, 1993) (in Arabic). Similarly, the major biography of Hafez Assad by Patrick Seale does not feature any reference to the nuclear issue: Patrick Seale, *Asad: The Struggle for the Middle East* (Berkeley, CA: University of California Press, 1990).

is best exemplified by then defense minister Moshe Dayan, who spoke of Israel being on the brink of "destruction of the Third Temple" in reference to the potential destruction of the state of Israel itself.[11] As Israel suffered severe losses on both the Syrian and Egyptian fronts, with both Arab armies approaching the borders of Israel proper, the war proved to be precisely the type of existential threat that Israel's nuclear weapons were intended to deter.

It was in this context that Israel supposedly ordered a "nuclear alert" during the first week of the war in order to ready its nuclear weapons for possible delivery by way of its Jericho missiles. The available information, although sparse, also indicates that this was done in conjunction with a request by Dayan that Prime Minister Golda Meir authorize preparations for a "demonstration" of Israel's nuclear capability, presumably in the form of a high-altitude nuclear test.[12] The authors of the most authoritative study on the nuclear dimension of the 1973 war state that this suggestion was rejected outright by Meir with the support of others in the Israeli war cabinet.[13] The reasons cited for this refusal were primarily political rather than military. A demonstration of Israel's nuclear capability would have constituted a clear violation of Israel's non-introduction pledge and would have eroded the diplomatic cover Israel had thus far enjoyed from

---

11. This quote from Moshe Dayan has been referenced widely in the literature on the 1973 war. Forty years after the war, the Israeli government released transcripts of recordings of Israel's military leadership which show how Israel's military commanders reacted to Dayan's pessimistic assessment. See "Destruction of the Third Temple? I don't accept that," *Israel Hayom,* September 11, 2013, http://www.israelhayom.com/site/newsletter_article.php?id=11915.

12. See Avner Cohen "How Nuclear Was It? New Testimony on the 1973 Yom Kippur War," *Arms Control Wonk* (blog), October 21, 2013, http://lewis.armscontrolwonk .com/archive/6909/israel-nuclear-weapons-and-the-1973-yom-kippur-war. Cohen was also one of the lead authors in what is perhaps the most authoritative study on this subject: Elbridge Colby, Avner Cohen, William McCants, Bradley Morris, and William Rosenau, "The Israeli Nuclear Alert of 1973: Deterrence and Signaling in Crisis," Center for Naval Analysis, April 2013.

13. Colby et al., "The Israeli Nuclear Alert of 1973," 43–44.

the United States, a development that would in all likelihood have led to international pressure for Israel's nuclear disarmament.[14] In other words, the reasons attributed to Israel's decision not to conduct a demonstration of its nuclear capability—even in the darkest hour of the war—were anchored in an overwhelming reluctance not to abandon its posture of nuclear opacity. As for the alleged nuclear alert ordered by Israel, the authors conclude that it was not intended as a form of signaling to deter either the Arab states or the Soviet Union, but rather was undertaken as a precautionary measure at the height of the war.[15]

This leads to a rather stark conclusion regarding the nuclear dimension of the 1973 war: it was largely irrelevant. The outbreak of the war constituted a massive failure of Israeli nuclear deterrence. Furthermore, whatever military or symbolic value Israel could have derived from its nuclear weapons during the war was outweighed by political considerations that constrained Israeli decision-making regarding any overt demonstration of its nuclear capability.

The 1991 Gulf War provides another milestone by which to assess the efficacy of Israel's nuclear deterrent. The military dimension of the war unfolded within a unique political context that previaled during the conflict. Saddam Hussein sought to attack Israel with the explicit purpose of eliciting an Israeli military response in order to disrupt the broad international and Arab coalition arrayed against him. In other words, not only was Iraq undeterred by Israel's nuclear capability, it specifically sought to invite the consequences of Israel's deterrence failure.

The prevailing Israeli assessment on the eve of the war was that given the "irrational" and "suicidal" quality of Saddam's psyche, there was indeed a high probability that Iraq would follow through on its threat of targeting Israel militarily.[16] Moreover, recognition of the seriousness of

---

14. Ibid., 44–45.

15. Ibid., 46.

16. Gerald Steinberg, "Parameters of Stable Deterrence in a Proliferated Middle East: Lessons from the 1991 Gulf War," *Nonproliferation Review*, Fall/Winter 2000: 50.

the threat posed by Iraq's medium-range ballistic missiles and its significant CBW capability had prompted numerous Israeli public threats of
retaliation in the years leading up to the war. In 1988, then defense minister Yitzhak Rabin threatened to retaliate ten-fold should Iraq target Israel
with chemical weapons.[17] There is also evidence that Israel issued an
explicit warning to Iraq on the eve of the war via Jordan's King Hussein,
whereby it threatened to reduce Iraqi cities to ashes if unconventional
weapons, specifically chemical warheads, were used by Iraq.[18]

Iraq's missile strikes against Israel marked the first time that Israeli cities
were subjected to Arab attacks since the first Arab-Israeli war in 1948.
Although the inaccurate Iraqi Scuds failed to result in civilian casualties,
Israeli analysts acknowledge that this represented a clear failure of Israeli
deterrence. However, whether Israeli threats of massive retaliation successfully deterred Iraq from employing chemical weapons against Israel
remains an open question. Yet this clearly belies the prevailing assessment
in Israel at the time of the war. As stated by political scientist Zeev Maoz,
"At the time . . . nobody [in Israel] knew when or where the next missile
would hit, its payload, or its destructive potential." The question arises
as to whether Israel would have followed through on its implicit threat
to use nuclear weapons against Iraq if the latter had employed chemical
warheads. No doubt there would be internal pressure on Israel's leaders
to do so. However, there would also be grounds for restraint. An Israeli
nuclear strike against Iraq would have constituted a massively disproportionate response, especially if the casualties from Iraq's chemical attacks
were minimal. It would have also elevated the military dimension of the

17. Ibid., 52.

18. Israeli historian Avi Shlaim recounts in his biography of King Hussein that during
a secret Israeli-Jordanian meeting at Hussein's private residence in the English
countryside prior to the war, then deputy chief of staff of the IDF Ehud Barak
explained that ". . . we were gassed once . . . and that we are not going to be gassed
again." He added, "If one single chemical warhead falls on Israel . . . look at your
watch and forty minutes later an Iraqi city will be reduced to ashes." Avi Shlaim,
Lion of Jordan: The Life of King Hussein in War and Peace (New York: Alfred Knopf,
2008), 508.

Arab-Israeli conflict to the unconventional level with serious long-term implications for Israeli security. It is likely, or at the very least conceivable, that Israel's decision-makers would have factored in the potential military and regional response to a nuclear strike and concluded that the high costs entailed in such a response far outweighed the minimal benefits. It was precisely this dilemma that Israel's leadership grappled with at the height of the 1973 war.

Moreover, the claim that Israel's nuclear deterrence dissuaded Iraq from employing chemical weapons during the war rests on thin evidence.[19] The overall military and political context of the war suggests that the decision not to employ chemical weapons in the conflict was due to other factors, primarily the unreliability of Iraq's chemical weapons arsenal in producing mass casualties as was Saddam's intent and, more importantly, the deterrent effect of US retaliatory threats against Iraq should it resort to unconventional weapons.[20] Yet the more pertinent explanation probably lies in a completely different assessment of Iraqi strategy with regards to the employment of its unconventional weapons. A close examination of Iraqi documents captured after the US invasion in 2003 reveals that the primary purpose of Iraqi CBW was defensive rather than offensive.[21] Rather than Israel deterring Saddam from launching chemical strikes at Israeli cities, perhaps it is more appropriate to think of Iraq's acquisition

19. For analyses that credit Israel's nuclear deterrence with dissuading Iraq from using chemical weapons against Israel, see Steinberg, "Parameters of Stable Deterrence," and Amatzia Baram, "Israeli Deterrence, Iraqi Responses," *Orbis* 36, no. 3 (Summer 1992): 385–403.

20. Zeev Maoz offers the best counterargument to the claim that Israel's nuclear deterrence prevented Iraq from employing its chemical warheads. See Zeev Maoz, *Defending the Holy Land: A Critical Analysis of Israel's Security & Foreign Policy* (Ann Arbor, MI: University of Michigan Press, 2009), 322–325. See also Evron, *Israel's Nuclear Dilemma,* 209–214.

21. Conversations between Saddam and his commanders revealed that only extraordinary circumstances—such as an attack on Baghdad or an unconventional strike by either Israel or the United States—would trigger the use of such weapons. See Avner Golov, "Deterrence in the Gulf War: Evaluating New Evidence," *Nonproliferation Review* 20, no. 3 (2013): 453–472.

of CBW as part of an effort to establish a deterrent relationship vis-à-vis both Israel and the United States.

In all three cases mentioned here—the 1967 war, the 1973 war, and the 1991 Gulf War—Israel's concept of nuclear deterrence was put to the test in situations of actual military conflict. What emerges from this survey is an assessment that casts serious doubt on the deterrent value of Israel's nuclear capability and, more broadly, on the degree to which nuclear weapons have contributed in any tangible way to Israel's overall security.

The logical conclusion from this assessment is aptly stated by Cohen: "It appears that each war made it clearer how almost impossible it is that Israel could find itself in circumstances that would compel it to resort to nuclear weapons. All of these events revealed that, short of a direct nuclear attack, it is *almost* inconceivable that Israel would use nuclear weapons to defend itself against existential threats."[22]

Yet perhaps the most salient point in assessing the current utility of Israel's nuclear deterrent is the transformation of Israel's regional strategic environment since it became a nuclear-weapon state. The peace treaties with both Egypt and Jordan, the unanimous adoption of the Arab Peace Initiative by all members of the Arab League which offered full peace and normalization in return for Israel's complete withdrawal from occupied Arab territories, and the conventional military superiority of the IDF in both qualitative and quantitative terms over its neighbors have all rendered the initial scenarios for possible nuclear use implausible, if not completely unrealistic. Israeli politicians have often attributed much of this benign transformation, especially the Arab readiness to make peace, to the political utility of nuclear weapons in altering the Arab strategic calculus regarding Israel. Israeli leader Shimon Peres, one of the key architects of Israel's nuclear program, best captured this view when he

---

22. Avner Cohen, "Israel: A Sui Generis Proliferator," in *The Long Shadow: Nuclear Weapons and Security in 21st Century Asia,* ed. Muthiah Alagappa (Stanford, CA: Stanford University Press, 2008), 253 [emphasis in original].

stated that Israel "built the nuclear option not to have a Hiroshima but an Oslo."[23] The reality, however, is that Israel's nuclear capability has been irrelevant to the vicissitudes of Arab-Israeli diplomacy, which trace their origins to long before Israel's acquisition of nuclear weapons.[24] The Arab position toward Israel is, in essence, based on Israel's readiness to end its occupation of Arab territories, not on Israel's nuclear status.

Proliferation in the Absence of Regional Arms Control

Given the extent of the transformation in Israel's strategic environment, the logical consequence in terms of Israel's overall security policy would be a reassessment of its nuclear strategy that would lead to a gradual decoupling of nuclear weapons from Israel's strategic posture. This, of course, has not happened. To the contrary, the link between Israel's nuclear weapons and its security strategy has only been strengthened.

Why then has Israel maintained this posture in the face of such a profound transformation in the military balance and overall threat environment in its favor, as well as the dubious efficacy of its nuclear deterrent? The answer likely resides in what can be described as Israel's quest to maintain a situation of absolute security. It was this impulse that prompted the late Israeli Prime Minister Menachem Begin to articulate the doctrine that now bears his name by declaring, "Under no circumstances would we allow the enemy to develop weapons of mass destruction against our nation. We will defend Israel's citizens, in time, with all the means at our disposal."[25] Begin's announcement was made two days after Israel had successfully bombed Iraq's Osiraq reactor on June 9, 1981, and constituted, in essence, a policy of preemptive counter-proliferation against

---

23. Quoted in the *Jerusalem Post,* July 14, 1998.

24. The history of the secret Arab-Israeli negotiations conducted during the 1950s is chronicled by Itamar Rabinovich, *The Road Not Taken: Early Arab-Israeli Negotiations* (New York: Oxford University Press, 1991).

25. Cited in Shai Feldman, "The Bombing of Osiraq—Revisited," *International Security* 7, no. 2 (Fall 1982): 122.

adversary WMD capabilities, especially nuclear programs. Since then, Israel has applied this policy at least once in September 2007 to destroy Syria's nascent nuclear reactor at al-Kibar, and has repeatedly threatened, implicitly in Israeli official statements and explicitly through leaks to the media, to apply the same measure to destroy Iran's nuclear program.[26] By acting to preserve its regional nuclear monopoly, Israel in effect ensures that it will maintain escalation dominance in whatever future conflict might ensue with its adversaries.[27]

The diplomatic corollary of this strategy has been the formulation of an arms control policy designed to achieve the dual objectives of preserving Israel's posture of nuclear opacity and maintaining its military superiority in both conventional and unconventional weapons. Israel was the first country beyond the five declared nuclear powers to acquire a nuclear weapons capability, and the first to do so before the entry into force of the Non-Proliferation Treaty. A central purpose of opacity, therefore, was to keep Israel outside of the global nuclear nonproliferation regime. This objective entailed the adoption of a rejectionist policy toward the NPT, citing the treaty's inability to address Israel's "exceptional" security situation.[28] As a result, Israel has stood outside the global nuclear order not only with respect to its position not to join the NPT, but also by its refusal thus far to become a full member of any of the major nonproliferation

---

26. For an account of the developments leading up to the al-Kibar strike, see David Makovsky, "The Silent Strike: How Israel Bombed a Syrian Nuclear Installation and Kept it Secret," *The New Yorker,* September 17, 2012, 34–40.

27. The term "escalation dominance" was coined by Herman Kahn. See Herman Kahn, *On Escalation: Metaphors and Scenarios* (Baltimore: Penguin Books, 1968), 290. Paul Bracken uses the term to describe Israel's strategy in maintaining its nuclear monopoly in the Middle East. See Paul Bracken, *The Second Nuclear Age: Strategy, Danger, and the New Power Politics* (New York: Times Books, 2012), 138.

28. See Cohen, *Israel and the Bomb,* 293–322, for an overview of the historic evolution of Israel's position toward the NPT. For an analysis of Israel's contemporary posture toward the treaty, see Gerald Steinberg, "Examining Israel's NPT Exceptionality: 1998–2005," *Nonproliferation Review* 13, no. 1 (2006): 117–141.

treaty regimes.[29] Moreover, external pressure to bring Israel into global arms control negotiations has met with little success since, in the words of Marvin Miller and Lawrence Scheinman, "it is very difficult to discuss constraints on a weapons program that does not officially exist."[30] The exceptional difficulty of engaging Israel in the global arms control process was exemplified by the inability of the Clinton administration to bring Israel into the negotiations on a global Fissile Material Cut-off Treaty (FMCT). Israel's reluctance in this regard stemmed from the fact that the objectives of the treaty, especially with respect to its verification requirements, would undermine Israel's nuclear opacity.[31]

Israel's aversion to engage in arms control is not confined to the global level but extends to the regional context as well. Israel has always emphasized the primacy of regional considerations as a central tenet for any viable arms control process. However, this position has entailed a list of prerequisites that places any Israeli concessions in the form of tangible arms control commitments at the end of a long and drawn-out political process that is often referred to by observers as the long-corridor approach.[32] The milestones for this process entail the achievement of

---

29. Israel has not signed the Biological and Toxins Weapons Convention and has signed but not ratified the Comprehensive Test Ban Treaty and the Chemical Weapons Convention.

30. Marvin Miller and Lawrence Sheinman, "Israel, India, and Pakistan: Engaging the Non-NPT States in the Nonproliferation Regime," *Arms Control Today* 33, no. 10 (December 2003), https://www.armscontrol.org/act/2003_12 /MillerandScheinman.

31. For Israel's position on the FMCT, see Cohen, *The Worst Kept Secret*, 214–240; and Shlomo Ben-Ami, "Nuclear Weapons in the Middle East: The Israeli Perspective," paper presented at the September 2009 meeting in Cairo of the International Commission on Nuclear Non-proliferation and Disarmament, 12–14.

32. Avi Beker, "Israel's Long Corridor: Ambiguity and Nuclear Non-Proliferation," *Institute of the World Jewish Congress,* no. 7, 1995; and Avner Cohen and Patricia Lewis, "Israel and the NWFZ in the Middle East: Tiptoeing Down a 'Long Corridor,'" in *Arms Control and Missile Proliferation in the Middle East,* ed. Bernd W. Kubbig and Sven-Eric Fikenscher (London: Routledge, 2012).

comprehensive peace in the region, including normalization between Israel and its neighbors, confidence- and security-building measures involving all states in the Middle East, and the achievement of overall stability in the region. Furthermore, any regional arms control process should take into account Israel's special security requirements (such as the need to counterbalance potentially hostile coalitions of states) which require Israel to retain a distinct advantage in the overall balance of regional military forces, as well as maintain those security capabilities that offset its perceived strategic vulnerabilities.[33]

This approach is derived from a highly distinct conception of arms control at the core of which is a deep-seated skepticism that any such process can have a positive effect in ameliorating regional conflicts. According to the Israeli view, it is incumbent first to address the political basis of the conflict before engaging in any meaningful arms control, irrespective of the strategic military asymmetries in Israel's favor.[34] The Israeli approach thus rests on a gradual sequential process designed to limit the overall level of arms once the political conditions have been met, after which, according to former prime minister Ehud Barak, Israel would still be required to retain a strategic deterrent "for as long as necessary in

---

33. Shlomo Brom offers a succinct explication of Israel's position on arms control as articulated by Ambassador Eytan Bentsur, former director general of the Israeli Foreign Ministry. Shlomo Brom, "Israel's Perspective on the Global Elimination of Nuclear Weapons," in *Unblocking the Road to Zero: Pakistan and Israel,* ed. Barry Blechman (Washington, DC: The Stimson Center, 2009), 47–51. See also Shai Feldman, *Nuclear Weapons and Arms Control in the Middle East* (Cambridge, MA: MIT Press, 1997), 243–262.

34. This of course runs counter to the history of arms control between the superpowers during the Cold War. The gamut of agreements negotiated between the United States and the Soviet Union that stabilized the strategic competition between them—ABM, SALT, INF, START, and CFE, to name only a few—were all negotiated while the fundamental issues of the Cold War remained unresolved.

terms of geography and time."[35] At the end of the long corridor, Israel would remain the dominant military power in the region in terms of both conventional and unconventional weaponry.

Predicated on such a highly conditional approach, Israel's position has obstructed every major arms control endeavor for the Middle East. Although Israel accepts in principle the long-standing objective of establishing a nuclear-weapon-free zone in the Middle East, as proposed by Egypt and Iran since 1974, this acceptance is dependent on the prerequisite of reaching full peace and normalization between Israel and its neighbors. Similarly, when Egypt developed the zone proposal in 1991 following the Gulf War, calling for a zone free of all weapons of mass destruction in the Middle East, Israel's position was that such an objective cannot be realized, and negotiations toward its achievement cannot even be initiated, without a fundamental political transformation in the region.[36]

The objective of establishing a WMD-free zone was referenced in the 1991 UN Security Council Resolution 687 that ended the Gulf War in recognition of the threat posed by the proliferation of weapons of mass destruction in the region. More importantly, the zone proposal was enshrined in a special resolution adopted by the 1995 NPT Review and Extension as part of the package of measures that allowed for the indefinite extension of the treaty. Since then, efforts to institute a negotiating process to realize this objective have met with no success. The latest of these efforts, focused on convening a conference in Helsinki

---

35. *Haaretz,* October 5, 1999. Quoted in Ben-Ami, "Nuclear Weapons in the Middle East: The Israeli Perspective," 3.

36. The literature on the zone concept for the Middle East is voluminous. For an overview of the history of the proposals see Patricia Lewis, "All in the Timing: The Weapons of Mass Destruction Free Zone in the Middle East," Chatham House, Royal Institute of International Affairs, August 5, 2014; and Jozef Goldblat, "Nuclear-Weapon-Free Zones: A History and Assessment," *Nonproliferation Review,* Spring/Summer 1997: 18–32.

on the establishment of the zone as mandated by the 2010 NPT Review Conference (RevCon), floundered after the conference failed to convene by its original date in late 2012 due to Israel's refusal to attend and has therefore been postponed indefinitely.[37]

Israel's reservations toward the conference related to the fact that it was initiated within the NPT framework, to which it is not a party, rather than in a regional context that would address Israel's specific political and security concerns. But the more fundamental reason relates to Israel's distinct approach to arms control, which was inherently incompatible with the zone proposal. The objective of establishing a WMD-free zone is, in its essence, anchored firmly within a disarmament approach to addressing the proliferation problem in the region. In contrast, Israel's conception eschews disarmament, viewing it (correctly) as a means to diminish its strategic capabilities and eventually bring about its nuclear disarmament, in favor of a process that emphasizes political recognition, confidence- and security-building measures, and at best limited steps toward arms control.

This fundamental divergence in the basic underpinnings of arms control and disarmament was reflected most clearly in the Arms Control and Regional Security (ACRS) working group, one of the five working groups established as part of the Middle East peace process following the Madrid Peace Conference in 1991. The ACRS working group began its work in 1992 and constituted the only serious attempt at instituting a viable arms control process for the Middle East.[38] Israel's approach to

---

37. The 2010 NPT Review Conference mandated the convening of a conference in 2012 "to be attended by all states of the Middle East, on the establishment of a Middle East zone free of nuclear weapons and all other weapons of mass destruction, on the basis of arrangements freely arrived at by the states of the region, and with the full support and engagement of the nuclear-weapon states." NPT 2010 Final Document—Volume I, http://www.un.org/en/conf/npt/2010.

38. Ambassador Nabil Fahmy, who headed Egypt's delegation to the ACRS talks (and later Egypt's Foreign Ministry), best articulated the Egyptian perspective: see Nabil Fahmy, "Reflections on the Arms Control and Regional Security Process in the

ACRS prioritized an extensive confidence-building framework that would foster the necessary trust to enable the working group to address the hard security issues related to arms control. These issues, including the central question of nuclear arms control, would be deferred until an overall regional political settlement was achieved. This stood in marked contrast to Egypt's approach, which—while not opposed to a robust confidence-building agenda—argued that the ACRS process could not be sustained without a serious focus on arms control and disarmament in order to address the prevailing military and strategic imbalance in the Middle East. The suspension of the ACRS working group in 1995 came after three years in which Israel adamantly refused to engage in any such process. To quote Egypt's former Foreign Minister Nabil Fahmy who at the time headed Egypt's delegation to the ACRS working group, "In the end, it was not simply a deadlock over the nuclear issue that was behind the demise of ACRS, but the absence of any serious arms control or disarmament agenda for any class of weapons, conventional or unconventional."[39]

In short, Israel's distinct conception of arms control, based as it is on a highly conditional approach that defers any tangible commitments in this regard to an undefined political end state, has stood in the way of every major arms control proposal for the Middle East over the past four decades. Consequently, the Middle East remains among the few regions

---

Middle East," in *New Horizons and New Strategies in Arms Control,* ed. James Brown (Albuquerque, NM: Sandia National Laboratories, 1998). See also "Prospects for Arms Control and Proliferation in the Middle East," *Nonproliferation Review,* Summer 2001: 1–7; and "Special Comment" in *Disarmament Forum,* The Middle East, no. 2, 2001, United Nations Institute for Disarmament Research: 3–5. The Israeli perspective can be found in Emily Landau, "Egypt and Israel in ACRS: Bilateral Concerns in a Regional Arms Control Process," Memorandum no. 59, June 2001, Jaffee Center for Strategic Studies, Tel Aviv University.

39. Nabil Fahmy and Karim Haggag, "The Helsinki Process and the Middle East: The Viability of Cooperative Security Frameworks for a Region in Flux," in *Regional Security Dialogue in the Middle East: Changes, Challenges and Opportunities,* ed. Chen Kane and Egle Murauskaite (New York: Routledge, 2014), 64.

lacking a viable arms control framework to stem the tide of proliferation. The consequences for the region have been dire. Over the last half century, the Middle East has seen a rising proliferation trend in every class of weapons of mass destruction and their delivery systems, together with unprecedented levels in overall military expenditures.[40] To the extent that these trends have been ameliorated, this was achieved not through a negotiated process but by diplomatic and military coercion. In the absence of a regional disarmament framework, the Middle East has witnessed perhaps the most frequent instances of coercive arms control in the post-Cold War era: Israel's military actions against Iraq's Osiraq reactor in 1981 and Syria's al-Kibar facility in 1997; the US-led coalition in the 1991 Gulf War which destroyed Iraq's nuclear infrastructure, followed by the establishment of an extensive inspection regime in the form of the UN Special Commission to ensure the dismantlement of the remainder of Iraq's WMD programs; the international pressure that brought about Libya's decision to relinquish its WMD programs; and, most recently, the forced dismantlement of Syria's chemical weapons arsenal following its accession to the Chemical Weapons Convention in the face of an explicit threat of military intervention by the United States.[41] Such a record does

40. The compilation by the Center for Nonproliferation Studies provides the most comprehensive data on Middle East country programs and regional proliferation trends: www.nonproliferation.org. See also Sami G. Hajjar, *Security Implications of the Proliferation of Weapons of Mass Destruction in the Middle East* (Carlisle, PA: United States Army War College Strategic Studies Institute, 1998); Anthony H. Cordesman, "Weapons of Mass Destruction in the Middle East: Regional Trends, National Forces, Warfighting Capabilities, Delivery Options, and Weapons Effects," Center for Strategic and International Studies, Washington, DC, September 2000; and Ian O. Lesser and Ashley J. Tellis, *Strategic Exposure: Proliferation Around the Mediterranean* (Santa Monica, CA: RAND, 2007). According to the Stockholm International Peace Research Institute, Middle East military expenditures increased by 56 percent between 2004 and 2013. See Sam Perlo-Freeman and Carina Solmirano, "Trends in World Military Expenditure, 2013," SIPRI Fact Sheet, April 2014.

41. For Libya's decision to relinquish its WMD programs, see John Hart and Shannon N. Kile, "Libya's Renunciation of Nuclear, Biological and Chemical Weapons and Ballistic Missiles," SIPRI Yearbook 2005: 629–648. Regarding Syria's chemical

not bode well for a political process that can potentially draw the region into a global nuclear disarmament framework.

The resort to coercion, however, has not been able to arrest, let alone reverse, the unconventional arms race in the region. Today, the major challenge to the prevailing nuclear status quo comes from Iran's development of its nuclear program. Yet the intense preoccupation with Iran's nuclear capability ignores the fact that it constitutes only one element of a broader dynamic that is gradually leading to the emergence of a new nuclear order in the region. It is in this context that the implications for nuclear deterrence, and how the Middle East relates to any future endeavor to achieve global nuclear disarmament, should be assessed.

The Emerging Nuclear (Dis)order in the Middle East

Three developments are converging to produce the gradual emergence of a new nuclear order in the Middle East: the prospects of a nuclear renaissance as regional states look to civilian nuclear power to address their increasing energy demands; the emergence of Iran's nuclear program as a factor in the regional security landscape irrespective of the outcome of the nuclear negotiations between Iran and the P5+1 (the permanent five members of the UN Security Council plus Germany); and the erosion of the global nuclear nonproliferation regime due in part to a lack of progress in achieving the universality of the NPT or the establishment of a WMD-free zone in the Middle East. Each of these factors on its own will no doubt affect the regional security environment. However, it is the synergistic interaction of these trends that will determine the contours of the emerging nuclear order in the region.

---

weapons disarmament, see Jean Pascal Zanders and Ralf Trapp, "Ridding Syria of Chemical Weapons: Next Steps," *Arms Control Today,* 2013, https://www .armscontrol.org/act/2013_11/Ridding-Syria-of-Chemical-Weapons-Next-Steps; and Ralf Trapp, "Elimination of the Chemical Weapons Stockpile of Syria," *Journal of Conflict and Security Law* 19, no. 1 (2014): 7–23.

Given the fact that the Middle East is a major energy producer, it would seem odd that the region would be a prime candidate for a major expansion in the use of civilian nuclear power. Most projections, however, point to long-term energy deficits as economic growth, demographic trends, and increased urbanization drive overall regional energy demand by 2050.[42] It is this overriding factor that has prompted Saudi Arabia, Egypt, Turkey, Jordan, Algeria, and the United Arab Emirates to announce major plans for nuclear power development, with the latter being the first to have already made major strides toward constructing an operational nuclear power program. Although still at an early stage, the latest projections by the International Atomic Energy Agency (IAEA) put the low estimate for the expansion of nuclear power in the region at 8.9 gigawatts of electricity by 2030, with the high estimate at 13.4 gigawatts of electricity during the same time frame. Either would constitute an increase by orders of magnitude from the current level of nuclear-generated electricity at 0.9 gigawatts of electricity.[43] Significantly, these trends do not appear to

---

42. BP Global, *BP Energy Outlook 2035: The Middle East,* http://www.bp.com/content /dam/bp/pdf/Energy-economics/Energy-Outlook/Regional_insights_Middle_East _2035.pdf; "Future Energy Challenges in the GCC Region," *Forum,* no. 96 (May 2014), Oxford Institute for Energy Studies; John Everington, "Middle East Energy Consumption Could Rise 114% by 2050," *The National,* October 14, 2013; *The Economist,* "The GCC in 2020: Resources for the Future," 2010; Glada Lahn and Paul Stevens, "Burning Oil to Keep Cool: The Hidden Energy Crisis in Saudi Arabia," Chatham House Report, Royal Institute for International Affairs, 2011; *The Economist,* "Securing MENA's Electric Power Supplies to 2020," 2011.

43. International Atomic Energy Agency, "International Status and Prospects for Nuclear Power 2014," IAEA Report by the Director General, August 4, 2014. For an overview of the drivers of the nuclear renaissance in the Middle East, see Laura El-Katiri, "The GCC and the Nuclear Question," Oxford Institute for Energy Studies, December 3, 2012; Adnan Shihab-Eldin, "Why Are Oil Exporting Countries Pursuing Nuclear Energy?" presentation before the Kuwait MIT Center for Natural Resources and the Environment, February 27, 2013; Melanie Grimmitt, "The MENA Nuclear Renaissance," *Energy and Environment* 22, nos. 1–2 (February 2011): 37–46.

have been affected by the Arab revolutions or Japan's Fukushima nuclear accident.[44]

The prospects for such a significant expansion of nuclear power programs in the region have generated significant interest among Western analysts regarding the proliferation risk this would entail.[45] As the only country in the region to actually have a nuclear power reactor, Iran has advanced its enrichment capability and other aspects of its nuclear infrastructure under the guise of its civilian nuclear program. Given that energy concerns constitute a less-than-convincing rationale for embarking on costly nuclear power programs in the view of some Western nonproliferation policy circles, the real motivation for Iran's neighbors to develop civilian nuclear programs is seen to be driven by the need to acquire a measure of nuclear technical proficiency as part of a hedging strategy against the prospects of a nuclear Iran.[46] The technical expertise, nuclear infrastructure, and large stocks of nuclear fuel that would accumulate from operating nuclear reactors would put countries in the region in a

44. Adnan Shihab-Eldin, "Nuclear Power in the Middle East Following Fukushima," presented to the International Seminar on Nuclear War and Planetary Emergencies, Erice, Italy, August 19–24, 2012.

45. Matthew Fuhrmann. "Spreading Temptation: Proliferation and Peaceful Nuclear Cooperation Agreements," *International Security* 34, no. 1 (Summer 2009): 7–41; Harold Feiveson, Alexander Glaser, Marvin Miller, and Lawrence Scheinman, *Can Future Nuclear Power Be Made Proliferation Resistant?* Center for International and Security Studies at Maryland, University of Maryland, College Park, July 2008; George Michael, "Assessing the Link Between Civilian Nuclear Assistance and the Proliferation Risk," *International Studies Review* 15 (September 2013): 444–450; Matthew Kroenig, "The Nuclear Renaissance, Sensitive Nuclear Assistance, and Nuclear Weapons Proliferation," in *The Nuclear Renaissance and International Security,* ed. Matthew Fuhrmann and Adam Stulberg (Stanford, CA: Stanford University Press, 2013); Steven E. Miller and Scott Sagan, "Nuclear Power Without Nuclear Proliferation?" *Daedalus,* Fall 2009: 7–18.

46. See for example, United States Institute of Peace, "Report of the Technical Advisory Group on Nuclear Energy in the Middle East," in *Engagement, Coercion, and Iran's Nuclear Challenge,* ed. Barry Blechhman and Daniel Brumberg (Washington, DC: Henry L. Stimson Center, 2010).

position to be able to address the challenge of a nuclear-capable Iran should the need arise.[47]

To counter such an eventuality, there has emerged an informal consensus, especially in the United States, on an approach that would curb the proliferation risk entailed in the global expansion of nuclear energy through a series of policy measures that would operate both at the country-specific level and at the level of the global nuclear nonproliferation regime. Countries that aspire to acquire nuclear energy programs should agree to submit to the IAEA's more rigorous safeguards system by signing the Additional Protocol to their original safeguards agreement with the agency and relinquish their right to access sensitive aspects of the nuclear fuel cycle, preferably through a voluntary commitment to forgo uranium enrichment as a condition for nuclear cooperation. The UAE's nuclear cooperation agreement with the United States, in which it committed to forgo any enrichment activity, is now considered the "gold standard" for civilian nuclear cooperation that should be emulated.[48] These measures would be complemented by steps designed to address the perceived loopholes in the NPT that have allowed states to abuse their treaty rights to access nuclear technology for peaceful purposes in order to acquire the precursors of a nuclear weapons capability: making the Additional Protocol mandatory for all states; limiting the ability of states to withdraw from the NPT under Article X after they have acquired the benefits of treaty membership in terms of nuclear cooperation;

---

47. For example David Albright and Andrea Scheel estimate that regional civil plutonium production in the form of spent fuel from regional nuclear energy reactors could total more than 13,000 kilograms (thirteen tons) by 2020, and nearly forty-five tons by 2030, enough for almost 1,700 nuclear weapons. See Institute for Science and International Security, "Unprecedented Projected Nuclear Growth in the Middle East: Now Is the Time to Create Effective Barriers to Proliferation," November 12, 2008.

48. Bryan R. Early. "Acquiring Foreign Nuclear Assistance in the Middle East: Strategic Lessons from the United Arab Emirates," *Nonproliferation Review* 17, no. 2 (July 2010): 259-280; Center for Strategic & International Studies, "The UAE 123 Agreement: A Model for the Region?" Gulf Roundtable Summary, October 23, 2009, http://csis.org/files/attachments/091023_Pickering%20Summary.pdf.

ensuring that states' safeguards agreements remain in perpetuity should they withdraw from the NPT; denying states access to sensitive fuel cycle technologies despite this being within their "inalienable right" under Article IV of the NPT while encouraging multilateral approaches to managing the nuclear fuel cycle; and instituting a robust enforcement mechanism for addressing cases of noncompliance through the UN Security Council.[49]

It becomes readily apparent from the issues raised here that the future trajectory of the nuclear renaissance in the Middle East is intimately tied to the other two drivers of the emerging regional nuclear order: the implications of Iran's nuclear program and the weakening of the nuclear non-proliferation regime. The latter issue has been a cause of concern for more than a decade as reflected in the UN Report of the High-Level Panel on Threats, Challenges and Change issued in 2004 which warned that "the nuclear non-proliferation regime is now at risk because of lack of compliance with existing commitments, withdrawal or threats of withdrawal from the Treaty on the Non-Proliferation of Nuclear Weapons to escape those commitments, a changing international security environment and the diffusion of technology." As a result of the cumulative effect of these developments, the report concluded, "We are approaching a point at which the erosion of the non-proliferation regime could become irreversible and result in a cascade of proliferation." The implication is that countries that possessed the requisite nuclear infrastructure would be able "to

---

49. This approach is best summarized in Henry Sokolski and Victor Gilinsky, "Serious Rules for Nuclear Power Without Proliferation," in *Moving Beyond Pretense: Nuclear Power and Nonproliferation,* ed. Henry Sokolski (Carlisle, PA: US Army War College Press, June 2014), 457–500. See also Pierre Goldschmidt, "Lecture delivered to the 24th Conference of the Nuclear Societies," Israel, February 19–21, 2008, http://carnegieendowment.org/files/nuclearsocieties.pdf. For the application of these measures in the Middle East context, see *Nuclear Energy in the Middle East: Implications, Challenges, Opportunities,* Report and Recommendations of the Global Nuclear Future Initiative, presented in Abu Dhabi, December 13–15, 2009, http://www.amacad.org/pdfs/abudhabiReport.pdf.

build nuclear weapons at relatively short notice *if the legal and normative constraints of the Treaty regime no longer apply* [emphasis added]."[50]

The Middle East occupies a central place in this context. Israel's hold-out status has always presented a particularly vexing problem in terms of realizing the universality of the NPT. Moreover, the near complete lack of progress toward implementing the 1995 Resolution adopted by the NPT Review and Extension Conference on establishing a WMD-free zone in the Middle East has taken its toll on subsequent NPT Review Conferences that have failed to achieve consensus. The similar lack of progress with regards to the proposed Helsinki conference threatens to adversely affect the upcoming 2015 NPT Review Conference. The ramifications, as stated by Patricia Lewis, are potentially severe: "The NPT would be damaged in the immediate aftermath and, unless there were clear and prompt moves to rectify the situation, the long-term impact on the treaty and on Middle East regional security would be negative."[51]

While the long-term consequences of the erosion of the global nonproliferation norm could prompt states to reassess their commitment under the NPT, the more immediate effect would be a reluctance on the part of those states that aspire to acquire civilian nuclear power to undertake commitments that would limit their access to nuclear technology and material, or agree to the proposed reforms to the treaty regime that would entail additional obligations and constraints on their nuclear programs. The result would be a trend toward greater nuclear sovereignty and the assertion of national control over nuclear programs in the Middle East and elsewhere. In this context, states would be reluctant to relinquish control

---

50. United Nations, *A More Secure World: Our Shared Responsibility,* Report of the Secretary-General's High-level Panel on Threats, Challenges and Change, 2004: 39–40, http://www.un.org/en/peacebuilding/pdf/historical/hlp_more_secure _world.pdf.

51. Lewis, *All in the Timing,* 19. For an analysis of how the Middle East issue has impacted the legitimacy of the nonproliferation regime, see Steve Miller, "Nuclear Collisions: Discord, Reform and the Nuclear Nonproliferation Regime," American Academy of Arts and Sciences, April 2012: 15–19.

of the nuclear fuel cycle, or agree to any constraints on their "inalienable right" to access nuclear technology under Article IV of the NPT.

This trend would not necessarily be driven by a motivation for acquiring an advanced nuclear breakout capability. Rather, it would be the byproduct of the steady erosion of the legitimacy of the nonproliferation regime. Yet the trajectory of the region's nuclear program will also no doubt be influenced by the overall course of the Middle East security environment, and in particular changes to the nuclear status quo in the region. Should this occur, states will begin to rely on their civilian nuclear programs as a form of hedging in a manner that would provide them with future options toward a nuclear capability to counterbalance what they perceive to be threats to their security.[52]

This is precisely why the developments relating to Iran's nuclear program, and the possible regional reactions they elicit, especially with regard to Israel, present the most significant potential to alter the regional nuclear status quo. Despite successive rounds of negotiations between Iran and the P5+1, several Security Council Resolutions sanctioning Iran, and the most comprehensive international sanctions regime ever to be imposed on a state since the end of the Cold War, Iran's nuclear program has steadily advanced over the last decade to the point where it has developed a diversified nuclear infrastructure, a mastery of the complete nuclear fuel cycle, including an advanced fuel enrichment program which has produced a growing stock of low-enriched uranium. According to the IAEA, Iran's nuclear program has also acquired a military dimension including research related to nuclear warhead design and assembly.[53]

Irrespective of their ultimate outcome, three aspects stand out regarding the current nuclear negotiations with Iran. First, the Joint Plan of

---

52. Ariel Levite provides a framework for assessing the concept of nuclear hedging, "Never Say Never Again: Nuclear Reversal Revisited," *International Security* 27, no. 3 (Winter 2002/2003): 59–88.

53. International Atomic Energy Agency, *Implementation of the NPT Safeguards Agreement and Relevant Provisions of Security Council Resolutions in the Islamic Republic of Iran,* report by the director general of the IAEA, November 8, 2011.

Action agreed to by Iran and the P5+1 in November 2013 already concedes Iran's right to retain an enrichment program while leaving the issue of its size and scope to a final comprehensive agreement. This constitutes a significant shift from the original US position (and UN Security Council Resolutions) which insisted on zero enrichment. The political recognition of Iran's right to retain even a minimal enrichment program in whatever agreement is reached is likely to create what may be referred to as the "Iran standard" that will compete with the UAE "gold standard" for defining the scope of regional nuclear programs in the future, in particular with respect to enrichment capability. Second, should a final comprehensive agreement be reached it is unlikely that it will lead to the dismantlement of Iran's nuclear infrastructure, given Iran's insistence on retaining an industrial-size enrichment program. Finally, whatever agreement is reached will be time-bound, meaning that any limitations imposed on Iran's program for the duration of the agreement will no longer be binding once the agreement expires.

The current negotiations, therefore, are unlikely to reverse the reality of Iran's latent nuclear capability. Short of a comprehensive approach to deal with the nuclear question in the Middle East including Israel, Iran's nuclear capability will remain a fixture of the region's security environment. Determining the degree of separation between this capability and the acquisition of a nuclear weapons option lies at the heart of the nuclear negotiations. However, even in the event that the negotiations produce a successful outcome, it is likely that at some point the potential for Iran's nuclear program to alter the nuclear status quo in the region will resurface, bringing Iran closer to attaining a nuclear threshold status. Failure to reach an agreement, on the other hand, will inevitably bring that point closer. Similarly, in the absence of a comprehensive agreement, extending the Joint Plan of Action is unlikely to be sustainable as was the case with the 2003 agreement between Iran and the E3 (Germany, France, and the United Kingdom) to suspend its enrichment activity, which broke down two years later leading to Iran resuming its enrichment program.

The Fragility of Deterrence
beyond the Middle East Nuclear Tipping Point

The eventuality of Iran crossing the nuclear threshold naturally raises the question of the prospects for a stable nuclear deterrence regime in the Middle East between Iran and Israel, and Iran and the United States, similar to that which prevailed in the Cold War between the United States and the Soviet Union. The specific deterrent relationship that emerges will of course depend on whether and how Iran chooses to cross the nuclear threshold. The prospect of Iran emulating the North Korean model—whereby it declares its nuclear capability, tests a nuclear device, and announces its formal withdrawal from the NPT—constitutes one possible scenario. However, most analyses tend to agree that there is no discernible decision on the part of Iran's leadership to reach for a nuclear weapons capability. Short of a military confrontation over Iran's nuclear program which would constitute yet another case of coercive nuclear disarmament in the region, a more likely scenario is that Iran continues to develop its nuclear program just short of full-fledged weaponization. By opting for a virtual capability without an overt nuclear posture, Iran would possess the requirements for a rapid breakout toward a nuclear weapons capability while avoiding a crisis with the international community by remaining within the NPT.[54] If some variant of the latter scenario prevails, the Middle East will feature another case of nuclear opacity, whereby both Iran and Israel possess an undeclared nuclear weapons capability, the major differences being the

---

54. Melissa G. Dalton, Colin H. Kahl, and Matthew Irvine, "Risk and Rivalry: Iran, Israel and the Bomb," Center for a New American Security, June 6, 2012: 10–12; Jacques E.C. Hymans and Matthew S. Gratias, "Iran and the Nuclear Threshold: Where is the Line?" *Nonproliferation Review* 20, no. 1 (2013): 13–38; Geoffrey Kemp, "Iran's Nuclear Options," *Iran's Nuclear Options: Issues and Analysis,* The Nixon Center, January 2001: 1–17; Jacques E.C. Hymans, "When Does a State Become a 'Nuclear Weapon State?' An Exercise in Measurement," *Nonproliferation Review* 17, no. 1 (March 2010): 161–180.

scope and sophistication of their respective nuclear arsenals and their different position vis-à-vis the NPT.[55]

However, under whatever scenario that emerges, the Middle East context will differ radically from that which governed the emergence of the classic US-Soviet deterrent relationship during the Cold War, and from which the more optimistic assessments for a stable Iranian-Israeli deterrent system are derived. Those who look to the Cold War as a model that can be successfully replicated in the Middle East argue that Iran is cognizant of Israel's nuclear capability and therefore will operate under the certainty that any use of nuclear weapons will lead to the destruction of the Islamic Republic itself. Nuclear weapons, according to this view, will exert the same stabilizing effect on decision-makers in the Middle East as they did in Washington and Moscow. The inherent logic of deterrence will therefore prevail.[56]

Yet it is highly unlikely that the mere introduction of nuclear weapons will constitute a sufficient basis for stable deterrence in the Middle East. The elements that underpinned the US-Soviet deterrent relationship are entirely or partially absent from the region: effective early warning and nuclear command and control systems; a viable second strike option; secure delivery systems that can survive a first nuclear strike; communications links between decision-makers during times of crisis; enunciated nuclear doctrines that allow for accurate assessments of adversary intentions and red lines; and a process of nuclear arms control negotiations, all of which made for a stable regime of deterrence that developed and matured over time.

---

55. Jean-Loup Samaan. "Revisiting Nuclear Opacity in the Middle East: A Scenario," *Orbis* 57, no. 4 (Autumn 2013): 627–642.

56. Kenneth Waltz, "Why Iran Should Get the Bomb: Nuclear Balancing Would Mean Stability," *Foreign Affairs* (July/August 2012): 2–5; Barry Posen, "A Nuclear-Armed Iran: A Difficult but Not Impossible Policy Problem," A Century Foundation Report, 2006. For an Israeli assessment of the potential for a stable deterrent relationship with a nuclear Iran, see Ofer Israeli, "An Israeli Plan B for a Nuclear Iran," *Middle East Review of International Affairs* 16, no. 2 (June 2012): 52–60.

In stark contrast to the Cold War model, the structural factors that differentiate the nuclear context in the Middle East would instill a highly unstable dynamic. In the absence of effective channels of communication, it is difficult to perceive that any of the actors would have a sound appreciation of adversaries' decision calculus, which is precisely what accounts for the repeated deterrence failures in the Middle East. A scenario of nuclear opacity between Iran and Israel would only exacerbate the problem. Unlike the South Asian context in which both India and Pakistan have signaled the various threat scenarios that would govern their use of nuclear weapons, and where nuclear issues are the subject of public debate,[57] deterrence in the Middle East would operate in the absence of any declared nuclear doctrine on the part of either Israel or Iran.[58] Consequently, the region would not benefit from what Joseph Nye referred to as "nuclear learning," a cognitive process by which nuclear states adjust their perception of adversary intent, capability, and political will over the course of decades of strategic interaction, as has taken hold between India and Pakistan.[59]

Moreover, there is the question of how nuclear weapons will intersect with the region's volatile conflict environment. If, indeed, nuclear

---

57. V. R. Raghavan, "Limited War and Nuclear Escalation in South Asia," *Nonproliferation Review,* Fall-Winter 2001: 1–18; Ashley J. Tellis, India's *Emerging Nuclear Doctrine: Exemplifying the Lessons of the Nuclear Revolution* (Seattle: National Bureau of Asian Research, May 2001); Namrata Goswami, "The Essence of the South Asian Nuclear Debate," *Strategic Analysis* 30, no. 3, Institute for Defence Studies and Analyses, July 2006; Rifaat Hussain, *Nuclear Doctrines in South Asia* no. 4, South Asian Strategic Stability Institute, December 2005; and two chapters in *Deterrence Stability and Escalation Control in South Asia,* ed. Michael Krepon and Julia Thompson (New York: The Stimson Center, 2013): Christopher Clary and Vipin Narang, "Doctrine, Capabilities, and (In)Stability in South Asia," and Michael Krepon, "Pakistan's Nuclear Strategy and Deterrence Stability."

58. Yair Evron, "An Israel-Iran Balance of Nuclear Deterrence: Seeds of Instability," in *Israel and a Nuclear Iran: Implications for Arms Control, Deterrence and Defense,* ed. Ephraim Kam (Tel Aviv: Institute for National Security Studies, July 2008), 47–64.

59. Joseph S. Nye, "Nuclear Learning and US-Soviet Security Regimes," *International Organization* 41, no. 3 (Summer 1987); and Jeffrey W. Knopf, "The Concept of Nuclear Learning," *Nonproliferation Review* 19, no. 1 (March 2012): 79–93.

weapons afford Iran a sense of immunity at the conventional level from the overwhelming military superiority enjoyed by the United States and Israel, the potential for conflict escalation at the sub-conventional level can increase considerably. Under the cover of its newly acquired nuclear capability, Iran can significantly elevate the level of material and political support to its regional proxies, thus shifting the spectrum of conflict to the level of asymmetric conflict where it enjoys a distinct advantage. The propensity for miscalculation in such a context can only increase with the fault lines between conventional, sub-conventional, and nuclear conflict becoming increasingly blurred. A repeat of, for example, the 2006 Israeli-Hezbollah war in Lebanon in a regional nuclear context would pose the possibility of uncontrolled escalation to the nuclear level given the fluid nature of the conflict and the lack of clarity as to the red lines of the various protagonists.

Just as these factors would preclude the emergence of a stable deterrence relationship between Israel and Iran, they would similarly undermine the prospects for a regional system of extended deterrence underpinned by the United States. Here, again, the Middle East presents a wholly different context from the European and Asian theaters that have come to define the model for successful extended nuclear deterrence. In both Western Europe and East Asia, the credibility of the US security and nuclear guarantee has been proven throughout the Cold War and more recently in the face of North Korea's nuclear escalation. However, the qualitatively different nature of the United States' political relationships with its allies in the Middle East would cast doubt over the credibility of such a guarantee should it be invoked. Despite the formidable US military presence in the region, the credibility of its defense commitments has suffered as a result of the withdrawal from Iraq and Afghanistan, the pivot to Asia, the failure to contain the fallout from the Syrian civil war, and the inability to check Iranian adventurism throughout the Levant.[60] The very fact that the United States would move to adopt a posture of

---

60. Kathleen J. McInnis, "Extended Deterrence: The US Credibility Gap in the Middle East," *Washington Quarterly* 28, no. 3 (Summer 2005): 169–186; and Carlo Masala,

extended deterrence would mark the failure of its efforts to prevent Iran from acquiring nuclear weapons.

Moreover, as already mentioned, Iranian acquisition of nuclear weapons would constitute a drastic shift in the region's conflict environment to the sub-conventional level, which will pose an acute security challenge for US allies in the region. Here, the reluctance of the United States to engage militarily at this level—notwithstanding the military campaign against the Islamic State in Syria and Iraq, which is narrowly focused on containing the terrorist threat in the region—would erode the credibility of whatever nuclear guarantee the United States would provide to protect its allies. The link between the United States' extended deterrence posture in the Middle East and the security calculus of its regional allies will remain weak, in marked contrast to the US nuclear commitment in Asia and Western Europe.[61]

Perhaps the most explicit testament to the fragility of a mutual nuclear deterrence scenario in the Middle East comes from Israel's position. The Begin Doctrine rested on an explicit rejection of deterrence, a position that was best articulated by Ariel Sharon following Israel's bombing of Osiraq: "Israel cannot afford the introduction of the nuclear weapon. For us it is not a question of a balance of terror but a question of survival. We shall therefore have to prevent such a threat at its inception."[62] It is this assumption of the fragility of nuclear deterrence that has driven Israel's significant investment in strategic offensive and defensive systems since the 1991 Gulf War in the areas of missile defense, extensive homeland defense systems (including the creation of a Home Front Command within the IDF), early warning satellites, and the development of a nuclear

---

"Extended Deterrence in the Middle East: A Fuzzy Concept that Might Work?" *Strategic Assessment* 14, no. 4 (January 2012): 115–122.

61. Masala, "Extended Deterrence . . . A Fuzzy Concept," 121. See also Yair Evron, "Extended Deterrence in the Middle East," *Nonproliferation Review* 19, no. 3 (2012): 377–390; and James A. Russell, "Nuclear Reductions and Middle East Stability: Assessing the Impact of a Smaller US Nuclear Arsenal," *Nonproliferation Review* 20, no. 2: 263–278.

62. Quoted in Shai Feldman, "The Bombing of Osiraq—Revisited," 112.

second-strike option through a sea-based nuclear arm based on its German-manufactured submarine fleet. As stated by Zeev Maoz, "these measures reflect a strategic admission that nuclear deterrence cannot be relied on to guarantee Israel's security."[63]

The development of these systems predates the emergence of the Iranian challenge to the nuclear status quo in the region and therefore indicates the propensity for vertical proliferation in Israel's nuclear arsenal even in the absence of any direct nuclear threat. It is therefore important to examine the long-term impact on Israel's nuclear posture in the eventuality that Iran does indeed acquire a nuclear weapons capability. As with most aspects related to Israel's nuclear program, much of the analysis must remain speculative. Yet the South Asian context provides a template for the dynamics of nuclear modernization on the part of India and Pakistan to cope with the demands imposed by augmenting their nuclear deterrent capability.[64]

Extrapolating from this template, we can discern that the effect on Israel's overall nuclear posture is likely to unfold on three interrelated levels. First, there is likely to be a shift in Israel's nuclear strategy from

---

63. Zeev Moaz, "Mixed Blessing,," 57–58. See also E. L. Zorn, "Expanding The Horizon: Israel's Quest for Satellite Intelligence," US Central Intelligence Agency, https://www.cia.gov/library/center-for-the-study-of-intelligence/kent-csi/vol44no5/html/v44i5a04p.htm; Uzi Rubin, "Missile Defense and Israel's Deterrence Against a Nuclear Iran," in *Israel and a Nuclear Iran: Implications for Arms Control, Deterrence and Defense,* ed. Ephraim Kam (Tel Aviv: Institute for National Security Studies, July 2008), 65–82; Cohen, "Israel: A Sui Generis Proliferator," 254–255; and "Operation Samson: Israel's Deployment of Nuclear Missiles on Subs from Germany," *Der Spiegel,* June 4, 2012, http://www.spiegel.de/international/world/israel-deploys-nuclear-weapons-on-german-built-submarines-a-836784.html.

64. Peter R. Lavoy, "Managing South Asia's Nuclear Rivalry: New Policy Challenges for the United States," *Nonproliferation Review,* Fall/Winter 2003: 84–94; and two chapters in Feroz Hassan Khan, Ryan Jacobs, and Emily Burke, *Nuclear Learning in South Asia: The Next Decade* (Monterey, CA: Naval Postgraduate School, June 2014): Mansoor Ahmed, "Trends in Technological Maturation and Strategic Modernization: The Next Decade," and Vipin Narang, "Military Modernization and Technological Maturation, An Indian Perspective: Stabilizing the Instability-Stability Paradox."

deterrence to preemption, with a corresponding reconfiguration of the operational mission ascribed to Israel's nuclear weapons. As Iran's nuclear capabilities develop over time in terms of number of warheads and accuracy of its missile delivery systems, the issue of the survivability of Israel's nuclear arsenal will emerge as a key concern. However the Iranian-Israeli deterrent relationship unfolds, it will operate in a context of limited early warning given the short missile flight times and the vulnerability of Israel to the effects of a nuclear attack given its lack of strategic depth. These pressures will likely prompt Israel to adopt a preemptive nuclear strategy alongside its strategy of deterrence. In order to mitigate the vulnerabilities Israel will likely face in a nuclear context, the role of nuclear weapons will be to preempt a potential Iranian nuclear first strike should Israel perceive that deterrence will fail. This in turn will require placing its nuclear force on a heightened alert status by mating nuclear warheads to its missile force, and possibly deploying nuclear warheads at or near Israeli airbases in order to ensure a rapid arming of its bomber fleet.[65] If Israel has indeed kept its nuclear weapons in unassembled mode in accordance with its pledge not to be the first to introduce nuclear weapons to the Middle East, it is unlikely that such a posture will be sustainable in the context of a nuclear deterrent relationship with Iran.

Secondly, one can anticipate that Israel's nuclear force structure will also be affected. Here it is important to note that Israel's nuclear arsenal is already structured around a triad of air-, land-, and sea-based delivery systems. Accordingly, one can also assume a degree of sophistication in the nuclear arsenal itself around a variety of warhead designs that could be fitted onto the various delivery platforms. In addition, several reports have surfaced regarding Israel's large-scale production of tritium

---

65. Andrew F. Krepinevich, "Critical Mass: Nuclear Proliferation in the Middle East," Center for Strategic and Budgetary Assessments, 2013: 28–29; Steven R. David, "Armed and Dangerous: Why a Rational Nuclear Iran is an Unacceptable Risk to Israel," Begin-Sadat Center for Strategic Studies, Mideast Security and Policy Studies no. 104, November 2013: 39–41; Louis Rene Beres, "Israel's Uncertain Strategic Future," *Parameters,* Spring 2007: 37–54.

for a weapons-boosting program.[66] The possibility that Israel had developed tactical nuclear weapons has always been a subject of speculation among analysts of Israel's nuclear program.[67] If this did indeed occur it would seemingly contradict a purely deterrent role for Israel's nuclear arsenal. One possible explanation is that the development of a tactical nuclear capability could be the result of bureaucratic inertia divorced from a clear strategic rationale and without political guidance.[68] Given the sophistication of Israel's military-nuclear capability, therefore, it is unlikely that the impact from the emergence of a nuclear deterrent relationship with Iran will lead to a qualitative shift in Israel's force structure. Rather, one can assume that whatever change will occur will be in the form of incremental refinements to aspects of Israel's nuclear force; for example, enhancing the range of its nuclear armed submarines, improving the accuracy of its missile force, updating its nuclear targeting to cover

66. Israel's tritium production was one of the elements contained in the revelations by Mordechai Vanunu regarding Israel's nuclear program. See Amy Goodman, "An Interview With Mordechai Vanunu," *Counterpunch,* August 18, 2004, http://www.counterpunch.org/2004/08/18/an-interview-with-mordechai-vanunu. In addition, Israel reportedly exported quantities of tritium to South Africa in 1977. See Peter Liberman, "Israel and the South African Bomb," *Nonproliferation Review,* Summer 2004: 1–35.

67. Seymour Hersh provides the earliest claim that Israel did indeed produce tactical nuclear weapons. See Hersh, *The Samson Option: Israel's Nuclear Arsenal and American Foreign Policy* (New York: Random House, 1991), 216, 239. For others who lean toward this assessment, see Ben-Ami, *Nuclear Weapons in the Middle East,* 8; Hans M. Kristensen, "Non-Strategic Nuclear Weapons," Federation of American Scientists, May 2012: 9; and Anthony Cordesman, "Israel's Weapons of Mass Destruction: An Overview," Center for Strategic & International Studies, June 2, 2008, http://csis.org/files/media/csis/pubs/080602_israeliwmd.pdf. Avner Cohen argues that Israel opted not to produce tactical nuclear weapons in keeping with its nuclear strategy of existential (strategic) deterrence: *The Worst Kept Secret,* 83.

68. Avner Cohen argues that Israel's crossing the threshold to become a nuclear weapon state in 1967 was done without an explicit directive from the political echelon: *The Worst-Kept Secret,* 175–176.

both counter-value and counter-force targets, and upgrading its nuclear command and control system.

Finally, there is the question of whether Israel will rethink its doctrine of opacity which will inevitably come under stress in the context of a nuclear deterrence relationship with Iran. Given the unique quality of Israel's nuclear opacity, there is no indication as to how it will operate when faced with a challenge from another nuclear-weapon state. Thus far, opacity has had a remarkable longevity through numerous crises, most notably the 1973 war. Yet it will be hard to reconcile such a posture with the requirements of a robust deterrence system between Israel and Iran.[69] Without conveying a clear articulation of intent to uphold defined red lines, deterrence would fail in a volatile nuclear environment prone to miscalculation. Moreover, if indeed Israel does shift to a strategy of nuclear preemption, it will have to contend with the implications of nuclear use without a prior explicit warning, precisely the dilemma that confronted Israeli decision-makers during the height of the 1973 war.

Much of the analysis regarding possible proliferation scenarios in the Middle East is focused on the potential for a regional "nuclear cascade" in response to Iran acquiring a nuclear weapon capability. The underlying assumption is that Iran crossing the nuclear threshold would set off a wave of horizontal proliferation prompting a major reevaluation on the part of Saudi Arabia, Egypt, and Turkey, among others, to embark on a serious drive to acquire a similar capability. However, the trajectory of the proliferation trend in the region in response to this eventuality is likely to

---

69. Louis Rene Beres, "Changing Direction? Updating Israel's Nuclear Doctrine," *Strategic Assessment* 17, no. 3, (October 2014); Cohen, *The Worst Kept Secret,* 217; Cohen, "Israel: A Sui Generis Proliferator," 259–261. For an assessment of the merits of preserving Israel's nuclear ambiguity or opting for a declared nuclear deterrent posture, see Reuven Pedatzur, "The Iranian Nuclear Threat and the Israeli Options," *Contemporary Security Policy* 28, no. 3 (December 2007): 513–541; and Gerald Steinberg, "Walking the Tightrope: Israeli Options in Response to Iranian Nuclear Developments," in *Reassessing the Implications of a Nuclear-Armed Iran,* Judith S. Yaphe and Charles D. Lutes (Washington, DC: National Defense University, 2005).

be vertical and only subsequently horizontal. Rather than a nuclear cascade which is likely to unfold over an extended period of time, the more immediate impact will be on Israel's overall nuclear posture. How Israel chooses to respond to a nuclearized Middle East will constitute a development no less transformative than Iran's crossing of the nuclear threshold. Should Israel forgo its nuclear opacity, the regional ramifications are likely to be severe, both in terms of the security calculus of regional states and with respect to the integrity of the nuclear nonproliferation regime. The alternative scenario of extended nuclear opacity—with both Iran and Israel maintaining their status as undeclared nuclear powers—will perhaps lessen the damage to the nonproliferation regime, but its impact on the region's security landscape will be profound. Caught between two nuclear powers, it is unlikely—in the context of the uncertainty that will pervade the regional security environment—that other regional powers will not come under pressure to follow suit.

The Urgency of Reversing
the Slide toward a Nuclearized Middle East

The evolution of the nuclear question in the Middle East reveals two overriding trends. The first is the declining efficacy of nuclear deterrence. Rather than afford a measure of security, nuclear deterrence threatens to become a highly destabilizing factor as the region moves beyond Israel's nuclear monopoly. This, however, has not led to a reassessment of the utility of nuclear weapons nor has it galvanized efforts to move the region towards nuclear disarmament. To the contrary, the second trend is the creeping nuclearization of the region driven by the pressures of both horizontal and vertical proliferation.

The outcome of these trends will constitute a major challenge for regional arms control, and a potentially insurmountable obstacle toward the goal of global nuclear disarmament. In a nuclearized Middle East, nuclear weapons will gain a greater salience in the security calculus of those states that possess them, while spurring those who do not to achieve the precursors that will provide them with a potential nuclear option in the future. This would hold true not only for regional states, but also for external actors, primarily the United States, which might feel compelled to rely on an extended deterrence posture for its allies in the region. Irrespective of whether this would actually forestall the proliferation trend in the region, a US posture of extended deterrence would have major implications for US nuclear declaratory policy, its approach to global and regional arms control, and potentially its advocacy for the goal of global nuclear disarmament. Moreover, the shift in the nuclear status quo in the Middle East will likely constitute a key factor in the erosion of the global nuclear nonproliferation regime, not only with respect to the normative aspect related to the double standard that exempts Israel from any arms control or disarmament commitments, but also because the reality of a nuclearized Middle East can potentially bring about the collapse of the regime itself. There can be no greater setback to the cause of global nuclear disarmament.

The only way to forestall such an eventuality is through devising a comprehensive arms control framework for the Middle East that can halt the slide to a nuclearized future and eventually put the region on a path toward nuclear disarmament. This would require, however, a fundamental reevaluation on the part of regional states and international actors, in particular the United States, regarding their approach to the nuclear question in the Middle East. This is because the region poses a special set of political and techno-political challenges that need to be addressed in the context of integrating the Middle East into any future global nuclear disarmament process.

Reassessing the US-Israel nuclear bargain

As Cohen's masterful history of Israel's nuclear program shows, the United States is an active partner in Israel's policy of nuclear opacity. The secret bargain between President Richard Nixon and Prime Minister Golda Meir in 1969, subsequently reaffirmed by successive US administrations, constituted a tacit acceptance by the United States of Israel's nuclear capability. It "exempted Israel from the United States' nonproliferation policy as long as Israel kept these weapons invisible."[70] This was to have enormous implications for US policy toward regional nuclear disarmament, including the objective of establishing a WMD-free zone in the Middle East to which the US ostensibly subscribes and its position on the universality of the NPT.

The United States has effectively adopted the Israeli view that the creation of such a zone is a long-term objective and that "a comprehensive and durable peace in the region and full compliance by all regional states with their arms control and nonproliferation obligations are essential precursors for its establishment."[71] For Israel's part, the diplomatic cover provided by the United States for its nuclear program allowed Israel to adopt its highly conditional approach to regional arms control while forestalling any domestic debate on the nuclear question. Given that the original purpose of opacity was to keep Israel out of the global nuclear regime, and the complicity of the United States in this objective constitutes a serious obstacle that must be overcome.

For any progress to be made in halting the trend toward regional nuclearization, advancing the goal of NPT universality, and fostering the objective of a world without nuclear weapons, the US-Israel nuclear bargain must be reassessed. This is imperative not only to bring about a relaxation of Israel's negotiating posture to enable a more forthcoming Israeli position regarding regional and global arms control, but also with respect to the objective of achieving global nuclear disarmament. After all, it should be no surprise that Israel evinces the same skepticism to the goal of global

---

70. Cohen, *The Worst-Kept Secret,* xiii. Cohen describes the diplomacy surrounding the Nixon-Meir meeting in pp. 23–33. For a concise account of the US-Israel secret bargain, see Avner Cohen and William Burr, "Israel Crosses the Threshold," *Bulletin of the Atomic Scientists* 62, no. 3 (May 30, 2013): 22–30.

71. Office of the White House Press Secretary, "Statement by National Security Advisor General James Jones on the Non-Proliferation Treaty Review Conference," May 8, 2010, http://www.whitehouse.gov/the-press-office/statement-national-security-advisor-general-james-l-jones-non-proliferation-treaty-

nuclear disarmament as it does to any form of regional arms control process.[72] It is also imperative because it is a necessary prerequisite for the United States to broaden its approach to regional nonproliferation and arms control. The current US effort with Iran is divorced from any comprehensive framework to address the proliferation problem in the Middle East. For the United States to adopt such an approach, however, it would have to revise its long-standing nuclear bargain with Israel.

The need for an interim regime
of nuclear control in the Middle East

The current deadlock on regional arms control stems from a fundamental incompatibility in the position of the major actors involved. Consequently, the goal of establishing a WMD-free zone in the Middle East is one that will only be realized after a lengthy negotiating process that is liable to face serious setbacks before any meaningful progress is made. This means that even under an optimistic scenario whereby negotiations on the creation of a zone are successfully launched, this in itself may not halt the slide toward regional nuclearization.

What might be required therefore is an interim regime of nuclear control, coupled with steps toward nuclear confidence-building, with the objective of breaking the proliferation trend in the region and gradually reducing nuclear asymmetries. This would not be a substitute for the zone, but rather a precursor to its establishment, through a series of voluntary steps undertaken by all countries in the region subject to IAEA verification, with the active engagement of the P5 and especially the United States.

The proposed interim regime would be based on three pillars. The first would rest on a system of fissile material control in the Middle East. This would entail a voluntary moratorium on enrichment and reprocessing which would effectively create an enrichment/reprocessing-free zone

---

72.   See Ariel E. Levite, "Global Zero: An Israeli Vision of Realistic Idealism," *Washington Quarterly* 33, no. 2 (April 2010): 157–168; and Brom, "Israel's Perspective, 51–55.

in the Middle East through voluntary steps that would not entail a renunciation of states' rights to peaceful nuclear energy under Article IV of the NPT. This should be followed by a baseline declaration by each country on its fissile material inventory that would include both military and civilian stocks, and a commitment to IAEA verification of its declaration. At a subsequent stage, this should be followed by a commitment to place existing stocks of fissile materials under IAEA safeguards as an interim measure until a mechanism can be devised to allow for the gradual drawdown and eventual elimination of fissile material stocks.[73]

The second pillar would focus on transparency and nuclear confidence-building measures. As a first step, a time frame for bringing all nuclear facilities in the region under IAEA safeguards should be agreed upon. This could be done in conjunction with allowing nationals from neighboring countries to join IAEA inspection teams during their visits to nuclear facilities on a case-by-case basis. This approach can also draw on the South Asian context where there has been progress on establishing a nuclear confidence-building agenda.[74] This can include a commitment, deposited with the P5, not to attack any nuclear facilities in the region, a similar commitment to observe a moratorium on nuclear tests, and declaratory statements of no first use of WMD.

Complementing this approach would be the third pillar of the proposed regime which would focus on options for multilateral assurances

---

73. Many of these steps are elaborated in Frank N. von Hippel, Seyed Hossein Mousavian, Emad Kiyaei, Harold A. Feiveson, and Zia Mian, *Fissile Material Controls in the Middle East: Steps Toward a Middle East Zone Free of Nuclear Weapons and All Other Weapons of Mass Destruction,* Research Report no. 11, International Panel on Fissile Materials, October 2013.

74. Tariq Rauf, "Confidence-Building and Security-Building Measures in the Nuclear Area With Relevance for South Asia," *Contemporary South Asia* 14, no. 2 (June 2005): 175–189; Umbreen Javaid, "Confidence Building Measures in Nuclear South Asia: Limitations and Prospects," *South Asian Studies* 25, no. 2 (July–December 2010): 341–349; Michael Krepon and Chris Gagne, eds., *The Stability-Instability Paradox: Nuclear Weapons and Brinksmanship in South Asia* (Washington, DC: The Stimson Center, June 1, 2001).

of fuel supply to countries embarking on a civilian nuclear program. The objective would be to tie the emerging regime of nuclear control to one of the various multilateral arrangements for nuclear fuel supply such as the IAEA's low-enriched uranium fuel bank or the German Multilateral Enrichment Sanctuary Program.[75]

The advantage of this approach is that it would not target any particular state but would focus on steps to be undertaken by all states in the region. It would also avoid the protracted negotiations involved in lengthy arms control processes. Rather it would focus on unilateral voluntary commitments that would be encouraged and facilitated by the P5. This approach, however, would no doubt bump up against the obstacle of Israel's opacity posture as was the case with its opposition to the FMCT process.[76] This is why the active involvement and leadership of the United States will be key to its success. Israel will have to be persuaded of the merits of this approach in that it would foster a more benign regional security environment that would benefit its long-term security.

Avoiding conferring a special status to non-NPT states

This is an issue of process and relates to the question of how to draw Israel and the other NPT holdout states—India, Pakistan, and North Korea—into an arms control process without according them a special status outside the global nuclear nonproliferation regime. Integrating the NPT holdouts has been a long-standing issue of concern for arms control

---

75.   For an overview of the various arrangements for multilateral management of the nuclear fuel cycle, see Mary Beth Nikitin, Anthony Andrews, and Mark Holt, "Managing the Nuclear Fuel Cycle: Policy Implications of Expanding Global Access to Nuclear Power," *Congressional Research Report,* October 19, 2012.

76.   Israel is favorable to multilateral approaches in the region, but is unwilling to subject its nuclear program to any of the limitations that would be entailed by such an approach. See Thomas Lorenz and Joanna Kidd, "Israel and Multilateral Nuclear Approaches in the Middle East," *Arms Control Today* 10, 2010, http://www.armscontrol.org/act/2010_10/Lorenz-Kidd.

advocates.[77] Since the NPT only recognizes two categories of states—nuclear-weapon states and non-nuclear-weapon states, a categorization which cannot accommodate the four hold-out states—the dilemma lies in devising an arms control framework to incorporate these states outside the NPT. In part, this was the intent of the CTBT and FMCT regimes. The danger, however, lies in the risk that such an endeavor would in effect create a third class of states outside the NPT framework. Had these states engaged fully in the test ban treaty and FMCT process, the likely outcome would have been that they would have their own set of arms control obligations and possibly be subject to different verification provisions than the non-nuclear-weapon states. This would have bestowed de facto recognition of the special status that these states occupy outside the NPT regime. An alternative would be to formalize the status of the holdouts by conferring "associate membership" through a special protocol to the NPT as advocated by US lead arms control negotiator Thomas Graham.[78] This would do untold damage to the integrity of the nonproliferation regime as it would reward, rather than proscribe, non-adherence to the NPT, which would undermine the core bargain of the treaty itself.

This is the dilemma that will resurface in the context of any endeavor to advance the goal of global nuclear disarmament. Formulating the diplomatic framework to advance this objective would require devising a process to incorporate the NPT holdout states without conferring a special

77. Jenny Nielsen, "Engaging India, Israel and Pakistan in the Nuclear Non-Proliferation Regime," *Disarmament Diplomacy* no. 86, Autumn 2007, http://www.acronym.org.uk/dd/dd86/contents; Natasha Barnes, Tanya Ogilvie-White, and Rodrigo Alvarez Valdes, "The NPT Holdouts: Universality as an Elusive Goal," *Nonproliferation Review* 17, no. 1 (March 2010): 95–113.

78. Avner Cohen and Thomas Grahamn, "An NPT for Non-Members," *Bulletin of the Atomic Scientists* 60, no. 3 (May/June 2004): 40–44. See also Sverre Lodgaard, "Making the non-proliferation regime universal: Asking non-parties to behave 'as if' they were members," The Weapons of Mass Destruction Commission, Paper no. 7. http://www.un.org/disarmament/education/wmdcommission/files/No7-Lodgaard%20Final.pdf.

status that would legitimize their non-adherence to the treaty. Should the process stall at some interim point, the fact that these states had acquired some form of special recognition along the way would have serious implications for the overall integrity of the regime.

Related to this is another issue of process which revolves around whether the focus of the arms control process should be regional or global. Israel insists on a purely regional process divorced from any linkage with the global level, especially the NPT. In this, Israel stands in marked contrast to India which adamantly rejects any form of regional arms control in favor of a global approach that would address the discriminatory nature of the global nonproliferation regime. Integrating India and, by extension, Pakistan into a global disarmament effort would therefore conceivably be much easier than the dilemma presented by Israel's position on arms control. As previously stated, Israel's approach is not tied to global disarmament concerns or principled arguments regarding nonproliferation, but rather hinges solely on regional security concerns.

However, it is inconceivable that the nonproliferation agenda can be advanced in the Middle East while being completely delinked from the global level. The nuclear negotiations between the P5+1 and Iran clearly demonstrate this. Similarly, it is hard to imagine that the ACRS process could have been initiated without the active involvement of the United States, which co-chaired the working group. This also applies to the interim regime of nuclear control described above, which cannot be advanced in the absence of serious engagement by the United States. A creative framework that combines both regional and global approaches would therefore be required.

Peace and cooperative security: A necessary prerequisite?

As previously stated, Israel's core approach to regional arms control, one that is shared by the United States, is predicated on the approach of peace first, arms control and disarmament last. According to this view, a fundamental transformation in the region's politics and overall security environment is an essential prerequisite for agreeing to any serious arms control or disarmament process for the Middle East. Yet this concept ignores the degree to which Israel's regional security environment has already been transformed. Given Israel's qualitative and quantitative military superiority, the absence of any militarily significant threat, and a forward Arab position on peace, there is little to justify Israel's insistence on maintaining its nuclear monopoly until absolute peace is achieved. Rather than being anchored in a strategic calculus based on specific threat perceptions, Israel's nuclear posture derives its rationale from the influence of the Jewish historical narrative on Israel's national psyche, the corollary of which is a strategy based on the realization of absolute security. The argument that justifies Israel's retention of its nuclear capability to face the looming threat of a nuclear Iran implies the logic of a self-fulfilling prophecy. Israel's nuclear posture, together with its concept of arms control, has deprived the region of an arms control process that can forestall the eventuality of a nuclear-armed Iran. It is the failure to engage in such a process that is leading to the emergence of precisely the threat against which Israel's nuclear weapons were designed to defend.

There can be little doubt about the desirability of peace to foster an enabling environment for regional arms control. However, the region's conflicts are too intractable, too complex, and too volatile to hinge the promise, indeed the necessity, of arms control on their successful resolution. At the very least, peace should not be a condition for initiating the first stages of an arms control and disarmament process. Indeed, such a process can be a prelude to peace rather than the other way around in that it instills a mutual understanding of states' threat perceptions and fosters a semblance of trust as reciprocal limitations, and eventually drawdowns in the level of armaments, accommodate the security interests of the parties involved.

Related to this is the notion that nuclear disarmament would necessitate some form of cooperative security framework, to ensure that states do not suffer from a security deficit after they had relinquished their nuclear capability. Yet if anything, the analysis presented throughout this chapter shows that nuclear weapons have been superfluous as a factor in the region's conflicts and have failed to provide an adequate deterrent for Israel despite its regional nuclear monopoly. It appears that there is a growing recognition of this reality in Israel. The experience of the nuclear dimension of recent conflicts has "deepened the basic Israeli outlook that nuclear weapons may have important symbolic and political value but lack genuine military value and should not be recognized as military weapons systems."[79]

Furthermore, the Middle East does not provide an environment conducive to the establishment of such a regional cooperative security framework, given the multiple conflicts, the persistence of strategic asymmetries between states, and the domestic upheavals brought about by the Arab uprisings and escalating ethnic and sectarian divisions.[80] This point aside, however, it is far from clear that such a framework is necessary for the objective of nuclear disarmament in the Middle East.

Nuclear latency in the Middle East

This is an issue that relates to the end-state of global nuclear disarmament. The concept of latency rests on the proposition that in the post-disarmament stage, former nuclear-weapon states would be permitted to retain elements of their nuclear infrastructure in order to be able to reconstitute their nuclear arsenals should the need arise. Retaining such a capability will enable nuclear-weapon states to take serious strides toward global nuclear disarmament with the confidence that they have an option to guard against a possible breakout scenario in the future.[81]

---

79. Cohen, *The Worst-Kept Secret,* 81.

80. See Fahmy and Haggag, "The Helsinki Process."

81. Sidney D. Drell and James E. Goodby, *A World Without Nuclear Weapons: End-State Issues* (Stanford, CA: Hoover Institution Press, 2009), 6–8; Sukeyuki Ichimasa, "The Concept of Virtual Nuclear Arsenals and 'a World Without Nuclear Weapons,'" *NIDS Journal of Defense and Security* 13 (December 2012); George Perkovich and James M. Acton, "Abolishing Nuclear Weapons," in *Abolishing Nuclear Weapons: A*

This concept poses serious questions related not only to its applicability but also its legitimacy. If the concept of nuclear latency were to be formalized in a future global disarmament treaty, meaning that some states would be allowed to retain such a capability while others would not, this would only perpetuate the discriminatory nature of the current nonproliferation regime in a different form. If, on the other hand, there were no formal prohibition on any of the members of the treaty to retain such a capability, then the nuclear arms race would be substituted by a nuclear latency race, with states striving to develop their nuclear infrastructure up to the point permitted by the treaty. The end result would be a world with multiple "virtual" nuclear-weapon states. It is hard to imagine how this could be the basis for a sustainable nuclear disarmament treaty regime with so many nuclear programs close to the point of breakout.

Furthermore, it is not clear what would constitute a legitimate justification for a state to actualize its virtual nuclear capability by rebuilding its nuclear weapons arsenal. In such a context, the propensity for instability would be quite high, with each state fearful that the other would move rapidly to reconstitute its military nuclear capability. As stated by Tom Schelling, "Every crisis would be a nuclear crisis, any war could become a nuclear war. The urge to preempt would dominate; whoever gets the first few weapons will coerce or preempt. It would be a nervous world."[82]

Beyond these questions, however, the Middle East poses unique challenges with respect to applying the concept of nuclear latency. Israel, after all, can be said to have presented the first example of nuclear latency with its non-introduction pledge. The definition of non-introduction was the subject of intense American-Israeli negotiations that preceded the Nixon-Meir 1969 meeting. Whereas the United States defined non-introduction

Debate, ed. George Perkovich and James M. Acton (Washington, DC: Carnegie Endowment for International Peace, 2009), 120–127.

82. Thomas C. Schelling, "A World Without Nuclear Weapons?" *Daedalus* 138, no. 4 (Fall 2009): 127.

to mean that Israel would refrain from manufacturing any nuclear weapons components, even if they were kept unassembled, Israel maintained that non-introduction meant refraining from conducting a nuclear weapon test and publicly acknowledging nuclear possession. Anything short of that would not constitute a violation of Israel's non-introduction pledge.[83] These negotiations provide what may perhaps be the first example of attempting to define the demarcation line between nuclear latency and actual nuclear weapons possession. The United States failed to impose a formulation for an advanced stage of latency on Israel, i.e., keeping nuclear weapons components unassembled. Wherever the dividing line is drawn between virtual and actual nuclear weapons capability, it is unclear how states with advanced nuclear infrastructures and know-how can be kept from crossing that line.

The other objections concerning latency are of particular relevance to the Middle East. Presumably, Israel would be the prime candidate that would be afforded the right to retain some form of latent capability, a fact that would either perpetuate the nuclear double standard that has traditionally been applied to Israel or pave the way for a virtual nuclear race in the Middle East. Iran's nuclear program offers another case where negotiations with the P5+1 are focused precisely on the issue of where to draw the line regarding Iran's nuclear latency. In Iran's case the line would be drawn much lower than with Israel. Would this create a different standard with respect to defining the virtual nuclear threshold? Would it be the case that some states would be allowed to progress toward a more advanced state of latency than others?

In the absence of a uniform standard that would define the scope of nuclear latency that would be applied to all states, such questions would bedevil the nuclear disarmament regime and could eventually undermine it altogether.

---

83. Cohen, *Worst-Kept Secret,* 4. See also Cohen and Burr, "Israel Crosses the Nuclear Threshold," 22–30.

Conclusion: Overcoming the Middle East
Roadblock toward Global Zero

Cohen recounts the first and only instance of public debate on the nuclear issue in Israel among a group of scientists and intellectuals during the early 1960s. The argument that appears to have prevailed in the course of this debate centered on the implications of Israel's nuclear project. Were Israel to acquire a nuclear capability, this would inevitably trigger a nuclear race in the Middle East. Nuclear weapons would afford Israel a measure of security only as long as it retained its nuclear monopoly. Once that monopoly was lost, the impact on Israel's security would be severe as Israel's size, demographic profile, and geopolitical situation would make it acutely vulnerable in the context of mutual nuclear deterrence, and more so in a situation of nuclear parity. "Hence, the argument went, Israel's nuclear program embodied the seeds of its own futility."[84]

More than fifty years since Israel became a nuclear weapon state, the prescience of this assessment is clear. In articulating their vision for global nuclear disarmament, Shultz, Kissinger, Perry, and Nunn offered a frank admission: "The steps we are taking now to address these [proliferation] threats are not adequate to the danger."[85] This was in reference to the global nuclear context. However, such an admission would also certainly apply to the Middle East. The region does not seem to have figured prominently in the global nuclear disarmament movement. This is probably due to the implicit assumption that the Middle East can wait until the endeavor to initiate a process to achieve a world without nuclear weapons gains momentum. But if the analysis presented here tells us anything, it is that the region cannot afford to wait. Left unchecked, the creeping nuclearization of the Middle East can present a set of challenges that jeopardize the vision of global nuclear disarmament.

---

84. Cohen, *Worst Kept Secret*, 37–38.

85. George P. Shultz, William J. Perry, Henry A. Kissinger, and Sam Nunn, "Toward a Nuclear Free World," *Wall Street Journal*, January 15, 2008.

The unique circumstances governing the nuclear question in the Middle East therefore reinforce the need for urgency. It is not too late to reverse the proliferation trend in the region. The Middle East has already crossed the nuclear threshold with Israel being the first country to go nuclear beyond the five recognized nuclear-weapon states under the NPT. But the region is not yet at the nuclear tipping point. Forestalling this eventuality will require a comprehensive approach that goes beyond the narrow focus on limiting Iran's nuclear program. This should begin by discarding the assumption that merely freezing the nuclear status quo in the Middle East will suffice to halt the proliferation dynamic that is now taking hold in the region.

Dealing with the nuclear question in the Middle East in its entirety is the only way to prevent the slide toward a nuclearized future. The "joint enterprise" put forward to establish the conditions for a world without nuclear weapons must therefore broaden its focus beyond the global level to articulate tangible steps to address the nuclear question at the regional level with a clear focus on the Middle East. The points of departure for such an endeavor must be a sober assessment of the nuclear context in the region and a roadmap to bring it closer to the vision enunciated for a nuclear-free world. Articulating such an agenda can help make the Middle East a pillar of a nuclear-free world, rather than an obstacle that would push this lofty goal further away.

CHAPTER 9

**A Middle East Free of
Weapons of Mass Destruction:
Moving beyond the Stalemate**

Peter Jones

Introduction

What appears to be an intractable standoff has characterized discussions
of Middle East arms control and disarmament for decades. On one side
are arguments, largely associated with Egyptian diplomacy, that a zone
free of weapons of mass destruction in the region can be accomplished
through accessions by all regional states to existing international arms
control and disarmament treaties, primarily the Nuclear Non-proliferation
Treaty (NPT). There will be a need for some regional add-ons for specific
matters, but these can be done quickly and should not get in the way
of the speedy creation of a zone. Above all, the control of the region's
weapons of mass destruction (WMD) can be achieved without the need
to mimic other regions in the creation of a regional security system as a
necessary accompaniment to arms control.[1]

---

1. For a statement of this view by two Egyptian diplomats (arguing that the European
   experience of regional security-building, which combined more general security
   issues with arms control, is not applicable to the Middle East), see Nabil Fahmy and

On the other hand are arguments, largely associated with Israeli diplomacy, that such a zone requires, as a pre-condition, that peaceful relations
exist in the region. In this view, the creation of a zone will be the cap-
stone to a process of regional peacemaking that will transform the region
into one where states no longer require WMD options because of their
sense of insecurity. Efforts should thus be made to begin the process of
creating such a new regional reality, and to keep WMD out of the hands
of especially dangerous regimes (in the Israeli view, essentially everyone
else in the region) in the meantime.[2]

Each of these arguments has a certain logic about it, and each serves
the narrowly defined interests of the country that makes it. For Israel, the
desire to avoid talking about, much less diplomatically dealing with, its
opaque nuclear status requires arguments which hold that this status is
not the real issue; that the real issue of regional security in the Middle
East is the lack of an inclusive, stable regional order. Once that has been
addressed, questions surrounding a WMD-free zone can begin to be tackled. For Egypt, the desire to pressure Israel into quickly renouncing its
nuclear option means that arguments that this cannot be done until the
region is at peace are unacceptable, as this may take decades—if it ever
happens at all. Egypt therefore believes that disarmament can take place
without the need for substantial revision to the regional order. Tangible
steps to create a Middle East WMD-free zone must begin immediately,
regardless of the broader issues of regional stability, and Israel's WMD

Karim Haggag, "The Helsinki Process and the Middle East: The Viability of Cooperative
Security Frameworks for a Region in Flux," in *Regional Security Dialogue in the
Middle East: Changes, Challenges and Opportunities,* ed. Chen Kane and Egle
Murauskaite (New York: Routledge, 2014).

2. This policy is sometimes known as the "long corridor" approach: disarmament will
only be possible once the region has passed down a "long corridor" of peacemaking
and transformation. See Avner Cohen and Patricia Lewis, "Israel and the NWFZ in the
Middle East: Tiptoeing Down a 'Long Corridor,'" in *Arms Control and Missile Proliferation in the Middle East,* ed. Bernd W. Kubbig and Sven-Eric Fikenscher (London:
Routledge, 2012).

capabilities are the place to start this, since they (in the Egyptian view) are at the root of the region's WMD problem.

This chapter argues that this debate is sterile. A way forward is required which cuts through the zero-sum nature of this exchange and which permits work on both objectives at the same time. The key to success is a process that creates an inclusive regional security system in the Middle East, which would include this crucial element: early and serious action on an ambitious arms control and disarmament agenda. This chapter begins with a brief review of the official efforts which have been made to create regional arms control systems in the Middle East. It then examines the kind of regional architecture that will be necessary to support the goal of creating a WMDFZ. It will propose some ideas on how to get there, over time. This last point is especially important: this will be lengthy enterprise of small steps, especially initially, toward great goals.

Section 1: Official Arms Control and Disarmament Efforts in the Region

There have been two official efforts to create a regional arms control and disarmament process in the Middle East. One lasted a few years and then fell apart over the differences between Egypt and Israel regarding the nuclear issue. The other has (thus far) not been able to begin, once again, because of the differences over this issue.

The group which existed was a creation of the Middle East Peace Process, specifically the multilateral talks which occurred within that process in the early 1990s. The Arms Control and Regional Security Working Group (known as ACRS) existed from 1992 to 1995. It was the first and, thus far, the only multilateral dialogue on regional security in the Middle East.[3] Though ACRS failed due to the growing difference between Israel

---

3. Several histories have been written of the ACRS process. For an Egyptian perspective, see Nabil Fahmy, "Reflections on the Arms Control and Regional Security Process in the Middle East," in *New Horizons and New Strategies in Arms Control,* ed. James Brown (Albuquerque, NM: Sandia National Laboratories, November 1998); Nabil Fahmy, "Prospects for Arms Control and Proliferation in the Middle East,"

and Egypt over the nuclear issue, it is often forgotten that all of the other multilateral groups failed shortly after, due to differences over the direction of the bilateral track of the peace process. Analysis of ACRS points to the following weaknesses in its composition and working methods:

- It was not sufficiently inclusive in either its composition (several key countries either stayed away, or were not invited) or its agenda.
- It conceived of the Middle East as one entity for arms control purposes, not recognizing that there are significant subregional issues, even as there are issues which must be tackled by the region as a whole.
- It conceived of Middle East regional security and arms control as being a sub-issue of the Arab-Israeli peace process, thereby creating a dynamic which did not recognize that the Middle East

---

Nonproliferation Review, Summer 2001: 1–7; and Nabil Fahmy, "Special Comment," United Nations Institute for Disarmament Research, *Disarmament Forum* 2, 2001: 3–5. An Israeli perspective can be found in Emily Landau, *Egypt and Israel in ACRS: Bilateral Concerns in a Regional Arms Control Process,* Memorandum no. 59, June 2001, Jaffee Center for Strategic Studies (Tel Aviv). For other perspectives see Michael D. Yaffe, "Promoting Arms Control and Regional Security in the Middle East," *Disarmament Forum* 2, 2001: 9–25; Peter Jones, "Arms Control in the Middle East: Some Reflections on ACRS," *Security Dialogue* 28, no. 1 (1997): 57–70; Peter Jones, "Arms Control in the Middle East; Is It Time to Renew ACRS?" *Disarmament Forum* 2, 2005; and Peter Jones, "The Arms Control and Regional Security Working Group: Still Relevant to the Middle East?" in *WMD Arms Control in the Middle East: Prospects, Obstacles and Options,* ed. Harald Müller and Daniel Müller (Farnham, UK: Ashgate, 2014); Bruce Jentleson, "The Middle East Arms Control and Regional Security Talks: Progress, Problems, and Prospects," University of California, Institute on Global Conflict and Cooperation, Policy Paper no. 26, September 1996; and Joel Peters, *Building Bridges: Arab-Israeli Multilateral Talks* (London: Royal Institute of International Affairs, 1994). In the interests of full disclosure, it should be noted that the present author was a member of the Canadian delegation to the ACRS process, which played a facilitative role in discussions of regional CBMs, during his service with Canada's Department of Foreign Affairs.

has been the scene of several overlapping conflicts, many of which have had nothing to do with the Arab-Israeli question.

- It failed to sufficiently explore the issue of how a regional security system might be created in the Middle East to support and be the framework for regional arms control and disarmament (though efforts were under way to begin this exploration when ACRS was suspended).

The question of an official, regional approach to arms control lay dormant after ACRS, despite a worsening regional security situation, particularly as regards concerns over WMD proliferation. In 2010, during the conference to review the implementation of the NPT, Egypt and others succeeded in getting the international community to agree to work toward a process intended to create an official arms control dialogue in the Middle East. By most accounts, the United States accepted this reluctantly and only because Arab countries, led by Egypt—by now very frustrated after many years of attempts to introduce the issue to the agenda of international disarmament talks—threatened to wreck the NPT review process.

The resolution that passed at the NPT 2010 Review Conference called for an official meeting to consider the question of creating a Middle East WMDFZ and begin steps toward this goal before the next NPT Review Conference in 2015.[4] It was clear from the beginning that the United States was not enthusiastic about this. Israel, noting that it never signed the NPT and was thus not even at the 2010 Review Conference, never formally stated that it would participate in the process. A host for the proposed Middle East WMDFZ conference was found—Finland—and

---

4. Specifically, the resolution adopted by the 2010 NPT Review Conference called for the convening of a conference in 2012 "to be attended by all states of the Middle East, on the establishment of a Middle East zone free of nuclear weapons and all other weapons of mass destruction, on the basis of arrangements freely arrived at by the states of the region, and with the full support and engagement of the nuclear-weapon states." NPT 2010 Final Document, vol. I, http://www.un.org/en/conf/npt/2010.

tentative preparations began. But the initial meeting, which was scheduled for 2012, was postponed by the United States, which argued that preparations were not sufficiently advanced to assure success. This was thinly veiled code for the fact that the basic differences which had killed ACRS twenty years before had not been resolved, and the United States saw no value in going forward with a process which would founder as ACRS had. Egypt and others took the view that it was up to the United States to bring Israel to the table with a changed position, but the United States has maintained that it is not able (nor does it appear to be willing) to do so.

Thus far, despite the valiant efforts of Finland and some Track 2 processes to generate some sort of dialogue which would advance the agenda,[5] it seems unlikely as of this writing that any official meeting will take place pursuant to the 2010 NPT mandate before the 2015 Review Conference.

Section 2: A Middle East Regional Security Architecture and the WMDFZ Question

The world is not without experience in the creation of zones free of weapons of mass destruction. There are nuclear weapon-free zones (NWFZs) in Latin America, Africa, Central Asia, and Southeast Asia which provide some basis for understanding the challenges facing the Middle East as it embarks upon this journey.[6] In looking at the NWFZs that exist, not one of

---

5. See, for example, the activities of the Academic Peace Orchestra, a German-based Track 2 project which has held several conferences and workshops to develop ideas in support of the goal. More information may be found at http://academicpeaceorchestra.com.

6. In 1996 two noted international disarmament experts did a major study on these zones and their possible lessons for the Middle East. See Jan Prawitz. and James F. Leonard, "A Zone Free of Weapons of Mass Destruction in the Middle East," United Nations Institute for Disarmament Research, 1996. Others studies of note on the subject include Patricia Lewis, "All in the Timing: The Weapons of Mass Destruction Free Zone in the Middle East," Chatham House, August 2014; and Jozef Goldblat,

them happened quickly or in the absence of a broader system or architecture of regional institutions and discussions on cooperation and security. Disarmament does not take place in a vacuum; it requires predictability and trust. These factors take time to nurture. Steps toward regional arms control are part of this, but not all of it. Though supporters of the "Egyptian position" will scoff, this is not an acceptance of "the Israeli argument." Rather, it is a recognition of reality. Indeed, one of the great tragedies of the past few decades has been that the relative strengths and weaknesses of the various positions are not debated on their merits. Merely by pointing out the obvious (that no other region which has achieved a NWFZ agreement has done so in the way Egypt proposes for the Middle East), one is subject to criticism for being a supporter of the "Israeli view." It is difficult to imagine how we might go forward with the atmosphere thus poisoned.

What is meant by "a regional architecture"? In essence, it is the creation of an ongoing process whereby the regional countries develop norms and mechanisms to assist them in managing their relations. Such architectures involve the creation of norms of conduct and means of communication which are then subject to ongoing review and implementation in a cooperative fashion. It is important to note that these regional architectures all began modestly and evolved. The intended objective of these systems is to assist the states of each region in creating stability and predictability in their relations. In doing so, each process has laid the ground for a fundamental reconsideration of basic security policies and assumptions—including, in some regions at least, the eventual renunciation of WMD options.[7]

"Nuclear-Weapon-Free Zones: A History and Assessment," *Nonproliferation Review,* Spring/Summer 1997.

7. There have been several books and papers published on the idea of a regional security architecture for the Middle East. For a selection, see Peter Jones, "Towards a Regional Security Regime for the Middle East: Issues and Options," Stockholm International Peace Research Institute, 1998, republished with an extensive new afterword in 2011, http://books.sipri.org/product_info?c_product_id=434; Peter Jones, "Structuring Middle

Principles for a Regional Architecture
to Support a WMDFZ in the Middle East

The Middle East is characterized by multiple, overlapping rivalries and security challenges. There has historically been enormous mistrust, and not only on the Israeli-Arab level. The region is the only one where WMD have actually been used since 1945, and there have been several attempts to clandestinely develop WMD, including by some regional countries in direct contravention of treaty obligations. Moreover, despite the argument advanced by some that the existence of Israel's clandestine nuclear capability is at the heart of the Middle East's WMD problem, the actual instances of WMD use in the region have had nothing to do with Israel. Clearly, though Israel's WMD program is a significant factor in the region's WMD problem, there is a wider set of causes for proliferation in the region. Finally, the recent series of uprisings and revolutions (beginning with the so-called Arab Spring) show that the region is in considerable flux, both socially and politically.

This is not the best of environments in which to embark upon the creation of a WMDFZ. But all of these factors also make the creation of such a zone of critical importance. The legacy of mistrust and rivalry and the current upheavals in the region suggest that the creation of a WMDFZ will be a long and slow process of developing trust and predictability concerning many issues. This process will have to be founded and developed according to some key principles. The following may be a starting point.

East Security," *Survival* 51, no. 6 (December 2009–January 2010); Shai Feldman and Abdullah Toukan, *Bridging the Gap: A Future Security Architecture for the Middle East* (Lanham, MD: Rowman and Littlefield, 1997); the collection of essays in the 2003 special issue of *The Journal of Strategic Studies* 26, no. 3 (2003) on "Building Regional Security in the Middle East: International, Regional and Domestic Influences"; the collection of papers in Kane and Murauskaite, *Regional Security Dialogue in the Middle East;* and the collection of papers in Müller and Müller, *WMD Arms Control in the Middle East.*

Principle 1: An Inclusive Process

"Inclusion" concerns both the *membership* and the *agenda* of a process. In terms of *membership,* it is generally agreed that the region should be defined as the states of the Arab League, plus Iran, Israel, and Turkey. It is likely that not all of these countries will join the process at the outset, but seats must be left for them when they are prepared to join. Another issue is the question of whether extra-regional partners can be included. These would be countries with interests in the region and whose support is vital if a process is to work. Finally, it will be necessary to include nearby states on issues where their presence is relevant. Concerning the WMDFZ issue, for example, it is likely that Pakistan and India would be involved in some way as their WMD activities affect the security of some nations within the proposed Middle East zone.

Turning to the *agenda,* inclusivity means that all issues of concern must be on the agenda. However, there is an interplay between what issues can productively be discussed and who agrees to join the discussions. For example, if one of the key states rumored to have, or be seeking, WMD refuses to join, it will be difficult to have conclusive discussions—though consideration of the issue can go forward with those who are at the table. Furthermore, while all issues should be on the agenda, the official process will probably begin with some issues for early work which hold out the prospect of success. This raises the issue of expectations. If the agenda deliberately avoids the toughest issues, many will regard it as not serious; but if it tackles the hardest issues right away, failure is likely. Instead, certain clusters of issues could be developed, with each being discussed in an appropriate forum, and with some having objectives that could be realized earlier than others. There are many ways to identify those issues which will be the subject of dialogue at different levels of the process.

Principle 2: A Multilayered Process

The second principle thus concerns the structure of the process. Since there will be some states unlikely to join an official process at the outset, how can an inclusive process be structured in terms of both agenda and membership? An answer could be to structure the process around interrelated and interlocking levels of dialogue. The first will be Track 1, government-level discussions. These, initially, will be low-key, issue- and results-oriented, and will go on between those states in the region willing to talk to each other, joined by invited extra-regional states and institutions. The usual diplomatic conventions, such as consensus decision-making, are likely to apply; a rigid structure should be avoided in the early stages. The key principle here is that the agenda will be initiated and developed by those parties operating within the process.

The second tier would be some sort of Track 2 process. This track would deal with issues which were not yet ready for inclusion on the official track, but on which focused, long-term, expert discussion could prepare the ground for eventual inclusion in the official talks. Officials could participate in these discussions, in their private capacities. This track could include institutes and individuals from the region and beyond, according to the subject to be discussed in each case. It might require a modest organizational structure, procedures to report to Track 1, and financial support from both regional and extra-regional states and foundations.[8]

---

8. The idea of creating a Track 2 process on regional security matters to complement and assist Track 1 is discussed in Jones, "Structuring Middle East Security," and Jones, "Towards a Regional Security Regime." The role of Track 2 in regional security discussions is further assessed in Peter Jones, "Filling a critical gap or just wasting time? Track Two diplomacy and regional security in the Middle East," *Disarmament Forum*, no. 2 (2008); D.D. Kaye, *Talking to the Enemy. Track Two Diplomacy in the Middle East and South Asia* (Santa Monica, CA: RAND Corp., 2007); Emily Landau, *Arms Control in the Middle East: Cooperative Security Dialogue and Regional Restraints* (Eastbourne, UK: Sussex Academic Press, 2006), chapter 2; Hussein Agha, Shai Feldman, Ahmad Khalidi, and Zeev Schiff, *Track II Diplomacy: Lessons from the Middle East* (Cambridge, MA: MIT Press, 2004); and D.D. Kaye, "Track Two Diplomacy and Regional Security in the Middle East," *International Negotiation* 6, no. 1 (2001). There are also chapters devoted to the idea in Kane and Murauskaite, *Regional Security Dialogue in the Middle East*.

Principle 3: "Variable Geometry"

In a multilayered process, the membership and topics to be discussed will vary by level. If only certain states are prepared to join the official layer for the time being, the structured Track 2 layer could have many more members, including from countries that do not yet formally recognize each other. Because of the current situation in the region, dialogue mechanisms will develop in a flexible manner according, at least in the early years, to the concept of "variable geometry" (as sometimes proposed for the European Union). This idea holds that different issues will be discussed in different fora and at different rates of speed, according to the requirements of the topic at hand. Different constellations of actors may attend different discussions, but the whole will be bound together by an overarching framework of principles and objectives which will have to be agreed upon by the region's states. This raises the question of who might be the core states necessary to get the process going. There is no obvious answer to this question; much will depend on who steps forward to lead.

Principle 4: Regional and Subregional Dimensions of a WMDFZ Process

The fourth key principle has to do with the relationship between the proposed new process and other, existing bodies. In other regional cases (such as the Association of Southeast Asian Nations and the Organization for Security and Co-operation in Europe), other multilateral bodies coexisted and evolved with those processes. The key to success was for these bodies to take the attitude that they were not in competition and that their basic objectives were complementary in many ways. In the Middle East case, there are already interstate bodies, groups, and initiatives, such as the Arab League, the Maghreb Arab Union, and the Gulf Cooperation Council. If a wider, regional cooperation and security process is to be developed in the Middle East, it will likely evolve in a way which fills niches that these standing bodies do not already fill. It will also be necessary in the Middle East case to consider how subregional dynamics might affect the creation of a region-wide process. A Middle East WMDFZ will require the ultimate creation of a region-wide security architecture, even as processes on other issues would continue to exist on the subregional level and should be encouraged. The key is to find a way in which region-wide and subregional agendas can go forward together and complement each other. Ideally, an emerging global architecture for disarmament, such as the proposed Joint Enterprise (see chapter 3) would also strengthen regional attempts at security and disarmament.

Principle 5: A WMDFZ Process and the Peace Process

Central to this issue is the question of whether the region has to wait until the Arab-Israeli issue is resolved before tackling the WMDFZ issue and launching such a cooperation and security process. Though it is difficult, the lesson from other regions, such as Southeast Asia, Africa, and Latin America, is that the creation of a regional architecture should go forward with a commitment from regional governments that they will not allow the inevitable ups and downs of the peace process to derail the broader discussions. Solving existing problems while also looking ahead is not contradictory. This will require leadership from some regional governments to ensure that the daily vicissitudes of public opinion do not block the process. It also argues for a quiet approach which eschews attempts to court public attention, at least at the beginning.

Principle 6: Latency

The question of WMD latency will be critical.[9] Certain states in the region have achieved real WMD capabilities, and others have progressed far along in their search for such capabilities. Even if agreement to eliminate

---

9. For a discussion of latency as it relates to nuclear disarmament generally, see Wolfgang Panofsky, "Capability versus Intent: The Latent Threat of Nuclear Proliferation," *Bulletin of the Atomic Scientists,* June 14, 2007. A critique of the intellectual and methodological poverty which has attended most discussions of latency may be found in Scott Sagan, "Nuclear Latency and Nuclear Proliferation," in *Forecasting Nuclear Proliferation in the 21st Century: The Role of Theory, vol. 1,* ed.

WMD from the region could be achieved, the knowledge of how to do it will not. Moreover, it seems likely that some degree of suspicion may exist in the region for some time, even if relations between all its states do achieve a better footing. It seems naïve to expect that at least some regional states will not hedge their bets by retaining some residual capability to reconstitute WMD programs quickly.[10] This problem points to the need for a comprehensive regional verification system to be developed, which will accompany the international verification systems which now exist. It should not be forgotten that at least two regional states (Iran and Iraq) achieved considerable progress toward developing nuclear weapons capability while they were part of the NPT. It also speaks to the need identified earlier for a much greater degree of trust to exist between regional states. In all likelihood, then, as the region evolves toward a WMDFZ, there will have to be a tacit recognition that some level of hedging will exist for some years of the process. The regime would seek to set some rules for such behavior and encourage the eventual renunciation of hedging.

Getting Started and Keeping Up the Momentum

As noted at the outset of this chapter, a WMDFZ will not magically appear in a region which is otherwise unstable and dangerous. Thus, the process could concentrate on the key issues in the following broadly thematic areas, according to the concept of "variable geometry." "Success" does not necessarily mean the achievement of a solution to all of these issues. But intensive dialogue to better manage their effects and develop possible longer-term solutions can be an important element in setting the stage

---

William C. Potter and Gaukhar Mukhatzhanova (Stanford, CA: Stanford University Press, 2010).

10. For a discussion of nuclear hedging, see Ariel E. Levite, "Never Say Never Again: Nuclear Reversal Revisited," *International Security* 27, no. 3 (Winter 2002/03).

of their eventual resolution. Not all issues can be initially tackled at the Track 1 level. The fact that some countries are not likely to participate in official talks over given issues (for reasons of not being willing to recognize each other, for example) means that a creative, flexible structure will be required which blends Track 1, Track 1.5, and Track 2 discussions. Finally, discussions over some of these issues are going to be happening at the global level. A creative way to blend regional and global discussions will be required to ensure that the two do not go off in mutually contradictory directions. This might be an area for a Joint Global Enterprise to play a useful role. With these points in mind, an illustrative list of issues which could be worked on at various levels in the coming years might include:[11]

Biological:

- Development of standards for the peaceful uses of biological science and technology in the region (following Biological Weapons Convention article X), perhaps leading to discussion of a regional Code of Conduct for work in this area
- Information-sharing on relevant activities, as described in the Biological Weapons Convention
- Studies by regional experts on verification techniques and lessons from various historical cases (e.g., the United Nations Special Commission in Iraq)
- Establishment of regional cooperation for disease surveillance (both human and animal)

Chemical:

- Studies by regional experts on verification lessons from other cases

---

11. This list of possible areas for CBM discussions at the Track 1, Track 1.5, and Track 2 levels in support of a Middle East WMDFZ process is illustrative only and is not meant to be exhaustive. Some discussions around some of these topics are already under way, but they could be brought under a single roof as part of a process arising from the implementation of the 2010 NPT Resolution.

- Development of standards for the peaceful operation of chemical industries in the region, perhaps leading to discussion of a regional code of conduct for work in this area
- Development of cooperation in the field of environmental standards and protection

Nuclear:

- Development of regional standards for the safe and transparent development of peaceful nuclear capabilities, such as power generation (drawing on relevant international agreements as appropriate)
- Development of regional standards for the safe and transparent handling and storage of nuclear waste (drawing on relevant international agreements as appropriate)
- Development of a regional agreement for assistance in the case of a nuclear accident (drawing on relevant international agreements as appropriate)
- Development of a regional inspection and verification model for a Middle East without nuclear weapons (drawing on relevant international and regional agreements as appropriate)
- Studies by regional experts on nuclear weapons dismantlement technologies (such as the recent Norway-United Kingdom project)
- Development of regional verification cooperation mechanisms relevant to the Comprehensive Test Ban Treaty, in cooperation with the Comprehensive Nuclear-Test-Ban Treaty Organization

Delivery Systems:

- Regional experts' study on the relevance for the Middle East of proposals made in other regional contexts for limitations on methods of WMD delivery
- Regional experts' study on the relevance for the Middle East of missile test notification agreements (such as the India-Pakistan agreement)

- Regional experts' study on historical cases of delivery system dismantlement (e.g., intermediate-range nuclear forces dismantlement under the Intermediate-Range Nuclear Forces Treaty)

General and Political:

- Regional experts' study on no-first-use agreements and their applicability to the Middle East
- Regional experts' study on other regional NWFZ cases and their applicability to the Middle East
- Establishment of a regional communications network for the sharing of notifications and other information relevant to a WMDFZ
- Regional experts' study on non-attack agreements and their applicability to the Middle East (e.g., India-Pakistan agreement on non-attack on nuclear facilities)
- Regional experts' study on conventional confidence-building measures and arms control measures which could assist in the creation of a WMDFZ

Other security issues:

- Confidence-building and security-building measures in the conventional military sphere
- Discussion of the broader regional security implications relating to specific conflicts such as the Arab-Israeli dispute and the situation in Syria
- Other issues of concern (e.g., criminal activity which has a security dimension)
- Other issue(s) to be agreed upon.

Conclusion

None of this will be terribly satisfying to those who want to see the creation of a WMDFZ in the Middle East right away. Their frustrations are understandable. But simply expressing those frustrations in such a way as to perpetuate the standoff over the issue is not going to make progress possible. In every other region where tangible progress has been made on the elimination of WMD, the process took years of patient diplomacy and dialogue. In each case, a few key states stepped forward to lead and others joined in later.

Moreover, other critical differences were ongoing in these regions even as the WMD process was under way, and no one took the view that disarmament discussions could not progress until one particular view of another specific question was accepted by everyone. All states of the region eventually came around to the view that a wider regional process for cooperation and security was an essential component in the creation of the zone. It seems highly unlikely that the Middle East—riven as it is with crises in Syria, the violent actions of sub-state actors such as the Islamic State, suspicions of WMD activities in Iran, and an Arab-Israeli peace process that seemingly will not end—can escape these realities.

If progress is to be made, pursuant to the 2010 NPT mandate, what is required is for all sides in the debate to show leadership. This will require the modification of long-held positions on all sides. Simply put, a WMDFZ cannot be created in the absence of progress toward the creation of a regional security system. But it is also unreasonable to hold that serious discussions around the creation of such a zone, and serious steps to begin bringing it about, cannot begin until all of the region's problems are solved. Both positions are unrealistic. The stalemate which has characterized discussions of the issue cannot be allowed to endure, if progress is ever to be made.

CHAPTER 10 **Decoupling Nuclear Weapons and Deterrence in South Asia**

S. Paul Kapur

One of the strongest arguments in favor of nuclear weapons is deceptively straightforward: states need nuclear weapons to ensure their survival in a dangerous world. By threatening to inflict incalculable horrors on the combatants, nuclear weapons can make war prohibitively costly[1] and prevent it from occurring. For no benefit that a state might seek by waging war, regardless of how important it might be, could possibly outweigh the catastrophe of nuclear devastation.[2] According to this logic, halting the spread of nuclear weapons across the globe, or disarming states that already possess nuclear weapons, could actually be counterproductive,

---

1. In a conventional world, defeat requires military victory that can take months or years to achieve, and probably does not entail the total destruction of an adversary. In a nuclear environment, by contrast, a state can in a matter of minutes not only defeat an adversary, but also destroy it as a functioning society. Thus, although the costs of conventional war can be significant, the costs of nuclear war are likely to be truly catastrophic. See Robert Jervis, *The Meaning of the Nuclear Revolution: Statecraft and the Prospect of Armageddon* (Ithaca, NY: Cornell University Press, 1989), 4–8.

2. As one scholar put it, "There is no more ironclad law in international relations theory than this: nuclear weapon states do not fight wars with each other." See Devin Hagerty, *The Consequences of Nuclear Proliferation: Lessons from South Asia* (Cambridge, MA: Massachusetts Institute of Technology Press, 1998), 184.

as it would make conflict safer and therefore more likely. Nuclear weapons thus represent an awful bargain, in which nuclear states accept a small likelihood of calamity in order to avoid conventional war. But given the high cost and frequency of conventional conflict in a non-nuclear world, it is a bargain worth making.[3]

This pro-nuclear argument presumes the existence of a close relationship between nuclear weapons and deterrence. The nuclear bargain is acceptable only because nuclear weapons are highly effective deterrent tools, more effective than any other means that states have at their disposal. If this assumption of a tight linkage between nuclear weapons and deterrence were in fact incorrect, it would change the contours of the debate, and the nuclear bargain outlined above would seem far less attractive.

Scholars skeptical of nuclear weapons' stabilizing effects have long sought to problematize their presumed tight link with deterrence. Some have focused on the organizations that controlled nuclear weapons, arguing that they would commit errors that would undermine nuclear weapons' deterrent effects. For example, militaries would devise standard operating procedures for managing the weapons that increased the likelihood of accident. Or they would permit military officers to adopt the destabilizing, offensive nuclear strategies that they would tend to prefer, but that could also lead to the outbreak of conflict. This argument did not deny the existence of a tight logical link between nuclear weapons and deterrence. The argument claimed, rather, that in practice, organizational pathologies would short-circuit the nuclear weapons-deterrence connection, preventing states from adopting the cautious, stabilizing policies that they might otherwise have embraced in a nuclear environment.[4]

---

3. See, e.g., Kenneth Waltz, *The Spread of Nuclear Weapons: More May Be Better*, Adelphi Papers 171, International Institute for Strategic Studies (1981), 1–37; and John J. Mearsheimer, "The Case for a Ukrainian Nuclear Deterrent," *Foreign Affairs* 72, no. 3: 65.

4. See Scott D. Sagan, *The Limits of Safety: Organizations, Accidents, and Nuclear Weapons* (Princeton, NJ: Princeton University Press, 1993).

A second major approach to decoupling nuclear weapons from deterrence directly addressed the logical link between the two. Unlike the "organizational" argument outlined above, this "strategic" approach maintained that nuclear weapons could increase the likelihood of war not because of bureaucratic pathologies, but because of decision-makers' rational calculations regarding nuclear weapons' coercive utility. A state that was dissatisfied with the status quo, and militarily weak relative to its adversaries, could be emboldened to challenge existing territorial or political arrangements through military action that it would have deemed excessively dangerous in a non-nuclear environment. This would occur because of nuclear weapons' ability to insulate the weak state from its adversary's conventional superiority; the stronger state, fearing nuclear escalation, would refrain from retaliating against the weak state's provocations with the full weight of its conventional capabilities. Thus, nuclear danger could actually create incentives for rational policymakers to choose to engage in aggressive behavior.[5] This meant not only that nuclear weapons might not generate deterrence in practice. It meant that nuclear weapons could fail to generate deterrence because the two were logically opposed to one another.[6]

This volume takes an eclectic approach to problematizing the relationship between nuclear weapons and deterrence. In the opening chapter, Benoît Pelopidas advances both of the above arguments. He explains that organizations can short-circuit rational nuclear decision-making, leading

---

5. The Kargil conflict, which erupted when Pakistan seized Indian territory in Kashmir soon after the two countries' 1998 nuclear tests, illustrates this logic. As I explain below, this and other aggressive Pakistani behavior following the tests was encouraged by the Pakistanis' belief that their new nuclear capacity insulated them from India's conventional superiority. This allowed the Pakistanis to challenge the Indians in a variety of ways, from waging an anti-Indian campaign using Islamist militants to flouting regional territorial boundaries.

6. See my discussion of the differences between organizational pessimism and strategic pessimism in Sumit Ganguly and S. Paul Kapur, *India, Pakistan, and the Bomb: Debating Nuclear Stability in South Asia* (New York: Columbia University Press, 2010).

to accidents and conflict. He also notes that nuclear weapons can create incentives for aggressive behavior by rational decision-makers. In addition, the chapter advances a number of other arguments that do not fall neatly into either of the above schools. For example, it highlights the issue of historical uncertainty, pointing out that we do not actually know why past cases that are often cited as successful examples of nuclear deterrence either remained peaceful or did not escalate. Close examination of these cases suggests that nuclear weapons may not have been responsible for their favorable outcomes. The chapter also emphasizes the possibilities for what one might call "nuclear substitution," generating deterrence through the use of tools other than nuclear weapons. As Pelopidas points out, conventional weapons systems can, in some cases, protect states as well as or better than nuclear weapons, without subjecting them to nuclear weapons' costs and dangers. Indeed, in a variety of situations, nuclear weapons may simply be inappropriate to security challenges that a state faces. Some of the authors of this volume thus seek to show that, for a wide range of theoretical, empirical, and practical reasons, nuclear weapons and deterrence should be decoupled from one another.

If this approach is correct, and states really can decouple nuclear weapons from deterrence, one of the most important arguments against nuclear arms control is considerably weakened. This creates new possibilities for states either to undertake serious reductions in their nuclear arsenals or to forgo nuclear weapons entirely. For, by doing so, states will not necessarily forfeit the deterrence that they need to survive. Indeed, doing so may actually help states to avoid deterrence failure and to protect themselves more effectively from the dangers of a violent and competitive world.

Even if nuclear weapons and deterrence can be decoupled in principle, however, achieving such an outcome could be difficult in practice. Decision-makers might fail to recognize security organizations' propensity for mismanaging nuclear weapons; might not understand that nuclear weapons can create incentives for aggressive behavior; might not know that the historical evidence linking nuclear weapons and deterrence is tenuous; might not realize that they could generate deterrence using non-nuclear tools; or might want nuclear weapons for reasons unrelated to deterrence. In any of these scenarios, the nuclear-deterrence decoupling outlined above would have limited relevance for real-world policy-making. It is also possible that decoupling logic could have an impact in one region of the world, where decision-makers recognize the tenuousness of the relationship between nuclear weapons and deterrence, but be irrelevant in another, where leaders still believe that nuclear weapons and deterrence are logically or practically connected, or want nuclear weapons for reasons unrelated to deterrence. The real-world applicability of decoupling logic must therefore be examined on a case-by-case basis.

South Asia is an important area in which to assess the applicability of the nuclear decoupling approach. It is one of the world's most volatile regions. India and Pakistan have fought four wars and engaged in innumerable skirmishes in the roughly six decades since independence. Their relations remain highly antagonistic. And the two countries possess sizable nuclear arsenals. If a decoupling of nuclear weapons from deterrence could lead to significant Indian and Pakistani nuclear reductions, it would thus make the region and the world considerably safer. This chapter attempts to determine the potential for nuclear decoupling to do so.

I argue that South Asia does not offer a single answer to this question; Indian and Pakistani positions regarding the relationship between nuclear weapons and deterrence diverge significantly. In the Indian view, deterrence and nuclear weapons are not wholly synonymous. Indian leaders not only believe that nuclear weapons can fail to deter conflict, but realize that nuclear weapons can actually encourage aggressive behavior that leads to the outbreak of conflict. They also recognize that, in certain situations, conventional capabilities can generate deterrence more effectively than nuclear weapons. Finally, Indian leaders value nuclear weapons' political symbolism and believe that they hold considerable value even apart from their deterrent effects. Nonetheless, the Indians also value what they view as nuclear weapons' robust deterrent characteristics, which they believe can protect them from stronger powers such as China. As a result, the Indians will not merely maintain their existing nuclear capabilities for the foreseeable future—they plan to augment them both qualitatively and quantitatively. Thus India is a mixed case. Indian leaders do not entirely conflate nuclear weapons and deterrence, but do believe that nuclear weapons' deterrent effects can help to ensure their security against particular dangers.

Pakistani leaders, by contrast, believe that deterrence and nuclear weapons are very closely linked. The Pakistanis are convinced that, just as nuclear weapons helped to prevent a Warsaw Pact conventional attack against weaker NATO during the Cold War, Pakistan's nuclear capacity has historically prevented aggression by a conventionally stronger India. They also believe that, in the absence of a robust nuclear capability, Pakistan will be unable to generate sufficient deterrence in the future to protect itself from a growing Indian conventional threat. As a result, the Pakistanis plan to rely even more heavily on nuclear weapons in the future than they have previously, lowering the nuclear threshold on the subcontinent in order to deter a catastrophic Indian conventional attack.

Although the differences between Indian and Pakistani understandings of the relationship between nuclear weapons and deterrence are real, one should not overstate their significance. For, at bottom, the practical reality for both countries is similar. Despite divergent views, neither side is going to eradicate or significantly reduce its nuclear weapons capacity in the foreseeable future. In fact, both sides are increasing their nuclear capabilities—though they are doing so in ways, and for reasons, that are quite different from one another. Below, I explore the strategic views, and resulting nuclear policies, of the two countries in turn.

India

Indian security managers do not generally conflate nuclear weapons with deterrence; they recognize that the two do not necessarily go hand in hand. The reason for this recognition is two-fold. First, Pakistan has waged a decades-long asymmetric warfare campaign against India, using Islamist militants supported by Pakistani forces, in hopes of coercing India into relinquishing Kashmir. The campaign has succeeded in attriting, or wearing down, Indian military and economic resources; in provoking New Delhi to employ heavy-handed counterinsurgency tactics that have tarnished India's international image; and in challenging the legitimacy of India's control of Kashmir. One of India's main national security goals has been to deter Pakistan from continuing to wage this militant campaign. But India has never been able to achieve this end, even after acquiring nuclear weapons. Indeed, some of the most spectacular militant attacks against India, including an assault on the Indian parliament in 2001 and attacks on Mumbai in 2008, occurred well after the Indian nuclear tests of 1998.

In addition, significant state-level disputes have erupted between India and Pakistan despite the two countries' possession of nuclear weapons. Regional conflict data show that these disputes increased in frequency and severity as the nuclear proliferation process progressed through the 1980s and the 1990s. In fact, the first outright war that India and Pakistan had fought in twenty-eight years occurred in 1999 in the Kargil area of Kashmir, when Pakistani forces seized a swath of territory on the Indian side of the Line of Control (LoC) dividing the disputed territory. The Indians, while remaining on their side of the LoC and avoiding horizontal escalation, fought a high-intensity conventional military campaign over several months to eject the intruders. The Kargil conflict occurred approximately one year after India and Pakistan tested nuclear weapons.[7]

This increased Indo-Pakistani conflict occurred largely because the Pakistanis were emboldened by their new nuclear capability; they realized that India could not unleash the full weight of its conventional advantage in retaliation against them for fear of triggering nuclear escalation. As

---

7. Note that the Indians refrained from crossing the LoC and escalating Kargil horizontally despite the fact that doing so would have facilitated their efforts to eject the intruders. See S. Paul Kapur, *Dangerous Deterrent: Nuclear Weapons Proliferation and Conflict in South Asia* (Stanford: Stanford University Press, 2007), 115–131; and Sumit Ganguly, *Conflict Unending: India-Pakistan Tensions Since 1947* (New York: Columbia University Press, 2002), 114–129.

a result, the Pakistanis could be far more aggressive in attempting to force India to relinquish Kashmir than they otherwise would have been. Thus, not only did nuclearization fail to prevent the outbreak of Indo-Pakistani militarized disputes—it increased their frequency and intensity.[8]

What lessons have the Indians taken from this experience regarding the relationship between nuclear weapons and deterrence? The Indians have learned that nuclear weapons cannot prevent significant Indo-Pakistani conventional conflict. Specifically, their inability to deter continued Pakistani provocations has demonstrated that nuclear weapons can encourage aggressive behavior on the part of a state anxious to challenge the status quo, but are blunt instruments in the hands of a state seeking to preserve it. Although they may be able to insulate a defender from catastrophic defeat, nuclear weapons can prove unhelpful in achieving more fine-grained, defensively oriented security goals. In the case of Kargil, nuclear weapons encouraged Pakistan to alter the status quo but did not enable India to restore it; India had to achieve that goal with conventional military forces, which were able to eject the Pakistanis and restore the Line of Control despite Pakistan's nuclear capability. In the case of Pakistan's militant campaign, nuclear weapons have not enabled India to prevent militants from launching attacks or to foil militant operations once they are underway. Also, India cannot credibly threaten to use nuclear weapons against Pakistan in retaliation for Pakistani support of militant groups; this type of threat would be so disproportionate as to wholly lack credibility. The Indians have thus found nuclear weapons to be of limited utility in achieving their most pressing security goals regarding Pakistan.[9]

8. Kapur, *Dangerous Deterrent,* 122–127.

9. See V. R. Raghavan, "Limited War and Nuclear Escalation in South Asia," *Nonproliferation Review,* Fall/Winter 2001; Ali Ahmed, "India's Limited War Doctrine: The Structural Factor," IDSA Monograph Series, no. 10 (December 2012); Rajat Pandit, "Nuclear Weapons Only for Strategic Deterrence: Army Chief," *Times of India,* January 16, 2012; C. Raja Mohan, "Fernandes Unveils 'Limited War' Doctrine," *The Hindu,* January 25, 2000; Suba Chandran, "Limited War with Pakistan: Will It Secure India's Interests?" Occasional paper, Program in Arms

As a result of these lessons, Indian efforts to deter Pakistan's asymmetric warfare campaign now focus mostly on limited conventional military operations.[10] Specifically, the Indians are developing a new conventional strategy, often referred to as Cold Start, for use against Pakistan. Traditionally, Indian offensive forces were garrisoned deep in the Indian heartland and required weeks to mobilize for operations against Pakistan. They therefore lost strategic and operational surprise when mobilizing during an Indo-Pakistani crisis, enabling Pakistan to take defensive measures and allowing the international community to pressure Indian leaders not to launch offensive military operations.[11] Cold Start, by contrast, would position offensive forces closer to the border, enabling the Indians to move quickly into Pakistan from multiple directions in the event of a

---

Control, Disarmament, and International Security, University of Illinois at Urbana-Champaign, August 2004: 41–42; Ganguly and Kapur, *India, Pakistan, and the Bomb,* 92–94; and Angel Rabasa, Robert D. Blackwill, Peter Chalk, Kim Cragin, C. Christine Fair, Brian A. Jackson, Brian Michael Jenkins, Seth Jones, Nathaniel Shestak, and Ashley J. Tellis, "The Lessons of Mumbai," RAND occasional paper, 2009: 14. Note that a threat to retaliate with nuclear weapons against Pakistan for prosecuting its militant strategy would also violate India's pledge not to use nuclear weapons against an adversary first. That pledge was articulated in India's 1999 draft nuclear doctrine and reiterated, with some caveats, in a 2003 restatement. See http://fas.org/nuke/guide/india/doctrine/990817-indnucld.htm and http://pib.nic.in /archieve/lreleng/lyr2003/rjan2003/04012003/r040120033.html.

10. The fact that Kargil remained at the conventional level and did not escalate convinced the Indians that they could wage carefully calibrated conventional military operations against Pakistan without triggering nuclear confrontation. See V. P. Malik, "Limited War and Escalation Control," article no. 1570, Institute of Peace and Conflict Studies, November 30, 2004; Chandran, "Limited War with Pakistan": 19; and Mohan, "Fernandes Unveils 'Limited War' Doctrine."

11. An example is the Indo-Pakistani military standoff following a terrorist attack on the Indian Parliament in December 2002. The Indians mobilized approximately 500,000 troops along the international border during this confrontation, but ultimately decided not to attack Pakistan. See V. K. Sood and Pravin Sawhney, *Operation Parakram: The War Unfinished* (New Delhi: Sage Publications, 2003); and Praveen Swami, "Gen. Padmanabhan Mulls Over Lessons of Operation Parakram," *The Hindu,* February 6, 2004.

provocation. This would allow the Indians both to wear down Pakistani forces by attrition and to seize Pakistani territory for use in post-conflict negotiations before the Pakistanis could adequately prepare and before outside states could convince Indian political leaders to stand down.[12]

India is coupling these doctrinal changes with significant additions to its conventional arsenal, including jet fighter and refueling aircraft, submarines, tanks, and artillery. Such purchases made India the world's largest arms importer between 2005 and 2011. Indian leaders plan to spend $80 billion on further modernization programs by 2015. The Indians hope that these conventional measures will succeed where nuclear weapons have failed, generating the deterrence necessary to convince Pakistani leaders to abandon their asymmetric warfare campaign.[13]

---

12. The Indians plan to limit their forces to shallow attacks of roughly 20 kilometers, to avoid presenting Pakistani leaders with an existential threat and crossing their nuclear thresholds: author's interviews of senior Indian strategists, New Delhi, July and September 2010; and Walter C. Ladwig III, "A Cold Start for Hot Wars? The Indian Army's New Limited War Doctrine," *International Security* 32, no. 3 (Winter 2007/2008): 159–160, 164–166. Note that Indian leaders have denied the existence of Cold Start. US officials have also expressed skepticism regarding India's willingness or ability to execute a Cold Start-like doctrine. See Manu Pubby, "No 'Cold Start' Doctrine, India Tells US," *Indian Express,* September 9, 2010; and Amol Sharma, "U.S. Envoy Tells of India Battle 'Doctrine,'" *Wall Street Journal,* December 3, 2010.

13. See S. Paul Kapur, "Ten Years of Instability in a Nuclear South Asia," *International Security* 33, no. 2 (Fall 2008): 71–94; Mark Magnier, "India on Military Buying Spree," *Los Angeles Times,* April 2, 2012; and Nicholas R. Lombardo, "India's Defense Spending and Military Modernization," *DIIG Current Issues No. 24,* Center for Strategic and International Studies, March 29, 2011. Much of India's enhanced conventional capability is sure to be directed against China, which the Indians view as their primary strategic competitor. But a significant portion of it is likely to be used against Pakistan and could help to make a Cold Start-like approach a reality. Note that the Indian government has yet to articulate exactly how its new military acquisitions are related to its broad strategic goals. For a discussion regarding the apparent absence of any overarching strategy to employ Indian military acquisitions, see Stephen P. Cohen and Sunil Dasgupta, *Arming Without Aiming: India's Military Modernization* (New Delhi: Penguin, 2010).

The second reason that the Indians do not conflate deterrence and nuclear weapons is that a large degree of their motivation for acquiring a nuclear capability had nothing to do with deterrence or even with security interests generally. To an important extent, the Indians wanted to acquire a nuclear weapons capability because of the political significance of doing so.[14] The Indians had long viewed Western non-proliferation efforts as hypocritical and deeply discriminatory. They were unwilling to accept what they saw as second-class status while an elite group of countries was permitted to monopolize nuclear weapons. The Indians were especially sensitive to this inequity given their colonial past, and even referred to efforts to prevent them from acquiring nuclear weapons as "nuclear apartheid."[15] Thus, for India, overcoming a form of international discrimination was an important purpose in acquiring a nuclear capability, quite apart from the achievement of any specific security goals. On this count, the Indians were in little danger of confusing nuclear weapons with deterrence; deterrence simply was not part of their nuclear calculus.

This is one of the reasons that Indians ascribed such importance to the United States-India agreement on civilian nuclear cooperation, which made civilian nuclear material and technology available to India. Under the Treaty on the Non-Proliferation of Nuclear Weapons, only states that are legitimate possessors of nuclear weapons, or that have signed the treaty and agreed to forgo nuclear weapons, are permitted access to such materials and technologies. Since India both refused to sign the NPT as a non-nuclear state and developed a nuclear weapons capability, Indians interpreted the US-India nuclear agreement as an implicit recognition of the legitimacy of their nuclear weapons status. And they saw this

---

14.   This is not to suggest that Indian leaders are indifferent to nuclear weapons' strategic effects. As I explain below, the Indians very much value nuclear weapons' deterrent qualities, particularly with regard to conventionally stronger China. My point here is simply that an important part of the Indian motivation for acquiring a nuclear capability was not related to such strategic calculations.

15.   See Jaswant Singh, "Against Nuclear Apartheid," *Foreign Affairs* 77, no. 5 (1998).

recognition, in turn, as a validation of their broader desire for increased international status.[16]

Indian security leaders, then, do not make the analytic mistake of wholly conflating nuclear weapons with deterrence. They recognize, in the security realm, that nuclear weapons not only can fail to deter, but can actually encourage adversary states to engage in aggressive behavior. And they believe that, to an important extent, nuclear weapons are about political symbolism, quite apart from their ability to make India more secure. This does not mean, however, that New Delhi is likely to be amenable to implementing significant nuclear reductions in the near future. The truth is quite the opposite: the Indians not only are unlikely to cut their nuclear arsenal, they are actively working to increase its size and efficacy.

India's unwillingness to reduce its reliance on nuclear weapons stems from two main causes. The first is that, while the Indians do not make the mistake of assuming that nuclear weapons and deterrence are synonymous, they do not believe that nuclear weapons are incapable of generating deterrence. Indeed, they believe that in some cases nuclear weapons can serve as useful deterrent tools. One such case is India's relationship with China. China worries Indian security elites for a number of reasons. China possesses a more powerful military than does India.[17]

---

16. See S. Paul Kapur, "More Posture than Review: Indian Reactions to the 2010 Nuclear Posture Review," *Nonproliferation Review* 18, no. 1 (2011).

17. China's defense budget is roughly 2.5 times that of India and the Chinese active-duty armed forces are approximately 1.7 times the size of India's. China also outmatches India in a range of conventional military capabilities, possessing about twice as many combat aircraft as India, four times as many submarines, and five times as many battle tanks. China's prowess is likely to grow further as it devotes more resources to defense in the coming years. Indeed, China appears likely to become the world's largest military spender in the next two decades. See Binoy Prabhakar, "How India Compares with China in Military Prowess," *Economic Times,* March 11, 2012; "China's Military Rise: There are ways to reduce the threat to stability that an emergent superpower poses," *The Economist,* April 7, 2012; and "The Dragon's New

The Chinese economy is significantly bigger and growing faster than India's.[18] A number of Sino-Indian border disputes have led to military confrontations in the past, including a bloody 1962 war in which India was badly beaten, losing 14,000 square miles of territory to the Chinese. These disputes remain unresolved, and periodically result in diplomatic spats and even militarized confrontations. Given its authoritarian political system, China's decision-making is opaque, making its actions hard to predict and forcing Indian planners to adopt worst-case assumptions about future behavior. And what the Indians do know of Chinese behavior is disconcerting, particularly with regard to other regional powers, which have recently been the object of Chinese military and economic coercion.[19]

Indian strategists would like to maintain the Indian Ocean region as an open international commons free from domination by any single power. The Indians fear, however, that given current economic growth trajectories, they may eventually be forced to recognize Chinese hegemony in the region and operate according to a hierarchical set of rules set in Beijing. Indian strategists recognize that avoiding such an outcome will be a complicated task comprised of multiple components, such as the maintenance of robust trading relationships with China and other regional

---

Teeth: A rare look inside the world's biggest military expansion," *The Economist,* April 7, 2012.

18. China's Gross Domestic Product (GDP) is approximately $7 trillion and growing at about 9 percent per year, while India's GDP is less than $2 trillion and growing at slightly under 7 percent per year. See Central Intelligence Agency World Factbook, available at https://www.cia.gov/library/publications/the-world-factbook/geos/ch.html; and https://www.cia.gov/library/publications/the-world-factbook/geos/in.html.

19. Examples include China's confrontations with Vietnam, the Philippines, and Japan. See "The Bully of the South China Sea," *Wall Street Journal,* August 10, 2012; and Keith Bradsher, "Amid Tension, China Blocks Vital Exports to Japan," *New York Times,* September 22, 2012.

powers;[20] continued Indian economic growth;[21] the cultivation of partners with similar interests regarding China and the broader region; and the pursuit of good diplomatic relations with China, enabling India to avoid needless tensions that will drain its resources and prevent it from focusing on other essential goals.[22]

Although the above policies focus on diplomacy and economics rather than military capabilities, nuclear deterrence will also comprise an important part of India's overall approach to the problem of rising Chinese power. Nuclear weapons will not, of course, be useful to the Indians in every area of Sino-Indian security relations. There are many problems below the level of general war that nuclear weapons will be unable to address. For example, nuclear weapons will not be able to prevent China from encroaching on Indian or other states' territorial waters; from contesting current Sino-Indian border arrangements; or from engaging in economic coercion against India or other countries in the region. Nuclear weapons can, however, provide India with a final backstop, preventing China from engaging in behavior so aggressive as to threaten India's sovereignty or survival. Given China's significant conventional military superiority, this offers the Indians important reassurance, limiting how

---

20. China is India's largest trading partner, and the two countries have recently signed a raft of agreements designed to increase bilateral trade. See "India, China Sign Trade Agreement," *Journal of Commerce,* December 17, 2010; and "India, China Ink 11 Pacts to Boost Trade," *Deccan Herald,* November 26, 2012.

21. Indian leaders view continued rapid economic expansion as a vital national security goal. See "India PM Says Economic Growth Issue of National Security," Reuters, August 15, 2012.

22. See, for example, Prashant Kumar Singh and Rumel Dahiya, "China: Managing India-China Relations," in *India's Neighbourhood: Challenges in the Next Two Decades,* ed. Rumel Dahiya and Ashok K. Behuria (New Delhi: Institute for Defence Studies and Analyses, 2012), 86–91; and Raja Menon and Rajiv Kumar, *The Long View from Delhi: To Define the Indian Grand Strategy for Foreign Policy* (New Delhi: Academic Foundation, 2010), 38–39.

dangerous the Chinese can potentially become.[23] As a result, the Indians are unlikely to reduce their reliance on nuclear weapons. Instead, they will seek to improve their arsenal, both qualitatively and quantitatively.

To this end, the Indians continue to produce fissile material; India and Pakistan are the only countries in the world that are currently believed to be doing so.[24] India probably possesses enough weapons-grade plutonium to produce between one hundred and one hundred thirty nuclear warheads, and is increasing its production capacity with projects such as an unsafeguarded fast-breeder reactor, which is under construction near Kalpakkam.[25] In addition, the Indians are significantly improving their delivery capabilities. For example, the recently tested Agni V intermediate-range ballistic missile, with a range of approximately five thousand kilometers, is capable of reaching targets anywhere in China, a fact that Indian

---

23. Note that, following India's 1998 nuclear tests, Prime Minister Atal Bihari Vajpayee wrote a letter to US President Bill Clinton explicitly stating that India's purpose in acquiring a nuclear capability was to protect itself against China. See "Nuclear Anxiety: Indian's Letter to Clinton On the Nuclear Testing," *New York Times,* May 13, 1998. For a discussion of the Sino-centric nature of Indian nuclear policy see also Toby Dalton and Jaclyn Tandler, "Understanding the Arms 'Race' in South Asia," Carnegie Endowment for International Peace, September 13, 2012. The above sections are based in part upon the author's private discussions with Indian diplomatic officials, military officers, and strategists in New Delhi from 2010–2012.

24. Peter Crail, "P5 to Take up Fissile Material Cutoff," *Arms Control Today,* September 1, 2011.

25. See Hans M. Kristensen and Robert S. Norris, "Indian Nuclear Forces, 2012," *Bulletin of the Atomic Scientists* 68, no. 4: 96-97; and Alexander Glaser and M.V. Ramana, "Weapon-Grade Plutonium Production Potential in the Indian Prototype Fast Breeder Reactor," *Science and Global Security* 15, no. 2: 85–105. Safeguards are measures designed to ensure that states do not use nuclear materials or facilities to produce nuclear weapons. They include site inspections as well as examination of nuclear materials. See International Atomic Energy Agency, "How We Implement Safeguards," available at http://www.iaea.org/safeguards/what.html; and Office for Nuclear Regulation, "What Are Nuclear Safeguards," available at http://www.onr.org.uk/safeguards/what.htm.

officials have publicly highlighted. And the BRAHMOS cruise missile, developed in tandem with Russia, will be able to deliver conventional or nuclear warheads at supersonic speeds on targets at ranges of three hundred to five hundred kilometers.[26] The Indians are also diversifying their delivery platforms, working to develop the land-, air-, and sea-based capabilities needed to field a full nuclear triad.[27] Thus, while in principle Indian leaders do not wholly conflate nuclear weapons with deterrence, in practice they rely heavily on nuclear weapons' deterrent capabilities to protect them from a stronger regional adversary.

The second reason that Indian leaders are unlikely to agree to significant nuclear disarmament in the foreseeable future, despite their recognition of the fallacy of conflating nuclear weapons and deterrence, was discussed above: a major motivation underlying the Indian nuclear weapons program has nothing to do with deterrence or even with security issues generally. This motivation is instead rooted in domestic political sensibilities regarding Indian national identity. The Indian leadership and public view the possession of nuclear weapons as a symbol of independence from foreign domination and of major-power status.[28] Since this view is not security-based, technical arguments about deterrence are unlikely to alter it. Rather, significant change will require a considerable

---

26. Vladimir Radyuhin, "BrahMos Gains Sub-strategic Super Weapon Capability," *The Hindu*, October 13, 2012.

27. See Kelsey Davenport, "India Moves Closer to Nuclear Triad," *Arms Control Today*, September 2012, and Kristensen and Norris, "Indian Nuclear Forces 2012": 96.

28. Note that Indian leaders also periodically decry the evils of nuclear weapons and call for their global elimination. The Indians have made clear, however, that until "universal" and "nondiscriminatory" disarmament occurs, they have no intention of forgoing their nuclear capability. See, for example, Rajiv Gandhi, speech to the United Nations General Assembly, June 9, 1988, available at http://www.nti.org/media/pdfs/Gandhi_1988.pdf; "India Subjected to Nuclear Blackmail Before 1998 Pokhran Tests: NSA Shivshankar Menon," *Times of India*, August 21, 2012; and "India to Revive Rajiv Gandhi's Global Disarmament Vision," *Times of India*, August 22, 2012.

cultural shift, which does not appear to be in the offing in the mainstream political arena.[29]

From the standpoint of decoupling deterrence and nuclear weapons, then, India is a mixed case. The Indians do not view deterrence and nuclear weapons as being synonymous. They recognize that nuclear weapons are often unable to prevent adversaries from engaging in unwanted behavior, and in some cases can even encourage them to do so, thereby directly contributing to deterrence failure. In addition, they realize that, in some instances, conventional weapons will offer India the best hope of achieving the deterrence that it requires. Nonetheless, the Indians also believe that nuclear weapons can, in particular circumstances, serve as important deterrent tools, especially with regard to a conventionally stronger power such as China. In addition, the Indians value nuclear weapons because of their inherent political qualities, which they view as symbolizing autonomy and major-power status. For both strategic and symbolic reasons, then, the Indians are not likely to reduce their reliance on nuclear weapons in the near future, despite their implicit recognition of decoupling logic. Instead they are likely to remain on their current path of increasing their nuclear capabilities.

Pakistan

India is not the only nuclear power in the South Asian region. Pakistan also possesses nuclear weapons. How do the Pakistanis view the link between nuclear weapons and deterrence? Do they believe that nuclear

---

29. In theory, significant nuclear reductions by major powers such as the United States could generate normative pressure for India to follow suit with limits on its own nuclear program. This seems unlikely to occur in the foreseeable future, however, since 1) the Indians view contemplated major-power cuts, such as those envisioned in the 2010 US Nuclear Posture Review, as more symbolic than substantive; and 2) the Indians have not shown much propensity for emulating major powers such as the United States when formulating nuclear policy. See Kapur, "More Posture Than Review": 73–75.

weapons and deterrence are one and the same? Or do they recognize the logical weakness of the deterrence-nuclear weapons link?

The Pakistani case provides even less reason for optimism than that of India. The Pakistanis believe that history clearly demonstrates the deterrent efficacy of nuclear weapons. Indeed, they are convinced that nuclear weapons are the only tools that have prevented India from both initiating conflicts with Pakistan and escalating ongoing Indo-Pakistani confrontations. Moreover, the Pakistanis believe that in the future, as India outpaces them economically and on the conventional military front, nuclear weapons will have to play an even greater role in deterring the Indians.

Given these beliefs, the Pakistanis are increasing the importance of nuclear weapons in their security posture. And they are doing so in a way deliberately calculated to lower the nuclear threshold on the subcontinent, thereby increasing the likelihood than any Indo-Pakistani conventional conflict will escalate to the nuclear level. Thus, Pakistani leaders are betting their country's survival on the existence of an extremely close link between nuclear weapons and deterrence.

At one level, Pakistani leaders recognize that not all deterrence is nuclear. They long focused their military efforts on conventional deterrence[30] and believed that the might of their army prevented aggression by an extremely hostile but militarily ineffective India.[31] For a time, the outcomes of India-Pakistan confrontations appeared to justify the Pakistanis' confidence in their conventional prowess. In the first two Indo-Pakistani wars, Pakistan managed to fight India to a standstill despite suffering from significant material disadvantages.[32] In recent years, however, the Pakistanis have moved away from that view and no longer believe that

---

30. The Pakistanis called this approach "offensive defense." See R.S.N. Singh, "Pakistan's Offensive-Defence Strategy," *Indian Defence Review,* February 18, 2011.

31. Stephen Cohen, *The Idea of Pakistan* (New Delhi: Oxford University Press, 2004), 121.

32. See Ganguly, *Conflict Unending,* 15–50.

conventional forces can generate the deterrence that they need to protect themselves against India.

The reasons for this change are fourfold. First, the Pakistanis' crushing defeat in the 1971 Indo-Pakistani war, which vivisected the country and created Bangladesh out of East Pakistan, demonstrated that Pakistan was the weaker power in South Asia not only on paper; it was also weaker on the battlefield. Indeed, in a head-to-head conventional contest with the Indians, Pakistan risked suffering catastrophic defeat. Thus, in the future, the Pakistanis would need to avoid fighting a conventional war with India. Not surprisingly, Pakistan began to pursue a nuclear weapons program in earnest following the Bangladesh conflict.[33]

Second, the lesson that the Pakistanis learned after the nuclearization of the subcontinent was that nuclear weapons protected them from India, deterring the Indians either from initiating conflict or from escalating conflict that already was in progress. The Pakistanis' learning in this regard was essentially opposite to that of the Indians. For example, as noted above, the Indians believed that the Kargil conflict demonstrated that nuclear weapons would not necessarily prevent significant conventional Indo-Pakistani confrontation. The Pakistanis, by contrast, believed that Kargil's lack of horizontal escalation demonstrated that catastrophic Indo-Pakistani conventional war would not occur against a nuclear backdrop. They therefore concluded that they had the freedom to pursue their security goals aggressively despite Indian conventional superiority.[34] Thus, while militarized disputes in a nuclear South Asia led Indian leaders to

---

33. See Samina Ahmed, "Pakistan's Nuclear Weapons Program: Turning Points and Nuclear Choices," *International Security* 23, no. 4 (Spring 1999): 178–204.

34. See, e.g., S. Paul Kapur, "Revisionist Ambitions, Conventional Capabilities, and Nuclear Instability: Why Nuclear South Asia Is Not Like Cold War Europe," in *Inside Nuclear South Asia,* ed. Scott D. Sagan (Stanford: Stanford University Press, 2009), 202; and Ashley J. Tellis, C. Christine Fair, and Jamison Jo Medby, "Limited Conflicts Under the Nuclear Umbrella: Indian and Pakistani Lessons from the Kargil Crisis," RAND Monograph Report, 2001: 48–49.

believe that nuclear weapons and deterrence are not always tightly coupled, they enhanced Pakistani leaders' belief in a close linkage between
nuclear weapons and deterrence.

Third, recent economic trends have badly damaged Pakistan, both
in absolute terms and in relation to India. The Indian economy has
grown in the high single digits for most of the past decade, averaging
8.6 percent from 2006–2011.[35] Pakistani growth, by contrast, averaged
only 4.4 percent during the same period, declining from a high of about
6.5 percent in 2006 to under 2.5 percent in 2011.[36] In addition to creating
severe domestic challenges,[37] this growth differential has led to increasing
asymmetries in defense spending. Pakistan's defense budget grew 10 percent from 2012–2013. India's budget, however, expanded even faster
during this period, with growth nearing 18 percent. And India's overall
defense expenditures, at over $40 billion, dwarfed Pakistan's expenditures
of under $6 billion.[38] In addition, the Pakistanis must now contend with
significant reductions in US military aid, which could lead them to fall
even further behind India in the years ahead.[39]

---

35. See indexmundi, "India GDP Real Growth Rate," http://www.indexmundi.com/g/g
    .aspx?c=in&v=66.

36. See indexmundi, "Pakistan GDP Real Growth Rate," http://www.indexmundi.com
    /g/g.aspx?v=66&c=pk&l=en.

37. For example, the Pakistani state is unable to provide its citizens with basic public
    goods such as primary and secondary education. Only 62 percent of Pakistani
    primary school-age children, and 23 percent of secondary school-age children, are
    enrolled in school. Douglas Lynd, *The Education System in Pakistan: Assessment of
    the National Education Census* (Islamabad: UNESCO, 2007), 7.

38. Press Trust of India, "Pakistan Defence Budget Goes Up by 10%," *Hindustan
    Times,* June 1, 2012; and Laxman K. Behera, "India's Defence Budget 2012-2013,"
    Institute for Defence Studies and Analysis, March 20, 2012, http://www.idsa.in
    /idsacomments/IndiasDefenceBudget2012-13_LaxmanBehera_200312.

39. Anwar Iqbal, "US House Reduces Pakistan Military Aid by $650m," *Dawn,*
    July 20, 2012.

Fourth, the Pakistanis view Indian conventional military advances outlined above, including Cold Start, as highly threatening and have made countering them a top priority. Given their lagging economy, however, they simply do not have the financial resources to match Indian improvements at the conventional level. The Pakistanis have therefore decided to rely even more heavily than they did in the past on nuclear weapons to generate deterrence and protect themselves from India.[40] If they are to achieve such deterrence, however, the Pakistanis must overcome a significant strategic challenge.

Pakistan has long reserved the right to use nuclear weapons first in the event of an Indo-Pakistani conventional conflict.[41] But this policy faced an inherent credibility problem. For the Pakistanis were threatening nuclear retaliation against an Indian conventional attack, thereby deliberately transforming a dangerous situation into a disaster of potentially catastrophic proportions. Would Pakistan actually take such a step? If their deterrent threat was to be effective, the Pakistanis had to convince the Indians that they were in fact likely to do so. Now, as the Indians outstrip

---

40. See "Force Cannot Be Caught Unawares: Kayani," *Indian Express,* February 24, 2010; S. Paul Kapur, "Ten Years of Instability in a Nuclear South Asia," *International Security* 33, no. 2 (Fall 2008): 90–91; Zahir Kazmi, "SRBMs, Deterrence and Regional Stability in South Asia: A Case Study of Nasr and Prahaar," Institute of Regional Studies, 2013: 23–25; and Maria Sultan, "Cold Start Doctrine and Pakistan's Counter-Measures: Theory of Strategic Equivalence," South Asian Strategic Stability Institute, 2011. During a December 2011 trip to Pakistan, the author's conversations with senior Pakistani military officers, diplomatic officials, and academics were dominated by Cold Start.

41. In an interview with an Italian arms control organization, Lt. Gen. Khalid Kidwai, director of the Pakistan Army's Strategic Plans Division, specified four conditions under which Pakistan would use nuclear weapons: India conquered a large portion of Pakistani territory; India destroyed a large portion of Pakistani air or ground forces; India economically strangled Pakistan; or India caused the internal destabilization of Pakistan. See "Nuclear Safety, Nuclear Stability, and Nuclear Strategy in Pakistan: A Concise Report of a Visit by Landau Network," available at http://www.centrovolta.it/landau/content/binary/pakistan%20Januray%202002.pdf.

Pakistani conventional capabilities, and the Pakistanis consequently rely more heavily on their nuclear deterrent, this problem is becoming even more urgent than it was previously.

The Pakistanis are addressing the problem by developing a battlefield nuclear capability, which will employ small, short-range weapons stationed close to the Indo-Pakistani border, potentially with launch authority pre-delegated to officers in the field in the event of a crisis. This will enhance the credibility of Pakistan's first-use threat in two ways. First, because battlefield nuclear weapons are relatively small and will be employed against military targets, their use will be less momentous than a decision to launch all-out counter-value attacks against the Indians. The choice to escalate to the nuclear level will thus theoretically be easier for the Pakistanis to make. Second, during a crisis, the decision to employ battlefield weapons may not be fully in the hands of Pakistani national leaders. Rather, the decision may be delegated to a field commander embroiled in a conventional fight, who could prove more willing to choose escalation than would senior leadership making decisions in relative calm far from the front lines.[42]

The development of a Pakistani tactical nuclear capacity thus increases the likelihood that a conventional Indo-Pakistani conflict will escalate to the nuclear level, and thereby can enhance the credibility of Pakistan's first-use posture. The Pakistanis hope that, even in the event of a significant provocation such as a major terrorist strike, fear of such escalation

---

42. See Rajesh Basrur, "South Asia: Tactical Nuclear Weapons and Strategic Risk," RSIS Commentaries 65, April 27, 2011; Kazmi, "SRBMs, Deterrence, and Regional Stability in South Asia": 22–29; Shireen M. Mazari, "Battlefield Nukes for Pakistan: Why Hatf IX (Nasr) Is Essential for Pakistan's Deterrence Posture & Doctrine," Project for Pakistan in 21st Century, September 2012; and Rodney Jones, "Nuclear Escalation Ladders in South Asia," Defense Threat Reduction Agency, Advanced Systems and Concepts Office, April 2011: 13. This discussion is also based on the author's private interactions with Pakistani military officers and strategic analysts.

will deter India from attacking them. For in the Pakistani view, the Indians' increasing conventional military advantage is eroding Pakistan's other means of ensuring its security.[43]

For Pakistan, then, the link between nuclear weapons and deterrence has become even tighter than it was in the past. The Pakistanis are responding to a growing conventional threat with nuclear weapons because they do not believe that they possess the resources to generate sufficient deterrence in any other way. In theory, then, nuclear weapons and deterrence may not be synonymous for Pakistan. But in practice they have essentially become so. As long as deep material imbalances between India and Pakistan remain, Pakistan will not view itself as having many realistic non-nuclear means of ensuring its security.

Conclusion

A convincing case for the decoupling of nuclear weapons from deterrence is made in this volume. Though they have long been conflated with one another, the logic underlying this conflation is questionable. Nuclear weapons can fail to deter aggression and can even encourage destabilizing behavior. They have been credited with preventing war in cases where the historical record is murky. And other capabilities, such as conventional weapons systems, could potentially substitute for nuclear weapons in a range of military scenarios, generating the deterrence that was previously believed to be nuclear weapons' exclusive purview. The analytic

---

43. In addition to enhancing the overall credibility of Pakistan's first-use threat, tactical nuclear weapons could potentially augment Pakistan's denial capability, facilitating the destruction of conventional Indian forces crossing into Pakistani territory. Such an enhanced denial capability could both contribute to Pakistani battlefield success and help to deter an Indian attack. See Jones, "Nuclear Escalation Ladders in South Asia": 18.

case for separating nuclear weapons from deterrence is thus strong. As a result, states should in theory be able to de-emphasize the role of nuclear weapons in their security postures, or potentially forgo them altogether, while generating sufficient deterrence to ensure their survival.

In the real-world context of regional security politics, however, this analytic case for decoupling may not result in nuclear retrenchment. In South Asia, despite the strength of decoupling logic, neither India nor Pakistan plans to reduce the role that nuclear weapons play in security policy. Indeed, both states plan to augment their nuclear capabilities quantitatively and qualitatively, for both strategic and political reasons, in the years ahead. Given this apparent disconnect between decoupling logic and South Asian security postures, what policies or regional developments might potentially improve the situation?

Three possibilities exist, though none offers easy or quick solutions. First, India and Pakistan could take steps to reduce the likelihood that they will have to deter one another from engaging in aggressive behavior. By improving the overall South Asian security environment, such measures could lower the two countries' perceived need for nuclear weapons, even if Indian and Pakistani leaders do not fully accept or appreciate decoupling logic. Such an approach would require significant concessions from both the Pakistanis and the Indians. The Pakistanis would need to abandon their support for anti-Indian Islamist militants and act decisively to defeat those still operating within the country. Supporting asymmetric warfare was useful to Pakistan in the past, as it attrited Indian economic and military resources, contributed to Pakistani domestic political cohesion, and enabled Pakistan to continue to contest territorial boundaries in Kashmir. But the strategy has now outlived its utility. Pakistan has begun losing control of its proxies, who challenge the government for control over large swaths of Pakistani territory; the country has suffered from damaging trade-offs between supporting militancy and promoting domestic development; and continued militant attacks have provoked India to adopt a more aggressive conventional military posture, which threatens

Pakistan and is leading it to rely more heavily on nuclear weapons to ensure its security.[44]

India could facilitate Pakistan's efforts to abandon jihad by mitigating Pakistani external security concerns, thereby enabling Pakistan to concentrate on the resolution of its internal security problems. Postponing the implementation of Cold Start-like policies would be helpful in this regard. Cold Start is a source of considerable worry for the Pakistanis and has spurred the adoption of some of their most dangerous policies, such as the development of a battlefield nuclear weapons capability. The Indian government might find it politically difficult to reduce external pressure on Pakistan, given the Pakistanis' close connection to the militants who regularly attack India. As Indian officials have told the author on numerous occasions, most Indians do not believe that it is their responsibility to make a hostile Pakistan feel more secure. In truth, however, India has a stake in the creation of a more stable Pakistan that is better able to address the problem of Islamist militancy within its borders. Thus, taking steps to increase Pakistani security, such as scaling back Cold Start-like policies, need not be seen simply as an Indian concession to Pakistan. Rather, it could be understood as an act of enlightened Indian self-interest. And, of course, if Indian forbearance did not lead to improvements in Pakistani behavior, the Indians could always resume Cold Start-like planning and policies.

If a reduction in Indian military pressure made the Pakistanis feel more secure, they might agree to limit or avoid the development of a battlefield nuclear weapons capability. The Indians might then join them in a pledge similarly to restrict the development of any battlefield nuclear capability of their own. This would significantly mitigate nuclear danger on the subcontinent. For, as noted above, Pakistan's battlefield nuclear weapons program is designed deliberately to lower South Asia's nuclear threshold.

---

44.   See S. Paul Kapur and Sumit Ganguly, "The Jihad Paradox: Pakistan and Islamist Militancy in South Asia," *International Security* 37, no. 1 (Summer 2012): 111–141.

An Indian battlefield nuclear program would have similar effects. Limiting or abolishing such programs would constitute a significant step toward stabilizing the region.

Second, China could decide to limit or scale back its nuclear weapons program. Since Indian leaders view China as their primary strategic threat, such Chinese retrenchment could reassure the Indians, thereby facilitating the adoption of less ambitious Indian nuclear policies. India would be even more likely to respond favorably if China's nuclear retrenchment were accompanied by reductions in conventional arms, which the Indians also find highly threatening and which drive a good deal of the Indian demand for a robust nuclear weapons capability. Indian moderation could, in turn, reassure the Pakistanis, perhaps enabling them to consider more moderate nuclear policies of their own. It is beyond the scope of this paper to determine whether the Chinese would ever seriously consider such a move. Even if they did, there is no guarantee either that India would reciprocate or that scaled-back Indian policies would have any effect on Pakistan's nuclear posture. In the absence of significant Chinese nuclear and conventional retrenchment, however, the likelihood of major Indian nuclear reductions is essentially zero. Thus, despite these uncertainties, Chinese nuclear and conventional military moderation would be a positive development for the strategic environment in South Asia.

Third, scholars and analysts can continue to problematize the relationship between nuclear weapons and deterrence, showing that the two are not synonymous and may even work at cross-purposes. This could help to make nuclear weapons less strategically desirable and also less prestigious. Such developments would, of course, give rise to new challenges. For example, if India and Pakistan were to de-emphasize nuclear weapons in their security postures, they would probably rely more heavily for deterrence upon conventional weapons, which can have destabilizing effects of their own. In addition, without the threat of nuclear escalation, the likelihood of large-scale conventional war between the two sides could increase. Nonetheless, eliminating or reducing India's and Pakistan's reliance on the awful nuclear bargain that I described at the beginning of this chapter would help insulate them from the even greater catastrophe of a nuclear exchange. To that end, discussions such as the one in this volume, which critically examine the nuclear weapons-deterrence link, are valuable. They will not, of course, lead to immediate policy change. They can, however, increase the likelihood that decoupling logic assumes a prominent place in nuclear discourse and debate. This, in turn, increases the likelihood that informed publics and political leaders in South Asia and elsewhere will recognize that nuclear weapons may not always make them more secure, and that they will formulate their strategic policy accordingly.

CHAPTER 11 **Getting to the Table: Prospects and Challenges for Arms Control with China**

Michael S. Gerson

Introduction

On November 11, 2014, US President Barack Obama and Chinese President Xi Jinping announced an important agreement to combat the growing threat of climate change. The agreement, apparently worked out over many months of quiet negotiations between Washington and Beijing, pledges that the United States intends to reduce its emissions by 26–28 percent below 2005 levels by 2025, and that China would reach its peak carbon emissions around 2030 and would increase its share of non-fossil fuels in primary energy consumption.[1] The climate change plan marks an important step forward in US-China relations and for the prospect of further cooperation between Washington and Beijing. At a joint press conference Xi spoke of developing a "new model of major country relations between China and the United States" and discussed the importance of deepening military exchanges, mutual trust, and cooperation to

---

1. See "U.S.-China Joint Announcement on Climate Change," November 11, 2014, http://www.whitehouse.gov/the-press-office/2014/11/11/us-china-joint-announcement -climate-change.

create a "new type of military-to-military relations between the two countries." Obama struck a similar tone, emphasizing the long-standing US policy of welcoming and supporting China's rise and welcoming opportunities for expanding cooperation "where our interests overlap or align."[2]

The climate change agreement is important not only because it addresses a pertinent global issue between two of the world's largest polluters, but also because it presents a new opportunity for the kind of cooperation upon which sustained mutual trust, respect, and stability are built. But while the climate change announcement is a useful development in the continued effort to foster positive and productive US-China relations, significant uncertainties and mistrust persist between Washington and Beijing—and perhaps nowhere is this greater than in the realm of military forces and capabilities. China's impressive economic growth has brought with it an expansive program to modernize its conventional and nuclear forces (as well as its space and cyber capabilities) and develop new anti-access/area denial (A2/AD) systems that threaten the United States' unfettered power projection in the region. These initiatives, in turn, have raised concerns in Washington and allied capitals about Beijing's true intentions in the region and around the world.[3] At the same time, emerging US capabilities such as ballistic missile defense and conventional prompt global strike, along with the US "pivot" to

---

2. "Remarks by President Obama and President Xi Jinping in Joint Press Conference," November 12, 2014, http://www.whitehouse.gov/the-press-office/2014/11/12/remarks-president-obama-and-president-xi-jinping-joint-press-conference.

3. For the United States and its allies in Asia, the rise of China threatens to upset the regional order built and maintained by the United States over the last several decades. The United States' role as the "regional sheriff" in Asia, an extra-regional power that provides security and maintains stability, is fundamentally tied to its ability to maintain unfettered access and power projection in the region. Now, however, the growth in the size and sophistication of China's military capabilities—including, for example, the development and deployment of anti-access/area denial weapons such as the DF-21D anti-ship ballistic missile—creates new challenges and poses new risks for US foreign and defense policy in the Asia-Pacific region.

Asia and the strengthening of alliance relationships in the region, have generated trepidations in Beijing about Washington's objectives and intentions with respect to China's rise and its position in the Asia-Pacific region.[4]

The changing security environment in the Asia-Pacific region driven by the rise of China, and the US reaction to it, has important implications for the goal of a nuclear weapons-free world. With China's ascent to great power status and its significant expenditures associated with the expansion and modernization of its military capabilities, continued progress toward a nuclear weapons-free world requires bringing China into the process. Yet, continued mistrust and mutual uncertainty regarding each other's military capabilities and strategic intentions present a formidable challenge to deep, meaningful engagement on nuclear issues. Washington and Beijing may be able to agree to cut their carbon emissions, but agreeing to cut or limit their nuclear arsenals is an entirely different matter.

Absent a fundamental shift in international relations or a catastrophic event, such as the use of nuclear weapons in war, it is likely that the process leading to a nuclear weapons-free world will occur slowly and

---

4. On mistrust and suspicion in US-China relations, see, for example, Kenneth Lieberthal and Wang Jisi, *Addressing U.S.-China Strategic Distrust,* John L. Thorton China Center Monographic Series No. 4 (Washington, DC: Brookings Institution, 2012); J.M. Norton, "The Sources of US-China Strategic Mistrust," *The Diplomat,* April 24, 2014, http://thediplomat.com/2014/04/the-sources-of-us-china-strategic -mistrust; and David M. Lampton, *Power Constrained: Sources of Mutual Strategic Suspicion in U.S.-China Relations,* NBR Analysis (Seattle, WA: National Bureau of Asian Research, 2010). Thomas Fingar and Fan Jishe contend that US-China relations are more stable than many realize, though they agree that US suspicions about China's growing military power and long-term intentions, along with Chinese concerns regarding missile defense and strategic conventional weapons, threaten to weaken Sino-American stability. See Thomas Fingar and Fan Jishe, "Ties that Bind: Strategic Stability in the U.S.-China Relationship," *Washington Quarterly* 36, no. 4 (Fall 2013): 125–138.

incrementally through a series of carefully crafted, verifiable arms control agreements. Such a process represents an important shift in the logic and objectives of arms control from the Cold War, where strategic stability—not abolition—was the central objective.[5] While strategic stability remains an important goal of arms control, modern proponents of nuclear abolition view arms control as a means through which to achieve eventual abolition, with strategic stability being an important and necessary interim product along the path to nuclear zero.

If arms control is to be the means through which verifiable and permanent abolition will be achieved, then analyzing China's commitment to nuclear zero requires first understanding China's perspectives on nuclear arms control. This paper will identify and analyze how Chinese officials and scholars view arms control, and assess how these views might affect China's willingness to engage in formal nuclear arms control and make serious moves toward nuclear zero.

Any assessment of China's historical and current view of arms control is necessarily speculative given the opaque nature of China's government, especially concerning issues associated with nuclear weapons. There have been, of course, a handful of official public pronouncements and documents over the years discussing the Chinese leadership's views on arms control. But, given China's absence from previous rounds of formal negotiations to limit or reduce nuclear weapons, there is relatively little to provide precedent or serve as a guidepost. Consequently, this paper seeks to get at the question of how China thinks about nuclear arms control—and thus if and how China will make real strides toward nuclear abolition—by examining the debates about arms control among Chinese scholars and defense analysts in the belief that at least some of the key themes that emerge from this literature reflect the debates and concerns about arms control among China's key decision-makers.

---

5. The classic text on arms control and strategic stability is Thomas C. Schelling and Morton H. Halperin, *Strategy and Arms Control* (New York: The Twentieth Century Fund, 1961).

China and Nuclear Arms Control: The Early Years

At first glance, China would appear to be a "natural" for nuclear arms control. Immediately following its first nuclear test on October 16, 1964, China declared a no-first-use (NFU) policy and encouraged the other nuclear-armed states (the United States, the Soviet Union, Great Britain, and France) to work toward the elimination of nuclear arms. Beijing's declaratory policy on arms control and abolition has remained essentially unchanged since that time. China welcomed Obama's April 2009 speech in Prague embracing the vision of a nuclear weapons-free world, proclaiming in August 2009 that it was ready to "make unremitting efforts to further promote the nuclear disarmament process and realize the goal of a nuclear weapons-free world at an early date." The following month, President Hu Jintao told the UN General Assembly that China "has consistently stood for the complete prohibition and thorough destruction of nuclear weapons" and called on the international community "to take credible steps to push forward the nuclear disarmament process."[6]

Yet, despite its consistent rhetoric in favor of arms control and abolition, China has been reluctant to get down to the actual business of limitations and/or reductions in nuclear arms. To be sure, China has not eschewed any kind of restraint with regard to nuclear weapons. Despite the contention of a February 2012 editorial in the *Washington Times* that China "has never agreed to be part of any strategic nuclear framework," China is, in fact, a signatory to several international agreements and is involved in multilateral fora associated with nuclear weapons.[7] China

---

6. These quotes are from Hui Zhang, "China's Perspective on a Nuclear-Free World," *Washington Quarterly* 33, no. 2 (April 2010): 142–43. The following year, China declared in its defense white paper that it has "always stood for the complete prohibition and thorough destruction of nuclear weapons." See People's Republic of China, *China's National Defense in 2010,* March 31, 2011, http://www.china.org.cn /government/whitepaper/node_7114675.htm.

7. For the original editorial, see "Obama's Unilateral Disarmament," *Washington Times,* February 16, 2012. For an excellent analysis of the factual errors made in this

joined the Conference on Disarmament in 1980; joined the International Atomic Energy Agency in 1984; announced in 1986 that it would suspend atmospheric nuclear tests (although it has not signed the 1963 Limited Test Ban Treaty); signed the Non-Proliferation Treaty in 1992 and supported its indefinite extension in 1995; signed the Comprehensive Test Ban Treaty in 1996 (though it has not yet ratified it); joined the Zangger Committee in 1997; and joined the Nuclear Suppliers Group in 2004. Moreover, China acceded to both the Chemical and Biological Weapons Conventions and has been an active participant in multilateral discussion on a Treaty on the Prevention of an Arms Race in Outer Space.

Nevertheless, China has been ambivalent and noncommittal at best—and outright belligerent at worst—when it comes to formal nuclear arms control with the United States or any other nuclear power. As early as the 1970s, Beijing called the Strategic Arms Limitation Talks (SALT I) between the United States and the Soviet Union "sham disarmament" and accused the superpowers of using arms control as a smokescreen for the continuation of the nuclear arms race.[8] At least part of this hostility toward early US-Soviet arms control was likely driven in part by Beijing's fear of some kind of collaboration or alliance between Washington and Moscow against China. By the time of SALT I the alliance between Moscow and Beijing was completely broken, and the two countries had participated in a series of conflicts along their border on the Ussuri River that included veiled Soviet threats of an attack on China's nuclear facilities.[9] US-China relations, while moving in a positive direction, were not yet solidified,

---

editorial, see Gregory Kulacki, "Washington Times is Wrong on China and Nuclear Arms Control," February 17, 2012, http://allthingsnuclear.org/washington-times -is-wrong-on-china-and-nuclear-arms.

8. See Banning N. Garrett and Bonnie S. Glaser, "Chinese Perspectives on Nuclear Arms Control," *International Security* 20, no. 3 (Winter 1995–1996): 47.

9. The Chinese leadership took these threats quite seriously—so seriously, in fact, that in October 1969 Mao Tse-tung ordered the senior leadership to flee Beijing and China's nascent nuclear forces were put on alert in the belief that the Soviet Union was planning to launch a surprise attack. See Michael S. Gerson, *The Sino-Soviet*

and thus some in Beijing's senior leadership almost certainly remained concerned about a threat from the United States. As such, the leadership in Beijing was more inclined to view SALT I as a strategic ploy rather than a genuine attempt to curb the arms race and reduce the danger of nuclear war.

Another factor likely contributing to Beijing's hostility toward nuclear arms control in the decade following its entrance into the nuclear club had to do with China's domestic situation. The years immediately following China's first test were chaotic. The Cultural Revolution that began in 1966 swept over the country, diverting manpower, money, and other resources away from the military and limiting attention and study to military matters, especially new and arcane topics like nuclear strategy and arms control. China did not establish an office or group within its military or political structures tasked with focusing on nuclear issues in the years immediately preceding its nuclear test. Rather, nuclear issues were treated with extreme secrecy and limited to a small group of the most senior military and political officials, thereby limiting opportunities for dialogue and debate. Consequently, while there was obviously sufficient technical expertise on nuclear weapons in China, in the 1960s and 1970s few had any real expertise on—and certainly no one had any experience with—nuclear arms control.[10]

Over the next few decades, China appears to have gone through a learning period with respect to nuclear strategy and arms control.[11] Beginning

---

Border Conflict: Deterrence, Escalation, and the Threat of Nuclear War in 1969 (Alexandria, VA: Center for Naval Analyses, 2010).

10. This paragraphs draws from M. Taylor Fravel and Evan S. Medeiros, "China's Search for Assured Retaliation: The Evolution of Chinese Nuclear Strategy and Force Structure," *International Security* 35, no. 2 (Fall 2010): 66–73.

11. See Gu Guoliang, "Chinese Arms Control and Nonproliferation Policy," in *Perspectives on Sino-American Strategic Nuclear Issues,* ed. Christopher P. Twomey (New York: Palgrave Macmillan, 2008), 176. Alastair Iain Johnston claims that the shift in China's positions on arms control is more akin to "adaptation" rather than "learning," though Johnston is using a more academic definition of these terms than

in 1978 the Second Artillery, the military component of the People's Liberation Army responsible for nuclear weapons, opened a research office, and through the 1980s the Second Artillery studied nuclear strategy and published operational documents. In addition, beginning in the 1980s a small community of arms control specialists emerged within Chinese think tanks and government-funded research institutes. Emblematic of the broader political reforms taking place in China, these experts had more leeway for open discussion and began publishing papers and attending international conferences on nuclear issues and arms control. The result was a more robust and sophisticated debate among Chinese nuclear specialists and, equally (if not more) important, the opportunity for dialogue with foreign arms control experts. As the importance of these topics grew, Beijing funded more research to build a cadre of arms control and nuclear strategy specialists. In 1988, for example, the Institute of Applied Physics and Computational Mathematics, a research component of the nuclear labs, created a program to train younger scientists about arms control. By 1997, China had created a specific department in its Foreign Ministry dedicated to arms control and disarmament.[12]

China's Changing Criteria and Evolving Concerns

As China devoted more attention and study to nuclear issues, the leadership in Beijing softened its tone on arms control. By the late 1980s, China moved from skepticism and even antagonism toward arms control to indications of a willingness to participate in the process at some point in the

---

is Gu Guoliang. See Alastair Iain Johnston, "Learning Versus Adaptation: Explaining Change in Chinese Arms Control Policy in the 1980s and 1990s," *China Journal* 35 (January 1996): 27–61.

12. See Bates Gill and Evan S. Medeiros, "Foreign and Domestic Influences on China's Arms Control and Nonproliferation Policies," *China Quarterly* 161 (March 2000): 66; Fravel and Medeiros, "China's Search for Assured Retaliation," 67; and Johnston, "Learning Versus Adaptation," 38–46.

future. In doing so, however, China placed some specific requirements that had to be met by the superpowers in order for it to consider engaging in arms control. And yet, as the United States came closer to meeting these stipulations, especially after the collapse of the Soviet Union, Beijing has proceeded to modify these requirements to push the timeline for its participation further into the future. For example, in 1982 the Chinese leadership indicated that it would participate in arms control when the United States and the Soviet Union had cut their nuclear arsenals by 50 percent and ceased testing, manufacturing, and deploying their nuclear weapons. Then, in 1988, China modified its position and instead argued there must be "drastic reductions" in US and Soviet nuclear arsenals before it would join. This shift from a numerical requirement—a 50 percent reduction— to a vaguer and more subjective standard served to put Beijing in firm control of when it would participate, since China could easily argue that reductions were not "drastic" enough in its view rather than risk being held to the numerical standard that it had previously set for itself.

Following the end of the Cold War, China's leadership continued to modify the conditions necessary for its involvement in formal nuclear arms control. In 1995 Beijing said that it would not participate until the United States and Russia reduced their nuclear arsenals well below START II levels, gave up tactical nuclear weapons, halted ballistic missile defenses, and committed to no-first-use nuclear policies. In one of the highest-level declarations about China's views on arms control, Chinese President Jiang Zemin argued at a meeting of the Conference on Disarmament in March 1999 that the United States and Russia must "substantially" reduce their nuclear forces in order for China to participate in a "multilateral nuclear disarmament process."[13] As recently as 2010, China declared in its defense white paper, "When conditions are appropriate,

---

13. See Robert A. Manning, Ronald Montaperto, and Brad Roberts, *China, Nuclear Weapons, and Arms Control: A Preliminary Assessment* (New York: Council on Foreign Relations, 2000), 65–66; and Brad Roberts, "Arms Control and Sino-US Strategic Stability," in *Perspectives on Sino-American Strategic Nuclear Issues*, 186–187.

other nuclear-weapon states should also join in multilateral negotiations on nuclear disarmament."[14] Consistent with earlier claims, China did not define what would be required for the strategic situation to be "appropriate." And, interestingly, China said only that "other nuclear-weapon states" should join in negotiations at an appropriate time, thus leaving it unclear as to whether China was even referring to itself as opposed to Britain and France. Consequently, while the rhetorical shift in China's position on arms control is certainly a welcome development, actual movement toward China's participation in a bilateral or multilateral process has been almost nonexistent.

In examining recent official statements by Chinese leaders as well as the positions and debates among Chinese scholars, several key themes emerge that underpin China's continued reticence to engage in formal nuclear arms control. Understanding these issues and concerns—and developing solutions to assuage them—is essential for bringing China into the process and, ultimately, for achieving a nuclear weapons-free world.

In terms of declaratory policy, the Chinese leadership continues to argue that the countries with the largest nuclear arsenals, the United States and Russia, shoulder a "special and primary responsibility" for leading the charge for further arms control and eventual global abolition.[15] Whereas in many international arenas Beijing has seemingly been eager to play a leading role, when it comes to nuclear arms control China continues to be quite comfortable on the sidelines. Washington and Moscow, according to this view, must lead by example.

Beyond this consistent policy position lie several deeper, more challenging issues that continue to complicate US efforts to bring China into an arms control process. The first is the lurking suspicion among some in China's strategic community that the US effort to engage China in arms control is really a trick—a Trojan Horse of sorts—intended to lock

---

14. *China's National Defense in 2010.*

15. Ibid.

in the United States' superior power position over China. According to this view, the US interest in arms control with China is driven less by a desire to reduce nuclear danger and enhance stability and more by the realities of China's rise and subsequent shift in the global balance of power. The United States, the argument goes, wants to engage in arms control negotiations in order to constrain China's nuclear modernization and buildup and maintain its dominant position in the international order.[16]

This skepticism about Washington's true motives applies not only to arms control but also to the entire abolition agenda. Some in China contend that the objective driving the US-led push for global nuclear abolition is Washington's desire for "absolute advantage" and "absolute security."[17] If nuclear weapons serve not only to prevent nuclear coercion and deter nuclear attacks—the two stated purposes of China's nuclear weapons—but also to deter conventional attacks by a superior opponent, then nuclear abolition would essentially give the United States a free hand to project power and attack any country it wished with its superior conventional forces. As one scholar argued, "The existence of nuclear weapons on the contrary weakens the conventional weapons advantages of the United States military. . . . Yet promoting global denuclearization is conducive to the maintenance of US conventional military resources to maximize the benefits of US national security."[18]

The second challenge relates to China's views on transparency. According to classic nuclear theory developed during the Cold War, transparency is a core component of strategic stability and arms control.

---

16. See Lora Saalman, "How Chinese Analysts View Arms Control, Disarmament, and Nuclear Deterrence After the Cold War," in *Engaging China and Russia on Nuclear Disarmament,* ed. Cristina Hansell and William C. Potter, Occasional Paper 15, James Martin Center for Nonproliferation Studies, Monterey Institute of International Studies, April 2009: 51–52.

17. See Lora Saalman, *China and the U.S. Nuclear Posture Review,* Carnegie Endowment for International Peace, February 28, 2011: 15.

18. Ibid., 23.

In terms of stability, the ability of nuclear-armed opponents (or, at least, countries not firmly allied with each other and with which there is some potential for conflict) to have insight into each other's nuclear capabilities and force structure helps tamp down arms races, assuages the need to base force planning solely on "worst case" assumptions about the other's forces, and helps alleviate concerns about a disarming first strike. Under this logic, transparency leads to predictability which, in turn, leads to stability. For arms control, transparency serves as a basic starting point for negotiations, since states cannot begin to find mutually agreeable limits unless they know what the other side possesses. Upon the completion and signing of an arms control accord, transparency serves as a central pillar of a verification regime to ensure that the parties are in compliance with their obligations.

China, however, has a different perspective on transparency. Given its relatively small nuclear arsenal, China relies on secrecy and opacity as core components of its strategic deterrent.[19] Given the limited size of its nuclear arsenal, China believes that a lack of transparency contributes to deterrence by enhancing the survivability of its nuclear arsenal; after all, if an enemy doesn't know where its nuclear weapons are or how many it has, they can't accurately and reliably be targeted for destruction. Whereas Western nuclear theory posits that transparency underpins stability, China's nuclear theory holds that a lack of transparency creates uncertainty which, in turn, encourages caution and restraint. For the United States, deterrence has rested on convincing an opponent of the *certainty* of unacceptable retaliation in response to a nuclear attack; for China, deterrence has traditionally rested on creating *uncertainty* in an opponent's strategic calculations about its ability to successfully eliminate China's minimal nuclear arsenal in a first strike.[20] Given the long-standing

---

19. Ibid., 17–18.

20. However, as Fravel and Medeiros argue, China's current nuclear modernization efforts are focused in large part on enhancing survivability. China, according to this argument, is seeking "assured retaliation," suggesting that China is trying to move

centrality of opacity in China's strategic thinking, efforts to convince the leadership in Beijing to be more forthcoming about its strategic capabilities have been met with fierce resistance. Moreover, consistent with the view that the United States' real interest in arms control and abolition is to restrain China and maintain a dominant power position, some in China contend that US efforts to convince Beijing to be more transparent about its nuclear capabilities are really designed to collect valuable targeting intelligence for US strategic war plans.[21]

Consequently, on the issue of transparency the United States and China find themselves holding diametrically opposed positions. Whereas the United States views transparency as a necessary first step for arms control and strategic stability, China believes that transparency is the product or outcome of better overall strategic relations. In China's view, Washington and Beijing must first establish "strategic trust" before there can be transparency and stability; in the United States' view, transparency is one of the important mechanisms for creating strategic trust.[22]

The Emergence of Non-Nuclear Concerns

In addition to the concerns outlined above, two additional issues have proved to be major stumbling blocks in US and international efforts to bring China into the nuclear arms control process: US ballistic missile defense (BMD) capabilities and US plans to develop and deploy strategic conventional weapons such as conventional prompt global strike (CPGS). That these two capabilities are central irritants in US-China (as well as

---

away from uncertainty of retaliation as the basis of its deterrent and toward certainty of retaliation due to a more varied, mobile, and thus survivable force. See Fravel and Medeiros, "China's Search for Assured Retaliation."

21. On China's views on transparency, see Li Bin, "China and Nuclear Transparency," in *Transparency in Nuclear Warheads and Materials: The Political and Technical Dimensions,* ed. Nicholas Zarimpas (Oxford: Oxford University Press 2003), 50–57.

22. Saalman, "China and the U.S. Nuclear Posture Review," 17–18.

US-Russia) nuclear relations exemplifies the increasingly important—and potentially dangerous—interplay between nuclear and conventional forces in the modern era. BMD and CPGS are, of course, non-nuclear systems. But because of what Beijing—and Moscow—believe they are potentially capable of doing, they pose threats to the stability of the nuclear balance and risk causing an escalatory spiral in a conflict.

Indeed, Beijing's concerns about BMD and CPGS highlight a central tension in current US nuclear policy: in seeking to reduce the role of nuclear weapons in its national security strategy, the United States has subsequently elevated the role and importance of conventional systems like BMD and CPGS. Yet, BMD and CPGS are precisely the US capabilities that China is so deeply concerned about, and this concern helps drive Beijing's resistance to greater transparency and encourages China's leaders to increase the size and sophistication of their nuclear and conventional forces in order to offset these systems.[23] Paradoxically, then, the means by which the United States has sought to diminish the role of nuclear weapons to pave the way for further arms control and eventual abolition is one of the things that is making those objectives so difficult.

While China's initial response to the US withdrawal from the Anti-Ballistic Missile Treaty was muted, its opposition has steadily grown over the past decade as US BMD plans and capabilities have evolved.[24] And

---

23. For example, according to Yao Yunzhu, a well-respected Chinese scholar on nuclear weapons and general officer in China's military, "BMD development and deployment is by far the most significant factor impacting China's nuclear calculus." See Yao Yunzhu, "Chinese Nuclear Policy and the Future of Minimum Deterrence," in *Perspectives on Sino-American Strategic Nuclear Issues*, 120. According to the US Department of Defense's 2014 China report, China is "working on a range of technologies to attempt to counter U.S. and other countries' ballistic missile defense systems, including MIRVs, decoys, chaff, jamming, and thermal shielding." See *Military and Security Developments Involving the People's Republic of China 2014*, Annual Report to Congress (Washington, DC: Office of the Secretary of Defense, 2014), 30.

24. For an excellent history of China's reactions to US BMD plans, see Brad Roberts, "China and Ballistic Missile Defense: 1955 to 2002 and Beyond," Institute for

despite repeated assurances that BMD is not designed for—and is, in fact, incapable of—defending against large-scale, sophisticated attacks like the kind that China could mount, many in Beijing remain unconvinced.[25]

China contends that US BMD systems could undermine its strategic deterrent by potentially shielding the United States from retaliation in kind after a US first strike had eliminated the majority of China's nuclear forces. The United States, Chinese policymakers argue, might be more willing to use nuclear weapons if it did not fear unacceptable retaliation. BMD not only might make US leaders more likely to use nuclear weapons against China, but it also might provide Washington with an incentive to engage in nuclear coercion or take greater risks in a crisis or conflict with China in the belief that its BMD capabilities effectively neutralize China's deterrent.[26] With an effective (or at least a perceived effective)

Defense Analyses, Alexandria, Va., September 2003.

25. According to the Ballistic Missile Defense Review, "While the GMD [ground-based midcourse defense] system would be employed to defend the United States against limited missile launches from any source, it does not have the capacity to cope with large scale Russian or Chinese missile attacks, and is not intended to affect the strategic balance with those countries." See *Ballistic Missile Defense Review Report,* US Department of Defense, February 2010, 13.

26. On Chinese concerns about US BMD, see, for example, Li Bin, "China and the New U.S. Missile Defense in East Asia," Carnegie Endowment for International Peace, September 6, 2012; Zhang, "China's Perspective on a Nuclear-Free World," 149–150; Jing-dong Yuan, "China and the Nuclear Free World," in *Engaging China and Russia on Nuclear Disarmament,* 32; Shen Dingli, *Toward A Nuclear Weapons Free World: A Chinese Perspective,* Lowry Institute for International Policy, Sydney, Australia, November 2009, 10; Saalman, "China and the U.S. Nuclear Posture Review," 24; Paul H.B. Godwin, "Potential Chinese Responses to U.S. Ballistic Missile Defense," paper prepared for the Stimson Center-CNA NMD-China Project, January 2002; and Li Bin, "The Impact of U.S. NMD on Chinese Nuclear Modernization," Pugwash Online, April 2001. It is important to note that China's concerns about BMD are not new and, in fact, predate the Obama administration's BMD plans and even the US withdrawal from the ABM Treaty. See, for example, *China, Nuclear Weapons, and Arms Control,* 45–50, which was published in 2000 by the Council on Foreign Relations.

BMD system, deterrence in US-China relations would become decidedly one-sided.

Whereas China worries that BMD threatens to destroy its missiles in flight, CPGS threatens to destroy its missiles before they are even launched. CPGS is intended to provide US decision-makers with a prompt, non-nuclear capability to strike targets anywhere in the world within a short time.[27] While US officials have posited a number of potential missions for CPGS—including striking high-value terrorist targets, countering anti-satellite weapon (ASAT) attacks, and countering anti-access/area denial strikes—the nuclear-related missions have focused exclusively on North Korea and Iran.[28] But despite the US focus on so-called rogue states in discussing potential nuclear scenarios for CPGS, China views this capability as posing an equally dangerous threat to its nuclear deterrent. If CPGS can target North Korean or future Iranian nuclear forces, Beijing reasons, it can also target China's nuclear arsenal. China worries that CPGS could give the United States a non-nuclear counterforce capability against China's nuclear-armed ballistic missiles. In this situation, the United States could theoretically launch a disarming first strike without having to first cross the nuclear threshold.[29] This non-nuclear counterforce capability, whether real or merely perceived by Beijing, risks encouraging

---

27. For an insightful analysis of CPGS, see James M. Acton, *Silver Bullet? Asking the Right Questions about Conventional Prompt Global Strike* (Washington, DC: Carnegie Endowment for International Peace, 2013). For several years after the initial launch of the CPGS program the stated objective was to strike targets anywhere in the world within one hour. However, as Acton notes, the one-hour time frame appears to be more of a guide than a firm requirement, and in any case there may be a program reassessment under way that is shifting the program's focus to shorter-range weapons for regional contingencies. See Acton, 4–5.

28. Ibid., 12–27. While official US statements about CPGS's potential counter-nuclear missions do not involve China, the counter-ASAT and counter-A2/AD missions do have China in mind.

29. On this point, see Rong Yu and Peng Guangqian, "Nuclear No-First-Use Revisited," *China Security* 5, no. 1 (Winter 2009): 85.

China to operate its forces in ways that could increase the chances of accidents, miscalculations, or nuclear escalation in a crisis or war.[30]

While many in China believe that BMD and CPGS separately pose threats to its strategic deterrent, Chinese policymakers and defense analysts are even more concerned about them being used together. With effective conventional strike capabilities and missile defense, China worries that the United States could launch a non-nuclear counterforce first strike and then use its BMD to destroy any remaining nuclear-armed missiles launched in retaliation. In this scenario the United States would, in effect, engage in nuclear war without having to fire a nuclear shot.[31]

Organizational and Bureaucratic Challenges

The preceding discussion demonstrates that there are some important challenges and obstacles to convincing China to participate in meaningful nuclear arms control that might pave the way for eventual global abolition. And, if the challenges outlined above were not enough, it is likely that China must also contend with some organizational and bureaucratic

---

30. For example, China could reverse a long-standing policy and start deploying its forces with warheads mated to missiles. In a crisis or conflict with the United States, Beijing, fearing a US first strike with CPGS systems, might be encouraged to disperse its mobile forces at an earlier time or even pre-delegate launch authority to field commanders.

31. On these concerns, see, for example, Christopher P. Twomey, "Nuclear Stability at Low Numbers: The Perspective from Beijing," *The Nonproliferation Review* 20, no. 2 (June 2013): 296; Acton, *Silver Bullet,* 120–126; Fingar and Jishe, "Ties that Bind," 133; Fravel and Medeiros, "China's Search for Assured Retaliation," 83; and Saalman, *China and the U.S. Nuclear Posture Review,* 22–23. For an analysis of the US ability to destroy Chinese nuclear forces in a conventional counterforce strike, see Tong Zhao, "Conventional Counterforce Strike: An Option for Damage Limitation in Conflicts with Nuclear-Armed Adversaries?" *Science and Global Security* 19, no. 3 (October 2011): 195–222.

hurdles that likely affect its willingness and ability to participate in arms control. As noted earlier, China was slow to develop formal governmental offices and expertise in nuclear weapons and deterrence, and its development of expertise specifically in arms control is likely to have been even slower. If US-Soviet/Russian arms control is any guide, the actual mechanics of arms control are complicated and esoteric, involving painstaking detail in definitions, counting roles, and verification procedures, to name only a few. Without direct experience in the business of negotiating and implementing a nuclear arms control agreement, some elements of China's governmental apparatus may be reticent—and possibly even obstructionist—in participating in arms control even when the strategic situation is deemed "appropriate" by Chinese standards, whatever they may be.

To be sure, China has been steadily developing academic expertise in nuclear weapons and arms control for several decades, and Chinese experts have participated in numerous unofficial Track II strategic dialogues, nuclear policy conferences, and technical meetings. In 2008 the U.S. National Academy of Sciences published the *English-Chinese, Chinese-English Nuclear Security Glossary,* a joint project by US and Chinese experts to create agreed-upon definitions of key nuclear terms. The issue, however, is whether this academic expertise, and some of the experts themselves, can filter up to China's key decision-making circles and turn China's learning in arms control theory into practice.

The Way Ahead

While none of the challenges outlined in this paper are insurmountable, China's concerns are real and firmly held, thus necessitating careful and culturally sensitive solutions. As such, this paper concludes with some modest recommendations.

A first step—and emphasizing the use of the word "modest" above—is to manage expectations about what is feasible and realistic in the near and medium term with respect to arms control with China. Given Beijing's lack of experience with formal nuclear arms control and both recent and long-standing concerns about US strategic capabilities and its true intentions with respect to arms control with China, efforts to find a neat, all-encompassing solution or framework are likely to fail. The United States must sufficiently address each of China's concerns about arms control, and some may be able to be dealt with together or on parallel tracks whereas others might need to be handled sequentially. US policymakers—and, equally important, the US arms control community—should therefore expect a long and complicated process to get China to the negotiating table, one that will almost certainly be filled with frustrations, false starts, limited successes, and even occasional setbacks. This should not be met with criticism, frustration, and calls for speedier progress. Rather, it should be viewed as an important and necessary strategic challenge that requires patience, persistence, and fortitude.

Managing expectations about what is realistic in the near and medium term is especially important because it may be the case that formal nuclear arms control negotiations with China might only be possible once China has "risen," rather than during its rise. The uncertainties and mistrust that are hampering efforts to bring China into formal nuclear arms control are driven in part by the fact that China is still in ascendance and the full strategic consequences and implications of its rise are as yet unclear. The history of China's rise, and the history of the US reaction to it, are still being written. It is possible that some of Beijing's trepidations about engaging in formal arms control—particularly the concern about Washington using arms control as a means to contain China's rise and lock in a superior power position—are driven at least in part by China's perception of itself as a weaker state that is still emerging as major power, one that has in the past been bullied and taken advantage of by larger powers. Consequently, Beijing might be willing to consider engaging in formal negotiations on limitations or cuts only after its military modernization is completed and its emergence as a great power is solidified.

Equally important, despite the desire among some in the US arms control community for significant limitations or cuts in the next round of arms control, US national security interests—and the broader abolition agenda—are better served by modest cuts over a series of agreements spanning several years, perhaps even decades. Not only is an initial proposal for substantial cuts likely to fail, thereby saddling the arms control record with a failure and setting back the arms control and abolition agendas, but calls for dramatic cuts might also scare off Beijing from participating in the first place. As a newcomer to arms control, it is likely that China would prefer quite modest cuts in its first round to become acquainted with the process and subsequent verification measures, and to ensure that it can still maintain security and protect its interests at lower levels.

The second recommendation is to refrain from forcing US strategic concepts and definitions on China. There seems to have been a view over the last few decades among some in the US nuclear community that the United States must "teach" China about nuclear strategy and arms control. This belief stems from the fact that some Chinese nuclear concepts have differed from those in the West. One example is the traditional Chinese word for deterrence, weishe, which has a more offensive connotation—more akin to the US concept of compellence—than in the West.[32] Another more recent example involves the concept of strategic stability. The 2010 US Nuclear Posture Review's call for maintaining and enhancing strategic stability with China was met with some confusion in Chinese strategic circles, as some in China view the concept of strategic stability as a relationship between relatively equal nuclear powers (such as the United States and Russia) and therefore not immediately applicable to

---

32. See, for example, Evan S. Medeiros, "Evolving Nuclear Doctrine," in *China's Nuclear Future,* ed. Paul J. Bolt and Albert S. Wilner (Boulder, CO: Lynne Rienner, 2006), 52, 65–66; Forrest E. Morgan, Karl P. Mueller, Evan S. Medeiros, Kevin L. Pollpeter, and Roger Cliff, *Dangerous Thresholds: Managing Escalation in the 21st Century* (Santa Monica, CA: Rand Corp., 2008), 65; and Jeffrey Lewis, "China's Nuclear Posture and Force Modernization," in *Engaging China and Russia on Nuclear Disarmament,* 40.

US-China nuclear relations.[33] Importantly, the Nuclear Posture Review did not define strategic stability, perhaps deliberately so in order to create an opportunity for Washington and Beijing to jointly agree on a definition. Whatever the reason, however, Chinese officials and nuclear experts responded to the review's call for strategic stability with China not by calling for bilateral work but by calling for the United States to provide a definition.[34]

While there are certainly some important differences in definitions and concepts in Washington's and Beijing's nuclear lexicons, these disparities should not be overstated. China's behavior over its nearly five-decade-long history with nuclear weapons demonstrates that it understands and abides by the core logic of nuclear weapons as developed in the West, even if the concepts and terms are somewhat different. At the most fundamental level, China views nuclear weapons not as militarily useful tools for aggression and coercion but rather as a means of preventing the threat or use of nuclear weapons against it. China's ongoing nuclear modernization programs (including the deployment of land-based mobile missiles and the introduction of a new class of ballistic missile submarines) are driven in part by the need to increase the survivability of its forces—*the central tenet of Western deterrence theory.* As such, the United States should avoid trying to force precise definitions or concepts on China. These efforts are not only unnecessary but, equally important, are counterproductive, as Beijing almost certainly would interpret these actions as condescending and emblematic of Washington's desire to maintain dominance over China.

---

33. For China's views on strategic stability, see PONI Working Group on U.S.-China Nuclear Issues, *Nuclear Weapons and U.S.-China Relations: A Way Forward,* Center for Strategic and International Studies, March 2013, 14. The author was a member of the committee upon which this report is based. See also Saalman, "China and the U.S. Nuclear Posture Review," 3, 7, 26–29; and Twomey, "Nuclear Stability at Low Numbers: The View from Beijing," 292–297.

34. I thank James Acton for this point.

The United States should instead seek, through both formal and informal channels, to better understand China's strategic concepts and work to ensure that China's policymakers and nuclear analysts understand US concepts and terms. This approach is already occurring through Track II channels and is exemplified by the development and publication of the *English-Chinese, Chinese-English Nuclear Security Glossary*. Precision and specificity are extremely important in dialogue and negotiations between nuclear-armed powers. But the point is that as long as each side understands exactly what the other means when it uses a term, it does not matter if both countries are using the same lingo. In fact, in US-China nuclear relations it may well be worth dispensing with traditional Western buzzwords such as strategic stability given the Cold War baggage they carry and instead focus only on the core issues encompassed by the concept, perhaps even under the banner of a new term jointly coined by Washington and Beijing.[35]

In terms of practical steps to assuage Chinese concerns about participating in arms control, the United States should consider how to involve China in some practical aspects of existing arms control agreements. Given China's lack of experience in this arena, appropriate first-hand exposure could help familiarize Beijing with what arms control looks like in practice and help minimize the inherent trepidations involved in getting involved in something of this magnitude for the first time. As just one example, the United States could consider allowing China to observe a practice inspection of Russia's strategic forces allowed under New START.[36]

Perhaps the most important issues that need to be resolved in order to pave the way for China's participation have to do with BMD and CPGS.

---

35. For a similar point, see "Nuclear Weapons and U.S.-China Relations," 14.

36. Ibid., 25. It is important to emphasize that this would be observation of a practice inspection conducted in the United States, as Russia would be unlikely to allow Chinese observes to accompany US officials on a real inspection.

Short of halting these programs—which would be politically unpalatable in America and unwise strategically given the myriad of threats to US security interests and its extended deterrence commitments—the United States must find credible ways to assure China that these systems are not a threat. Such efforts could include visits to US and Chinese missile defense sites, invitations to observe missile defense tests, joint technical assessments of BMD and CPGS capabilities, and joint threat assessments and scenario exercises analyzing the range of contingencies in which these capabilities might be used. Of course, all of these initiatives involve two critical elements of mutual trust: first, belief that these confidence-building efforts won't be used solely as intelligence-gathering efforts designed to collect information that can then be used to counter the other side's capabilities; and, second, faith that what each side is showing and communicating to the other about its capabilities and strategic thinking with regard to these weapons is, in fact, accurate.

Finally, beyond alleviating concerns about US capabilities and intentions, the United States can also encourage China's participation in formal nuclear arms control and the abolition agenda by adopting a no-first-use nuclear policy. China has repeatedly called for the United States and the other declared nuclear-weapon states under the Non-Proliferation Treaty to adopt NFU, going so far as to introduce in January 1994 a draft "Treaty on Mutual No-First-Use of Nuclear Weapons" and to propose that the nuclear-weapon states begin the first round of negotiations on the treaty in Beijing. Russia, however, was the only state that took interest in the proposal. In September 1994, China and Russia issued a joint statement committing to a mutual no-first-use policy and the de-targeting of nuclear weapons against each other.[37] With renewed global interest in nuclear abolition, China has stated that it believes a critical first step

---

37. Information Office of the State Council of the People's Republic of China, "China's Endeavors for Arms Control, Disarmament, and Non-Proliferation," September 2005, http://www.china.org.cn/english/features/book/140320.htm.

in realizing the goal of a nuclear weapons-free world is for the other nuclear powers to reduce the role of nuclear weapons in their national security strategies by foreswearing the option to use nuclear weapons first in conflict.[38] NFU, Chinese nuclear scholars argue, would enable further reductions because a nuclear posture designed for NFU can be much smaller than a posture that leaves open the option of first use.[39] For the United States, adopting NFU would not only meet one of China's concrete recommendations for creating the conditions for a nuclear-free world and potentially pave the way for Chinese participation in arms control, but it could also enhance national security by reducing fears of a US first strike in a crisis or conflict.[40] Adopting NFU would not be easy, as Washington would have to credibly convince its allies that it can still meet its extended deterrence commitments and would have to work to mitigate domestic political fallout. But, if reducing nuclear dangers and laying the groundwork for nuclear abolition are to remain important long-term US policy objectives, adopting NFU could be a meaningful step forward.

---

38. According to China's 2010 Defense White Paper, "China holds that, before the complete prohibition and thorough destruction of nuclear weapons, all nuclear-weapon states should abandon any nuclear deterrence policy based on first use of nuclear weapons. . . ." See *China's National Defense in 2010.*

39. See, for example, Zhang, "China's Perspective on a Nuclear-Free World," 145–146; Gregory Kulacki, "Chickens Talking with Ducks: The U.S.-Chinese Nuclear Dialogue," *Arms Control Today* 41 (October 2011), http://legacy.armscontrol.org /act/2011_10/U.S._Chinese_Nuclear_Dialogue; and Lu Yin, "Building a New China-US Strategic Stability," *Contemporary International Relations* 22, no. 6 (November/December 2012), http://www.eastviewpress.com/Files/CIR_6_2012 _China%20US%20Stability.pdf.

40. For arguments in favor of the United States adopting NFU, see Michael S. Gerson, "No First Use: The Next Step for US Nuclear Policy," *International Security* 35, no. 2 (Fall 2010): 7–47; and Scott D. Sagan, "The Case for No First Use," *Survival* 51, no. 3 (June–July 2009): 163–182.

Conclusion

After the initial excitement and euphoria that followed President Obama's embrace of the vision of a nuclear weapons-free world, the practical aspects of arms control and abolition have tempered any hope that may have existed for a smooth path to zero, even if over many decades. While the role and salience of nuclear weapons in international politics have certainly declined since the end of the Cold War, many nuclear-armed states continue to believe that nuclear weapons are a symbol of great power status and the ultimate guarantor of security and sovereignty. As one of the five declared nuclear-weapon states under the Non-Proliferation Treaty, China's embrace of abolition and its willingness to participate in formal arms control are crucial next steps in sustaining the momentum for global abolition. Indeed, China's participation may hold the key to multi-lateralizing what has historically been only a bilateral endeavor. As with many other aspects of modern international political and economic issues, the future of arms control is in the East.

CHAPTER 12 **China and Global Nuclear Arms Control and Disarmament**

Li Bin

Lack of Chinese-US Cooperation on Nuclear Arms Control

From 1993 to 1996, China and the United States made constructive joint efforts in negotiations on the Comprehensive Test Ban Treaty (CTBT). Since then, the two countries have made little progress in their cooperation on nuclear arms control, although they have significantly widened and deepened their cooperation on nuclear nonproliferation and nuclear security issues. The only recent notable progress in nuclear arms control between the two countries is a bilateral agreement on nuclear de-targeting announced in 1998.[1] In the first several years of this century, the topic of nuclear arms control was even excluded from semiofficial ("track 1.5") dialogues between the two countries.[2]

---

1. Howard Diamond, "Sino-U.S. Summit Yields Modest Advances in Arms Control Agenda," *Arms Control Today,* June 1, 1998, http://www.armscontrol.org/print/381.

2. For example, the serial US-China Conference on Arms Control, Disarmament and Nonproliferation usually divides its time half by half on the two topics of arms control and disarmament, but the Sixth Conference in 2006 did not include any arms control topic. See Stephanie C. Lieggi, "U.S.-China Nonproliferation Cooperation," Sixth U.S.-China Conference on Arms Control, Center for

It is worrisome if China and the United States cannot develop cooperation over nuclear arms control to help build trust between them. Both countries are concerned about each other's development of strategic nuclear capabilities. For example, the United States worries about the future development of the Chinese nuclear force while China is concerned about the development of the US missile defense program. These worries could eventually lead to a security dilemma for the two countries if they cannot develop an effective mechanism for cooperation.

In the global context, there has been no negotiation since 1996 at the Conference on Disarmament, the most important multilateral arms control negotiation forum. The five nuclear-weapon states (P5) are receiving growing pressure from the non-nuclear-weapon states for their inefficiency in implementing Article VI (which promotes disarmament) of the Nuclear Non-Proliferation Treaty (NPT). If P5 members can make some progress in global nuclear arms control and disarmament, they would be in a more favorable position to work with the non-nuclear-weapon states in promoting new nonproliferation arrangements.

This chapter focuses on nuclear arms control cooperation between China and the United States. It analyzes the opportunities in—and obstacles to—such cooperation by examining the differences and similarities in the Chinese and US approaches and makes recommendations about how to promote cooperation.

Chinese Views on the Roles of Nuclear Weapons and National Security

China and the United States have made little progress in nuclear arms control cooperation in the last one and a half decades partially because

---

Nonproliferation Studies, October 2006, http://cns.miis.edu/archive/cns/programs/eanp/research/uschina6/US_China_Conf06.pdf.

they have different agendas derived from their different security concepts and paradigms. When the strategists in the two countries design their own nuclear agendas, they use their traditional paradigms. However, when each views the agenda of the other side, each sometimes uses "mirror theory," assuming that the two sides have the same security philosophy. Failure to take note of these paradigm differences is a serious problem in Chinese-US nuclear dialogues.

The core concept in the American security paradigm is "national security threat." A national security threat is usually defined as a rival who has the capability and intention to hurt the United States. If a rival is believed to have nuclear weapon capability and an intention to use that capability to hurt the United States, it is indentified by the United States as a nuclear threat. During the Cold War, the Soviet Union was regarded by the United States as a primary nuclear threat. Today, nuclear terrorists and proliferators are considered by the United States as first-tier nuclear threats and Russia and China as second-tier nuclear threats.[3]

In China, there is an indigenous security paradigm in which "national security challenge" is a core concept. Unlike "national security threat" in the American paradigm, a "national security challenge" in the Chinese paradigm is a situation in which China is vulnerable. The origins of the challenge may be inside China or outside China—or both. For example, it is a belief in China that lagging behind technologically leaves China vulnerable to attacks. "Lagging behind" is a situation and the causes of the situation could be both inside and outside China. National security challenges and their origins include both military and non-military factors. For example, natural disasters and safety accidents are considered national security challenges, as illustrated in Chinese national security

---

3. US Department of Defense, "Nuclear Posture Review Report," April 2010, vi, http://www.defense.gov/npr/docs/2010%20Nuclear%20Posture%20Review %20Report.pdf.

white papers.[4] The Chinese security paradigm is sometimes called a "comprehensive security concept" or "comprehensive security theory."[5]

When the Chinese strategists consider nuclear weapon issues, their conclusions are sometimes different from those of their American counterparts because they use different paradigms in their analyses. This is an important concept for us to grasp as we try to understand the differences between Chinese and US nuclear arms control policies.

Security challenges related to nuclear weapons may be divided into two categories for the purpose of this chapter. The first category includes nuclear proliferation and nuclear terrorism. China identifies the dangers of nuclear proliferation and nuclear terrorism as serious challenges to its national security[6] and has developed a wide range of cooperation with the United States to curb the dangers. The second category of security challenges includes nuclear coercion, nuclear attack, and nuclear accidents; these challenges may be mitigated by nuclear arms control and disarmament efforts. This chapter discusses only the second category and explores how China and the United States can develop cooperation on it.

Nuclear coercion has long been identified as a challenge to China's security. The American security experts divide nuclear coercion into two categories: nuclear deterrence and nuclear compellence. According to the American definition, nuclear *deterrence* means forcing a rival to stop a move by threatening use of nuclear weapons, while nuclear *compellence* means forcing a rival to make a move by threatening use of nuclear weapons. The key difference here is that nuclear deterrence maintains the

---

4. Information Office of the State Council of the People's Republic of China, "China's National Defense in 2010," March 31, 2011, http://www.china.org.cn/government /whitepaper/node_7114675.htm; Information Office of the State Council of the People's Republic of China, "The Diversified Employment of China's Armed Forces," April 16, 2013, http://www.china.org.cn/government/whitepaper/node_7181425.htm.

5. Information Office, PRC, "Diversified Employment."

6. Information Office, PRC, "China's National Defense in 2010."

status quo while nuclear compellence changes the status quo.[7] Nuclear deterrence seems to be a positive action compared to nuclear compellence, so the United States chooses "nuclear deterrence" as the brand of its nuclear policy.

The Chinese strategists see the dynamics of nuclear coercion in a different way. Nuclear deterrence and compellence may be distinguishable if a conflict includes only one round of interactions: a country launches an act of aggression and its rival strikes back with nuclear weapons. A real conflict may include an escalation of interactions and it is sometimes difficult to identify who changes the status quo first in the escalation. As a result, it is difficult to identify a coercive threat as a deterrence or compellence in an escalation. For Chinese strategists, a policy identified as deterrence may actually be one of compellence.

China feels that it has been a victim of nuclear coercion and it criticizes the policies that leave space for nuclear compellence.[8] If a country cuts the linkage between its nuclear weapon use and conventional escalation, there is no chance for that country to send a nuclear compelling signal. If a country links its nuclear weapon use to conventional escalation, it can actively send a nuclear compelling signal. If a country does not exclude its nuclear weapon use in responding to conventional conflict, the policy still has some passive compelling effects. China always wants to reduce the chance of nuclear compellence by promoting a no-first-use policy. This is a major goal in China's nuclear arms control and disarmament agenda.

The danger of receiving a nuclear attack is also considered a challenge to China's security. Both the United States and Soviet Union threatened to

---

7. Thomas C. Schelling, "Arms and Influence: With a New Preface and Afterword" (New Haven, CT: Yale University Press, 2008), 70–71.

8. Li Bin, "Understanding China's Nuclear Strategy" (in Chinese), *World Economics and Politics* 9, 2006: 16–22.

use nuclear weapons against China at different times.[9] China was under the pressure of possible nuclear attacks for a few decades, and it had to spend its resources to build a nuclear arsenal and to develop civil defense.

For China, the challenges of nuclear coercion and nuclear attack are two sides of a coin. If the potential danger of nuclear attack can be stopped by China's small nuclear deterrent, China's civil defense effort, or a worldwide taboo against nuclear weapon use, nuclear coercion would become impossible. In the American view, nuclear attack is considered to be much more serious than nuclear coercion, at least in public discussions.

A third security challenge is the risk of nuclear accidents.[10] Nuclear accidents here include nuclear safety problems and the accidental or unauthorized launch of nuclear weapons. According to the Chinese view, the consequences of a major nuclear accident are as serious as receiving a nuclear attack. This is why China chooses a very low level of nuclear alerting. In the United States, the safety and security of nuclear weapons are very important issues, but they are not categorized as security threats as they cannot be measured by the "capability" and "intention" of a rival.

---

9. Regarding US threats of using nuclear weapons, see Hans M. Kristensen, Robert S. Norris, and Matthew G. McKinzie, "Chinese Nuclear Forces and U.S. Nuclear War Planning," Federation of American Scientists & Natural Resources Defense Council, November 2006, 127. Regarding Soviet threats of using nuclear weapons, see Michael S. Gerson, "The Sino-Soviet Border Conflict: Deterrence, Escalation, and the Threat of Nuclear War in 1969," Center for Naval Analyses, November 2010, http://www.cna.org/sites/default/files/research/D0022974.A2.pdf.

10. It is reported that "nuclear security" is one of the major issues addressed by China's National Security Commission. See Shannon Tiezzi, "China's National Security Commission Holds First Meeting," The Diplomat, April 16, 2014, http://thediplomat.com/2014/04/chinas-national-security-commission-holds-first-meeting. However, the original Chinese words, he anquan (核安全), primarily mean nuclear safety. See Liu Hua, "Preliminary Comment on the Position and Roles of Nuclear Safety in the Comprehensive National Security" (in Chinese), http://theory.people.com.cn/n/2014/0428/c40537-24952712.html.

The Chinese Nuclear Weapon Policy

Facing challenges related to nuclear weapons, the first-generation leaders of the People's Republic of China decided to develop the nation's own nuclear weapon capability. The purposes of Chinese nuclear weapons are to counter nuclear coercion[11] and to deter nuclear attack.[12] China has its own particular calculations on the balance among the quantity, quality, safety, and security of its nuclear arsenal.

For China, the most important step is to understand and demonstrate nuclear weapon technologies, rather than to produce and deploy the weapons. China's concern is that if it does not understand the technical and political nature of nuclear weapons, other nuclear-armed states would see this as a chance to coerce China by creating nuclear terror. It is unnecessary for China to weaponize all nuclear technologies it understands. An example is that China tested the principle of a neutron bomb but never used it to create actual weapons.[13]

Since developing nuclear capability, China has been comfortable with a small nuclear force. Many American strategists have predicted a dramatic increase in Chinese nuclear forces. One famous theory is the "spring to parity" proposed by former US Secretary of Defense Donald Rumsfeld.[14] The fact is that the size of China's nuclear force has been changing very slowly over the last few decades, during which China's economic growth has been very fast. China's economic capacity does not appear to be an important driver in its nuclear force development.

---

11. Li Bin, "Understanding China's Nuclear Strategy."

12. Sun Xiangli, "China's Nuclear Strategy," in *Comparative Study on Nuclear Strategies* (in Chinese), ed. Zhang Tuosheng et al. (Beijing: Social Science Academic Press, November 2014), 12.

13. Zheng Shaotang et al., *Yu Min—A Famous Scientist in Contemporary China* (in Chinese) (Guiyang: Guizhou People's Publisher, 2005), 112–114.

14. Brad Roberts, "On Order, Stability, and Nuclear Abolition," in *Abolishing Nuclear Weapons: A Debate,* ed. George Perkovich and James M. Acton (Washington, DC: Carnegie Endowment for International Peace, 2009), 167.

A much more important factor in China's quantitative requirement of nuclear weapons is the security situation it perceives. Some new evidence suggests that the quantitative requirement today may be smaller than in the second half of the 1960s, when both superpowers were hostile to China.

In 1966, China launched Project 816 to build a plutonium production facility in a tunnel in southwest China. The facility includes three graphite-moderated, water-cooled reactors. Each of them has a thermal power of eighty megawatts.[15] If operated for ten years at full capacity, this facility could produce about 900 kilograms of weapons-grade plutonium, or two hundred nuclear devices. The project was suspended in 1981 and permanently terminated in 1984 when the major construction of the facility was almost finished. Now the facility is open to the public as a museum. The Chinese government explained the reason for the termination of the project as "improvement of the international security situation."[16] This explanation is supported by some other evidence. In 1984, Chinese leader Deng Xiaoping told his German guest, Chancellor Helmut Kohl, that the Chinese leaders changed their assessment about the international security situation.[17] As the Chinese security perception changed, the Chinese decision-makers apparently lowered their quantitative requirements in nuclear weapons. They believed that they had redundant capacity for the production of weapon-usable fissile materials.[18]

---

15. Video, "The First Discovery of the Project 816 in Fulin" (in Chinese), http://v.youku .com/v_show/id_XMTY4MDU3ODgw.html.

16. Wei Weian, "Declassifying the Reasons Why Project 816 in Fuin, Chongqing Was Terminated" (in Chinese), http://info.gongchang.com/news/2010-04-27/96136.html.

17. Deng Xiaoping, "We Regard Reform as a Revolution" (in Chinese), October 10, 1984, http://zg.people.com.cn/GB/33839/34943/34944/34947/2617883.html.

18. The Chinese decision-makers had reached consensus on the redundancy of highly enriched uranium for weapons when they debated the production of low enriched uranium in 1981. See Zhang Sheng, "Coming from Wars—Record of Zhang Aiping's Life" (in Chinese), http://news.163.com/09/0511/09/5918LQK700013A68_2.html.

The history of the 816 Project suggests the following points: (1) China's quantitative requirement in nuclear weapons varies according to its security perception; (2) China lowered its quantitative requirement in nuclear weapons in the early 1980s; and (3) if China feels the danger of its security situation has become as serious as it was in the late 1960s, it may raise the number of its nuclear weapons by about two hundred warheads. The American concern that China would seek quantitative parity with the United States cannot be supported by Chinese security philosophy and practice.

According to the Chinese comprehensive security concept, safety problems and security problems are similar in their consequences and therefore should be treated equally. China carefully manages the balance between the deterrent effects of its nuclear weapons and their safety and security. It would not choose a nuclear weapon policy that protects its traditional military security but at a significant risk of a nuclear accident. This is a major reason China puts its nuclear weapons off alert in peacetime. The Chinese government has confirmed that its nuclear weapons are at low or appropriate alerting status.[19] A few years ago, the *People's Liberation Army Daily* published articles to explain how the Chinese nuclear force trains its soldiers to prepare for retaliatory nuclear attacks. According to the articles, China's nuclear retaliation is designed to be launched a few days after receiving a nuclear attack. Nuclear warheads are mounted on Chinese missiles just before launch.[20] The strategy of postponing retaliation does not change the deterrent effects of China's nuclear weapons as long as their survivability does not decrease significantly during the period between the attack and the retaliation. This

---

19. Information Office, PRC, "China's National Defense in 2010" and "Diversified Employment."

20. Li Bin, "Tracking Chinese Strategic Mobile Missiles," *Science & Global Security* 15, no. 1 (2007): 1–30.

delayed launch strategy can avoid misjudgments that could lead to unauthorized and accidental nuclear weapon launches.

Chinese Concerns over Emerging Security Challenges

Some origins and causes of the challenges to China's security are the capabilities and intentions of foreign countries. It is not difficult for American security experts to understand Chinese concerns on these challenges. For example, the United States has been developing a missile defense program since 1983. If the US missile defense capability grows, it would undermine China's nuclear deterrence. Another similar case is the US development of long-range precision conventional strike capability. If the US conventional precision strike capability became real, it would allow the United States to disarm China's nuclear deterrent force by conventional means. Some other US policies and practices have similar effects on the Chinese nuclear deterrent capability—for example, increasing US intelligence efforts aimed at locating the Chinese nuclear forces. Although the two countries have not yet found solutions to these problems, nuclear experts in China and in the United States understand each other's logic and have dialogues on these topics by using the capability and intention paradigm.

Other factors could also make China's leaders feel that they are in a dangerous situation, but it is difficult to attribute these factors to the capability and intention of a specific country. In these cases, the Chinese concerns are not always explicit to the American experts. For example, a traditional Chinese concern is that lagging behind technologically would leave China vulnerable to attacks but it is difficult for China to identify where the attack would come from. From a Chinese perspective, the most dangerous situation would occur when China does not understand the nature or the importance of a new technology, and it would be too late for China to respond to it. In other words, a "science surprise" could create a security challenge for China.

China's primary concern regarding US missile defense involved uncertainties about development of a new defense technology in new realms. China was on the US side in the early 1980s in criticizing Soviet global military expansions when the United States started its Strategic Defense Initiative (SDI). Although China understood that SDI was not aimed at China, and the capability was still far from mature, China was still very cautious about the new moves in defense research caused by SDI. China regarded SDI, EUREKA (European Research Coordination Agency), and some Soviet defense research as a new wave of efforts to seek technical superiority by the Western powers.[21] The concern is still there that China could fall further behind other countries in defense technologies. China's call for space arms control is a diplomatic approach to mitigate scientific surprises in a new defense technology race. China's worries about long-range precision strike capabilities, information warfare, and other new military technologies are based on similar considerations.

Some factors do not significantly change the nuclear weapon capability of any specific country, but they may change the relations between nuclear and conventional weapons. China is very cautious about any move that narrows the gap between nuclear and conventional weapons.

As mentioned earlier, nuclear weapons could play compelling roles if a country were to link the use of its nuclear weapons to conventional conflicts in its declaratory policy. Such a policy would allow the country to send compelling signals when it wants to use the influence of its nuclear weapons to support its conventional aggression. China views any reservation of using nuclear weapons in conventional conflict in declaratory policy as a potential danger of nuclear coercion.

Tactical nuclear weapons are also a serious concern for China as their existence sends a message to the world that nuclear weapons

---

21. Editorial of Chinese Communist Party's News, "Deng Xiaoping Made the Decision to Launch Project 863" (in Chinese), http://dangshi.people.com.cn/n/2014/1223 /c85037-26258764.html.

may be used in battlefields in the same way as conventional weapons. Tactical nuclear weapons are a negative factor for the nuclear taboo in international society. When the George W. Bush administration considered developing nuclear penetration warheads, the Chinese strategic community had very strong, critical reactions. This concern was not because the project would add to the US nuclear weapon capability against China. Rather, the worry was that the development of tactical nuclear weapons would lower the threshold of nuclear weapon use.[22] China now is also very concerned about the discussions in the United States concerning redeployment of tactical nuclear weapons in East Asia.[23]

The context of China's nuclear weapon policy includes the postures and structures of foreign nuclear forces, the international nuclear arms control regimes, international nuclear norms, and regional and global conventional military situations. If some of the factors change, China may have to make reactive adjustments in its nuclear weapon policy. From the capability perspective, the adjustments could be simple and straightforward. The effects of US missile defense on China could be compensated for by a buildup of Chinese offensive missiles; the danger of a conventional strike against Chinese nuclear targets can be avoided by a strategy of launch-on-warning. However, the adjustments would change some core values of China's nuclear policy and would be considered as harmful to China's security, according to its theory of comprehensive security.

---

22. Hu Siyuan, "Nuclear Shadow Moving Around: U.S. Research on Nuclear Penetration Warhead" (in Chinese), http://www.china.com.cn/xxsb/txt/2004-04/15/content _5545602.htm.

23. Zou Zaijian, "U.S. House Proposes Redeployment of Tactical Nuclear Weapons in South Korea" (in Chinese), http://js.people.com.cn/html/2012/05/15/108455.html.

China's Priorities and Pragmatic Policy
in Nuclear Arms Control

China has strong interests in nuclear arms control and disarmament and hopes to stop the origins and causes of the challenges to its security by arms control approaches. It has its own nuclear disarmament agenda based on its calculation of security challenges. Before China deepened its openness policy in 1980s, it always emphasized its independent views on nuclear disarmament and exercised unilateral self-constraints on its nuclear force—for example, a small force, low-alerting status, and a no-first-use commitment. After the 1980s, China joined more and more international arms control forums and regimes and began to seek compromises with other countries on global arms control issues. Now China's nuclear arms control and disarmament policy has become more pragmatic, but its disarmament goals are visible through its arms control statements and activities.

When China is pushed to join the nuclear disarmament agenda led by the United States, it sometimes feels reluctant as its national security interests may be omitted in the process. To promote Chinese-US cooperation on nuclear arms control and disarmament, it is important for America to understand which disarmament goals are most important to China. This would allow the two countries to find their common interests and to make use of Chinese political wisdom.

China's goal is to reduce challenges to its national security. Its agenda includes immediate efforts to curb emerging security challenges and a long-term blueprint to abolish nuclear weapons. China's immediate arms control approaches involve strengthening existing nuclear arms control agreements and norms and preventing the emergence of military competition in new realms. Missile defense, space arms control, counter-nuclear intelligence, and cybersecurity are outstanding issues China wants to discuss with the United States.

There are both similarities and differences between the Chinese and American blueprints of nuclear elimination. Both countries agree on strengthening the control and management of nuclear weapons and fissile materials before reaching a nuclear weapons-free world. However, the two countries have different preferences in choosing the path of nuclear disarmament. Basically, there are two kinds of arms control: (1) controls on the quantity of weapons and (2) controls on their use. The Washington Naval Treaty of 1922, which limited the number and size of deployed warships, is an example of quantitative control; the 1925 Geneva Protocol, which prohibited the use of chemical weapons, is an example of use control.

The American and Russian experiences in nuclear disarmament involve limiting and reducing the numbers of their nuclear weapons. China supports the US-Russian efforts toward reducing the sizes of their nuclear forces. But its preference in nuclear disarmament is to prioritize the control over nuclear weapon use. If nuclear weapons are not allowed to be used, their value would decline in the eyes of decision-makers and nuclear disarmament and abolition would face less resistance. It may be difficult to reach a prohibition on nuclear-weapon use in one step. So some gradual efforts are necessary. Nuclear-armed states may begin with no-first-use commitments. If all nuclear-armed states were to agree to a no-first-use policy, the overall effect would be similar to a policy of non-use of nuclear weapons. A parallel effort involves de-alerting nuclear weapons, which keeps nuclear weapons further away from use. China is the only nuclear-weapon state that supports the idea of nuclear de-alerting.[24] Chemical disarmament offers a useful experience for nuclear disarmament. When a nuclear taboo against use becomes robust enough, the condition of nuclear abolishment would be imminent.

---

24. United Nations, "General Assembly Adopts 63 Drafts on First Committee's Recommendation with Nuclear Disarmament at Core of Several Recorded Votes," press release, December 2, 2014, http://www.un.org/press/en/2014/ga11593.doc.htm.

The Chinese government now understands the importance of cooperation in nuclear arms control and disarmament. It pursues pragmatic diplomacy in this area, and its nuclear arms control and disarmament policy is a compromise between its desirable agenda and its cooperation with other countries. Although some of its agenda and priorities in nuclear arms control are not taken up by other countries, China still shows some flexibility if the general trend of disarmament is positive.

One example is negotiations on the Fissile Material Cut-off Treaty (FMCT) in the Conference on Disarmament. China once wanted to have parallel negotiations on FMCT and on space arms control. Now China supports the FMCT negotiations, although its proposed negotiation on space is denied by the United States.

On the Comprehensive Test Ban Treaty, China's position looks similar to that of the United States because neither of them has ratified the treaty. But actually their positions are very different. The United States cannot ratify the CTBT as it has doubts about verification under the treaty, especially the on-site inspection arrangements.[25] China does not have any problem with the content of the treaty and joins all activities of the treaty. The only Chinese concern is the future attitude of the United States toward the treaty. But China avoids publicly criticizing the United States in this regard.

Both China and the United States recognize the abolishment of nuclear weapons as the ultimate goal of nuclear disarmament. There are some slight differences in their formulations. In the United States, the statement by President Obama is "a world without nuclear weapons."[26] In China, the statement has been "complete and thorough nuclear disarmament"

---

25. Sean Dunlop and Jean du Preez, " The United States and the CTBT: Renewed Hope or Politics as Usual?" Nuclear Threat Initiative, February 1, 2009, http://www.nti.org /analysis/articles/united-states-and-ctbt.

26. "Remarks by President Barack Obama," Prague, April 5, 2009, http://www.whitehouse.gov/the_press_office/Remarks-By-President-Barack -Obama-In-Prague-As-Delivered.

since it first acquired nuclear weapons.[27] In recent years, China has proposed some formal language in various disarmament forums on the issue: "nuclear-weapon states should commit not to permanently possess nuclear weapons." The two countries apparently have a common goal in nuclear disarmament. The major difference between Chinese and US priorities is about the path of the disarmament. China is in favor of controls over the use of nuclear weapons while the United States prioritizes quantitative reductions. The positions of the two countries do not seem to be confrontational. Instead, they can be supplementary if the two can find a way to coordinate their positions.

China worries that some US activities—including missile defense development and intelligence activities aimed at locating Chinese nuclear weapons—would undermine the strategic stability between the two countries. China wants to deal with these issues by arms control approaches, but the efforts do not seem to be successful so far.

There is an endless loop between China and the United States on nuclear disarmament. Whenever there are problems and difficulties in the nuclear dialogues between the two sides, the discussions converge on two issues. One is why the United States avoids explicit commitment to a no-first-use policy and the other is why China cannot offer more nuclear transparency.

Moving Forward

Some American and Russian experts have called for bringing China into the process of their strategic nuclear reductions. There is a technical

---

27. "Statement by H.E. Ambassador Wu Haitao at the Thematic Debate on Nuclear Disarmament at the 69th Session of UNGA First Committee," October 20, 2014, New York, http://www.un.org/disarmament/special/meetings/firstcommittee/69/pdfs/TD_NW_20_Oct_China.pdf.

problem here. The US-Russian START strategic reductions are aimed at reducing the numbers of nuclear warheads on their operationally deployed strategic delivery systems. The number of operationally strategic nuclear warheads in China is zero, according to the START accounting rule, so the START-type nuclear disarmament in the United States and Russia cannot apply to China. Another problem is that it is difficult for China to play active roles in the START reductions that are designed for the bilateral US-Russian case.

As discussed above, China has its own special security paradigm and nuclear disarmament agenda. A good way to encourage China to play a more active role in nuclear disarmament is to take China's security concerns and disarmament proposals into serious consideration. China could therefore contribute its political wisdom and diplomatic resources to the broader nuclear disarmament process.

The five nuclear-weapon states have been working together toward nuclear disarmament although they have some different understandings on the issue. They have established working groups on the verification of deep nuclear reductions and on nuclear disarmament terminology. China is the coordinator of the working group on nuclear disarmament terminology. This is a good start and some more progress can be made in that direction if P5 can find a good means of cooperation.

This chapter offers four policy recommendations to promote cooperation among P5 members, especially between China and the United States, on nuclear arms control.

Both China and the United States need careful domestic reviews of their nuclear arms control policies to avoid misperceptions and internal contradictions

Both the Chinese and American policymakers have some misperceptions and misunderstandings about the real needs of their countries in this area. A typical example is the issue of on-site inspections. Chinese arms control experts always worry about the risk of abuse of on-site inspections in arms control verification. During CTBT and Chemical Weapon Convention (CWC) negotiations, they tended to tighten the regulations on inspections. In contrast, the American arms control experts always said they believed that more on-site inspections would better serve the security interests of the United States. In CTBT and CWC negotiations, they tended to push for an easy trigger of on-site inspections. It turned out that China feels comfortable with the on-site inspection arrangements of CTBT and CWC after the treaties were concluded, while the United States is nervous with the on-site inspection arrangements of the two treaties.[28] This fact is at odds with the perceptions of the Chinese and American strategic communities. If the Chinese and American arms control negotiators knew the real needs of their countries regarding on-site inspections, they could reach consensus more easily in the CWC and CTBT negotiations.

Some widely spread judgments on arms control in China and in the United States may be out of date as Chinese and American societies and the world situation in general have changed significantly in the last couple decades. If the old judgments are still influencing Chinese-US arms control discussions, the two countries will encounter unnecessary opposition and miss opportunities for cooperation. The Chinese and American security communities need to carefully reexamine their traditional views on arms control and the real security needs of their countries today so they can clarify their misunderstandings and misperceptions.

The Chinese strategic community needs interdisciplinary and interdepartmental discussions on two topics: (1) how to understand some important strategic terms, for example, *weishe* (a Chinese word associated

---

28. Concerning US worries about CTBT on-site inspections, see Dunlop and du Preez, "The United States and the CTBT." Concerning worries about Chemical Weapons Convention's on-site inspections, see Jonathan B. Tucker, "U.S. Ratification of the Chemical Weapons Convention," *Case Study Series,* Center for the Study of Weapons of Mass Destruction, National Defense University, December 2011, http://ndupress .ndu.edu/Portals/68/Documents/casestudies/CSWMD_CaseStudy-4.pdf.

with the meaning of coercion and deterrence) and deterrence; and (2) how to convert China's strategic goals into quantitative and qualitative requirements for its nuclear force. The balance of secrecy and transparency is also an important topic. At the least, the Chinese government should invest in nuclear auditing to better understand the technical and quantitative details of its nuclear capability and to prepare for future international discussions. Nuclear warhead counting rules are an important content in the audit.

The American strategic community needs serious debates on the following topics:

- What is the definition of strategic stability with China?
- Should the United States maintain strategic stability with China?
- Should the United States encourage engagements between Chinese and American nuclear scientists?

If the American strategic community could reach some basic consensus on these issues, Washington would become more capable and efficient in engaging with China on nuclear arms control.

The Chinese and American strategic communities need to improve their understandings of each other's security concerns and paradigms

There are more discussions between the Chinese and American arms control experts today than before but there is still room for them to improve mutual understandings. One example is the Chinese indigenous security paradigm. The American capability-intention paradigm is a dominant analysis framework in scholarly and policy research in the world. The Chinese security paradigm focusing on situation analysis is always ignored in international dialogues. When a security challenge to China is not the capability and intention of a specific country, the Chinese and

American security experts may have difficulties in their communication. If the strategic communities in the two countries paid attention to the differences in their analysis paradigms, mutual understandings would be significantly promoted.

China and the United States need more pragmatic discussions on current arms control issues

China and the United States have some disagreements on the current arms control issues and they have not made apparent progress in the last decade to solve their disputes. Yet, there are opportunities for cooperation if both sides slightly change their view angles. For example, there is an endless loop between China and the United States on no-first-use policies and on nuclear transparency. If China were to take a forward view, it would find that the United States is gradually moving toward a declaration that the sole purpose of US nuclear weapons is deterring nuclear attacks. The "sole purpose" declaration will be an American version of no-first-use if it becomes true. If the United States were to take a backward view, it would find that China offered a great nuclear transparency to the United States, including showing American nuclear scientists the Chinese preparation of a nuclear test at the test site. The Chinese nuclear transparency was obscured by US domestic politics, especially the 1999 Cox report that accused China of stealing nuclear weapon secrets from the United States.

When the United States is ready, it could issue a joint statement with China on a no-first-use agreement. In the statement, China could reaffirm its no-first-use policy while the United States could declare that the sole purpose of US nuclear weapons is to deter nuclear attack.

Nuclear transparency in China may be promoted in two parallel steps. The first step is to develop a method of counting China's nuclear weapons (including warheads, delivery systems, and fissile materials). Before China publicizes the numbers of its nuclear weapons, it could engage with

American and Russian disarmament experts on the counting rules. The second step is to resume and encourage engagements between Chinese and American nuclear experts and nuclear laboratories. To lay the basis for this step, the US government needs to acknowledge the benefits of such engagements in the past.

Besides breaking the loop of nuclear transparency and no-first-use, China and the United States can develop cooperation on many other issues. China and the United States could both ratify the CTBT (as long as the US Congress gets majority support for the treaty). Before that, the two countries could join the other three nuclear-weapon states to reaffirm their nuclear test moratoriums at the NPT review conference. They could also develop more cooperation on the improvement of CTBT verification on the basis of their current "track 2" discussions.

China and the United States should explore cooperation on long-term nuclear disarmament

China's disarmament priority is to control nuclear weapon use, while the US priority is to control nuclear weapon numbers. It seems that nuclear de-alerting could become an issue of common interest. For China, de-alerting is an effort to keep nuclear weapons further from use. In a recent United Nations vote, China was the only nuclear-weapon state publicly supporting de-alerting.[29] In the United States, there is growing support for this idea. When the four American statesmen—George P. Shultz, William J. Perry, Henry A. Kissinger, and Sam Nunn—published their appeal for a world free of nuclear weapons on January 4, 2007, the first step they suggested was changing the Cold War posture of deployed nuclear weapons to increase warning time and thereby reduce the

---

29. United Nations, "General Assembly Adopts 63 Drafts."

danger of an accidental or unauthorized use of a nuclear weapon.[30] The American decision-makers should take their advice. Actually, the START-serial treaties are also de-alerting arrangements by their nature, as the treaties require the United States and Soviet Union to download certain numbers of nuclear warheads from delivery systems. If China and the United States can develop some mutual understandings on nuclear de-alerting, other nuclear-weapon states will feel more enthusiastic about joining the process.

---

30. George P. Shultz, William J. Perry, Henry A. Kissinger, and Sam Nunn, "A World Free of Nuclear Weapons," *Wall Street Journal,* January 4, 2007, http://www.wsj.com /articles/SB116787515251566636.

CHAPTER 13 **Korea: Will South Korea's Non-Nuclear Strategy Defeat North Korea's Nuclear Breakout?**

Peter Hayes and Chung-in Moon

Introduction

When the US-DPRK Geneva Agreed Framework was signed in October 1994, it appeared that the North Korean nuclear breakout had been turned around. But the second North Korean nuclear crisis in 2002—triggered over Pyongyang's allegedly illicit program of producing highly enriched uranium—not only shattered the Agreed Framework. The issue now threatens to spiral out of control. The Six-Party Talks—involving North and South Korea, the United States, China, Japan, and Russia—have stalled and Pyongyang has conducted three underground nuclear tests. Claiming that it has been successful in diversifying as well as miniaturizing both plutonium and uranium bombs, North Korea (officially the Democratic People's Republic of Korea) on February 12, 2013, publicly

The authors thank Roger Cavazos, Elbridge Colby, John Delury, James Goodby, Jeffrey Lewis, John Merrill, Terrence Roehrig, Lee Sigal, and Christopher Twomey for review. The authors are solely responsible for this text.

proclaimed that it has become the ninth nuclear-weapon state. The North Korean nuclear threat is no longer hypothetical, but real and present.[1]

For now, South Korea (officially the Republic of Korea) still favors a peaceful settlement through dialogue and negotiations, especially the Six-Party Talks. But some South Korean conservatives are growing increasingly impatient. They argue that the United States should redeploy tactical nuclear weapons in the South, or that the South should develop its own nuclear weapons. This sentiment has been fueled by a recent debate in the United States as to whether it should reject or accommodate such a move, as well as by the prospect that North Korea eventually will develop the ability to hit the United States with a few nuclear weapons.

Against this backdrop, the paper examines the dynamics of the nuclear threat in Korea and explores options for reducing the role of nuclear weapons in regional security. The first section of the chapter traces the history of North Korea's nuclear weapons and analyzes its nuclear capabilities and motives. It also addresses the peninsular, regional, and global security implications of this nuclear breakout. The second section examines South Korea's response, especially focusing on recent debates about the United States reintroducing tactical nuclear weapons or the South developing its own nuclear weapons capability. The third section presents the option of developing a comprehensive security settlement and creating a Northeast Asian nuclear weapon-free zone as a way out of the Korean nuclear quagmire. Finally, we draw some policy implications about how to deal with the peninsular nuclear problems in the context of a revived global effort to abolish nuclear weapons.

---

1. See Gregory J. Moore, ed., *North Korean Nuclear Operationality* (Baltimore: Johns Hopkins University Press, 2013); and "Special Issue on Nukes, Succession Politics, and the Future of North Korea" *Global Asia* 4, no. 2 (Summer 2009).

North Korea's Nuclear Breakout and Implications

Like the South, North Korea initiated a nuclear program in the 1950s and 1960s. In 1965, it operated a tiny IRT-2000 research reactor with the help of the former Soviet Union.

The precise date when North Korea decided to pursue and develop nuclear weapons is not known. Kim Il Sung likely began thinking about nuclear weapons as a result of the Korean War, at which time American nuclear threats were aimed explicitly at China and the North Korean military. The United States deployed nuclear weapons in Korea in 1958. During the 1960s the former Soviet Union and its Eastern European allies consistently rebuffed North Korean requests for nuclear technology, perhaps worrying that any technology they provided the North would find its way to China. Some speculate that the North was matching South Korea's nuclear weapons program that began in 1971.

In April 1975, North Korean leader Kim Il Sung visited China and asked Mao Tse-tung for off-the-shelf nuclear weapons to allow him to take advantage of demonstrations in South Korea against President Park Chung-hee.[2] Kim's intention was to ride the revolutionary wave created by the fall of Saigon in South Vietnam and Phnom Penh in Cambodia and foment a popular revolution in the South. At that time, North Korea was at the apogee of its power and Kim Il Sung wanted nuclear weapons to limit US intervention if war broke out on the peninsula. There are also some scholars who believe that an active North Korean nuclear weapons program was triggered by the August 1976 crisis in which the United States deployed ground-based tactical nuclear weapons as part of

---

2. Balazs Szalontai and Sergey Radchenko, *North Korea's Efforts to Acquire Nuclear Technology and Nuclear Weapons: Evidence from Russian and Hungarian Archives*, Cold War International History Project, Woodrow Wilson International Center, Working Paper 53, August 2006: 12, http://www.wilsoncenter.org/sites/default/files /WP53_web_final1.pdf.

its response to the killing of two American officers at Panmunjom in the Korean Demilitarized Zone.

In any event, it is clear that by the mid-1980s, North Korea had begun to realign its nuclear program to produce weapons. In the late 1980s, the Department of Defense Industry of the Korea Workers' Party took over the management of nuclear facilities in Yongbyon. In 1986, the North began to build a five-megawatt graphite-moderated reactor that was able to produce plutonium and a "radioactive chemical lab" (that is, a reprocessing facility). Although the 1994 Geneva Agreed Framework froze nuclear facilities and activities in Yongbyon, the North tested the high explosives needed for detonating a nuclear weapon between 1993 and 1998 in the nearby mountains.[3]

After the Agreed Framework fell apart in the wake of the second nuclear crisis in 2002, Pyongyang reactivated its five-megawatt[4] nuclear reactor in Yongbyon and began to extract plutonium. As the Six-Party Talks stalled, the North tested nuclear weapons in October 2006, May 2009, and February 2013. North Korea referred to its nuclear weapons in discussions with American officials in 2003 and made many public references to its nuclear weapons between 2003 and 2010, when its foreign affairs ministry declared on May 26 that it was satisfied to be a nuclear-armed state (as against a nuclear-weapon state recognized as legitimate by the Nuclear Non-Proliferation Treaty [NPT], from which it had earlier departed). "The DPRK," averred the spokesman, "is just satisfied with the pride and self-esteem that it is capable of reliably defending

3. Chun-geun Lee, "Bukhanui Haekneungryok gwa Hyanghu Jeonmang (North Korea's Nuclear Capability and Prospects)," paper presented at a seminar organized by the Korea Peace Forum, April 17, 2014: 3–5.

4. This reactor produced thirty megawatts of heat or thermal output at maximum, but was rated at five megawatts-electric by the DPRK, serving only the local complex when it produced power.

the sovereignty of the country and the security of the nation with its own nuclear weapons."[5]

However, for a state to be recognized as effectively capable of detonating a nuclear warhead against a target—that is, to be nuclear-armed—it must not only blow up a nuclear device, but must meet four conditions: possession of nuclear warheads, demonstration of delivery capability, nuclear testing, and miniaturization of nuclear warheads to mount on missiles. We will examine each of these necessary conditions.

The first question is how much fissile material for nuclear weapons North Korea possesses. Until recently, most of the discussion has centered on how much plutonium was obtained from spent fuel at the Yongbyon graphite-cooled reactor frozen by the 1994 Agreed Framework.[6] Estimates vary, but the North's reprocessing campaigns from this reactor's spent fuel might have yielded as many as five bombs-worth of plutonium. (The exact amount depends on the warhead design as well as the burn-up of the fuel in the reactor and the efficiency of the reprocessing, and is possibly substantially less than five.) Reactivation of this reactor (which as of December 2014 was in progress but not complete) might produce an estimated six to seven kilograms of plutonium or about one warhead-per-year equivalent. When completed and operating, North Korea's new twenty-five-megawatt light-water reactor might yield about fifty-six kilograms of plutonium per year, enough to manufacture up to eleven bombs per year. In mid-2012, its plutonium inventory was estimated to be capped with enough for six to eighteen weapons-worth, and a midpoint of twelve

---

5. KCNA, "FM Spokesman on Right to Bolster Nuclear Deterrent," May 24, 2010, http://www.kcna.co.jp/item/2010/201005/news24/20100524-15ee.html.

6. See "KCNA Report on Nuclear Activities in DPRK," Korean Central News Agency, October 3, 2003, http://www.kcna.co.jp/item/2003/200310/news10/04.htm; "Spent Fuel Rods Unloaded from Pilot Nuclear Plant," Korean Central News Agency, May 11, 2005; and "DPRK Completes Reprocessing of Spent Fuel Rods," Korean Central News Agency, November 3, 2009, http://www.kcna.co.jp/item/2009/200911/news03 /20091103-08ee.html.

weapons-worth,[7] reduced by 2014 by one weapons-worth of plutonium used in the 2013 test. (These estimates might vary upward slightly if the North mastered small warheads using less fissile material very early in its development efforts.)

To the plutonium inventory we must add material produced by North Korea's highly enriched uranium (HEU) program. In this regard, the most serious uncertainty is whether it operated a clandestine enrichment plant and, if so, what size and for how long. There is also the question of the HEU production at the Yongbyon enrichment plant shown to Stanford University scholar Siegfried Hecker in 2010. One estimate, based on detailed open-source information, comparable programs in other states, and highly informed technical analysis of plutonium and enrichment technology, is that as of mid-2012, North Korea had between zero and twelve nuclear weapons-worth of highly enriched uranium (each assumed to contain twenty kilograms of weapons-grade HEU).[8] By 2014, this 2012 range for the total inventory of highly enriched uranium might have increased at most by ten weapons-worth,[9] depending on the number of centrifuges in operation, the plant operating factor, whether the North made low-enriched fuel for its small light-water reactor between 2012 and 2014, and the level of enrichment used for the weapon. Roughly, therefore, by 2014 North Korea could have had as few as five weapons-worth of plutonium and zero weapons-worth of highly enriched uranium, or as much as seventeen weapons-worth of plutonium plus, at most, ten weapons-worth of highly enriched uranium.

Delivering nuclear weapons, the second aspect of a nuclear weapons capability, is another matter altogether. North Korea has proved that

---

7. David Albright and Christina Walrond, *North Korea's Estimated Stocks of Plutonium and Weapon-Grade Uranium,* Institute for Science and International Security, August 16, 2012: 2, http://isis-online.org/uploads/isis-reports/documents/dprk_fissile _material_production_16Aug2012.pdf.

8. Ibid., 1.

9. Ibid., Table 2, 36.

it has credible short- and middle-range delivery capability including KN-02, Scud B and C, Nodong, and Musudan missiles. These missiles are known to be unreliable and inaccurate. But if it were firing nuclear weapons in an all-out attack on South Korean cities, this might not matter too much—although the plausibility of such a suicidal spasm is dubious. The five test-launchings of intercontinental range Daepodong-I missiles (1998) and Daepodong-II missiles (2006, 2009, and 2012) all failed. But the most recent launching of space launch rocket Eunha 3 with a dual-use application to long-range missiles, on December 12, 2012, succeeded. The rocket put a small satellite into orbit, although North Korea was unable to communicate with or control it.[10] Thus, Pyongyang does have some missile delivery capability—enough to cause considerable damage to South Korea, possibly to Japan, and, speculatively, even to the United States. Some analysts also argue that the North might use submarines, fishing trawlers, tunnels, or even foreign-flagged merchant vessels to deliver nuclear weapons outside its border. However, such means of delivery would require pre-delegated use authority along with small and reliable warheads, and would risk discovery and subsequent great-power intervention. Therefore, we believe such attacks are implausible.

The third prerequisite is well-tested nuclear warheads. Although its first test was likely a dud,[11] its second and third tests had yields of two to six kilotons and seven and a half kilotons, respectively. It is still not known if the third test used uranium or plutonium. But overall, to date North Korea's revealed nuclear device reliability is about 66 percent. Pyongyang is clearly preparing for a fourth test, but has delayed it since

---

10. David Wright, "North Korea's Satellite," Union of Concerned Scientists, December 15, 2012, http://allthingsnuclear.org/north-koreas-satellite/; also, William J. Broad and Choe Sang-hun, "Astronomers Say North Korean Satellite Is Most Likely Dead," *New York Times,* December 17, 2012, http://www.nytimes.com/2012/12/18 /world/asia/north-korean-satellite.html?_r=0.

11. Peter Hayes and Jungmin Kang, "Technical Analysis of the DPRK Nuclear Test," NAPSNet Special Reports, October 20, 2006, http://nautilus.org/napsnet/napsnet -special-reports/technical-analysis-of-the-dprk-nuclear-test.

early 2014, perhaps due to China's pressure. The North is likely to continue its nuclear testing unless some deals are made through the Six-Party Talks or DPRK-US bilateral talks, subject to having sufficient fissile material. (If the true stocks are very small, then additional tests for political or military reasons could reduce and even reverse the rate of weaponization and deployment.)

Finally, miniaturization of nuclear warheads is likely the biggest obstacle to a missile-deliverable nuclear weapon. After the 2013 test, Pyongyang announced that the test "physically demonstrated the high performance of the DPRK's nuclear deterrent which has become smaller, lighter and diversified as it was a primary counter-measure in which it exercised its maximum self-restraint."[12] Unsurprisingly, South Korea took this reference to a "smaller, lighter" weapon to mean that Pyongyang may be able to mount nuclear bombs on short-range missiles.[13] In October 2014, General Curtis Scarlatti, head of US Forces Korea, stated that North Korea has the technology to make a small nuclear warhead and put it on a missile. But, he also added, he did not know if they had done so, and if they had, it would likely have low reliability. "We've not seen it tested at this point," he stated. "Something that's that complex, without it being tested, the probability of it being effective is pretty darn low."[14]

In sum, North Korea has already acquired nuclear warheads, conducted nuclear tests, has short- and intermediate-range missiles, and may

---

12. KCNA, "DPRK's Underground Nuclear Test Is Just Measure for Self-defence," February 12, 2013.

13. Yong-soo Jeong and Sung-eun Yoo, "Buk, Gipok Silheom Geupjeung . . . Haemugi Sohyonghwa Bakcha" (The North, Accelerating High Explosive Tests, Entering the Final Stage of Miniaturization of Nuclear Bombs), *JoongAng Ilbo*, November 5, 2014 (Korean), http://article.joins.com/news/article/article.asp?total_id=16324150.

14. Marcus Weisgerber, "US Doesn't Know If North Korea Has a Nuclear Missile," *Defense One*, October 24, 2014, http://www.defenseone.com/threats/2014/10 /us-doesnt-know-if-north-korea-has-nuclear-missile/97364/?oref=defenseone _today_nl.

have miniaturized warheads. But, when mated with unreliable missiles, the overall system probability of North Korean nuclear-armed missiles is likely to be very poor. Nonetheless, from the viewpoint of those receiving its verbal nuclear threats in the region and beyond, it is necessary to attribute some capability to the North (not just in missile delivery, but by bombers, ship, or ground delivery systems) and to adopt countermeasures. In short, nuclear threats from the North are no longer hypothetical but real and present.

Unraveling North Korea's Nuclear Intention

By all accounts, North Korea is a failing, if not failed, state. A devastating famine in the 1990s compounded a collapsing economy. Today, most North Koreans still suffer from chronic food shortages and malnutrition, coupled with acute energy shortages.[15] The lack of energy and hard currency effectively paralyzed the North Korean economy by lowering its capacity utilization rates to below 20 percent, leading to a miserable quality of life.[16] North Korea's leaders have failed to satisfy the most basic human needs of its own people, yet it has continued to pursue nuclear

---

15. See Hazel Smith, *Hungry for Peace: International Security, Humanitarian Assistance, and Social Change in North Korea* (Washington, DC: United States Institute of Peace, 2005); Stephan Haggard and Marcus Noland, *Hunger and Human Rights: The Politics of Famine in North Korea* (Washington, DC: U.S. Committee for Human Rights in North Korea, 2005); and Peter Hayes and David von Hippel, "Foundations of Energy Security for the DPRK: 1990–2009 Energy Balances, Engagement Options, and Future Paths for Energy and Economic Redevelopment," NAPSNet Special Reports, December 18, 2012, http://nautilus.org/napsnet/napsnet-special-reports /foundations-of-energy-security-for-the-dprk-1990-2009-energy-balances -engagement-options-and-future-paths-for-energy-and-economic-redevelopment.

16. See *Global Asia*, "Dark and Mysterious: How Kim Jong Un is Reforming North Korea," special issue, 9, no. 1 (Spring 2014).

ambitions. Given this discrepancy, what motivates its pursuit of nuclear weapons?[17]

For the North Korean leadership and even its ordinary citizens, the fear of an American nuclear attack is not contrived, but real. They believe that the United States plans to stage nuclear attacks on the North, and the only way to deter the United States is to arm themselves with nuclear weapons, ultimately with a second-strike capability.[18] President Bush's labeling in 2002 of North Korea as a rogue nation reinforced North Korea's threat perception. Also, the explicit US nuclear preemption doctrine, its announcement in the 2001 Nuclear Posture Review that it might use tactical nuclear weapons, and the invasion of Iraq appear to have led North Korean policymakers to switch from using nuclear weapons as a way to compel the United States to change its policies toward their country to relying on nuclear weapons as a deterrent force. Thus, Nodong Shinmun, the daily newspaper of the Korea Workers' Party, editorialized in 2005: "American intention is to disarm us and to destroy us with nuclear weapons. . . . Whatever preemptive nuclear attacks the United States undertake, we are ready to meet them with powerful retaliatory strikes."[19]

Two factors further reinforce North Korea's deterrence motive. In the 1990s it exploited opacity and ambiguity similar to that used by Israel, characterized by "absence of testing, denial of possession, eschewal of

---

17. See Scott D. Sagan, "Why Do States Build Nuclear Weapons? Three Models in Search of a Bomb," *International Security* 21, no. 3 (Winter 1996/1997): 54–86.

18. Alexandre Mansourov, "Witnessing North Korea's Nuclear Breakout: What Everyone Needs to Know about Kim Jong Un's Nuclear Doctrine and Strategy," NAPSNet Special Reports, December 16, 2014, http://nautilus.org/napsnet/napsnet-special -reports/kim-jong-uns-nuclear-doctrine-and-strategy-what-everyone-needs-to-know.

19. *Nodong Shinmun*, September 21, 2005. This editorial appeared as a response to a *Washington Post* article which reported the Pentagon's proposed revision to its nuclear doctrine that "would allow commanders to seek presidential approval for using atomic arms against nations or terrorists who intend to use chemical, biological, and nuclear weapons against the U.S., its troops or allies." For the article itself, see Walter Pincus, "Pentagon May Have Doubts on Preemptive Nuclear Moves," *Washington Post*, September 19, 2005.

nuclear threats, and non-deployment."[20] However, as American pressure increased, it shifted from opaque to ambiguous to explicit, with the North declaring outright its possession of nuclear weapons in 2002. By testing and deployment, the North has become bolder in pursuing its peculiar version of nuclear deterrence. Another factor can be seen in the development of its delivery capability. Although still a long way from posing a credible threat of nuclear attack on the US mainland, and even further from matching the American ability to annihilate North Korea with nuclear attacks, the North has nevertheless been driven by the logic of nuclear weapons to seek to gain such a capacity in the future.

Deterrence is not the only rationale. North Korea's nuclear venture also seems to be closely associated with the domestic politics of legitimacy and coalition-building.[21] Current leader Kim Jong Un's legitimacy stems from his lineage with his father, Kim Jong Il, and grandfather, Kim Il Sung. After his political ascension in 1994, Kim Jong Il championed the slogan of *gangsung daeguk* (strong and prosperous great nation) as the new governing ideology. That strong and prosperous great nation is to be realized through *sungun jungchi* (military-first politics), which gives the military the preeminent position in North Korean politics.[22] Thus, the nuclear ambition satisfied several domestic political purposes. It not only enhanced Kim Jong Il's political legitimacy by symbolizing the vision of a strong and prosperous great nation, it also served as a vehicle for

---

20. Rajesh M. Basrur, *Minimum Deterrence and India's Nuclear Security* (Stanford: Stanford University Press, 2005), 28.

21. Mun-hyung Huh, "Bukhanui Haekgaibal Gyoehoick Injunggwa Hyanghu Jungchaek Junmang (North Korea's Admission of Nuclear Weapons Development Plan and Prospects of Future Policy)," in *Bukhaek Munjeui Haebopgwa Junmang* (Solution and Prospects of the North Korean Nuclear Problem), ed. Jung-Bok Lee (Seoul: Jungang M & B, 2003), 157–206.

22. Chung-in Moon and Hideshi Takesada, "North Korea: Institutionalized Military Intervention," in *Coercion and Governance: The Declining Role of the Military in Asia,* ed. Muthiah Alagappa (Stanford, CA: Stanford University Press, 2001), 257–282.

consolidating his political power through the co-option of the military. With the added benefit of enhancing North Korea's international status and prestige by joining the elite group of nuclear states, the possession of nuclear weapons strengthened Kim's domestic rule—as it no doubt does today for his son.

Nuclear weapons also helped the DPRK to maintain a military equilibrium on the peninsula through the acquisition of asymmetric military capabilities. Until the early 1970s, North Korea had military superiority over South Korea (leaving US forces out of the equation). However, the inter-Korean military balance began to shift in favor of the South beginning in the 1980s. South Korea surpassed the North's labor-intensive military by combining its enhanced defense industrial production with the acquisition of advanced foreign weaponry. The widening gap between their conventional forces was inevitable given the rapidly growing disparity in the two Koreas' economic and technological capabilities. While the South has emerged as the fourteenth largest economy in the world, greatly facilitating its defense buildup, the North's continued poor economic performance is reflected in its slower military buildup. North Korea's attempt to possess nuclear weapons can be interpreted as a calculated move to make up for its weakness in conventional forces by pushing for a non-conventional, asymmetric force buildup via weapons of mass destruction and missiles.[23] This approach provides a less expensive path of offsetting the growing gap in conventional forces.

Finally, North Korea appears to regard nuclear weapons as a valuable economic asset for two reasons. One is as bargaining leverage for economic gain; the other is as a tool for export earnings. As the 1994 Geneva Agreed Framework demonstrated, the North was able to win economic and energy concessions such as two light-water nuclear reactors, a

23. Taik-young Hahm, "Nambukhan Gunbi Gyongjaengui Ihae" (Understanding North-South Korean Arms Race), in *Bundaui Dueolgul* (Two Faces of Division), ed. Seung-ryol Kim and Jubaek Shin (Seoul: Yoksa Bipyong, 2005), 106–107.

supply of heavy oil, and other economic assistance in return for freezing its nuclear activities and returning to the NPT. Although these benefits did not for the most part materialize, Pyongyang learned that nuclear weapons offer bargaining leverage. Moreover, its track record on the export of missiles, weapons, and reactors to Syria shows that Pyongyang is willing to transfer nuclear materials to other states for export earnings.

Peninsular and Regional Security Impacts of a Nuclear North Korea

These explanations do not account wholly for the North's use of nuclear threats, however. Two incidents in 2010—North Korea's sinking of the South Korean naval ship Cheonan and its shelling of Yeonpyeong Island— were followed by nuclear testing and campaigns of outrageous rhetoric, including the threat in 2013 to annihilate cities in South Korea, Japan, and the United States and to conduct preemptive nuclear attacks. Pyongyang's actions have been aimed at compelling its adversaries, not deterring them from attack.[24] The effect of this opportunistic and extreme use of nuclear threat rhetoric and actions is compounded by uncertainty over new leader Kim Jong Un's capacities to be a responsible nuclear commander given

---

24. See Peter Hayes, "North Korean Nuclear Nationalism and the Threat of Nuclear War in Korea," NAPSNet Policy Forum, April 21, 2011, http://nautilus.org/napsnet /napsnet-policy-forum/11-09-hayes-bruce/; "Supporting Online Material: North Korean Nuclear Statements (2002–2010)," NAPSNet Special Reports, May 17, 2011, http://nautilus.org/napsnet/napsnet-special-reports/supporting-online-material-north -korean-nuclear-statements-2002-2010/; Peter Hayes and Roger Cavazos, "Rattling the American Cage: North Korean Nuclear Threats and Escalation Potential," NAPSNet Policy Forum, April 4, 2013, http://nautilus.org/napsnet/napsnet-policy -forum/rattling-the-american-cage-north-korean-nuclear-threats-and-escalation -potential-2/; and Hayes and Cavazos, "North Korean and US Nuclear Threats: Discerning Signals from Noise," *The Asia-Pacific Journal* 11, no. 14 (April 8, 2013), http://japanfocus.org/-Roger-Cavazos/3924#.

his inexperience and the apparent convulsions within the regime leading to the execution of his uncle in 2013.

The implications for peninsular security from this evolution of North Korea's nuclear threat are grave.[25] A nuclear North Korea is incompatible with peace-building on the Korean Peninsula. It not only threatens the South with nuclear attack, but also fundamentally alters the inter-Korean military balance and tempts the North to dictate the terms of eventual reunification to the South. Thus, nuclear armament dovetails with North Korea's governing ideologies of *gangsung daekuk* or making North Korea a strong and prosperous nation and *sungun jungchi*, which emphasizes military self-reliance and the unification of Korea on its own terms. Under these political and military circumstances, peaceful coexistence between the two Koreas is unlikely and conventional and non-conventional arms races between the two will intensify. This is not just a matter of the North's actions, but also of the South's response. The South is arming itself heavily with high-technology weapons such as Aegis destroyers, German-built submarines, amphibious assault ships, and stealth fast patrol boats armed with surface-to-surface and surface-to-air missiles. Even more troublesome is that North Korea's possession of nuclear weapons nullifies the 1992 Declaration on the Denuclearization of the Korean Peninsula, freeing South Korea to respond in kind.

South Korea's Response: Should It Go Nuclear?

Pessimism looms in South Korea because two decades of dialogue and negotiation failed completely to stop its neighbor's nuclear breakout. Many policymakers believe that resumption of the Six-Party Talks is futile and that there is simply no prospect of reversing the North's nuclear

---

25. Bruce Bennett, "Avoiding the Peacetime Dangers of North Korean Nuclear Weapons," *IFANS Review* 13, no. 2 (December 2005): 30–37.

armament. Military options have long been considered unrealistic, while the Bush administration pursued a hostile neglect strategy that ended as a failure. The strategic patience strategy of the Obama administration has not worked either.

In this bleak situation, hard-line military options are coming to the fore. Most salient for some is fielding an active defense such as interceptor missiles, including advanced Patriot missiles and even the THAAD (Terminal High Altitude Area Defense), and preparing for preemptive surgical strikes even at the risk of conflict escalation.

However, as we will argue below, it would be extremely difficult to rely on preemptive strikes since the key military targets in North Korea are concealed and likely underground in thousands of tunnels. Even if the underground locations were known and all entrances could be sealed by precision strikes, such an attack could lead to escalation with the prospect of enormous collateral damage.

Geopolitics also matter. North Korea is different from Iraq. China, Russia, and likely even South Korea would strongly oppose such military actions due to the likely catastrophic consequences that would ensue. For all these reasons, a growing number of hard-liners in South Korea are raising nuclear deterrence as an alternative, an argument to which we now turn.

Pro-Nuclear South Korean Voices

After North Korea tested a third nuclear device on February 12, 2013, many South Koreans felt helpless, frustrated, even outraged. For many years, a slight majority of South Koreans have supported obtaining an independent nuclear weapons program. Since the North began testing, this has increased. Before the 2013 test, one opinion poll showed 66 percent of respondents favored the South developing its own nuclear weapons. After the test, more than 70 percent were in favor (although far fewer were willing to end the US alliance to achieve that goal). Leading conservative politicians such as Chung Mong-joon advocate that South Korea "go nuclear." *Chosun Ilbo,* the leading conservative newspaper, backs this campaign. Thus, popular and elite opinions are shifting ground.[26]

US Nuclear Analysts on Implications of South Korean Nuclear Proliferation

A debate in the United States has complicated the dialogue in Korea. In the February 2014 issue of *The National Interest,* David Santoro, a non-proliferation specialist, wrote an article, "Will America's Asian Allies Go Nuclear?"[27] Santoro notes that there are powerful voices in South Korea and Japan who call for deployment of their own nuclear weapons rather than relying on US nuclear extended deterrence. He attributes this trend to North Korea's provocative behavior, China's aggressive rise, and the general perception that defense budget cuts in the United States represent a weakening of US security commitments in the region. Given their technology and financial resources, he worries that South Korea and Japan could develop nuclear weapons. He observes that their nuclear breakout would effectively end the global nonproliferation regime and collide with US efforts to reduce the role of nuclear weapons in international affairs.

26. D. J. Kim, "S. Korea needs to consider acquiring nuclear weapons," *Chosun Ilbo,* July 10, 2012 (Korean), http://srchdb1.chosun.com/pdf/i_service/pdf_ReadBody.jsp ?Y=2012&M=07&D=10&ID=2012071000058; G. J. Cho, "South Korea's Nuclear Armament for Self-Defense: Secret Story of Israel's Clandestine Nuclear Weapons Development," *Monthly Chosun,* February 2011 (Korean), http://monthly.chosun .com/client/news/viw.asp?ctcd=D&nNewsNumb=201102100029; see also Mong-Jun Chung's remarks: "The nuclear deterrence can be the only answer. We have to have nuclear capability," in K. J. Kwon, "Under Threat, South Koreans mull nuclear weapons," CNN, March 18, 2013, http://www.cnn.com/2013/03/18/world/asia /south-korea-nuclear/. On redeployment of US tactical nuclear weapons, see "'Unwanted Decision' should be made for the protection of the country and people," Editorial, *Chosun Ilbo,* February 13, 2013 (Korean), http://srchdb1.chosun.com/pdf /i_service/pdf_ReadBody.jsp?Y=2013&M=02&D=13&ID=2013021300002.

27. David Santoro, "Will America's Asian Allies Go Nuclear?" *The National Interest,* January 30, 2014,http://nationalinterest.org/commentary/will-americas-asian -allies-go-nuclear-9794.

Thus, he argues that the United States must threaten to end alliances with South Korea and Japan if they go nuclear.

Elbridge Colby, a fellow at the Center for a New American Security, rebuts Santoro's argument in the March issue of *The National Interest,* arguing that the United States should "Choose Geopolitics Over Nonproliferation."[28] Colby contends that the ultimate goal of US foreign policy is not nonproliferation but "protecting Americans' security, liberty and prosperity through moral means." He argues that nuclear nonproliferation should not be regarded as *summun bonum* and that the scenarios regarding nuclear-armed South Korea and Japan should be evaluated coolly, based on their likely impact on US national interests. Although he argues that there might well be situations in which South Korean or Japanese pursuit of nuclear weapons would justify Washington walking away from these bilateral alliances, Colby holds that it would be unreasonable to automatically scrap these alliances—ultimately instruments of geopolitics—solely based on nonproliferation considerations. He maintains that under certain conditions—for instance, if the threat from China were to grow dramatically—adjusting existing extended nuclear deterrence arrangements or even tolerating some form of proliferation might better suit US interests than simply terminating these alliances. Colby further notes that threatening to cut off these alliances, as Santoro suggests, would run the risk of both losing the proliferation game and weakening the US position in Northeast Asia. We note that it might also play into the hands of Japanese pro-nuclear nationalists, some of whom favor enlisting a nuclear-armed North Korea against China.

Perceived Advantages of Nuclear Weapons to South Korea

Colby's view gave new hope to South Korea's conservative pundits by hinting that, under certain conditions, maintaining the alliance and allowing

---

28. Elbridge Colby, "Choose Geopolitics Over Nonproliferation," *The National Interest,* February 28, 2014, http://nationalinterest.org/commentary/choose-geopolitics -over-nonproliferation-9969?page=6.

US allies to go nuclear are not necessarily incompatible, as the European experience has shown. Fear of losing their alliances with the United States is one reason why Japan and South Korea were hesitant in pushing for domestic nuclear weapons development in the past. These South Korean pundits offer several rationales.

First, they argue that North Korea has already become a nuclear-weapons state, profoundly altering the balance of power on the Korean Peninsula. The only way to cope with nuclear North Korea is to secure a credible nuclear deterrence capability, they say. This logic is based on the notion of "an eye for an eye" or, as we might say in this context, a "nuke for a nuke," a strategic approach termed "symmetric deterrence."

Second, some suggest that nuclear weapons would endow South Korea with a bargaining chip to compel North Korea to abandon its nuclear weapons. In this case, Seoul would go nuclear only when and if Pyongyang adheres to its nuclear weapons path, implying that this decision would not be irreversible, even if taken. A variant on this argument that one hears in Seoul is that South Korea's threat to go nuclear will push China to put much more pressure on North Korea out of fear that South Korean proliferation would result in Japanese nuclear weapons—a nightmarish outcome for China.

Third, many pundits voice doubt about the credibility of American extended deterrence as North Korea increases its nuclear capability. They are skeptical that the United States would use nuclear weapons if the North developed the capability to threaten the US homeland. This is the fear that was described as "decoupling" during the Cold War. The idea was that the credibility of US extended nuclear deterrence would recede as potential enemies developed the capability to threaten the United States itself. Thus, the argument goes that South Korea should have its own nuclear deterrent capability to substitute for dwindling US nuclear deterrence. We address this issue at the end of this section as it bears close examination once the DPRK is able to strike the US homeland.

Finally, enduring distrust of China, Russia, and Japan serves as another catalyst for pro-nuclear South Korean sentiment. China, Russia, and North

Korea already have nuclear weapons. And recent strategic moves by the Shinzo Abe government in Japan suggest to many South Koreans that it is simply a matter of time before Japan is armed with nuclear weapons. Should this come to pass, then South Korea would be the only non-nuclear-weapons state in the region, leaving it dependent *and* insecure in South Korean minds. Because American disengagement from South Korea and the region cannot be ruled out, this fear of abandonment is grounded in the real world, even if there is no immediate prospect of American withdrawal from the Asia-Pacific region or, indeed, of a nuclear-armed Japan.

Given these views, what are the pros and cons of an independent South Korean nuclear force or the alternative of redeployment of American nuclear weapons to South Korea? Below, we answer these two questions by measuring their security effects in comparison with the baseline present arrangement of extending nuclear deterrence from US-based nuclear weapons. In the following section, we will further question whether this arrangement is the best that can be done, especially in light of the North Korean nuclear breakout, by suggesting that with vision, leadership, and tough policies, a comprehensive regional security framework could be implemented that would reverse North Korea's nuclear armament *and* reduce the role of nuclear weapons in interstate relations of all powers in the region, nuclear and non-nuclear, as is demanded by the global nuclear weapons abolition enterprise. We do not suggest that achieving this outcome would be easy. But it may prove to be easier than continuing with the status quo that allows North Korea to expand its nuclear forces and requires that it be managed by a countervailing nuclear threat, with all the attendant hazards.

Disadvantages of Independent South Korean Nuclear Weapons

In reality, an ROK nuclear weapons option, be it independent or by redeployment of US nuclear weapons, is neither feasible nor desirable. As we shall see, it is not feasible due to severe credibility problems. The baseline measure of the credibility of an independent South Korean nuclear weapons program from the viewpoint of the North and, to a lesser extent, China is how it compares with the credibility of South Korea relying on nuclear extended deterrence based on US strategic nuclear forces.

Militarily, it would be undesirable. Two small nuclear-armed states would be trapped in an unstable "mutual probable destruction" relationship, each with incentive to use nuclear weapons first rather than lose them.[29] Inter-Korean psychological warfare would become even more ferocious than that seen over the last six decades.

Far from reinforcing South Korea's already overwhelming offensive military capabilities—including in almost every dimension where North Korea has tried to develop "asymmetric" capabilities—South Korean nuclear weapons would undermine conventional deterrence and even reduce South Korea's ability to use its conventional forces in response to a North Korean attack.

Above all, we see its feasibility as very low because of severe political, legal, and institutional obstacles. There is no doubt that South Korea has the technological and financial capability to develop nuclear weapons. But it has never been easy, and won't be so at any time soon, for South Korea to arm itself with nuclear weapons, let alone with a submarine or bomber-based nuclear retaliatory capacity that is immune from preemption—the basis of stable nuclear deterrence. It would take South Korea years to develop and deploy even a minimum deterrent. Until then, it would not possess a credible second-strike capability. Initially, a South Korean nuclear force would be vastly inferior to current US nuclear capabilities. It also lacks the space-based and high-altitude reconnaissance and other intelligence systems needed to accurately hit mobile military or leadership targets.

---

29. John on-fat Wong, *Security Requirements In Northeast Asia,* dissertation, University of Wisconsin, 1982, 77, http://nautilus.org/napsnet/napsnet-special-reports/security-requirements-in-northeast-asia. See also Peter Hayes, "'Mutual Probable Destruction': Nuclear Next-Use in a Nuclear-Armed East Asia?" NAPSNet Policy Forum, May 14, 2014, http://nautilus.org/napsnet/napsnet-policy-forum/mutual-probable-destruction-nuclear-next-use-in-a-nuclear-armed-east-asia.

While it develops its own nuclear weapons force—and assuming that doing so leads to rupture of the US-ROK alliance—South Korea would be vulnerable to a preemptive first strike by Russia or China, who would certainly target it. Seoul would lack a countervailing ability to strike back after suffering a nuclear attack. This may not be of concern in peacetime. But in wartime, these two nuclear-weapons states would be obliged to treat a South Korean nuclear force as a potential threat (as they may do already and likely already do so with regard to North Korea's nascent nuclear force). Where would South Korea test and deploy the weapons under such circumstances? In whose backyard?

The late American political scientist Kenneth Waltz argued that nuclear proliferation may lead to strategic stability based on the threat of mutual nuclear annihilation.[30] But John on-fat Wong argued decades ago that two small states armed with nuclear weapons in a military standoff are engaged in an unstable relationship that is best described as "mutual probable destruction" because of their incentive to use their nuclear weapons first rather than lose them.[31] That is, given the time it would take each side to strike, an independent South Korean force facing off against the North Korean nuclear force would be characterized by escalation imperatives that would make the peninsula highly unstable, with potentially catastrophic consequences. Far from reinforcing South Korea's already overwhelming offensive military capabilities—including in almost every dimension where North Korea has developed offsetting "asymmetric" capabilities—South Korean nuclear weapons would undermine deterrence based on conventional forces, and even reduce South Korea's ability to use its conventional forces in response to a North Korean attack (see below).

---

30. For arguments as to the impacts of more versus fewer nuclear weapons, see Scott D. Sagan and Kenneth N. Waltz, *The Spread of Nuclear Weapons: A Debate Renewed* (New York: W.W. Norton, 2003).

31. Wong, "Security Requirements in Northeast Asia," 77. See also Peter Hayes, "Mutual Probable Destruction."

Put in more theoretical terms, both Koreas would be faced with a nuclear-armed adversary with a mutual incentive to strike first. Each would therefore remain in a state of constant nuclear alert in case the other side intended to attack immediately (in contrast to general deterrence, where nuclear weapons cast a long shadow that makes commanders very cautious but there is no immediate intention to attack and therefore no reason to stay on constant high alert).[32] This state of constant fear of an immediate threat of preemptive nuclear attack would push both Koreas to invest heavily in improved surveillance and intelligence capabilities needed to pinpoint nuclear targets for successful preemption, especially given the potential for deception as to location and deployment of nuclear weapons. It would be difficult for either Korea to achieve sufficient confidence that such intelligence were reliable enough to launch a preemptive strike as soon as either gained more than a few warheads and dispersed them—which North Korea has likely done already. Indeed, for South Korea, going it alone without US support, and possibly losing the United States altogether as senior ally, implies reduced confidence in its intelligence, surveillance, and reconnaissance information, which is provided today mostly by US extra-peninsular assets, implying that the South's ability to identify targets to attack preemptively may be lacking.[33] However, it is also possible that in a crisis, intelligence that suggests a pending attack combined with partial but reliable data as to locations of a substantial fraction of the other's nuclear forces could lead either Korea to mount a damage-limiting preemptive strike.[34]

The complications that an independent South Korean nuclear weapons capability would cause for US Forces Korea and Combined Forces

---

32. The distinction between immediate and general nuclear deterrence was made by Patrick M. Morgan, *Deterrence: a conceptual analysis* (Beverly Hills, CA: Sage Publications, 1977).

33. The authors thank Christopher Twomey for this point.

34. We are indebted to Christopher Twomey for making this point in his review of an earlier draft of this essay.

Command would be enormous. Put simply, no US commander-in-chief is going to put American forces in harm's way in Korea if South Korea wields nuclear weapons outside of US political and military command-and-control. Since its creation in 1978, Combined Forces Command has been headed by an American and combines the US and ROK military leadership in South Korea to face North Korea. However, nuclear weapons remained under the sole command of the American general who also commanded US Forces Korea; nuclear command, control, and communications were never shared with ROK military counterparts when US nuclear weapons were deployed in South Korea (from 1958 to 1991).

In the European context, only one state in alliance with the United States—the United Kingdom with its "special relationship"—developed its own nuclear forces. Except for a few naval and aerial tactical nuclear weapons, all UK strategic and aerial nuclear weapons were dedicated to NATO and, ultimately, were commanded by NATO's American military head.[35] (French nuclear weapons were kept outside of NATO's integrated command after the *force de frappe* was created in 1966.) Given the stakes in Korea, it is incredible that the United States would violate the principles of unified command when it comes to nuclear weapons and accept a unilateral capacity by South Korea to start a nuclear war. Indeed, in the case of the United Kingdom, NATO commanders assumed that once released from direct US control in wartime, allied forces armed with nuclear weapons would rapidly lose communication with nuclear commanders, creating a risk of loss of control that would deter Soviet aggressors.[36] This is not a precedent that the United States will want to repeat in Korea.

To the extent that both Koreas became fully armed with operational nuclear forces targeting each other across the Demilitarized Zone (DMZ),

---

35. Shaun Gregory, "The command and control of British tactical nuclear weapons," *Defense Analysis* 4, no. 1 (1988): 39–51, http://dx.doi.org/10.1080 /07430178808405328.

36. Ibid., 49.

independent South Korean nuclear weapons would not only create a more volatile standoff than the Korean Peninsula already has. They would contribute to a rigid and permanent (until it failed) state of psychological warfare and nuclear threats even more ferocious than that seen over much (but not all) of the last six decades. Of course, it is possible that both sides would recognize the immense danger in escalation/de-escalation strategies involving nuclear threat, as did India and Pakistan in the 1999 Kargil crisis. But the opposite also seems just as possible given the nature of the Korean conflict which, unlike the India-Pakistan conflict, involves intense dimensions of a civil war as well as ideological collisions. In short, a nuclear-armed South Korea would ensure the continuing division and antagonism between the two Koreas and would undermine inter-Korean *trust politik, peace politik,* or anything other than *mutual destruction politik* for the indefinite future.

This nuclear standoff would be made even more volatile because one or both Koreas armed with nuclear weapons may believe that nuclear weapons provide a threshold below which covert or even overt conventional military provocations may be undertaken, because the aggressor Korea believes that the victim Korea would see the risk of escalation to nuclear war arising from retaliation as too great. This is the obvious lesson learned from the North's attack on the ROK warship *Cheonan* and the shelling of Yeonpyeong Island in 2010.[37] The same lesson has been learned by India facing Pakistani-originated violence in Kashmir and Mumbai.[38]

South Korea would face very high costs were it to move to nuclear armament because it is deeply embedded in a network of multilateral and bilateral treaty commitments and nuclear energy-supply trading networks.

---

37. Jerry Meyerle, with contributions from Ken Gause and Afshon Ostovar, *Nuclear Weapons and Coercive Escalation in Regional Conflicts: Lessons from North Korea and Pakistan,* CNA, November 20, 2014, http://www.cna.org/sites/default/files/research/DRM-2014-U-008209-Final2.pdf.

38. Terence Roehrig, "The case for a nuclear-free South," *JoongAng Daily,* June 19, 2014, http://koreajoongangdaily.joins.com/news/article/article.aspx?aid=2990820.

South Korea is a member of the Nuclear Non-Proliferation Treaty, and therefore cannot receive, manufacture, or get any assistance to produce nuclear explosive devices or weapons under Article 2. It is also obliged to comply with the safeguard regulations of the International Atomic Energy Agency (IAEA), whose alarm bells will ring loudly the moment that South Korea starts a nuclear weapons program.[39] It cannot emulate Israel, which has refused to sign the NPT and is believed to be one of the states with a clandestine nuclear weapons program. Seoul would have to emulate Pyongyang if it pursues nuclear weapons sovereignty. Like the North in 1994, the South would have to leave the NPT using the pretext of emergency. But unlike North Korea, which had almost no external nuclear ties or market relations to lose, South Korea is highly involved in global markets. The ROK's global reputation is exemplified by South Koreans serving as UN secretary-general and World Bank president. To say the least, it would undermine South Korea's claim to global middle power leadership as embodied in its hosting of such events as the 2012 Nuclear Security Summit.[40]

Pulling out of the NPT and the IAEA might lead to UN action, possibly UN Security Council sanctions as were imposed on North Korea, as well as national sanctions. It would certainly end South Korea's profitable reactor exports, never mind the loss of supply of uranium, enrichment services, and other materials and dual-use technology needed for South Korea's nuclear fuel cycle from the members of the Nuclear Supply Group such as the United States, Australia, Russia, and France. South Korea would face an even larger energy shortfall than Japan had to deal with after shutting down all its nuclear plants in 2011.

Also at risk would be the 1974 bilateral nuclear energy cooperation accord with the United States. The United States would be obliged by

---

39. Jungmin Kang, Peter Hayes, Li Bin, Tatsujiro Suzuki, and Richard Tanter, "South Korea's Nuclear Surprise," *Bulletin of the Atomic Scientists* 61, no. 1 (January 2005): 40–49, http://bos.sagepub.com/content/61/1.toc.

40. Roehrig, "The Case for a Nuclear-free South."

domestic law to cut off all ties in nuclear cooperation and demand restitution of uranium stock, including spent fuel. Bilateral relations could turn frigid fast, as in the 1970s when Seoul secretly pursued a nuclear weapons program.[41] Even if Seoul promised not to use nuclear weapons-related capabilities for anything but peaceful purposes, it would undercut its own attempt to rewrite the bilateral 123 nuclear agreement (Section 123 of the US Atomic Energy Act) that needs to be renewed after March 2016. Should the South start to acquire nuclear weapons, Washington would likely reject out of hand not only Seoul's request to reprocess or pyroprocess spent nuclear fuel, but also its desire to enrich uranium, even for research.

An independent South Korean quest for nuclear weapons will not only justify North Korea's nuclear status and diminish the opposition from China and Russia to the North's nuclear armament, but could also trigger a nuclear domino effect in Northeast Asia. South Korea would have to take into account hostile Japan and China armed with nuclear weapons in its defense planning. It should be noted that some ultra-rightists in Japan relish the prospect that Seoul might make such a move so that they can justify Japanese nuclear weapons. Generalized nuclear armament would be a nightmare for South Korean security.

In sum, South Korea would face significant—possibly highly significant—political, economic, and security costs if it were to develop and deploy its own nuclear weapons. Of course, if such a choice were made in a context in which the United States withdrew extended deterrence due to isolationism in Washington, or the North obtained substantial backing from other big powers for its provocative actions or outright military aggression against the South, or the North acted outrageously (such as conducting an atmospheric nuclear test), then some of these negative impacts might be

---

41. Peter Hayes and Chung-in Moon, "Park Chung Hee, the CIA and the Bomb," NAPSNet Special Reports, September 23, 2011, http://nautilus.org/napsnet/napsnet -special-reports/park-chung-hee-the-cia-and-the-bomb.

ameliorated. The United States might be persuaded to remain in alliance, albeit with major downgrading of South Korea's stature in American eyes, which it enjoys today due in large part to its restraint to date in responding to the North. Trading partners might be less damning and more willing to continue with business as usual.

What About Redeploying US Tactical Nuclear Weapons?

Instead of making its own, might South Korea ask the United States to redeploy nuclear weapons? Such redeployment is not inconceivable. However, considered carefully, the idea of redeploying US tactical nuclear weapons is as fantastic as South Korea going it alone.

First, a few air-delivered nuclear weapons based in Korea would add little to overall deterrence and pose the same use-them-or-lose-them dilemma as would South Korean nukes. Second, since 2009, the United States has downplayed the role of nuclear weapons in every aspect of its security posture. South Korea would be swimming against this tide. Third, far from asserting South Korea's military prowess against North Korea's nuclear weapons, these weapons would symbolize renewed subordination to the US military.

The United States will not commit thousands of nuclear-certified personnel and millions of dollars to redeploying nuclear weapons to Korea. The United States already extends nuclear deterrence with its home-based strategic nuclear forces, and will not pay twice for such an improbable mission, especially given the costs in reconfiguring and modernizing the US nuclear arsenal.

Political and Military Effects of Redeployment

Even if the United States returned tactical nuclear weapons to the peninsula, this would not help solve the North Korean nuclear conundrum. It would give Pyongyang a pretext to accelerate its weapons program. China would move closer to North Korea militarily, aggravating South Korea's insecurities.

From a military perspective, US nuclear weapons based in South Korea lack merit in supporting Combined Forces Command's most important mission: deterring a North Korean attack on South Korea.

In recent years, South Korea's missile capability has significantly improved. Its air superiority with F-16s, F-15s, and, eventually, F-35s provides an effective force with which to strike massing North Korean forces and to attrite the long-range artillery and rockets that threaten Seoul. When American conventional assets are added, ROK-US combined forces are formidable. With complete control of North Korea's airspace, it would not take them long to occupy key sites, even if unconventional warfare lingered in mountainous areas for some months.

To attack the South, North Korea would rely on its forward-deployed forces to threaten northern Seoul with long-range artillery and rocket fire. Kim Jong Un cannot hope to attack the South and achieve military victory.[42] The South's military and the DPRK's Korean People's Army (KPA) are opposing, immense military masses, both deterred from moving against the other, and locked in an inherently stable and—so far—permanent standoff. The North's nuclear weapons, and hypothetical South Korean nuclear weapons, make little marginal difference to these opposing tectonic forces.

Kim Jong Un's nuclear weapons capabilities provide at best little—and likely no—additional deterrence to that already sustained by his conventional forces. The combined probability of a North Korean missile-delivered nuclear warhead exploding over a target given all the systems that must work together—the rockets, the separating stages, the re-entry vehicle, the guidance system, the fuze, and the warhead itself—is likely less than 10 percent. If the North were to use a nuclear weapon, it would then face US-ROK and allied forces that would dismember the regime and kill its leaders or put them on trial for crimes against humanity and

---

42. Roger Cavazos, "Mind the Gap Between Rhetoric and Reality," NAPSNet Special Reports, June 26, 2012, http://nautilus.org/napsnet/napsnet-special-reports/mind-the-gap-between-rhetoric-and-reality.

nuclear aggression. Russia and China could well join this campaign. If Kim Jong Un is rational, his nuclear weapons are unusable and add nothing to the KPA's offensive capabilities.

If Kim Jong Un is misinformed or deluded, and launches an all-out attack on the South, then it's fair to ask whether having US nuclear weapons in South Korea could, first, deter and, if deterrence fails, then defeat the KPA, more than having them based in the United States. Of course, if Kim Jong Un is *truly* mad, then he is immune to deterrence, conventional or nuclear, in which case strictly military considerations based on uniquely nuclear weapons effects are what is important in evaluating their utility. In this instance, there is no difference between offshore and in-ROK deployments, and there are security advantages to having deliverable weapons kept outside of South Korea.

If a war began due to bad information, loss of control, or stupid decisions made by the North, US tactical nuclear weapons are no more useful on the battlefield than they were in the 1970s and 1980s, when the US military itself—led by General Jack Cushman at the time—concluded that the weapons were unusable, contributing to the eventual global withdrawal of nuclear weapons in 1991.[43] Authoritative analysis from that period describes the utter devastation that would arise from using nuclear weapons in Korea. In 1978, Bryan Jack and a team of analysts at Pan Heuristics asked how nuclear weapons might be used to blunt a North Korean all-out attack on the South.[44] Their analysis (which posited South

---

43. John H. Cushman, *Organization and Operational Employment of Air/Land Forces,* US Army War College, 1984; Cushman, "Military Options in Korea's End Game," NAPSNet Policy Forum, May 23, 1994, http://nautilus.org/napsnet/napsnet-policy -forum/military-options-in-koreas-end-game/; and Cushman, oral history and other papers that describe his internal battles in the US Army to remove fallacious nuclear weapon strategies from his plans to fight war in Korea, see volume 2, p. 8–23, and "Korea, 1976 to 1978: A Memoir," p. 26, http://www.west-point.org/publications /cushman.

44. This analysis draws on pp. II-85 to II-93 of Bryan Jack, Marcella Agmon, Steven L. Head, David McGarvey, Beverly Rowen, and Henry S. Rowen, "The South Korean Case: A Nuclear Weapons Program Embedded in an Environment of Great Power

Korean nuclear weapons, but the results are identical if American nuclear weapons are substituted) still pertains today because nothing has changed with regard to the effects of nuclear weapons. While the disposition of the bulk of North Korean forces moved forward in the early 1980s within a hundred kilometers of the DMZ, they must still pass through the same narrow corridors to attack the South.

What did Jack's team members find in 1978, other than the ruinous after-effects from radiological plumes after multiple nuclear strikes? In the most urgent case, the attempt by the KPA to seize Seoul, they calculated that roughly 120 American forty-kiloton nuclear weapons would have to be fired in the three attack corridors, in broader areas north of these corridors, and at point targets such as hardened airfields, to block an all-out North Korean attack. They also calculated that the same military effect could be achieved with conventional artillery and bombs already in the US-ROK arsenal in South Korea.

The same conclusion must be reached today, only more so due to the greatly increased numbers, precision, and lethality of US-ROK ground and aerial conventional forces and to vastly improved communications and battle-space awareness and management. Only in the case of attacking the North's cities did Jack's team find that nuclear weapons were more "efficient" because it was improbable that US-ROK conventional forces responding to a North Korean attack could reach that far northward to match the speed and scale of counter-city nuclear attacks inflicted by US nuclear forces. Their conclusions as to the relative utility of counter-force nuclear versus conventional strikes remain valid today, but the utility of a counter-city strike is dubious because there would be no political logic to punishing large numbers of innocent North Koreans for the actions of the leadership.

Concerns," vol. 2, *Regional Rivalries and Nuclear Responses,* Pan Heuristics Final Report to US Defense Nuclear Agency, February 28, 1978, http://nautilus.org /foia-document/regional-rivalries-and-nuclear-responses-voluume-ii-the-south -korean-case-a-nuclear-weapons-program-embedded-in-an-environment-of -great-power-concerns.

Even if Kim Jong Un was the target, not tanks or infantry or whole city populations, then the United States (or a nuclear-armed South Korea) likely would also kill vast numbers of innocent North Koreans with nuclear attacks. Such attacks would be disproportionate and reprehensible, even after North Korean nuclear first use.[45] Given the labyrinths of caves in the North in which Kim Jong Un and his nuclear weapons could hide, it is also unlikely that the success of such attacks could be assured. Then what? Today, the missions that were allocated to nuclear weapons in the mid-seventies are best accomplished by air-launched precision-guided munitions that have similar lethality without the side effects of massive collateral damage and radiation.

At bottom, redeployment rests on the argument that *"local* US nukes" would reduce the probability that, *in extremis,* North Korea would play its nuclear card more than *"distant* US nukes" would. Ironically, redeployment of US nuclear weapons might enhance nuclear risk-taking by the DPRK. Because the North's leaders would perceive in-ROK deployment to increase the risk of preemptive nuclear attack, long a North Korean concern, it would play into North Korean "crazy like a fox" strategy. To be effective, such an "irrational" strategy demands that it create and increase the risk to the United States of prosecuting the war to eliminate North Korea, not play it safe by avoiding or reducing such risk, in order to shift the American cost-benefit calculus. Presenting Kim Jong Un with the opportunity to do so is the opposite of what the US and South Korean military should be doing to shape his strategic options.

Credibility of US Nuclear Extended Deterrence?

What about the argument that when North Korea can strike the United States with nuclear weapons, the credibility of the US nuclear extended

---

45. Tom Nichols, "The Case for Conventional Deterrence," *The National Interest,* November 12, 2013, http://nationalinterest.org/commentary/the-case-conventional -deterrence-9381.

deterrent falls so much that it will no longer be sufficient?[46] This is an old argument in the NATO context. Now it must be examined in Korea.

In low-level military conflict, nuclear retaliation is implausible either because it would be disproportionate or even militarily counter-productive on the battlefield or because it could lead to condemnation and even intervention by third parties.

However, once an adversary like the DPRK can plausibly threaten to hit the United States itself, the sheer magnitude of nuclear detonations—even if they are too few to destroy the United States—could make Washington think twice about trading Guam for Seoul. The key elements of credibility are capacity and resolve from the perspective of the adversary.

In terms of capacity, the United States can reduce North Korea into a smoking, radiating ruin in a few hours, should it decide to do so, with only a small fraction of its missile force, either from submarines or from land-based missiles. These missiles are reliable and would be precision-targeted. There is no credibility gap here. Long-range bombers are equally capable, just a bit slower.

The second aspect of credibility is the resolve of the party issuing a nuclear threat to make good on it. "Hiroshima" and "Nagasaki" remind North Koreans of American resolve in the past and Korean survivors from the Hiroshima bombing are still alive to remind them. Moreover, any attack or threat of nuclear attack by the North on the South signals that an attack on the United States may be forthcoming and requires immediate response—although that response may not be nuclear.

Also, the United States has direct vital interests in South Korea, including Washington's credibility, its reputation given its investment of treasure and lives in Korea since the Korean War, and its economic interest in a vital South Korean economy. Any military attack on the ROK-proper will

---

46. See, for example, Ho-yeol Yoo, "Is It Right Time to Propose a Dialogue with North Korea?" April 18, 2013, JTBC (Korean), http://news.jtbc.joins.com/article/article .aspx?news_id=NB10266522; and Choon-geun Lee, "Nuclear Armament: An Interpretation from International Political Perspective," *Bukhan* (North Korea), no. 417 (2011): 22.

kill many American and Chinese civilians almost immediately, which will instantly involve the United States in a kinetic conflict. What happens in South Korea also directly affects Washington's strategic relationship with China, which also involves US and Chinese nuclear weapons. North Korean nuclear threats aimed at the South already reverberate instantly into the US-China relationship, as occurred in 2012 and 2013, resulting in high political and military response at a regional level, both unilateral and concerted between the two great powers. US stakes are vital, albeit different, to those of Seoul in responding credibly to North Korean nuclear threats. In short, there is no credibility deficit.

Psychological Dimensions of South Korean Nuclear Weapons or US Redeployment

The main driver of South Korean longing for nuclear weapons, whether independent South Korean nuclear forces or redeployed US nuclear weapons, is to offset North Korea's use of nuclear threats. This is not a deterrent use of nuclear weapons by the North, but a compellent one—that is, one that attempts to change existing US or South Korean policies by nuclear threat.[47] Historically, a major factor motivating a state to develop its own nuclear weapons, or for the United States to extend nuclear deterrence to an ally, has been for the leadership to reassure its

---

47. Patrick Morgan notes that the United States and North Korea used nuclear threats primarily for compellence in the 1991–2002 time frame in "Deterrence and System Management: The Case of North Korea," *Conflict Management and Peace Science* 23, no. 2 (April 2006): 121–138. The DPRK's nuclear threats from 2008 onward have been primarily compellent in nature, not deterrent, as documented in Peter Hayes and Scott Bruce, "North Korean Nuclear Nationalism and the Threat of Nuclear War in Korea," *Pacific Focus* 26 (2011): 65–89, http://onlinelibrary.wiley.com/doi/10.1111 /j.1976-5118.2011.01056.x/abstract; and also Peter Hayes and Roger Cavazos, "North Korean and US Nuclear Threats." For a careful examination of American nuclear compellence during the Cold War, see John Merrill and Ilan Pelig, "Nuclear Compellence: The Political Use of the Bomb," *Crossroads* 11 (1984): 19–39, http://nautilus.org/wp-content/uploads/2011/12/Merrill-Peleg-Nuclear-Compellence -Crossroads-11-1984-pp-19-39.pdf.

domestic population that it is not susceptible to nuclear coercion or to reassure an ally's leadership that it need not fear such coercive threats by a nuclear-armed adversary, regardless of popular perception.

The DPRK's actual use of nuclear threats since 2006 has been mostly aimed at compellence based on sowing terror in the minds of civilian populations, not just the minds of the leadership of South Korea and Japan, with the aim of extracting political and other concessions from the United States, South Korea, Japan, and even China and Russia (by attacking UN Security Council resolutions aimed at reversing its nuclear armament). Its propaganda has clearly addressed popular, not just elite, audiences. In some respects, it has succeeded. The entry of North Korean nuclear weapons into Western (and Chinese) popular culture, cartoons, and movies is partly the result of these threat campaigns. Moreover, the threats were not harmless. In Guam, for example, an emergency was declared and families kept their children home from school due to the threat of missile-delivered attacks made by Pyongyang in April 2013.[48]

Historically, nuclear weapons were forward-deployed by the United States for two reasons. The first was to increase the recognition by adversaries such as the former Soviet Union and North Korea that conventional attacks on US allies could evoke early and assured US nuclear retaliation. The second was to reassure US allies that its promise to use nuclear weapons in response to such aggression was credible. As we noted earlier, now that US tactical and theater nuclear weapons are no longer deployed in-country and in-region, the issue of credibility is a real one—especially in light of the total failure by the United States to halt, reverse, and overcome North Korean nuclear weapons proliferation.

But, as we argued already, South Koreans should examine this issue in the bigger geo-strategic picture. In effect, the United States recast nuclear *extended* deterrence in the 1991–2010 period to become nuclear *existential* deterrence, reserving nuclear weapons to respond only to

---

48. Brett M. Kelman, "N. Korean missile threats worry some on Guam," *USA Today*, April 12, 2013.

existential threats to the United States or its allies. No US nuclear forces are dedicated to deterring war against South Korea (or against Japan, for that matter). Even less understood is that both nations may have just as much nuclear existential deterrence as an American living in Idaho. Put baldly, because their vital interests are so intertwined, an existential threat to South Korea is inseparable from an existential threat to the United States. Any nuclear threat, let alone a nuclear attack, bears on these shared vital interests. Yet it is equally true that this residual nuclear existential deterrence may have little discernible impact on real military decisions and deployments given the conventional forces involved on the ground and the risks and benefits generated by nuclear threats, let alone nuclear use, by any of the parties involved in the Korean conflict.

South Koreans cannot pick and choose which benefits to take and which costs to avoid in their alliance with the United States. It's a package deal. Currently, the package is a region-wide strategy based on advanced conventional forces and on joint, cross-service capacities in the Western Pacific, integrated with interoperable allied forces. The question that South Koreans must answer is whether the putative reassurance that they would obtain from having their own nuclear weapons is worth rupturing this alliance—as likely would occur if they were to go it alone—and, if not, whether the costs and benefits of hypothetical redeployment of US nuclear weapons to South Korea would outweigh the destabilizing and counter-productive political and military effects that would follow.

What Should South Korea Do Instead?

South Korea's best military options to respond to the North's nuclear threat are to develop its conventional military forces in alliance with the United States and to develop cooperative military-military relations with all states in the region. South Korea should avoid a simplistic retaliatory response to North Korean provocations and instead work closely through Combined Forces Command to develop operational strategies underscoring the absolute and relative superiority of ROK-US allied forces while avoiding deployments and exercises that suggest preemptive attacks aimed at the leadership or positioning of forces that imply a pending all-out attack on the North (especially offshore US forces). Specifically recommended in this regard is avoidance of operations by Combined Forces Command designed to degrade KPA C3I (command, control, communications, and intelligence infrastructure), destroy its leadership, and strike strategic forces, including nuclear weapons, that may induce nuclear strikes from North Korean leaders, as they may believe they are in a "use or lose" situation.[49]

American and South Korean military strategy should *not* be based on preemptively attacking North Korea's nascent nuclear force, nor on retaliating against its first use with nuclear weapons. A US nuclear attack is improbable under any but the most extreme circumstances, in which case options are available to the United States that do not require redeployment or use of American nuclear weapons. Although it may seem counterintuitive to many, military strategies, exercises, and capacities that are designed to attack and kill North Korea's national political-military leadership are a particularly bad idea, because they impel these leaders to reflect on the utility of early first nuclear use and, if achieved, could lead to DPRK leaders' loss of control of whatever nuclear weapons they have to deliver against US and South Korean forces. If DPRK deployment of nuclear weapons is accompanied by pre-delegated use authority to nuclear units, successful decapitation could generate a nuclear attack. Some strategies to attack military command posts and communications links between nuclear forces and central commanders may also risk nuclear escalation if use authority has been pre-delegated. True, restraint may come at a cost to US-ROK conventional forces that would otherwise

---

49. Kier A. Lieber and Daryl G. Press, *Coercive Nuclear Campaigns in the 21st Century: Understanding Adversary Incentives and Options for Nuclear Escalation,* Center on Contemporary Conflict, Naval Postgraduate School, 2013, http://www.nps.edu/Academics/Centers/CCC/Research/PASCC.html.

gain relief due to the fragmentation and confusion created by such disabling retaliatory attacks against Pyongyang's conventional command posts and communications (assuming these are commingled with those supporting nuclear units). But strengthening US-ROK defenses, including adding counter-missile systems and hardening command posts against nuclear attack, reduces further the chance of a North Korean attempt to use nuclear weapons to decapitate the ROK and US military.[50]

The United States and South Korea should do everything possible to help stabilize the North economically to avoid it falling into desperate straits that could induce the leadership to lash out (although this assistance might not negate entirely this threat and military strategies must still be available to deal with such contingencies). Crisis avoidance is far cheaper than crisis management, let alone war and nuclear war. South Korea's best political and psychological strategy to counter the North's coercive use of nuclear threats and to reassure its own population is to deepen and expand its own non-nuclear nationalist credentials. In this regard, South Korea's use of creative and agile diplomacy that exploits its position as a medium-sized power surrounded by great powers is the best approach. South Korean leadership on nuclear security agendas, including post-Fukushima regional frameworks for emergency response to nuclear fuel-cycle incidents and large-scale accidents, exemplifies this powerful symbolic strategy. This non-nuclear national narrative should be extended to design and implement a regional treaty framework for comprehensive security. Within that framework, South Korea can lead the in-depth examination of the stabilizing effects of a regional nuclear weapon-free zone. This strategy can be implemented in concert with China and Mongolia, and could receive the support of the United States and Russia, leaving Japan nowhere to go but to join such a zone in the future. North

---

50. Chang Kwoun Park and Victor A. Utgoff, "On Strengthening Extended Deterrence for the ROK-US Alliance," *Joint Forces Quarterly* 68 (1st quarter 2013): 84–90, https://www.questia.com/magazine/1G1-323503436/on-strengthening-extended -deterrence-for-the-rok-u-s; see also, http://ndupress.ndu.edu/Portals/68/Documents /jfq/jfq-68.pdf.

Korea could be invited to join and comply over time, or disarm quickly to join as a non-nuclear state in return for guarantees from the nuclear-weapons states that it will neither be attacked nor threatened with attack by nuclear weapons. Incentives could include a non-hostility agreement, a peace treaty to end the Korean War, and economic assistance to enable the North to make the transition to a normal state and political economy. If North Korea balks, then eventually it will collapse into a unified Korea and become part of a regional nuclear weapon-free zone.[51]

To achieve this outcome, South Korea needs to redefine the goals of reviving the moribund Six-Party Talks toward achieving a comprehensive security settlement, not just the nuclear disarmament of North Korea. At the same time, South Korea must maintain an open door policy toward the North. The South is powerful enough today to wait for as long as it takes for the North to commence a genuine reconciliation process leading to rapprochement and eventually to peaceful reunification. In this ultimate end game, nuclear weapons have no role to play.

Comprehensive Security Settlement and Northeast Asian Nuclear Weapon-Free Zone

The implications of the argument advanced above—that reliance on the status quo of nuclear extended deterrence provided by the United States to South Korea is preferable to a go-it-alone South Korean nuclear break-out or a redeployment of US nuclear weapons to South Korea—is that this is the best that can be achieved, and that the status quo is stable, sufficiently secure, and therefore acceptable. This section challenges this bleak view that condemns South Korea and other regional states, and

---

51.   Binoy Kampmark, Peter Hayes, and Richard Tanter, *A New Approach to Security in Northeast Asia: Breaking the Gridlock Workshop,* NAPSNet Special Reports, November 20, 2012, http://nautilus.org/napsnet/napsnet-special-reports /gridlockworkshopsummary/#axzz31SQamTGM.

North Korea itself, to strategic drift with periods of confrontation and tension loaded with gunpowder and even the risk of nuclear war. Instead, we argue that it is critical that the nuclear tide be turned back in Northeast Asia, and that there are ways to do so that not only serve the region, but also can be implemented in tandem with a multifaceted effort at global and regional levels to jointly implement a nuclear abolition enterprise. This effort should target the resolution of regional conflicts; the de-emphasis and then removal of nuclear threat as a constitutive element of interstate relations in the region; and the leadership role of non-nuclear states, including even North Korea once it reverses gear and reverts to full non-nuclear status. This approach entails national leaders meeting at summits, regional monitoring, verification, and enforcement mechanisms that are consistent with but reinforce global obligations to comply with NPT and IAEA safeguards. Also crucial are tightened nuclear materials controls and, perhaps most important in Northeast Asia, ancillary arms control and disarmament agreements and precursory confidence-building measures on offensive conventional forces and on ballistic missile defenses.

These are factors that require extensive dialogue, joint research, and high-level political and military engagement involving all states before any state can move forward. Without leadership, none of this will come to pass. With leadership, many apparently insurmountable obstacles may disappear overnight to reveal the most important underlying insecurities that must be addressed to move forward quickly. There is much prior experience in nuclear and conventional arms control and disarmament measures to draw on in tackling the complex and uncertain security dilemmas that afflict the Korean Peninsula and the region. But ultimately, there is no substitute for political will and engagement to identify the limits of possible change and to create the transitional rules in the course of implementing collaborative security strategies.

The North Korean nuclear threat now involves all states in the region. Reversing the North Korean nuclear breakout is beyond the power of the United States and South Korea acting alone. Instead, what is needed is a robust adaptive strategy that *reshapes* the role of nuclear weapons in the range of possible multipolar, bipolar, and unipolar future regional orders. Instead of shaping behaviors incrementally, as was tried without success at the Six-Party Talks, future six-party negotiations need to focus on creating a new *comprehensive* security settlement in a treaty format, including an agreement modeled in some respects after the Southeast Asian Treaty of Amity and Cooperation to which the United States acceded without congressional approval.

By *comprehensive,* we mean that at the outset, nothing is agreed until everything is agreed. Only then does the negotiation concerning implementation and sequencing commence. This is the basis of multilateral negotiations with Iran. A similar approach that combines coercive aspects of sanctions and other political-military pressure with engagement and the prospect of constructive and positive shared outcomes is necessary in talks with North Korea.

By *reshape,* we mean that a comprehensive security settlement should create a new regional framework that:

- Recognizes that all parties wish to eliminate nuclear weapons as a basis of their security relationships
- Reflects the reality that nuclear weapons are of decreasing political and military value
- Facilitates reduction of the role of nuclear weapons in the parties' respective political and military policies and postures

The long-standing and well-tested framework for such a commitment is a legally binding nuclear weapon-free zone, for which there are many precedents around the world spanning four decades.[52]

---

52. Kerstin Vignard, ed., "Nuclear-weapon-free zones," United Nations Institute for Disarmament Research, *Disarmament Forum* 2 (2011), http://www.unidir.org/files /publications/pdfs/nuclear-weapon-free-zones-en-314.pdf. Also see Michael Hamel-Green, "Regions That Say No: Precedents and Precursors for Denuclearizing Northeast Asia," NAPSNet Special Reports, June 5, 2012, http://nautilus.org/napsnet /napsnet-special-reports/regions-that-say-no-precedents-and-precursors-for

A comprehensive security settlement requires a regional treaty framework, not just a political agreement, if it is to be meaningful to all the parties, including North Korea.[53] Anything less will fail and leave the states in the region to ride the roller coaster of confrontation and standoff, of semi-permanent crisis. This treaty, which might be titled A Northeast Asian Treaty of Amity and Cooperation, would have six key elements, all of which are necessary:

1. Termination of the state of war
2. Creation of a permanent security council to monitor and verify compliance and decide on violations

---

-denuclearizing-northeast-asia: "As of late 2011, 138 out of 193 UN member states have entered into, and ratified, legally binding treaties to reduce or constrain nuclear weapon proliferation, development and basing in their own regions (or other regions over which they have territorial claims). These include the 1959 Antarctic Treaty (47 states with interests in Antarctica), the 1967 Tlatelolco Treaty (33 Latin American states), the 1985 Rarotonga Treaty (13 South Pacific States), the 1995 Bangkok Treaty (10 Southeast Asian states), the 1996 Pelindaba Treaty (30 African states, with a further 21 signed but not yet ratified), and the 2006 Semipalatinsk Treaty (5 Central Asian States). NWFZs now cover almost the entire Southern Hemisphere, and wide swathes of the Northern Hemisphere, including the most recent Central Asian zone, which is entirely in the Northern Hemisphere." Other treaties also denuclearize geographic areas: the Outer Space Treaty, the Moon Agreement, and the Seabed Treaty. Mongolia's 1992 self-declared nuclear-weapon-free status has been recognized internationally through the adoption by consensus of UN General Assembly Resolution 53/77D in December 1998 on "Mongolia's international security and nuclear weapon free status."

Arguably, *the Korean Joint Denuclearization Declaration* (1992) also established a limited NWFZ in Korea, now moribund. Thousands of cities and provinces have established local NWFZs. Some states, like New Zealand, have written their non-nuclear status into their legal systems or, like the Philippines, into their constitutions. However, these are not treaty-based zones, nor are they recognized by the United Nations under international treaty law. The Comprehensive Nuclear-Test-Ban Treaty, not yet in force, will ban nuclear explosions and will prohibit and prevent any such nuclear explosion at any place under a state party's jurisdiction or control.

53. Kampmark, *A New Approach to Security in Northeast Asia.*

3. Mutual declaration of no hostile intent
4. Provision for assistance for nuclear and other energy
5. Termination of sanctions
6. Establishment of a nuclear weapon-free zone

A comprehensive regional agreement on security requires ratification by a number of states, although adherence to sections would be specific to the signatory states. Provisions would come into effect in a staggered manner—immediately upon ratification or when various conditions are met. A seventh element—inter-Korean reconciliation leading to peaceful reunification—could be included as part of this settlement, depending on the views of the two Koreas. It would be a working example of the global principle that would undergird nuclear abolition, namely, a new diplomatic mechanism that, by settling regional conflicts, encourages nuclear restraint.

Within this comprehensive framework, three of the hardest security issues—nuclear threats by the nuclear-weapons states to non-nuclear states in Northeast Asia, the provision of US nuclear extended deterrence to its allies in the region, and North Korea's breakout and nuclear threat—would be managed and resolved in a Northeast Asian nuclear weapon-free zone (NWFZ).

The North insists that any US nuclear threat toward it must cease before it will revert to non-nuclear-weapons status and that this guarantee must be legally binding rather than an executive branch policy recommendation that can disappear overnight after a presidential election. The only framework in which this combination is possible is a nuclear weapon-free zone treaty. Last July, the UN secretary-general urged states in the region to consider appropriate action to establish a nuclear weapon-free zone in Northeast Asia, "including by promoting a more active role for the regional forums in encouraging transparency and confidence-building among the countries of the region."[54] On October 21, 2014, Pyongyang

---

54. Work of the Advisory Board on Disarmament Matters, Report of the Secretary-General to UN General Assembly, July 26, 2013, https://disarmament-library

announced via its state news agency, KCNA, that it proposed "building a nuclear-free zone through peaceful dialogue and negotiations . . . combined with the method of removing the US nuclear threat by relying on international law,"[55] indicating that a dialogue with the North as to what it means by this proposal may be productive.

As we noted above, a nuclear weapon-free zone is a treaty, affirmed in the Nuclear Non-Proliferation Treaty, whereby states freely negotiate regional prohibitions on nuclear weapons.[56] Its main purposes are to strengthen peace and security, reinforce the nuclear non-proliferation regime, and contribute to nuclear disarmament. A Northeast Asian Nuclear Weapon-Free Zone would provide a stabilizing framework in which to manage and reduce the threat of nuclear war, eliminate nuclear threats to non-nuclear-weapons states in compliance with their NPT and IAEA obligations, and facilitate abolition of nuclear weapons. (It would apply to nuclear weapons only, not to other weapons of mass destruction.) It would also restrain and reverse the North's nuclear armament; build confidence that nuclear weapons will not be used either for political coercion or to fight wars; and reassure non-nuclear-weapon states that they are secure, thereby deepening commitment to non-nuclear-weapon status. In a Northeast Asian zone, US Forces Korea and a reconstituted UN Command[57] might become a

.un.org/UNODA/Library.nsf/a45bed59c24a1b6085257b100050103a /f82ba7fcf1be289085257bce006a670a/$FILE/A%2068%20206.pdf.

55. KCNA, "U.S. Can Never Evade Blame for Blocking Solution to Nuclear Issue: Rodong Sinmun," October 21, 2014, http://www.kcna.co.jp/item/2014/201410 /news21/20141021-11ee.html.

56. United Nations, "Establishment of nuclear-weapon-free zones on the basis of arrangements freely arrived at among the States of the region concerned," Annex 1, Report of the Disarmament Commission, General Assembly, 54th session, Supplement No. 42 (1999): 7.

57. This could possibly involve states already allied with the United Nations Command under a new Security Council mandate. The sixteen UNC member countries are Australia, Belgium, Canada, Colombia, Denmark, France, Greece, the Netherlands, New Zealand, Norway, the Philippines, South Africa (rejoined in 2010), Thailand, Turkey, the United Kingdom, and the United States. See "Statement Of General

pivotal,[58] rather than a partisan, deterrent, thereby creating an enduring geostrategic buffer between the two Koreas and between China and Japan.[59]

In such a zone, states would undertake differential obligations.[60] Non-nuclear-weapon states that are signatories to and in full compliance with the Non-Proliferation Treaty undertake to not research, develop, test, pos-

---

Walter L. Sharp, Commander, United Nations Command; Commander, United States-Republic Of Korea Combined Forces Command, and Commander, United States Forces Korea Before The Senate Armed Services Committee," April 12, 2011, http://www.dod.mil/dodgc/olc/docs/testSharp04082011.pdf: "The UNC continues to maintain a rear headquarters in Japan. Unique to that presence is a status of forces agreement that allows the UNC Commander to use seven UNC-flagged bases in Japan for the transit of UNC aircraft, vessels, equipment, and forces upon notification to the government of Japan. During 2010, four naval vessels and four aircraft called on ports in Japan under the auspices of the UNC. Almost 1,000 military personnel participated in these visits. The multi-national nature of the UNC rear headquarters is reflected in its leadership. Last year for the first time, a senior officer from Australia assumed command of the headquarters, while the deputy is an officer from Turkey."

58. Peter Hayes and Richard Tanter, "Beyond the Nuclear Umbrella: Re-thinking the Theory and Practice of Nuclear Extended Deterrence in East Asia and the Pacific," *Pacific Focus* 26, no. 1 (April 2011): 8–9, http://onlinelibrary.wiley.com/doi/10.1111/pafo.2011.26.issue-1/issuetoc: "*Pivotal deterrence:* This concept captures the possibility for nuclear weapons states to arbitrate between two adversarial states, and to deter them from attacking each other. This pivotal role does not imply impartiality, but it further complicates an already complex strategic situation and may supplant or be superimposed on old forms of strategic deterrence. Relevant contexts for the USA may be the Korean Peninsula, China-Japan relations, and Taiwan-China relations." The concept was first explicated fully in Timothy W. Crawford, *Pivotal Deterrence: Third-Party Statecraft and the Pursuit of Peace* (New York: Cornell University Press, 2003).

59. As argued by Shinichi Ogawa, "Link Japanese and Koreans in a Nuclear Weapon-Free Zone," *New York Times,* August 29, 1997, http://www.nytimes.com/1997/08/29/opinion/29iht-edskin.t.html.

60. This section draws on Peter Hayes and Richard Tanter, "Key Elements of Northeast Asia Nuclear-Weapons Free Zone (NEA-NWFZ)," NAPSNet Policy Forum,

sess, or deploy nuclear weapons, and to not allow nuclear weapons to be stationed on their territory.[61] Their ratification would bring the zone into

61. The exact mix of these prohibitions varies across zones. Recent zones prohibit more activities. Two issues are important in the Northeast Asia context. The first is *stationing* of nuclear weapons. Secret US-Japan agreements provided for US storage and/or re-introduction of nuclear weapons. President George Bush's 1991 statement that "under normal circumstances, our ships will not carry tactical nuclear weapons," and that land and sea-based warheads not withdrawn, dismantled, and destroyed "will be secured in central areas where they would be available if necessary in a future crisis" also left open the possibility that the United States might, presumably subject to consultation with allies, redeploy such weapons into Japan and the ROK. At the time, then chairman of the Joint Chiefs Colin Powell said that only twenty-four hours would be needed to reverse the order. Since 1991, many of the tactical and theater nuclear weapons in the US arsenal no longer exist. The only salient non-strategic weapon today is the aging B-61 thermonuclear warhead that is stored in the United States and forward-deployed in some NATO countries. Practically speaking, redeployment and forward stationing of nuclear weapons would be very difficult to achieve. Home-porting strategic nuclear submarines in allied ports is physically possible but politically difficult, and would affect greatly a United States second-strike capability by increasing the vulnerability of these submarines to a first strike. The second important issue is *transit*. To avoid conflict between Japan's domestic non-nuclear principles and transit of its narrow straits leading from the Sea of Japan (called the East Sea of Korea by North Korea) to the Pacific Ocean by US and Soviet warships, Japan limited its coastal jurisdiction in these straits to three nautical miles, allowing free international passage through a narrow strip of international waters. Leaving aside apparently commonplace past transit of US nuclear weapons via airfields and ports, not just innocent passage in the territorial waters of Japan, the adoption of a zone-wide twelve-mile nautical limit for a Northeast Asia nuclear weapon-free zone would change current Japanese legal treatment of the straits and the related legal regime under which transit could occur. President Bush's statement is "Bush's arms plan; Remarks by President Bush on Reducing U.S. and Soviet Nuclear Weapons," *New York Times*, September 28, 1991, http://www.nytimes .com/1991/09/28/us/bush-s-arms-plan-remarks-president-bush-reducing-us-soviet -nuclear-weapons.html?pagewanted=all&src=pm. Powell is cited in Eric Schmitt, "Bush's Arm[s] Plan; Cheney Orders Bombers Off Alert, Starting Sharp Nuclear Pullback," *New York Times*, September 29, 1991, http://www.nytimes.com/1991

force even if the nuclear-weapon states take their time to commit (as they have done in all the other zones).

Nuclear-weapon states that are NPT signatories, unlike North Korea, give negative security assurances to not use or threaten to use nuclear weapons against the non-nuclear-weapon states that are party to, and in compliance with, the nuclear weapon-free zone treaty.[62] Their only obligations are to extend negative assurances to non-nuclear-weapon states party to the agreement and to accept those nations' restrictions on stationing nuclear weapons (and, depending on how the treaty is formulated, restrictions on nuclear weapons transit).

/09/29/world/bush-s-arm-plan-cheney-orders-bombers-off-alert-starting-sharp
-nuclear-pullback.html?pagewanted=all&src=pm. On Japan's transit policy and
territorial waters, see Chi-Young Pak, *The Korean Straits* (Leiden: Martinis Nijhoff,
1988), 79–81; on recent Chinese naval surface and submarine transit of the straits
and Japanese response, see Peter Dutton, *Scouting, Signaling, and Gatekeeping:
Chinese Naval Operations in Japanese Waters and the International Law Implications,*
China Maritime Studies Institute, US Naval War College, February 2009,
https://www.usnwc.edu/Research---Gaming/China-Maritime-Studies-Institute
/Publications/documents/CMS2_Dutton.aspx.

62. Article 2 of the Protocol of the Southeast Asian NWFZ specifies that: "Each State
Party undertakes not to use or threaten to use nuclear weapons against any State Party
to the Treaty. It further undertakes not to use or threaten to use nuclear weapons
within the Southeast Asian Nuclear-Weapon-Free Zone." To date, the nuclear-
weapon states have resisted this provision, partly because the Southeast Asian NWFZ
covers the Exclusive Economic Zone, but also because it implies restrictions on the
use of nuclear weapons from within the zone against adjacent zones. Eventually, the
mosaic of such stringent zones could reinforce each other to prohibit all threat and
all use of nuclear weapons, as envisioned by Seongwhun Cheon as a "Pan-Pacific
nuclear weapon free zone (PPNWFZ), encompassing East Asia, South Pacific and
Latin America." See Cheon, "The Limited Nuclear Weapon Free Zone in Northeast
Asia: Is It Feasible?" *The Mongolian Journal of International Affairs,* 14 (2007): 115,
http://www.google.com/url?sa=t&rct=j&q=the%20limited%20nuclear%20weapon
%20free%20zone%20in%20northeast%20asia%3A%20is%20it%20feasible
&source=web&cd=10&ved=0CGIQFjAJ&url=http%3A%2F%2Fjournals.sfu.ca
%2Fmongoliajol%2Findex.php%2FMJIA%2Farticle%2Fdownload%2F31%2F31&ei
=FrRoUM_1CeaZiAKPmIHYAg&usg=AFQjCNF3AKPQtXpEK97pNQshHqF6o9JA7w.

In early "3+3" proposals,[63] three nuclear-weapon states (the United States, China, and the Soviet Union) plus three non-nuclear-weapon states (North and South Korea, plus Japan) were proposed as parties. In 2010, the Nautilus Institute proposed a 3+2 version (starting with South Korea and Japan only, leaving an open door for North Korea to join later or collapse into the zone). Today, it seems sensible (and consistent with other zones) for all five NPT nuclear-weapon states to join and for at least four NPT non-nuclear-weapon states to join at the outset (Japan, South Korea, Mongolia, and possibly Canada)—and possibly North Korea in a contingent status (explained below). This "5 + 4.5," later "5+5" (ignoring Taiwan, see below) model of a Northeast Asian zone takes time (but not without limit) to fully integrate North Korea.

---

63. Endicott's fifteen-year series of workshops first proposed a thousand-kilometer range from the Korean DMZ that covered parts of Alaska, China, Mongolia, and Russia as well as Korea and Japan, and later an ellipse that covered northeastern China, Mongolia, the Russian Far East, part of Alaska, the two Koreas, Japan, and Taiwan at the southern end. See John E. Endicott, "Limited nuclear-weapon-free zones: the time has come," *Korean Journal of Defense Analysis* 20, no. 1 (2008): 17, http://dx.doi .org/10.1080/10163270802006305. Endicott's concept was reviewed critically by Cheon, "Limited Nuclear Weapon Free Zone": 106–115. The 3+3 concept is advanced by Hiromichi Umebayashi, "A Northeast Asia Nuclear-Weapon-Free Zone with a Three Plus Three Arrangement," East Asia Nuclear Security Workshop, Tokyo, November 2011, http://nautilus.wpengine.netdna-cdn.com/wp-content/uploads /2011/12/UMEBAYASHI---A-NEA-NWFZ-with-3-3-Arrangement-_2011--Tokyo_.pdf; and similarly, Kumao Kaneko, "Japan needs no umbrella," *Bulletin of the Atomic Scientists,* March/April 1996: 46–51, http://books.google.ca/books?id =ygwAAAAAMBAJ&printsec=frontcover&source=gbs_ge_summary_r&cad=0#v =onepage&q&f=false The first proposal for phased implementation of a 3+3 concept is found in Seongwhun Cheon and Tatsujiro Suzuki, "The Tripartite Nuclear-Weapon- Free Zone in Northeast Asia: a Long-Term Objective of the Six Party Talks," *International Journal of Korean Studies* 12, no. 2 (2003): 41–68, http://www.kinu.or .kr/eng/pub/pub_03_01.jsp?page=2&num=42&mode=view&field=&text=&order =&dir=&bid=DATA03&ses=&category=11. Nautilus's 3+2 concept was advanced in "Korea-Japan Nuclear Weapon Free Zone (KJNWFZ) Concept Paper," May 6, 2010, in English, Korean, and Japanese, http://nautilus.org/projects/by-name/korea -japan-nwfz.

This zone would require a stringent monitoring and verification regime satisfactory to all parties. At minimum, all non-nuclear-weapon states in the zone should accept the IAEA Additional Protocol. Specific monitoring and verification provisions would be needed during and after dismantlement in North Korea.[64] The North would also need to meet all the requirements of the IAEA to restore confidence in its nuclear weapons intentions, as has South Africa since it dismantled its nuclear weapons. Conversely, North Korea (and other parties) could demand inspection of US facilities in South Korea (perhaps reactivating the moribund 1992 Joint Denuclearization Declaration inspection mechanism) and Japan, with reciprocal challenge inspection rights in the North. Specific arrangements will be needed to control the North's nuclear weapons-capable personnel. Challenge inspections might be built into the treaty itself. Non-intrusive inspections of transiting ships and aircraft might use state-of-the-art anti-terrorist monitoring techniques at airfields and in ports but not in innocent oceanic or aerial transit. The treaty may want to invite parties to adopt more stringent inspection arrangements as technology evolves. For example, parties to a nuclear weapon-free zone could create a regional nuclear forensics network and database to control non-state actor nuclear proliferation. Also, plutonium-based fuel cycles, as in Japan and under discussion in Seoul, may require more stringent transparency in real time than current safeguard systems allow to preserve a meaningful diversion-detection-to-response-time ratio. The parties

---

64. There is extensive precedent in the case of South Africa, Iraq, and Libya for documenting such dismantlement. See David Albright and Corey Hinderstein, "Cooperative Verified Dismantlement of Nuclear Programs: An Eye Toward North Korea," June 1, 2003, http://isis-online.org/conferences/detail/cooperative-verified -dismantlement-of-nuclear-programs-an-eye-toward-north-/10 and Andre Buys, "Proliferation Risk Assessment of Former Nuclear Explosives/Weapons Program Personnel: The South African Case Study," University of Pretoria, South Africa, July 21, 2007, http://nautilus.org/wp-content/uploads/2012/01/Buys-research-report -final.pdf. Also see Buys, *Tracking nuclear capable individuals,* Nautilus Institute Workshop, April 4–5, 2011, Washington, DC, http://nautilus.wpengine.netdna-cdn .com/wp-content/uploads/2011/12/Tracking_Nuclear_Individuals_Buys.pdf.

may need to create a regional inspectorate, as has occurred in the Latin American nuclear weapon-free zone; or determine that noncompliance would be determined by the council governing a regional treaty of amity and cooperation; or refer noncompliance to the UN Security Council.

The existing toolkit of sanctions, interdiction, and coercive diplomacy combined with engagement may not suffice to maintain compliance with a Northeast Asian Nuclear Weapon-Free Zone. Nuclear threats against non-nuclear-weapon states by nuclear armed states should be met in accordance with the 1994 UN Security Council resolution whereby the nuclear states undertook to respond to "nuclear aggression" against non-nuclear-weapon states. A nuclear weapon-free zone places the legal onus on all nuclear-weapon states that are party to the zone to respond, not merely those in bilateral alliances (US-South Korea, US-Japan, China-North Korea). Thus, it provides non-nuclear-weapon states with a multilateral, legally-binding guarantee that they may invoke if they are subjected to nuclear threat or attack. States generally are loath to break treaties, and a treaty-based commitment is more likely to be observed than one based on unilateral or executive branch declaratory policies which may vary between administrations and even be abandoned overnight.

As was noted above, a nuclear weapon-free zone treaty must specify if the conference of parties is unable to resolve a dispute on how noncompliance should be dealt with. The options would be to refer noncompliance to a superordinate regional council if such is created concurrently as part of a regional treaty of amity and cooperation; or to the IAEA (if the matter relates to a nuclear fuel cycle activity); or directly to the UN Security Council if it relates directly to nuclear weapons acquisition, deployment, or threats by or aimed at non-nuclear-weapon states.

No monitoring and verification system will provide absolute confidence. No means of guaranteed enforcement of such a treaty is possible. What is important is whether sufficient confidence can be achieved that monitoring and verification systems will work and that enforcement

is credible. This confidence should be compared with the security outcomes and confidence associated with not controlling nuclear threat and
nuclear weapons via a Northeast Asian zone—not with an abstract ideal
world in which nuclear weapons simply do not exist.

It is worth emphasizing that such a zone would *not* end nuclear
extended deterrence although it would require South Korea and Japan
to recast their perceptions of what constitutes nuclear extended deterrence from a Cold War concept based on forward-deployed weapons
and instant nuclear retaliation to a post-Cold War concept that we termed
above as "nuclear existential deterrence." Should a state renege on its
commitments under such a treaty, then all the nuclear-weapon states are
committed to countering nuclear aggression. Should the transgression be
from North Korea either halting its denuclearization to comply with a
zone treaty or initiating a new breakout, then US guarantees to not use
nuclear threat or attack would be moot.[65]

Of course, as a self-declared nuclear-armed state, North Korea's
nuclear aggression[66] presents a major obstacle, albeit primarily political-

---

65. Actual arrangements between nuclear-weapon states and non-nuclear-weapon states
     vary from zone to zone. Jayantha Dhanapala argues that they cannot do so in
     Dhanapala, "NWFZS and Extended Nuclear Deterrence: Squaring the Circle?"
     NAPSNet Special Reports, May 1, 2012, http://nautilus.org/napsnet/napsnet-special
     -reports/nwfzs-and-extended-nuclear-deterrence-squaring-the-circle/. The experts
     cited in the 1975 United Nations study of nuclear-weapon-free zones split on
     whether nuclear deterrence could be extended to non-nuclear states who are party
     to such a zone. See *Comprehensive Study Of The Question Of Nuclear-Weapon-Free
     Zones In All Its Aspects,* Special report of the Conference of the Committee
     on Disarmament, http://www.un.org/disarmament/HomePage/ODAPublications
     /DisarmamentStudySeries/PDF/A-10027-Add1.pdf.

66. The phrase "nuclear aggression" is used deliberately, and refers to UNSC Resolution
     255 on June 19, 1968, which "Recognizes that aggression with nuclear weapons or
     the threat of such aggression against a non-nuclear-weapon State would create a
     situation in which the Security Council, and above all its nuclear-weapon State
     permanent members, would have to act immediately in accordance with their
     obligations under the United Nations Charter." This commitment was reaffirmed and
     strengthened in UNSC Resolution 984 on April 11, 1995, which states that nuclear-

psychological, rather than military, to realization of a Northeast Asian zone. However, the main reason to establish such a zone is not just to respond to Pyongyang, but also to address the proliferation potential of Japan, South Korea, and Taiwan and to create a stabilizing framework in which to manage strategic deterrence between the nuclear nations. The North should not be allowed to shape the strategic environment. Rather, a sound strategic environment should be created that shapes its choices. This approach requires that the United States revive its commitment to setting global geo-strategic goals and acting in concert with other great powers to implement game-changing strategies. The last time the United States did so in East Asia was when President George Bush unilaterally removed US forward-deployed non-strategic nuclear weapons in 1991.[67] It's time for the United States to revive its great-power diplomacy in a

---

armed members of the UNSC will also investigate and take measures to restore the situation, offer the victim technical, medical, scientific, or humanitarian assistance, and to recommend compensation under international law from the aggressor for loss, damage, or injury sustained as a result of the aggression. See "Programme for Promoting Nuclear Non-Proliferation," *Treaties, Agreements and other relevant documents,* vol. 2, 8th edition, 2000, chap. 6, "Security Assurances," http://www .ppnn.soton.ac.uk/bb2table.htm.

Since 2009, North Korea's nuclear threats arguably fall into the category of such aggression, as is argued by Peter Hayes and Scott Bruce, "North Korean Nuclear Nationalism and the Threat of Nuclear War in Korea" and "Supporting Online Material: North Korean Nuclear Statements (2002–2010)", May 17, 2011, http://nautilus.org/napsnet/napsnet-special-reports/supporting-online-material -north-korean-nuclear-statements-2002-2010. However, any nuclear threat, whether clinical or flamboyant, may be perceived as aggressive, especially (as was the case in the last *US Nuclear Posture Review*) where specific countries are named. It likely would be counterproductive to refer to nuclear aggression in a Northeast Asia NWFZ, and no other NWFZ treaty text has done so. (Source: Personal communication from Ambassador Thomas Graham to Peter Hayes, September 30, 2012.)

67. Susan J. Koch, "The Presidential Nuclear Initiatives of 1991–1992, WMD Case Study 5," Center for the Study of Weapons of Mass Destruction, US National Defense University, October 1, 2012, http://wmdcenter.dodlive.mil/2012/10/01 /wmd-case-study-5.

similar far-reaching manner instead of attempting to manage Pyongyang's bad behaviors at the margin.

In a legal sense, there are two ways to deal with North Korea in a Northeast Asian Nuclear Weapon-Free Zone treaty.[68] The first is to simply leave the door open for non-nuclear-weapon states to join the treaty. Thus, if only Japan, South Korea, Mongolia, and possibly Canada were to sign at the outset, the North could later join after denuclearization (or collapse into the South, making the issue moot). More desirably, it could join the Northeast Asian zone treaty at the outset, but not waive the provision that the treaty only come into force when all parties have ratified it, while the other parties would waive this provision.[69] North Korea thereby

---

68. There actually are three additional possibilities to the two provided in the text, all improbable: (1) the DPRK collapses into the ROK, at which point ROK obligations in a Northeast Asian nuclear weapons-free zone would cover the DPRK's nuclear weapons, which would be removed by the nuclear-weapons states and certified as gone by the IAEA; (2) the DPRK disarms first in some separate agreement, then joins the zone as a non-nuclear weapons state in full compliance already with its IAEA and NPT obligations—in this case, we don't need a zone to achieve denuclearization of the DPRK although it might be needed to sustain it, and also for non-DPRK nuclear risk management reasons in Northeast Asia, for example, the nuclear element of Sino-Japanese relations; (3) DPRK stays outside of the zone altogether, with or without nuclear weapons, but ROK and Japan implement it for their own security reasons, which is vanishingly improbable given their perceptions of DPRK and Chinese nuclear threats respectively. Thus, we ignore these three conceptual possibilities.

69. This approach is transposed from the Tlatelolco Treaty which established an ingenious and innovative legal mechanism by which reluctant states could be encouraged to join the zone at a later date. It consists of a provision in Article 28 (3) that allows a signatory state to "waive, wholly or in part" the requirements that have the effect of bringing the treaty into force for that state at a particular time. As Mexican diplomat Alfonso Garcia Robles noted in his commentary on Article 28: "An eclectic system was adopted, which, while respecting the viewpoints of all signatory States, prevented nonetheless any particular State from precluding the enactment of the treaty for those which would voluntarily wish to accept the statute of military denuclearization defined therein. The Treaty of Tlatelolco has thus contributed effectively to dispel the myth that for the establishment of a nuclear-weapon-free-zone it would be an essential requirement that all States of the region concerned should become, from the very outset, parties to the treaty establishing

would reaffirm its commitment to become a non-nuclear-weapons state in compliance with its NPT-IAEA obligations, but would take time to comply fully. The other non-nuclear-weapons states could set a time limit for this to happen and reserve the right to abandon the treaty if the North has not denuclearized sufficiently by that time. Concurrently, the nuclear armed states (hopefully all of them, not just the United States) would qualify their guarantees to not use nuclear weapons to attack the non-nuclear-weapons states party to the treaty so as to specifically exclude North Korea from the guarantee, or would calibrate their guarantee to the extent that it has come into full compliance.

In this manner, the North's nuclear armament, such as it is, would not be recognized as legitimate in any manner; the standards that it must meet when denuclearized would equal those for all non-nuclear-weapons states in the nuclear weapon-free zone, including monitoring and verification requirements; and, most important, North Korea would be offered a legally binding, multilateral guarantee by all the nuclear-weapons states that it will not face nuclear threat or the use of nuclear weapons against it. Based on North Korea's history and its weak strategic situation, we judge this benefit to be of great significance to it. The only way to find out how valuable this guarantee would be to the North is to engage it. Whether the executive branch could get such a treaty ratified by the US Senate is an open question; but even if it only signed but did not ratify the treaty for many years, over time the weight of precedent under international law as well as state practice will put increasing pressure on the United States to ratify the treaty, especially if US security goals in the region become intertwined with the successful operation of a nuclear weapons-free zone.

Designing, negotiating, and implementing a Northeast Asian zone would not be easy. Indeed, there are many difficult issues that would

---

the zone. In this way, the normative framework for a non-nuclear region can be established before all states are ready to actually implement the framework." See Michael Hamel-Green, "Implementing a Korea-Japan Nuclear-Weapon-Free Zone: Precedents, Legal Forms, Governance, Scope, Domain, Verification, Compliance and Regional Benefits," *Pacific Focus* 26, no. 1 (April 2011): 97–98, http://onlinelibrary.wiley.com/doi/10.1111/pafo.2011.26.issue-1/issuetoc.

require it to be tailored to the region's specific circumstances. Taiwan, for example, presents a special problem. However, it could solve this problem by declaring that it will fulfill the non-nuclear-weapons states' obligations in the treaty. China can declare that its commitment covers Taiwan as part of China (nuclear-weapons states have made such declarations in other zones with regard to trust territories). A zone that de facto includes Taiwan could reduce Pyongyang's leverage on China and the United States via the threat that it might share nuclear weapons with Taiwan or that it might attack the South in the midst of a Taiwan Straits crisis involving a US-China confrontation. However, Taiwan's participation in the regime as a non-member is not integral to the creation of the zone covering the core non-nuclear territories of Korea and Japan.

One key question for a Northeast Asian Nuclear Weapon-Free Zone is whether the nuclear armed states should impose on their own territory a geographic restriction on deployment of nuclear-armed ground-launched ballistic and cruise missiles in a verifiable zone as part of the nuclear weapon-free zone—in effect, the price charged by the United States and Russia to China for delivering Japan, South Korea, and, de facto, Taiwan into a nuclear weapon-free zone. Another is whether nuclear fuel cycle cooperation should be included as part of the treaty or as a separate set of parallel side agreements (some regional in scope, some likely DPRK-specific). A third question is whether a parallel agreement on a regional space launch cooperation program under the regional security settlement treaty would facilitate Japanese, South Korean, and North Korean commitment to a Northeast Asian zone.

Other important questions include whether side agreements are needed to restrain arms races with offensive conventional weapons that undermine strategic stability and even restore the threat of mass destruction—only, this time, by non-nuclear weapons; whether a Northeast Asian zone would commit nuclear-weapons states to not fire nuclear weapons out of a zone, not just to not station them in the zone or to transit them through via innocent passage; and what provisions for emergency redeployment, as apparently exist in the case of Japan and were implied in the 1991 withdrawal, would be allowed. (Otherwise, wittingly or unwittingly, a non-nuclear-weapons state can become party to nuclear threat or nuclear use, transgressing its non-nuclear status to other parties of the treaty.)

Also, does a Northeast Asian zone precede or follow from a comprehensive security settlement? How would a Northeast Asian zone complement adjacent zones, and how would it facilitate a Middle East nuclear weapon-free zone (and vice versa) as part of a global nuclear abolition enterprise that builds a global mosaic of such zones?

Although a Northeast Asian zone is likely the only way now that Pyongyang could denuclearize safely, and would present all regional states with an improved security environment, a comprehensive security settlement framework of which a nuclear weapon-free zone is only part is consistent with some of the possible regional futures. These are a "business-as-usual" competitive-cooperative future regional order in which the United States exercises leadership, a cooperative democratic liberal regional order (in which China has become a democratic as well as a market state), and a Sino-US condominium.

To succeed, a comprehensive security settlement framework achieved in any of these possible regional orders requires US leadership and a joint vision with all the states in the region, most importantly with China. It offers the United States and China a common security objective that, while tough to realize, is achievable. And it offers an engagement opportunity for the United States and China to work together in a way that provides diplomatic and economic collaboration to match the military-led US rebalancing.

A number of pathways can be envisioned whereby such a zone might be brought into existence. One plausible process would entail taking the following steps to activate a regional dialogue:

- North and South Korea renew their support for a nuclear weapon-free Korean Peninsula.
- Japan, Mongolia, and possibly Canada declare jointly that they will join North and South Korea in a treaty that will establish a Northeast Asian nuclear weapon-free zone and accept stringent

monitoring and verification common to all nations that are parties
to the zone.

- China, Russia, and the United States declare that each of them will
sign and seek to ratify a protocol to that treaty which will commit
each of them to act in accordance with the terms of that treaty's
provisions regarding stationing and transfer of nuclear weapons,
and which also will extend assurances to the parties regarding
non-use of nuclear weapons against any of them. The protocol
would also state that existing defense commitments between the
nuclear-weapon states and the non-nuclear-weapon states would
not be affected by this protocol. The protocol might also commit
the nuclear-weapon states to join in a negotiation to expedite the
reduction of the nuclear threat, and outline the calibration of these
assurances to the degree to which state parties covered by the
zone have disarmed and are in compliance with their NPT and
IAEA obligations (that is, North Korea).

- While negotiations are proceeding pursuant to this agreed framework, two other working groups, appropriately configured as to
membership, would begin negotiations on arrangements to replace
the 1953 armistice agreement and to normalize relations between
North and South Korea.[70]

Although American leadership and the exercise of great power is critical to realize a constructive outcome that overcomes the threat of nuclear
proliferation and reduces the risk of nuclear war in the region, South
Korea as a middle power is well-positioned not only to prompt the United
States to lead in this manner, but also to exploit its location in regional
interstate relationships to conceptualize and promote a comprehensive
security settlement strategy with each of the six parties and with other
partners such as the European Union, Mongolia, Canada, the members
of the Association of Southeast Asian Nations, and Australia. Thus, some

---

70. We are grateful for James Goodby's suggestions in this regard.

South Koreans believe that the four steps outlined above might be best kick-started by a six-party summit of heads of state.

Conclusion

Koreans have a special understanding of nuclear weapons due to the tens of thousands of Koreans who perished in Hiroshima on August 6, 1945.[71] This appreciation is not pacifist in nature, as in the Japanese Left after World War II, or the unilateral disarmament movement in Europe during the Cold War. Many Koreans who survived the nuclear bombing at Hiroshima wished that the United States had used more nuclear weapons at that time to punish the Japanese for crimes against Koreans in the colonial period and the war effort. This experience gives Koreans insight into the absolute nature of nuclear weapons that is unmatched in most societies.

Koreans on both sides of the DMZ have also spent decades observing carefully the political and military strategies and operational doctrines employed by the nuclear-weapon states in the exercise of great power. Neither Korea can emulate any of these strategies. They are too small and vulnerable to become nuclear-weapon states with secure retaliatory forces. As Robert Zarate observed recently, even the British gave up an independent missile force and the French nuclear bombers were aptly called Mirage.[72] Many small and medium states have looked over the nuclear precipice, pulled back, and committed themselves to non-nuclear national narratives. The sky did not fall down, their economies and soci-

71. See Peter Hayes, "Pikaton," chap. 17 in *Pacific Powderkeg: American Nuclear Dilemmas in Korea* (Lexington, MA: Lexington Books, 1990), 241ff., http://nautilus .org/wp-content/uploads/2011/04/PacificPowderkegbyPeterHayes.pdf.

72. Robert Zarate, "America's Allies and Nuclear Arms: Assessing the Geopolitics of Nonproliferation in Asia," Foreign Policy Institute, May 6, 2014, http://www .foreignpolicyi.org/content/america%E2%80%99s-allies-and-nuclear-arms -assessing-geopolitics-nonproliferation-asia.

eties became highly developed and secure, and, in the case of Germany, reunification was achieved without war. Israel is the sole exception to this rule; but the two Koreas may have more ability to establish a modus vivendi and eventual peaceful rapprochement and even reunification than Israel does facing its neighbors.

The division of Korea, the failure of the great powers to achieve a political settlement of the Korean War, American inability to deal with Pyongyang's demands in a way acceptable to Washington and Seoul, and the spiraling internal crisis that grips the DPRK today all present South Korea with immense security challenges at a national, regional, and global level. In contrast to the outrageous nuclear threats issued by the North since 2006, the South has exhibited a mostly calm, reasoned, and proportionate non-nuclear response while situating itself in global and regional diplomacy as a friendly, desirable contributor to global and regional security. Most of the gains from two decades of investing in profoundly non-nuclear credentials and reputation would be lost immediately if the South were to match the North's primitive nuclear tactics (we hesitate to elevate its behavior to the level of strategy).

In short, we believe that most South Koreans are too smart to fall for the fairytale of a nuclear-armed future. Nuclear fantasies are a poor substitute for developing real political and military strategies to deal with the reality of Kim Jong Un's regime. South Korea's work is already cut out to implement fully its non-nuclear strategy and national narrative. We see no reason to abandon this path.

North Korea presents an enormous challenge to South Korea in this passage. But in time, even that threat is likely to fade away. Either at the outset, as a foundation on which this outcome is achieved, or as an end result whereby the regional strategic environment will be more conducive to reducing the role played by nuclear weapons in interstate relations in this region, a regional nuclear weapon-free zone seems a necessary (albeit not sufficient) means whereby this non-nuclear security system will be built in Northeast Asia. Meanwhile, South Koreans should be content to rely on the existing arrangement whereby conventional extended deterrence is buttressed, slightly, by nuclear extended deterrence in its current diluted form, as sufficient to countervail North Korea's nuclear threats. This is more effective and safer than obtaining an independent nuclear force or redeploying American nuclear weapons in Korea.

If South Koreans stay their non-nuclear course, therefore, they will contribute a cornerstone of the new security architecture that eliminates nuclear weapons not only from East Asia but from the whole world. To take this path will require an independent South Korean vision of a peaceful, non-nuclear peninsula and regional security framework. Many factors in domestic South Korean politics and dependency on the US-ROK alliance work against such a possibility. Equally, South Koreans understand that they have the most to lose in the current conflict and the most to gain from its peaceful settlement. That a pathway to a non-nuclear future in Korea can be visualized puts the onus on Koreans to find the pathway to that future, however difficult or unlikely it appears from the vantage of the present.

CHAPTER 14 **Japan's Disarmament Dilemma: Between the Moral Commitment and the Security Reality**

Nobumasa Akiyama

Introduction

Japan's attitude toward nuclear disarmament is often perceived as ambiguous, caught between a moralistic view on nuclear weapons and the reality of today's security environment. On the one hand, Japan claims a destiny as a strong advocate of total elimination of nuclear weapons as the only nation to experience nuclear attacks. On the other hand, in reality, Japan's security policy has relied on the United States' extended deterrence, including nuclear deterrence. Throughout its post-war history, Japan has reinforced its alliance with the United States in part to deter aggression by nuclear-armed states and to maintain stability in the East Asian security environment. Meanwhile, Japan has been extensively pursuing its nuclear energy program, including a nuclear fuel cycle program. Japan's uranium enrichment and reprocessing capabilities have been seen by outsiders as latent capabilities to develop its own nuclear weapons. Given a deteriorating political and security environment in East Asia, some observers believe that Japan could go nuclear at home and abroad.[1]

---

1. See, for example, Mark Erikson, "Japan Could 'Go Nuclear' in Months," *Asia Times*, January 14, 2003, http://www.atimes.com/atimes/Japan/EA14Dh01.html, and Oren

These contradictions puzzle outsiders and pose a dilemma for Japan's foreign and security policymakers.

This chapter addresses the question of Japan's posture toward nuclear disarmament by exploring the interactions among regional security dynamics, a global trend of nuclear disarmament norms, and the domestic social and political foundations of the policy. The conclusion is that a non-nuclear option is the rational strategic choice, not just an emotional choice based on history. This chapter also addresses Japan's view of the security environment in East Asia and the role of nuclear weapons in it, providing the basis for properly addressing the nuclear proliferation risk, an obstacle for nuclear disarmament. Finally, we consider how to narrow the gap between the two positions—morality and reality—so that Japan can contribute to the goal of realizing a world free of nuclear weapons.

Japan's Disarmament Dilemma

Emergence of Japan's Disarmament Dilemma

In this section, we have an overview of how Japan's disarmament dilemma is positioned between its domestic political environment, with its nuclear taboo, and the East Asian security environment.

The vast majority of Japanese oppose a nuclear option. "Japan as the first victim of the atomic bomb" is a frequent introduction to official and private statements describing Japan's position on nuclear issues including peaceful use programs and disarmament efforts. Japanese point to the fates of Hiroshima and Nagasaki and of the *Daigo Fukuryu-maru* (Lucky Dragon No. 5), a fishing boat exposed to nuclear fallout in 1954 after a test by the United States at Bikini Atoll, as their moral authority for advocating nuclear disarmament.

Dorell, "Some suggest S. Korea should go nuclear," *USA Today*, March 11 2013, http://www.usatoday.com/story/news/world/2013/03/11/south-korea-thinks-nuclear/1979051/.

Until now, the Japanese public has maintained a strong sentiment against nuclear weapons. According to a 2010 survey, 79 percent of respondents opposed a nuclear option.[2] It is a clear contrast to the number shown on a survey in South Korea, which is located in a similar security environment. The survey conducted there by The Asan Institute for Policy Studies showed that 66 percent of respondents supported the development of a nuclear weapons program, a 10 percent increase from 2010.[3] While 68 percent of the Japanese feel more threatened by China,[4] the largest nuclear-weapon state in the region, this threat perception hasn't led Japan to a nuclear option, an indication of how strong the nuclear taboo is among the Japanese public.

This public attitude has affected politicians' discourse on a nuclear option. Former prime minister Yasuhiro Nakasone, who is often described as a nationalist, conservative politician, repeatedly denied a nuclear option, given that the US-Japan alliance would continue. Current Prime Minister Shinzo Abe said at the Budget Committee of the Japanese House of Representatives in October 2006, in his previous term, that Japan did not have an option to possess nuclear weapons at all and that the Three Non-Nuclear Principles would not be changed.[5] The Japanese Diet passed a resolution of the Three Non-Nuclear Principles—namely, not to possess, not to produce, and not to introduce nuclear weapons—in

2. Kumiko Nishi, "Genbaku toka kara 65 nen–Kienu kaku no kyoi" (65 years since the dropping of atomic bombs: nuclear threats not yet vanished), *Hosokenyu to Chosa* (Research and investigation on broadcasting), October 2010, http://www.nhk.or.jp /bunken/summary/research/report/2010_10/101005.pdf.

3. Kim Jiyoon and Karl Friedhoff, "The Fallout: South Korean Public Opinion Following North Korea's Third Nuclear Test," issue brief 46, February 24, 2013, The Asan Institute for Policy Studies, http://en.asaninst.org/contents/issue-brief-no-46-the-fallout -south-korean-public-opinion-following-north-koreas-third-nuclear-test.

4. Pew Research Global Attitudes Project, "How Asians View Each Other," July 14, 2014, http://www.pewglobal.org/2014/07/14/chapter-4-how-asians-view-each-other.

5. *Kokkai Kaigi-roku (The Diet Record),* Shugiin Yosan-iinkai (the Budget Committee of the House of Representatives), 165th Session of the Diet, October 10, 2006.

November 1971.[6] Despite their hawkish images, Nakasone and Abe have affirmed a non-nuclear policy in their official statements. By contrast, in 1999 the parliamentary vice minister for defense, Shingo Nishimura, who suggested the possibility of a Japanese nuclear option, was dismissed, as his statement was in contradiction with official government policy. Other politicians, such as Shintaro Ishihara, former governor of Tokyo and a former member of the House of Representatives, were severely criticized for their arguments suggesting a nuclear option for Japan.

In the meantime, Japan's security policy has relied on the role of nuclear weapons through the US-Japan alliance. Along with Japan's own conventional defense capability, Japan's security policy has consisted of reinforcing its alliance with the United States, in which US extended deterrence, including its nuclear element, played an important role in deterring potential aggression or other offensive actions by nuclear-armed states. The Japanese security policy establishment holds a long-standing consensus that there is no plausible scenario in which developing nuclear weapons would be advantageous. However, Japan's pursuit of nuclear disarmament greatly depends on the role that nuclear weapons play in the regional security environment in East Asia and on how nuclear weapons figure in America's strategic calculations at global and regional levels.

Globally, arms control efforts are hobbled by disagreements between the United States and Russia over the agenda for the next round of arms control after New START, as well as the great divide between the two due to Russia's actions in Crimea and involvement in violence in Ukraine.[7] Other nuclear-armed states—including China, the United Kingdom, France, and non-NPT states such as India, Pakistan, Israel, and North Korea—have not been engaged in any arms control or reduction

---

6. The resolution on the Three Non-Nuclear Principles was adopted as a supplementary resolution attached to a resolution on the return of the Ryukyu Islands (or Okinawa) and Daito Islands. The return of the Ryukyu Islands and Daito Islands was the most important disputed issue between Japan and the United States at that time.

7. Russia's action could be seen as a violation of the Budapest Memorandum on Security Assurances.

negotiations. (The United Kingdom recently announced that it would unilaterally reduce its nuclear arsenal as low as 150.) Furthermore, threats of nuclear proliferation and nuclear terrorism have not diminished. Iran poses a daunting threat, and the potential threat of spreading sensitive nuclear technology through illicit trade to state and non-state actors remains. As President Obama mentioned in his speech in Prague, the total elimination of nuclear weapons may not be realized in our lifetime.[8]

In East Asia, almost all major players possess military or civilian nuclear capabilities, or both. China, the largest nuclear power in the region, has become more assertive toward its neighbors. Although China's economic growth benefits its neighbors and the rest of the world, its increasing assertiveness in border and maritime disputes raises grave concerns. The US Defense Department reported that China has modernized its nuclear arsenal and expanded its conventional military capability, with military budgets growing by 9.4 percent annually from 2004 through 2013.[9] The modernization of Chinese maritime and air capabilities—including anti-access/area-denial (A2/AD) capabilities and an upgrade of its nuclear arsenal, with the introduction of Jin-class strategic nuclear submarines with ballistic missile-launching capability—could potentially undermine US power projection capability and threaten the status quo regional balance of power. Negotiations on the denuclearization of North Korea are at a standstill, and North Korea's nuclear threats, combined with uncertainties about its political and security actions, place Japan in a position of continued reliance on US extended deterrence.

Japan has been unable to establish a sound political confidence with South Korea and China, these relationships being overshadowed by recent history. Although the history issue has not become a major point

---

8. "Remarks by President Barack Obama," Hradcany Square, Prague, Czech Republic, April 5, 2009, http://www.whitehouse.gov/the_press_office/Remarks-By-President-Barack-Obama-In-Prague-As-Delivered.

9. Department of Defense, "Annual Report to Congress: Military and Security Developments Involving the People's Republic of China 2014": 43.

of contention in relationships with other Asian countries, including Australia, India, and the nations of Southeast Asia, the fact that the current government of Japan has not been successful in establishing trustworthy relationships with South Korea and China is seen to pose political risks to the rest of Asia and the United States, and to potentially constitute a basis for suspecting Japan's intentions on its nuclear policy.

Thus, changing configurations of the security environment in East Asia may widen a gap between the moralistic position that the Japanese try to maintain on nuclear disarmament discourse and the security policy reality that Japan has to face.

Japan's Disarmament Diplomacy in Multilateral Forums

Multilateral forums are platforms that the Japanese government has been utilizing for promoting its nuclear disarmament advocacy. Until 2014, Japan had submitted to the United Nations General Assembly, for twenty-one years in a row, a resolution requesting the total elimination of nuclear weapons.[10] Japan has been comfortably able to promote nuclear disarmament from the moralistic high ground. However, the global trend over the past decade has made Japan's position more complicated.

An essay written by the "Four Statesmen" for the *Wall Street Journal* in 2007[11] created momentum for nuclear disarmament. It was echoed by world leaders[12] and followed by a joint effort by Australia and Japan in

---

10. Press release by the Ministry of Foreign Affairs of Japan on the adoption by the UN General Assembly of resolutions on nuclear disarmament and small arms trade, December 3, 2014 (in Japanese), http://www.mofa.go.jp/mofaj/press/release/press4_001535.html.

11. George P. Shultz, William J. Perry, Henry A. Kissinger, and Sam Nunn, "A World Free of Nuclear Weapons," *Wall Street Journal,* January 4, 2007, http://online.wsj.com/articles/SB116787515251566636.

12. See also, Mikhail Gorbachev, "The Nuclear Threat," *Wall Street Journal,* January 31, 2007, http://online.wsj.com/news/articles/SB117021711101593402?mg=reno64-wsj&url=http%3A%2F%2Fonline.wsj.com%2Farticle%2FSB117021711101593402.html; Douglas Hurd, Malcolm Rifkind, David Owen, and George Robertson, "Start worrying and learn to ditch the bomb," *The Times,* June 30, 2008; and Helmut

2008 to create an International Commission on Nuclear Nonproliferation and Disarmament.[13] President Obama's historic speech in Prague in 2009 firmly consolidated a trend of pursuing the goal of a world free of nuclear weapons.[14] Agreement over the US-Russia New START treaty in 2010 reaffirmed the commitment of the Obama administration to nuclear disarmament.[15] Following this trend, the 2010 NPT Review Conference referred to the humanitarian dimension of nuclear weapons for the first time, and a global trend of nuclear disarmament seemed to be consolidated.

However, Japan's dilemma is amplified in multilateral disarmament diplomacy, with the rising debate on the humanitarian dimension of nuclear weapons. The humanitarian issue has been debated in various forums, including NPT Review Conferences. In 1996, in response to resolutions adopted by the World Health Organization and the United Nations General Assembly, the International Court of Justice issued an advisory opinion on the Legality of the Threat or Use of Nuclear Weapons. It said that "the threat or use of nuclear weapons would generally be contrary to the rules of international law applicable in armed conflict, and in particular the principles and rules of humanitarian law."[16] But the subsequent description with regard to situations of self-defense, where the very survival of a state was at stake, allowed the justification of use or threat of use of nuclear weapons.

Schmidt, Richard von Weizsäcker, Hans-Dietrich Genscher, and Egon Bahr, "Toward a nuclear-free world: a German view," *New York Times,* January 9, 2009, http://www.nytimes.com/2009/01/09/opinion/09iht-edschmidt.1.19226604.html?_r=0.

13. For details, see home page of ICNND, http://www.icnnd.org/Pages/default.aspx.

14. "Remarks by President Barack Obama," April 5, 2009.

15. For the New START, see US State Department, http://www.state.gov/t/avc/newstart/index.htm.

16. International Court of Justice, "Legality of the Threat or Use of Nuclear Weapons," advisory opinion, July 8, 1996, http://www.icj-cij.org/docket/files/95/7497.pdf. In the deliberation process of this case, mayors of Hiroshima and Nagasaki, along with government representatives, made oral opinion statements.

The 2010 NPT Review Conference, for the first time, referred to human-itarian concerns in its final document.[17] The Conference on the Humani-tarian Impact of Nuclear Weapons held its first meeting in Oslo in March 2013, the second one in Nayarit, Mexico, in February 2014, and the third one in Vienna in December 2014. The international community is still divided over whether this momentum should be further directed toward the establishment of a nuclear weapons convention, which would comprehensively prohibit use, possession, production, or other activi-ties related to nuclear weapons. Japan, which is likely to be affected by the consequences of the humanitarian debate on nuclear weapons, dis-patched a delegation of government and civil society representatives to these conferences.

Japan's dilemma is symbolically seen in the government's 2013 deci-sion to join two similar, but different, joint statements on the humanitar-ian consequences of nuclear weapons. One statement sponsored by New Zealand, with more than a hundred cosponsors, stated that it was "in the interest of the very survival of humanity that nuclear weapons are never used again, *under any circumstances* (emphasis added)."[18] Another spon-sored by Australia, and joined by seventeen states, mostly allies of the United States, noted the importance of recognizing the security dimen-sion as well as the humanitarian one in the nuclear weapons debate.[19] The difference between the two statements is whether to consider the

17. 2010 NPT Review conference, "Final Document," http://www.un.org/ga/search /view_doc.asp?symbol=NPT/CONF.2010/50%20(VOL.I) .

18. UNGA 68: First Committee, "Joint Statement on the Humanitarian Consequences of Nuclear Weapons," delivered by Ambassador Dell Higgle of New Zealand, October 21, 2013, http://www.un.org/disarmament/special/meetings/firstcommittee/68/pdfs /TD_21-Oct_CL-1_New_Zealand-(Joint_St).

19. UNGA 68: First Committee, "Joint statement on the humanitarian consequence of nuclear weapons," delivered by Ambassador Peter Woolcott of Australia, at UNGA68 First Committee, October 21, 2013, http://www.un.org/disarmament/special /meetings/firstcommittee/68/pdfs/TD_21-Oct_CL-1_Australia-%28Joint%20St %29.pdf.

security dimension of nuclear weapons, implying that the use of nuclear weapons shouldn't be denied when the very survival of the state is at stake. Japan was the only state that signed both statements. The Japanese government had not supported a similar joint statement sponsored by New Zealand the previous year, saying that non-use "under any circumstances" might contradict its security policy, as that phrase could deny the effectiveness of US extended nuclear deterrence. In 2013, the Ministry of Foreign Affairs explained the reversal of the decision by noting that the New Zealand-sponsored statement acknowledged that awareness of the catastrophic consequences of nuclear weapons must *underpin all approaches and efforts* toward nuclear disarmament, which could by implication include step-by-step approaches that Japan supported.[20] This awkward situation shows the dilemma embedded in Japan's multilateral diplomacy for nuclear disarmament.

Consolidating the Domestic Foundation of Japan's Disarmament Policy

Institutionalizing the Nuclear Taboo

This section reviews occasions during which some Japanese have discussed the possibility of developing nuclear weapons and describes the arguments that have led most Japanese to the conclusion that the nuclear option is neither practical nor wise. In order to properly frame a complex (and sometimes self-contradicting) picture of Japan's disarmament policy, it is essential to portray the domestic socio-political foundation of Japan's posture toward nuclear disarmament, in which the no-nukes mentality has been institutionalized into the Three Non-Nuclear Principles. The major elements of the socio-political foundation of Japan's posture

---

20.   Japanese Ministry of Foreign Affairs comment on "joint statement on humanitarian consequences of nuclear weapons" (in Japanese), October 22, 2013, http://www .mofa.go.jp/mofaj/press/page4_000254.html.

toward nuclear disarmament combines a strong sentiment against nuclear weapons at the grass-roots level with strategic calculations on the cost and benefits of nuclear weapons for Japan's security. Discussion in this section shows how the resilience of the non-nuclear norm in Japan was established in the midst of changes in the strategic environment.

As Japan experienced changes in its strategic environment and as concerns over security policy rose, there were voices for a nuclear option. But eventually, Japan chose to consolidate its non-nuclear policy. Such action often came with the consolidation of the US-Japan alliance and reaffirmation of alliance commitments from both sides.

Undoubtedly, Japanese public antipathy to nuclear weapons originated from the harsh experiences of Hiroshima and Nagasaki. Then the *Daigo Fukuryu-maru* incident in March 1954 and resulting casualties helped this anti-nuclear sentiment become a national movement against nuclear weapons. A grass-roots movement by a housewives' reading society against atomic and hydrogen bombs that began just after the incident rapidly developed into a nationwide movement. By the end of 1954, more than twenty million signatures had been collected.

The movement led to the formation of a nationwide anti-nuclear organization, the *Gensuikyo* (the Japan Council Against A and H Bombs) in 1955, which addressed support for victims of atomic bombs. The establishment of the *Gensuikyo* helped the experiences of Hiroshima and Nagasaki to be perceived by many Japanese as a national tragedy caused by nuclear weapons. The movement played a catalytic role in translating experiences and memories of only a part of the nation into a national experience and memory.[21]

While under the "Atoms for Peace" initiative the US and Japanese governments were discussing the introduction of peaceful uses of nuclear

---

21. Osamu Fujiwara, *Gensuibaku Kinshi Undo no Seiritsu: Sengo Nihon Heiwa Undo no Genzo 1954–1955* (The establishment of nuclear abolition movement: the origin of peace movement in post-war Japan, 1954–1955) (Tokyo: PRIME, Meiji Gakuin University, 1991).

energy into Japan, this big social movement against nuclear weapons naturally turned into a political issue. In April 1955, both the House of Representatives and the House of Councilors passed a resolution urging the international management of atomic energy and the prohibition of nuclear weapons. The proposal states, "We are the only nation in the world that knows the fear of nuclear weapons. Hence our nation has a reason to possess the sublime obligation to save the human race from the destruction by nuclear weapons, and have the largest voice on it."[22] This resolution marked the beginning of a process of consolidating and institutionalizing the "nuclear taboo" into Japanese politics.[23]

In 1958, Prime Minister Nobusuke Kishi said Japan would hold a policy not to possess any nuclear weapons, interpreting the constitution as allowing possession of nuclear weapons for defense.[24] While Kishi is famous for revising the US-Japan Security Treaty, correcting the inequality in 1960, he reaffirmed a non-nuclear policy in the same year, saying that Japan would not have nuclear weapons and would not let nuclear weapons be introduced.[25]

---

22. *The Diet Record,* Plenary Session, House of Representatives, the 19th Session, vol. 32, p. 2, April 2, 1954.

23. Ironically, when politics became involved in the anti-nuclear movement, the decline and split of the movement started. The anti-nuclear movement involved a wide spectrum of political forces ranging from communists to conservatives in the beginning. But such politicization later caused the split of the movement. The public did not want to be involved in ideological confrontations among political parties. The movement was successful at its initial stages because it eschewed any political elements, which made it possible to rally the masses to collectively support the anti-nuclear posture. In other words, by possessing particular political and ideological propensities, these organizations lost their function as a mechanism to convert widespread public sentiment into a political force.

24. *The Diet Record,* the Diet Committee, House of Councilors, the 28th Session, vol. 30, p. 18, April 18, 1958.

25. *The Diet Record,* the Special Committee on Japan-US Security Treaty, House of Representatives, the 34th Session, vol. 29, pp. 20–21, April 19, 1960.

In 1967, Prime Minister Eisaku Sato said, "We have clearly said that we do not produce, possess, nor allow to introduce nuclear weapons" during deliberations on a bill on the reversion of Okinawa to Japanese administrative control, where the issue of American possession of nuclear weapons in Okinawa was critical.[26] This strong no-nukes position was further consolidated by the Diet resolution on the Three Non-Nuclear Principles and non-nuclear Okinawa in 1971. And Prime Minister Sato issued a statement to affirm that his government would comply with the Principles.[27]

Japan's Non-Nuclear Option under Challenges: Japan's Strategic Choice

It should be noted that these commitments to a non-nuclear policy were made in spite of a major change in the strategic landscape in East Asia, namely China's acquisition of nuclear weapons capability, which was demonstrated by a successful nuclear test in Xinjiang Province in October 1964, while the Tokyo Olympic Games were being held. In 1966, a Dongfu 2 missile with a nuclear warhead was successfully delivered and exploded at a testing site. In the following year, China conducted its first hydrogen bomb test, which also turned out to be successful. This made China the fifth nuclear power in the world. Furthermore, in 1971, the government of the People's Republic of China (mainland China) replaced the Republic of China (Taiwan) as representing China in the United Nations and became a permanent member of the Security Council.

Although there were voices arguing for Japan's nuclear option to counter China's acquisition of nuclear weapons,[28] this didn't become a

---

26. *The Diet Record,* the Budget Committee, House of Representatives, the 57th Session, vol. 2, p.18, December 11, 1967.

27. *The Diet Record,* Plenary Session of the House of Representatives, the 67th Session, vol. 18, p. 20, November 24, 1971 (in Japanese).

28. Shintaro Ishihara, "Hikaku no Shinwa wa Kieta" (Myth of the Non-Nuclear Posture Disappeared), *Shokun,* October 1970: 22–40.

mainstream argument. The Japanese society wanted to maintain a relationship with China which could lead to a future rapprochement (which was not realized until the United States made a surprise rapprochement in 1972), and the government only expressed its regret.

Such a choice was based not only on a simple anti-nuclear mentality or the "nuclear taboo," but on profound political and strategic calculations. In December 1964, Sato expressed his personal view on the nuclear option to US Ambassador Edwin O. Reischauer, "stating his views coincided with those expressed to him by British PM Wilson that if other fellow had nuclears it was only common sense to have them oneself."[29] But at the same time, he was aware of a strong sentiment among the Japanese against nuclear weapons. Asked by Secretary of State Dean Rusk about the magnitude of change in Japanese public opinion due to China's nuclear test, Sato replied that the majority of Japanese felt that Japan should never possess nuclear weapons because of strong national anti-nuclear sentiment and the sense of security provided by the United States.[30] Certainly, the "nuclear taboo" had an impact on Sato's political calculation.

Meanwhile, in the late 1960s, upon China's nuclear acquisition, the Japanese government secretly examined the possibility of a nuclear option. The Minshushugi Kenkyukai, or Study Group on Democracy, completed the first part of a secret report in 1968 and the second part in 1970.[31] The first part reviewed technical and economic issues and the second

---

29. US State Department, "Foreign Relations of the United States, 1964–1968," vol. 29, document 37, "Telegram from the Embassy in Japan to the Department of State," December 29, 1964, https://history.state.gov/historicaldocuments/frus1964-68v29p2/d37#fn1.

30. Some argue that Sato's comments were intended to strengthen US commitment of its extended nuclear deterrence, rather than to express interest in a national nuclear option. See Mikio Haruna, "Itsuwari no heiwashugi-sha 'Sato Eisaku'" (Sato Eisaku as a forged pacifist), *Gekkan Gendai,* September 2008.

31. Minshushugi Kenkyukai was entrusted to commission a report by the Cabinet Information Research Office (Naikaku Chosa Shitsu).

part examined strategic, diplomatic, and political aspects of a nuclear option. The report concluded that Japan arming itself with nuclear weapons would cause a tremendous negative impact in international politics and the effectiveness of national security would significantly decrease.[32] Although it is not clear to what extent this internal report affected the actual decision on Japan's nuclear option, it is important to note that this analysis was shared within the political community surrounding the prime minister's office. It was not publicized because of three reasons: strong anti-nuclear sentiments among the Japanese public, the prospect of the renewal of the US-Japan security treaty, and concerns about hysterical responses from the Japanese media.[33]

Several other people expressed rationalist views against the nuclear option. Among them were Ambassador Atsuhiko Yatabe, who indicated the irrationality of Japan competing with China in nuclear armament,[34] and Nakasone Yasuhiro, then minister of state for defense. Nakasone revealed in his autobiography that, as minister for defense, he had concluded that although Japan was capable of possessing nuclear weapons, in reality, it would be impossible because there was no chance of securing a testing site in its territory.[35] In the meantime, Japan made an international legal commitment to forgo a nuclear option by signing the Nuclear Non-Proliferation Treaty (NPT) in 1970.[36]

---

32. Minshushugi Kenkyukai, "Nihon no kaku seisaku ni kansuru kenkyu" (Research on Japan's Nuclear Policy), vol. 2, 1970.

33. Yuri Kase, "The Costs and Benefits of Japan's Nuclearization: An Insight into the 1968/70 Internal Report," *The Nonproliferation Review,* Summer 2001: 55–68.

34. Atsuhiko Yatabe, *Kakuheiki Fukakusan Joyaku Ron* (On the Nuclear Non-Proliferation Treaty) (Tokyo: Yushindo, 1971), 193.

35. Nakasone Yasuhiro, *Jisei roku: Rekishi hotei no hikoku toshite* (On self-reflection: as a defendant of a court of history) (Tokyo: Shinchosha, 2004).

36. It should be noted that it took six years for Japan to ratify at the Diet. There were cautious views on the unequal nature of the treaty (in particular vis-à-vis China) and the potential restriction of peaceful use of nuclear technology.

The strong public antipathy to nuclear weapons can be characterized as a nuclear allergy, implying that the people do not make a choice
on nuclear policy following a thorough debate on the pros and cons of
a nuclear option. Proponents of a nuclear option complain that a nuclear
taboo inhibits any debate on the subject and suggest sarcastically that
the Three Non-Nuclear Principles should be *four* non-nuclear principles,
including a prohibition on debating nuclear weapons.

If the nuclear taboo in Japan were solely drawn from such an allergy,
Japan's non-nuclear choice would have a rather fragile foundation.
However, in reality, as seen above, Japan's non-nuclear choice in the
1960s and 1970s did not simply come from public sentiment but was
derived from strategic considerations. These rational strategic considerations provide a resilient foundation for Japan's non-nuclear posture. Even
in the midst of the recent deterioration of its political relationship with
China, Japan did not react to such a dramatic change of the strategic
landscape. It chose to reaffirm and strengthen its alliance with the United
States, rather than seek national nuclear capability.

Another official study on Japan's nuclear option was conducted by the
Japan Defense Agency (JDA—currently, Ministry of Defense) in 1995.[37]
The JDA report argued that the existential threats to the United States
from other nuclear-weapon states were gone, and it was unthinkable
for the United States to use nuclear weapons. With regard to China, the
report argued that there was virtually no possibility of a military conflict
between China and Japan involving China's use of nuclear weapons. Even
conventional conflict at a large scale was considered highly unlikely. The
JDA report did express concern about a possible scenario in which China
would use coercion against Japan, backed by nuclear capabilities, to force
concessions on bilateral disputes such as the sovereignty of the Senkaku

---

37.   This report was obtained by the Union of Concerned Scientists. See Gregory Kulacki,
Japan and U.S. Nuclear Posture, March 2010.

Islands or resource exploitation rights on the continental shelf.[38] In such a scenario, the utility of US extended nuclear deterrence would be significantly limited. This report suggested that US extended deterrence is the basis for arguments against Japan's own nuclear option. It also mentioned the risk of regional arms races, which, if caused, would not be preferable to Japan given its geostrategic vulnerabilities. This assessment can be applicable to the current security environment in East Asia in the midst of a rising China.

Political discourse in Japan over the nuclear option has occurred mostly in the context of changes in the East Asian strategic environment, leading it to bolster the US alliance commitment.[39] In other words, the formation of the foundation of Japan's non-nuclear choice in the post-war period has demonstrated that the credibility of the alliance and reassurance by the United States constituted a more credible and realistic option to cope with the rise of nuclear threats or changes of the strategic environment in East Asia.

US-Japan Dialogue on the Diminishing Role of Nuclear Weapons in the US Nuclear Posture

While US security assurances remain a key element of the security policies of non-nuclear-weapon states such as Japan and South Korea, unfortunately, the total elimination of the role of nuclear weapons would be a far-fetched goal under the current security environment in East Asia. If the

---

38. Japan Defense Agency, *Concerning the Problem of the Proliferation of Weapons of Mass Destruction,* 1995, http://www.ucsusa.org/sites/default/files/legacy/assets/documents/nwgs/1995jdastudy.pdf.

39. The linkage of the East Asian strategic environment and US nuclear deterrence in the Japanese attitude was also seen in the process of US-Soviet negotiations on the INF Treaty during the Reagan administration in the 1980s. Having learned that the US government was about to agree with its counterpart on the "relocation" of SS-20s to the east of the Ural Mountains as part of the deal, the Japanese government requested the United States not to accept such a relocation deal and to pursue the abolition of SS-20s, as the relocation option could undermine the nuclear security environment in East Asia.

region tries to reduce the role of nuclear weapons, alternative measures of security assurance for non-nuclear-weapon states should be pursued. If the United States plans to reduce the role of nuclear weapons in its security policy, there should be a mutual consent between allies on such a change.

The 2010 NPR (Nuclear Posture Review) process provided a typical example of how the alliance between a nuclear-weapons state and a non-nuclear-weapons state can reassure each nation about the security commitment (of the nuclear-weapons state) and the non-nuclear pledge (of the non-nuclear-weapons state). Major attention in the 2010 NPR process was paid to two points: first, whether the United States would decide to limit the role of nuclear weapons; and second, whether the retirement of TLAM-N (nuclear Tomahawk Land Attack Missile) would decrease the credibility of extended deterrence. The 2010 NPR narrowly defined the "fundamental role" of US nuclear weapons as "to deter nuclear attack on the United States, our allies, and partners." It suggested that the US alliance obligation could be achieved by limiting the role of nuclear weapons while others argued for maintaining the status quo. It also mentioned that, in the future, "the United States will consult with allies and partners regarding the conditions under which it would be prudent to shift to a policy under which deterring nuclear attack is the sole purpose of US nuclear weapons." But at the same time, it stated that "there remains a narrow range of contingencies in which US nuclear weapons may still play a role in deterring a conventional or CBW (chemical or biological weapons) attack against the US or its allies and partners."

The 2010 NPR also indicated the growing importance to extended deterrence of conventional elements, such as missile defense cooperation, counter-WMD capabilities, and conventional power-projection capabilities, in addition to the development of conventional prompt global strike capabilities. It mentioned that "enhancing regional security architectures are key parts of the US strategy for strengthening regional deterrence while reducing the role and number of nuclear weapons."

Although such a trend is generally favorable for reducing the role of nuclear weapons, some uncertainties must be addressed in order to avoid the stability-instability paradox. In comparison with nuclear deterrence, deterrence by conventional forces may increase uncertainty or difficulty in strategic calculations. First, conventional forces may have a lower threshold for actual use, compared to nuclear forces, and it would be difficult to calculate the costs and benefits of conventional military operations. Second, the inclusion of missile defense (although it may provide only limited capability against sophisticated long-range missile attacks) and conventional prompt global strikes in the formula of deterrence will make a formula of strategic stability more complicated, and obviously create even greater asymmetry in military doctrines between the United States and other nuclear-weapon states.

Another symbolic episode in the NPR process was the discussion between Japan and the United States over the retirement of TLAM-N. The United States confirmed the retirement of TLAM-N in drafting the 2010 NPR. Japanese officials at the bureaucratic level reportedly expressed concerns over this decision.[40] Their concern over the retirement of TLAM-N was that it would lose a step in the ladder to control escalation between a conventional war and a total war with nuclear exchange. The deployment of TLAM-N visibly demonstrated the US commitment of defending allies and hence (extended) deterrence with less possibility of escalation into a total nuclear war.

The role of nuclear weapons remains in establishing strategic relationships vis-à-vis Russia in the contemporary security environment, which maintains the role of strategic nuclear weapons. In a sense, however, in a response to threats from rogue states such as North Korea and Iran, which have become a critical issue to deal with in the context of the post-Cold War security environment, deterrence by denial has become

---

40. United States Institute of Peace, *Congressional Commission on the Strategic Posture of the United States,* May 6, 2009, 26, http://www.usip.org/sites/default/files /America%27s_Strategic_Posture_Auth_Ed_0.pdf.

more important while deterrence by punishment has become less relevant. Therefore, it was natural for the United States to build a nuclear deterrence architecture without relying on non-strategic nuclear weapons and thus to consider the retirement of TLAM-N.[41]

The gap between the two allies was solved through two means. One was political leadership. Katsuya Okada, then foreign minister, sent a letter to the secretaries of state and defense in December 2009, saying that requests for specific weapons systems did not reflect the views of the current Japanese government and affirming that Japan would not oppose the United States' decision to reduce the role of nuclear weapons. The other was the establishment of a bilateral extended deterrence dialogue, which provides an opportunity for the two governments to frankly exchange views on how to secure alliance deterrence as part of their security and defense cooperation.[42]

After all, "(t)he key argument for maintaining TLAM-N is to provide evidence of the United States' commitment towards Japan and hence assure—that is, provide psychological comfort to—Tokyo. Those who make this argument point both to the symbolism of maintaining a nuclear weapon system that would otherwise be scrapped and the fact that nuclear-armed submarines can be deployed in close proximity to Japan."[43]

Is an Institutionalized Nuclear Taboo Reversed?

Decades after the destruction of Hiroshima and Nagasaki, with a worsening security environment in East Asia (including North Korea's

---

41. TLAM-N has been considered unsuited for a first strike. See John E. Moore and Richard Compton-Hall, *Submarine Warfare: Today and Tomorrow* (Bethesda, MD: Adler & Adler, 1987), 258. Since deterrence by punishment has less of a role in deterring rogue states, the role of TLAM-N in a retaliatory capacity is limited.

42. Ministry of Foreign Affairs, "Japan-U.S. Extended Deterrence Dialogue," http://www.mofa.go.jp/press/release/press4e_000295.html.

43. James Acton, "Extended Deterrence and Communicating Resolve," *Strategic Insights* 8, no. 5 (Winter 2009): 5-15, http://www.nps.edu/Academics/Centers/CCC/Publications/StrategicInsights/2009/Dec/SI_V8_I5_2009_Acton_5.pdf.

brinkmanship with its nuclear capability and China's military modernization and upgrades), Japan's antimilitarism sentiment may be gradually
declining and its nuclear allergy may also be diminishing. A survey in
2006 showed that 61 percent of the Japanese think that discussion on
nuclear options should not be taboo.[44] Shigeru Ishiba, a former minister of defense, told an interviewer, in the context of Japan's choice on
nuclear energy, "although I do not think that Japan should have nuclear
weapons, keeping the nuclear energy program constitutes a latent nuclear
deterrence, with which Japan could make nuclear weapons in a certain
period of time."[45] Furthermore, in April 2014, the Japanese government
decided to change the interpretation of Article 9 of the constitution to
allow the state to exercise the right of collective self-defense. With his
visit to Yasukuni Shrine and remarks on history issues in the past, Abe has
been seen as leading Japan to a more assertive, militarist state.[46]

Abe's security policy is more proactive and robust than that of past
administrations. The establishment of a National Security Council of Japan
and the reinterpretation of the constitution as allowing Japan to exercise
the right of collective self-defense are seen as measures to strengthen
the security partnership with the United States, allowing more substantial
coordination and cooperation with the United States for regional stability as well as defense. The Japanese government has also sought robust
security ties with Australia and India, which could make a web (rather

44. "Abe naikaku: shijiritu kyuraku shusyou no shidoryoku miezu mitouha mo
    jiminbanare" (Abe Cabinet: sharp drop in approval rate, prime minister's leadership
    invisible, LDP lost non-partisan support), *Mainichi Shimbun,* November 27, 2006.

45. Interview with Ishiba Shigeru, "Kaku no senzaiteki yokushiryoku iji no tameni
    genpatsu tuzukeru beki" (Nuclear power program should be maintained in order
    to keep a 'latent nuclear deterrence'), *Sapio,* October 5, 2011, cited on the web
    magazine, *News Post,* September 21, 2011, http://www.news-postseven.com
    /archives/20110921_31301.html.

46. *The Economist,* "A slap in the face: Shinzo Abe takes a dangerous gamble,"
    January 4, 2014, http://www.economist.com/news/asia/21592659-shinzo-abe-takes
    -dangerous-gamble-slap-face?zid=315&ah=ee087c5cc3198fc82970cd65083f5281.

than hub-and-spoke) of US-led regional bilateral alliances. These steps are mostly welcomed by Southeast Asian states as well. These security policy measures for regional stability would reinforce the US commitment to extended deterrence rather than Japan's stand-alone security capabilities, which would reduce the possibility of Japan's nuclear option.

Contrary to the image of seeking a more robust security policy, Abe's government has taken cautious approaches toward nuclear issues. Currently, Japan is seen as a latent nuclear-weapons state because of its plutonium stockpile and possession of enrichment and reprocessing capabilities with a sophisticated space program. As of September 2013, Japan had roughly 36.3 tons of plutonium stored abroad and 10.8 tons of plutonium stored in Japan (of which 4.35 tons of plutonium is stored at the reprocessing facilities, 3.35 tons at the fuel fabrication facility owned by Japan Atomic Energy Agency, and 3.1 tons in other locations).[47] It is a daunting task for Japan to make this stockpile accountable. In a new Strategic Energy Plan issued in April 2014, the Japanese government decided to continue its fuel cycle program and to use Monju, a prototype fast breeder reactor, as "an international research center for technological development, such as reducing the amount and toxic level of radioactive waste and technologies related to nuclear nonproliferation."[48] Instead of maintaining Monju as a national center, Japan decided to make Monju open to the international community.

As a part of its commitments at the Nuclear Security Summit in March 2014, the Japanese government decided to return 300 kilograms of plutonium and ship 200 kilograms of UK-origin highly enriched uranium for

47. Cabinet Office Secretariat of the Atomic Energy Commission, "Wagakuni no plutonium kanri joukyo" (The current situation of plutonium management in Japan), September 16, 2014, http://www.aec.go.jp/jicst/NC/iinkai/teirei/siryo2014/siryo31/siryo3.pdf.

48. The Government of Japan, *Strategic Energy Plan,* April 2014, 54, http://www.enecho.meti.go.jp/en/category/others/basic_plan/pdf/4th_strategic_energy_plan.pdf.

458 | NOBUMASA AKIYAMA

fast critical assembly to the United States.[49] There was a rumor that the United States government pushed the Japanese government hard on this issue due to concerns over Abe's nationalistic nature. But it was not true. The negotiation started long before Abe took office, and the two governments had been negotiating for terms and conditions for the treatment of these nuclear materials. It was Abe's cabinet that decided to return plutonium to the United States. This mutual decision should be more or less interpreted as a mutual reaffirmation of each other's nuclear nonproliferation and nuclear security commitments based on a common perception, namely, US affirmation of trust in Japan's nonproliferation commitment and Japan's affirmation of commitment to the US-led nonproliferation regime.

Another recent news item which raised concern over Japan's nuclear policy was a Japanese news report in June 2014 on an "unreported" 640 kilograms of plutonium.[50] It was contained in MOX (mixed-oxide) fuel loaded in March 2011 into reactor 3 of Kyushu Electric Power's Genkai nuclear plant in Saga Prefecture during its regular checkup, but had been left there unused as the reactor could not restart in light of the disaster at Tokyo Electric Power's Fukushima No. 1 complex. The international community expressed concerns over Japan's failure to report the existence of plutonium. Some even brought up Japan's supposed hidden intention for a nuclear option, asking if it was an honest mistake.[51] In fact, that plutonium was properly and completely reported to the International Atomic

---

49. The White House, *"Joint Statement by the Leaders of Japan and the United States on Contributions to Global Minimization of Nuclear Material,"* March 24, 2014, http://www.whitehouse.gov/the-press-office/2014/03/24/joint-statement-leaders-japan-and-united-states-contributions-global-min.

50. "Japan failed to report 640 kg of nuclear fuel to IAEA," *The Japan Times,* June 7, 2014, http://www.japantimes.co.jp/news/2014/06/07/national/japan-failed-to-report-640-kg-of-nuclear-fuel-to-iaea/#.VMIS-UesXG8.

51. Hui Zhang, "China worries about Japanese plutonium stocks," *Bulletin of the Atomic Scientists,* June 17, 2014, http://thebulletin.org/china-worries-about-japanese-plutonium-stocks7248.

Energy Agency (IAEA) under Japan's safeguards obligation and did not constitute a violation. Rather, it was accidentally omitted from a voluntary reporting scheme Japan intended as an additional confidence-building measure.

Such a misunderstanding might come from perceptions of Prime Minister Abe's nationalist inclination based on his past words. However, Abe's realistic and internationalist—but not nationalistic—security policy stems from a concept of "proactive contribution to peace" (*sekkyokuteki heiwashugi*). This means trying to expand Japan's role in global peace and stability, in order to maintain the liberal international order, by partnering with the United States as well as Australia and other like-minded countries. With this understanding, the apparent gap between Abe's image of robustness in his security policy and cautiousness in his nuclear energy policy tells us that the nuclear option is being considered as a plausible option.

Toward Arms Control Dialogue in East Asia: Nuclear Threat Reduction in East Asia[52]

A Japanese Perception on the Security Environment in East Asia

For Japan's choice of a non-nuclear option, a real stress test will not be Abe's own ideology, but his government's choice of reaction to recent developments in the security environment in East Asia.

While the risk of nuclear war between major powers has declined with the end of the Cold War, the role that nuclear weapons plays in shaping security relationships in East Asia still remains. Three factors in particular

---

52. Analyses of the East Asian security environment in this section are based on my working paper prepared for the Hiroshima Round Table, "Laying the Groundwork for Promoting Nuclear Disarmament: An East Asian Perspective," http://www.pref .hiroshima.lg.jp/uploaded/attachment/145592.pdf.

affect the future of nuclear disarmament in the region: high nuclear density, persistent memories of the Cold War, and changes to the status quo with the rise of China and other emerging states in Asia.

North Korea, having conducted three nuclear tests and several missile launches, is assumed to be steadily developing its nuclear-weapon capabilities. Although it is not clear whether it has already acquired credible capability (such as miniaturization of warheads to load on missiles) to launch nuclear attacks on Japan, South Korea, and the United States, it certainly poses threats to regional stability, given its unpredictable behavior and efforts to exploit other states' willingness to engage it in order to extract benefits from negotiations. In this sense, North Korea's WMD threats remain an essential issue to be addressed in order to realize the denuclearization of Northeast Asia. North Korea may be able to detonate nuclear devices, has enough separated plutonium for several warheads, and has delivery capability with ballistic missiles reaching US territories as well as Japan.

China may have a stockpile of approximately 250 warheads, with more than 100 warheads deployed on ballistic missiles.[53] China has also constructed and put into operation three Jin-class ballistic missile submarines, each of which can carry twelve ballistic missiles. China's deployment of new road-mobile and sea-based ballistic missiles may afford China a more resilient second-strike capability.[54]

Although Russia is normally considered a European power, Russian officials have deployed a significant portion of their non-strategic nuclear weapons east of the Ural Mountains. Moreover, Russia has pointed to China's growing number of ballistic missiles as one possible rationale for withdrawing from the 1987 Intermediate-range Nuclear Forces (INF) treaty. At present, the United States government believes that Russia may

---

53. Stockholm International Peace Research Institute, *SIPRI Yearbook 2013: Armaments, Disarmament and International Security* (Oxford: Oxford University Press, 2012), 306.

54. Department of Defense, *Annual Report to Congress*, 7.

be circumventing or violating the INF treaty by deploying a new, two-stage intercontinental-range ballistic missile intended for regional deterrence missions, as well as a ground-launched cruise missile with a range of 2,000 kilometers.

Meanwhile, the predominance of the United States in the region, with its sound forward deployment capabilities, constitutes a major element of the stability in Asian regional security. Non-nuclear-weapon states such as Japan and South Korea are beneficiaries of US extended deterrence. Although there has been debate over the diminishing role of nuclear weapons in US security strategy and the increasing importance of conventional US forces, nuclear deterrence remains in a central role. With the rise of China's military capability and some constraints on the US "pivot" to Asia, along with North Korea's unpredictable provocations, US allies and partners seek reaffirming credible extended deterrence as long as such threats from nuclear-armed states exist.

Non-nuclear-weapon states in the region—Japan and South Korea—and the government of Taiwan have extensive civilian nuclear power programs. Japan is the only non-nuclear-weapon state that has nearly full-scale nuclear fuel cycle capacity, and South Korea is interested in recycling spent nuclear fuel, with its own research agenda for pyro-processing, a kind of reprocessing technology. Such technology may be diverted into the production of weapon-usable materials and be perceived as a latent nuclear weapon capability, which may potentially pose a sense of threats to others even if they are under IAEA's safeguards.

In the non-nuclear political and security environment, Asia is entering a period of great changes in the strategic landscape. Cold War-like logic overshadows the overall political and security environment in the region. US alliances with regional partners such as Japan and South Korea are linchpins of the regional security architecture. Due to historical legacies, however, US regional allies are not able to establish effective security relationships among themselves. For the same reason, Japan and China are not able to engage in sustainable strategic dialogue. Instead, accelerated by the historical legacy and territorial disputes in the East China

Sea, the two countries are competing for political influence over the rest of Asia and for the blessing of the United States on the legitimacy of their positions in the post-war international order.

The rise of China is a major factor shaping the regional strategic environment. China describes its rise as a peaceful one, saying it has no intention of challenging the international order. In the meantime, China seeks a "new model of major power relations" with the United States, the core notion of which is not yet clear to others. This notion is received by Japan, the United States, and other states with great caution, as they suspect China wants to reign over the region at the most, or at least deny US predominance and intervention in Asian strategic relationships. Although it may be natural for China to seek to increase its influence in regional politics as its power grows, its assertive maritime behavior in the East and South China seas, as it tries to change the status quo by coercion or pressure, certainly has had an adverse effect on the establishment of a peaceful and stable regional security environment.

China's actions will also reinforce the utility of alliances with the United States and justify other regional states' buildup of more robust defense and enforcement capabilities, which may eventually provoke an arms race in Asia. In fact, Southeast Asia is a hot spot of maritime capability buildup. Vietnam received its first submarine from Russia in December 2013, which will be followed by five more. In 2012, Indonesia concluded a contract with South Korea on acquisition of submarines. Myanmar (Burma) and Thailand are also interested in acquiring submarines. Japanese coast guard vessels are also high in demand in Southeast Asia.

In such a strategic environment, the role of nuclear weapons in deterrence, though remaining as an ultimate guarantor, may not be so big as it used to be in the US-Soviet bipolar system. Rather, the role of conventional deterrence has been increasing. Further, in such circumstances, non-military measures like diplomacy and dialogue should be given high priority.

In sum, in order to promote dialogue and subsequent implementation of nuclear threat reduction and disarmament in East Asia, it is necessary to address both nuclear and non-nuclear elements of strategic relationships among regional actors, as well as the balance among them.

The Need for More Strategic Dialogue among Major Stakeholders

While Japan's nuclear policy decisions rely heavily on the credibility of US extended deterrence, and it is unlikely the US commitment will significantly decline, uncertainty remains as to how China's nuclear and conventional military capabilities and strategic doctrine will develop.

While China maintains a relatively small-scale nuclear arsenal, its approach to deterrence relies on ambiguity. This lack of transparency is a strategic asset that helps China make up for the inferiority of its nuclear arsenal in both quality and quantity. China claims that it maintains a no-first-use policy, saying in "China's National Defense in 2010" that "China will not be the first to use nuclear weapons at any time and under any circumstance, and unequivocally commits that under no circumstances will it use or threaten to use nuclear weapons against non-nuclear-weapon states or nuclear-weapon-free zones."[55] China also claims that its warheads are not "mated with" delivery vehicles. The modernization of China's nuclear arsenal certainly poses questions over the sustainability and credibility of such declaratory policies. For example, introduction of ballistic-missile submarines inevitably changes the de-alert status of nuclear weapons, as nuclear warheads must be mated with delivery vehicles (submarine-launched ballistic missiles) in submarines while engaged in patrols.

While China has not developed its nuclear arsenal as much as expected, it takes a different approach to expanding its military influence in the region. China's anti-access and area-denial (A2/AD) capabilities may have a certain deterrence effect. With A2/AD capability, China could prevail militarily in a limited area (within the first island

---

55. Information Office of the State Council, People's Republic of China, "China's National Defense in 2010," March 2011, http://www.nti.org/media/pdfs/1_1a .pdf?_=1316627912.

chain, for example) in a relatively short time while it could conduct military operations to achieve a strategic (or sub-strategic) objective such as gaining control over Taiwan. The US Quadrennial Defense Review saw China's development of A2/AD capabilities as undermining the dominant US capabilities to project power,[56] which may threaten the integrity of US alliances and security partnerships, reduce US security and influence, and increase the possibility of conflict.

So far, neither China nor the United States has shown any interest in engaging in an arms control dialogue while both have started strategic dialogues at various levels on agendas related to their nuclear policies and strategic issues for confidence-building. But in the absence of a stable strategic relationship to provide a baseline for arms control, China and the United States may not be able to work together for nuclear arms reduction.

Two paradoxes must be resolved if the United States and China are to establish a stable strategic relationship which would lead them into nuclear threat reduction and disarmament. The first paradox is whether "symmetry" in nuclear arsenals and doctrines would be necessary for stability. Pursuit of "symmetry" in strategic forces and doctrine established the pro forma US-USSR balance of power during the Cold War. But if China does not seek parity with the United States, and the United States may not admit the vulnerability (officially), stability under asymmetries must be sought.

The second paradox is that asymmetric strategic relationships may require a fine-tuned modality of stability. However, the sophistication of the notion of strategic stability in this particular relationship may highlight the gaps that exist between two nuclear-armed states. Subsequently, the best mix of nuclear and conventional elements of deterrence in both punitive and denial capabilities and a combination of political and strategic (or military) stability must be taken into account in a formula of stability. As Chinese and US strategies are changing, stability is a moving

---

56. Department of Defense, "Quadrennial Defense Review 2014," 36, http://www
.defense.gov/pubs/2014_Quadrennial_Defense_Review.pdf.

target, and extensive political maneuvering will be required for both sides to agree on the state of stability.

In principle, Japan would welcome a common understanding on a stable strategic nuclear relationship between the United States and China. But, if such a deal were done without consultation with Japan, it might cause a rising sense of vulnerability among the Japanese. In that case, Japan could be more tempted to consider a nuclear option. Therefore, close consultation with US allies would be an important element for an effective arms control dialogue to succeed.

Implication of the Ukraine Situation on East Asian Non-Proliferation and Disarmament Scenes

The Ukraine situation may—correctly or not—provide Asia with lessons (applicable to nonproliferation and disarmament debates) on how the relationship between a major nuclear-weapon state and a non-nuclear-weapon state would take shape in the absence of mutual trust.

The international community perceived that Russia devalued legal and political commitments it made for security assurance to a non-nuclear weapon state, following the breakup of the Soviet Union (including the Budapest Memorandum on Security Assurance in 1994, the Helsinki Declaration in 1975, and the UN Charter) in its behavior toward Ukraine. Russia could do this because of the disparity between Russia and Ukraine in military capability and Ukraine's energy dependency. Ukraine had given up its nuclear weapons under the assumption that it would gain security benefits, which was the underlying assumption for the post-breakup security arrangements between Russia and former Soviet republics that transferred nuclear weapons to Russia. The ultra-nationalists in Ukraine claimed that Ukraine was threatened by Russia because it gave up nukes upon independence.[57] Such an argument suggests that the vulnerability of a non-nuclear-weapon state vis-à-vis the provocation or hostile attitude

---

57. "The Inquisitor: Nuclear weapons revival talked about by Ukrainian President Petro Poroshenko," *Kiev Post,* December 14, 2014, http://www.kyivpost.com/content

of a nuclear-armed state could be recovered by nuclear deterrence. Hence, a non-nuclear state in such a vulnerable position might be tempted to seek security assurance by other nuclear-armed states or by itself.

It should be emphasized that the situation of Asian allies such as Japan and South Korea under the formal arrangement of US extended deterrence is different from the situation of Ukraine, which is not in a legal security arrangement with the United States. The United States would be more committed to the security of formal allies. Therefore, US response to the situation of Ukraine is simply inapplicable to the US-Japan relationship.

However, when turning our eyes to other Asian countries, there are states, in particular the Philippines and Vietnam, which are confronted with China's pressure and assertive actions in the South China Sea without out extended deterrence by anyone, including the United States. The Philippines moved to reestablish a de facto alliance relationship with the United States, while Vietnam has so far not been seeking any security arrangement with others. Also important is how North Korea interprets the fate of Ukraine, along with the case of Libya.

Russia's behavior toward Ukraine may undermine the credibility of declaratory policy measures among non-nuclear states. Declaratory policies can effectively contribute to confidence-building and subsequent détente as well as arms control and threat reduction, when such policies are conceived as enduring commitments, resilient to the ups and downs of political relationships. Russia's violation of the political commitment of security assurance to Ukraine under the Budapest Memorandum may give an impression that declaratory policy is easily broken, and the principle of the rule of law may be too weak to guarantee the peace and the stability of strategic relationships.

Therefore, it is a daunting task for the international community, in particular nuclear-weapon states, to restore confidence in political and legal commitments on security arrangements by nuclear-armed states, in order to further promote nuclear disarmament.

Conclusion

As with the next round of US-Russian arms control negotiations, the United States and China will have many disagreements over setting a concrete agenda for arms control dialogue. China will not agree to disclose numerical information on its nuclear arsenal, including the number of warheads, the size of its fissile material stockpile, and the number and variety of ballistic missiles, until it is confident in its deterrence capability. It is understandable that China, given its inferior position vis-à-vis the United States and Russia, will try to secure nuclear deterrence with ambiguity or a lack of transparency. The United States may not want to acknowledge the vulnerability vis-à-vis China as this may force it to change its deterrence strategy against China. Such a situation implies that it is not likely, in the foreseeable future, that the United States and China will be engaged in formal arms control talks.

As long as nuclear weapons play a role in the security policy of East Asian countries, the Japanese government will continue relying on US extended deterrence. In order to narrow the gap between this reliance and the nation's non-nuclear philosophy, Japan must take a layered approach. At the global level, Japan's disarmament diplomacy acts to reinforce the norm of non-nuclear weapons. Since nuclear-armed states would not be likely to forgo a nuclear option when other states remain armed with nuclear weapons, Japan's disarmament diplomacy should focus on devaluing nuclear weapons by strengthening normative discourse on the humanitarian dimension of nuclear weapons. If norms of a reduced role for nuclear weapons and a higher threshold for their use are established, binding on all nuclear-armed states, a favorable environment for nuclear disarmament should emerge.

Japan will continue putting emphasis on reinforcing the US-Japan alliance and maintaining the role of nuclear deterrence in its security policy while upgrading its own capability to deny nuclear attacks by means of a missile defense system and the conventional capability to respond to relatively small-scale contingencies. Meanwhile, Japan will continue advocating the issue of humanitarian concerns over the use of nuclear weapons and urging the world to work toward the total elimination of nuclear weapons. This posture may cause criticism for its "double standard" at home and abroad. But Japan's choice of a non-nuclear option is strategic rather than emotional, and the basic assumption that US extended nuclear deterrence is more effective than national nuclear deterrence has not significantly changed. As long as the commitments by both Japan and the United States are reaffirmed by each other, Japan's rational choice of a non-nuclear option will be maintained. For Japan, the reliance on US extended nuclear deterrence is a response to the present situation, while efforts to advocate nuclear disarmament are a means to eliminate nuclear threats in a structural way.

In addition, Japan's nuclear choice has been rational, but adaptive. Japan has not been particularly proactive in setting conditions for nuclear disarmament, but has adapted its security policy to the changing environment. Thus, it can be assumed that essential conditions for Japan choosing a nuclear option would be when Japan believes, first, that the US-Japan alliance can no longer keep up with the expansion of Chinese military capabilities and, second, that the United States has lost its intention to maintain the credibility of extended deterrence, in particular of its nuclear element.

In order to avoid such a situation, confidence-building actions should be pursued which would lead to nuclear threat reduction with China and reassurance that the United States will continue its deterrence strategy. Non-military measures such as diplomacy and dialogue should be used to seek a common understanding on the modality of a stable strategic relationship among major players in East Asia, in particular the United States, China, and Japan.

Japan's disarmament dilemma can be solved by seeking the best mix of reinforced norms of non-use of nuclear weapons at the global level and of nuclear threat reduction with confidence-building measures through security dialogues at the regional level, as medium to long-term solutions. Meanwhile, Japan should seek robust reassurance of security through international cooperation including the US-Japan alliance and partnerships with other like-minded countries, as immediate responses to current security concerns.

Introduction to Part Three

On March 6, 2013, one of the co-editors of this volume, George P. Shultz, together with William J. Perry, Henry A. Kissinger, and Sam Nunn, wrote in the *Wall Street Journal:*

> The U.S. must work with other key states to establish a joint enterprise with common objectives to achieve near-term results. . . . The Nuclear Security Summits could provide a model for leaders working together to create a joint enterprise that would generate a coalition of willing states to establish priorities and achieve progress on specific steps. . . . Such a joint enterprise should include and be reinforced by regional dialogues.

In this final chapter, the authors lay out the considerations that might guide governments in moving from the current, increasingly dysfunctional methods of dealing with nuclear proliferation and threats of nuclear weapons use to a new institutional framework.

The previous chapters provided evidence that a successful effort to reduce and eliminate the nuclear threat must be based on a combination of regional and global joint enterprises. This chapter returns the focus to the global aspects of a joint enterprise committed to creating the conditions for a world without nuclear weapons. The cooperative nuclear restraint regime that was built up over decades has shown serious signs of decay. An effort, not just to bolster the old regime, but also to build a new conceptual and institutional foundation for nuclear restraint is urgently needed.

Creating the Conditions for a World without Nuclear Weapons

James E. Goodby and Steven Pifer

Introduction

The global nuclear challenge has changed dramatically over the past two decades. The bipolarity of the US-Soviet nuclear standoff during the Cold War has given way to a multilateral and, in some ways, more chaotic and perhaps more dangerous structure comprising nine states that possess nuclear weapons, several of which are situated in regions where

---

James Goodby and Steven Pifer are the principal authors of this paper. Others who contributed to its drafting or actively participated in substantive discussions regarding its content include: James Acton, Barry Blechman, Sid Drell, Bill Dunlop, Thomas Graham, David Holloway, Edward Ifft, David Koplow, Michael Mazarr, Gary Roughead, and Harry Rowen. Ideas in the paper also came from other participants in a workshop held at the Hoover Institution on July 25–26, 2012. The Hoover workshop and the subsequent meetings were part of the framework inaugurated by George Shultz, William Perry, Henry Kissinger, and Sam Nunn to promote a world without nuclear weapons. Goodby and Pifer, however, are responsible for the final product.

intense regional rivalries exist.[1] A factor almost completely absent in the middle years of the twentieth century is prominent today: the devolution of state authority to institutions and organizations, including terrorist groups, that can wield great power for either good or malign purposes. As a result, the odds of a nuclear weapon being used today are greater than during the Cold War, even if the prospect of a civilization-ending nuclear exchange between the United States and Russia has been dramatically reduced.

This problem led four Cold War statesmen—George Shultz, William Perry, Henry Kissinger, and Sam Nunn—to call for the elimination of the nuclear threat. The use of nuclear weapons is a real possibility. Yet the solidarity of nations needed to deal with this threat is not evident. This chapter outlines an approach for creating the conditions for a world without nuclear weapons. It centers on a global coalition of nations taking national initiatives to move the world back from the nuclear precipice by means of a long-term work plan. On the part of all nations engaged in this joint enterprise, there should be tangible, convincing commitments to near-term actions, agreed among the relevant nations, regionally as well as on the global level. These should be carried out at a brisk pace.

The political leadership in some nuclear-armed states won't initially be prepared to endorse the concept of a world without nuclear weapons. This is especially the case with those locked in fierce regional rivalries. But a gradual process of nuclear reductions combined with confidence-building measures—and progress in resolving regional security issues—could create, over time, a new consensus. This process would be a key element of a joint enterprise.

A joint enterprise as discussed in this chapter would be an effort by nations, launched at the summit level and conducted over a long period of time, to control the destructive nuclear forces that threaten to overwhelm

---

1. The nine states that currently possess nuclear weapons are the United States, Russia, Britain, France, China, India, Pakistan, North Korea, and Israel (which has not publicly acknowledged having nuclear arms).

them. The nuclear dimension is not the only element of the global trends that have been re-shaping the international system, but it remains perhaps the most deadly. It highlights several related international security challenges that also must be addressed more or less concurrently.

Steadiness of purpose over time will be required—not an easy thing to do. But this kind of persistence has been shown by many nations in recent history. It was shown by the United States during the more than four decades of the Cold War. This new struggle would become the defining hallmark of this era, which is still called "post-Cold War" because it has few defining features of its own.

Current international mechanisms necessary to create the conditions for a world without nuclear weapons are not adequate to do the job. Tinkering with the existing machinery will not magically make things possible that were not before. But some improvements in the way nations seek to build a safer global security environment would help. This will require leadership from the top on the part of several nations.

Shultz, Perry, Kissinger, and Nunn recognized in their five successive *Wall Street Journal* articles[2] that in focusing on nuclear weapons they were also bringing other big issues to the fore: the nature of deterrence, mitigation of regional conflicts, conventional force imbalances, safeguards for civilian nuclear power programs, and a variety of issues involving transparency of state behavior and international governance. They understood that nations are motivated and unified by visions of a brighter future, so they stressed the need for an overarching vision—the vision of a world without nuclear weapons.

The advice they offered in their first *Wall Street Journal* article was "first and foremost . . . intensive work with leaders of the countries in possession of nuclear weapons to turn the goal of a world without nuclear weapons into a joint enterprise." The article identified ambitious steps to "lay the groundwork for a world free of the nuclear threat." These included reducing substantially the size of nuclear forces in all states that

---

2. http://www.nuclearsecurityproject.org/publications/wall-street-journal-op-eds.

possess them and eliminating short-range nuclear weapons designed to be forward-deployed. The idea was that nations desiring to enter into a joint enterprise should be willing to sign on to the goal and to a series of steps that could be achieved via a sequence of agreements negotiated over time. That would, in turn, create the conditions for a world without nuclear weapons. This chapter describes a framework for seeking to make that objective a reality.

Conditions for a World without Nuclear Weapons

Creating the conditions for a world without nuclear weapons would require at least four developments.

1. The commitment of some nuclear-armed states might begin the process, but moving toward zero eventually will require a readiness on the part of all states with nuclear weapons to reduce and ultimately eliminate their nuclear arms.
2. New and strengthened verification measures would provide confidence that any nuclear cheating would be detected. A serious analysis of verification mechanisms for a world without nuclear weapons would be needed in order to demonstrate their feasibility.
3. An enforcement mechanism with teeth would dissuade both states that have nuclear weapons and those that do not from cheating on agreements. The mechanism would have to respond rapidly and effectively if violations occurred.
4. A changed international security framework would allow states to conclude that they could defend their vital interests through non-nuclear means.

Moreover, the key territorial and other interstate disputes that motivate states to acquire and maintain nuclear weapons in the first place must be resolved or at least mitigated. At the least, it would be important to gain acceptance by the contending states that nuclear arms will not help them resolve their disputes. Global agreements will have to be supplemented by regional agreements that will take into account specific conditions existing in each of those regions. Standards for effective verification of regional agreements would be a matter of international concern.

These are demanding requirements, which lead some people to conclude that a world without nuclear weapons is unattainable. It could turn out that they are right. But a failure to try amounts to acceptance of the current nuclear reality—and of the growing risk of the use of nuclear weapons with unpredictable consequences for mankind.

A joint enterprise process to create the conditions for a world without nuclear weapons could contribute to a broader effort to design and build the political and economic institutions that would succeed the post-World War II order. There is a question, of course—which would be resolvable only as events unfold and at the highest level of governments—as to how much progress on a new global security environment is needed to advance the goal of a world without nuclear weapons. But lack of progress in one area should not prevent progress in others, and progress in one area may create conditions that would promote progress in others.

Essential Features of a Joint Enterprise

The five articles written by Shultz, Perry, Kissinger, and Nunn imply that the elements of a joint enterprise could, and almost certainly must, develop at their own speeds and on their own merits in multiple channels. Some efforts would deal with nuclear arms reductions, some with regional conflicts, some with ancillary agreements such as conventional forces, and some with civil nuclear power.

A joint enterprise designed to create the conditions for a world without nuclear weapons will provide the conceptual glue to hold together these multiple endeavors as they advance toward that goal. It must be launched and overseen at the summit level: nothing less could hold all these disparate elements together and make possible the necessary collective decisions at critical junctures.

One such critical juncture noted in the March 7, 2011, article would be the "inherent limit to US and Russian reductions if other nuclear weapons states build up their inventories or if new nuclear powers emerge." This security dilemma means that, as Russia and the United States continue their reductions process, at some point other states possessing nuclear weapons must at least freeze their nuclear arsenals in place. Meanwhile, all states that do not possess nuclear weapons should take steps that will demonstrate their intention to refrain from acquiring them. The relationship is clearly a summit-level judgment.

As suggested in the five *WSJ* articles, a joint enterprise based on the principle of shared responsibility would contain some features that directly affect nuclear weapons reductions and some that would be necessary to create and sustain the conditions for a world without nuclear weapons. In that first category are the following features.

1. A joint enterprise should have a goal: achieving a world without nuclear weapons.
2. Whereas a joint enterprise might be launched with the participation of just some nuclear weapons states, its membership must include, at some stage in the process, all of the states possessing nuclear weapons, not just the five—the United States, Russia, Great Britain, France, and China— recognized in the Non-Proliferation Treaty (NPT).
3. Its membership should also include states not possessing nuclear weapons, especially those with advanced civil nuclear capabilities or otherwise in a position to contribute to preventing the spread of new nuclear weapons capabilities, such as Sweden and Japan.

4. As appropriate to their individual circumstances, members of a joint enterprise should negotiate and implement a program consisting of a series of separate, verifiable agreements that, by reducing the numbers and roles of nuclear weapons, would lay the groundwork for a world free of the nuclear threat.

5. The joint enterprise must aim at developing verification measures commensurate with increasingly deeper reductions of nuclear arms down to zero. These measures must be sufficient also to satisfy participants in a joint enterprise who may not be directly participating in such measures.

6. The joint enterprise will ultimately require an enforcement mechanism that would dissuade states from cheating on their obligations and that would respond rapidly and effectively to any cheating.

In the second category are the following additional features, which could perhaps be taken under the umbrella of a joint enterprise:

1. Mechanisms for mitigating or resolving regional disputes and conflicts that promote nuclear proliferation.

2. Ancillary agreements, such as limits on conventional forces and steps that reduce tensions over missile defenses.

3. Agreements and actions to tighten controls over nuclear materials globally, including more effective monitoring and internationalizing of some aspects of the nuclear fuel cycle.

To repeat: it is clear that a joint enterprise having these features must carry out its work through several channels, not in just one all-embracing forum. To have any realistic chance of succeeding, a joint enterprise must become the long-term, sustained business of heads of states and governments.

Principles and Process

In their essay published in the *Wall Street Journal* on January 4, 2007, the four statesmen asked, "Can a worldwide consensus be forged that defines a series of practical steps leading to major reductions in the nuclear danger?" The answer was not obvious—not then, not now. Shultz has called the present era "the Age of Diplomacy," and so it must be if nation-states are to get control not only of the nuclear threat but of all the global forces that are threatening to overwhelm them. In the nuclear arena, as the possessors of 90 percent or more of the world's nuclear weapons, the United States and Russia must lead. That means both championing the goal and actively promoting the steps it takes to get there: to think of the goal of a world without nuclear weapons as a compass guiding day-to-day decisions, not just an ideal. To develop traction, some diplomatic mechanisms must be created that will encourage many nations to rally around this standard—the United States in the role of lonely champion of the goal would quickly become a quixotic figure.

If the primary political objective is to achieve a world without nuclear weapons, then some diplomatic mechanisms must be found that will encourage many nations to sign up. The only such mechanism that exists today is the United Nations itself. Although it is not well-suited to negotiating, the United Nations can be a mechanism for recording and endorsing declaratory policies published by individual members. The Permanent Five members of the Security Council (all of whom possess nuclear weapons) also are beginning to act as a catalyst for broader support for key nuclear constraints.

American architect Louis Sullivan's dictum, "form follows function," is relevant here: before deciding how nuclear constraints should be negotiated, or otherwise put into effect, it would be wise to consider some principles that can be followed in creating new diplomatic mechanisms.

The first principle of a joint enterprise, of course, almost by its definition, is that *it should be global in scope*. But unless regional rivalries and conflicts are somehow brought under control, a joint enterprise will be limited in what it can achieve.

And so a second principle in considering how new diplomatic mechanisms might encourage nuclear restraint consists of *dealing with regional disputes*. This, too, was foreshadowed in the *Wall Street Journal* essays.

A third imperative is to *link further progress in US-Russian reductions in nuclear warheads with concrete, specific steps of nuclear constraints by other nations*. Many of these were listed in the *Wall Street Journal* articles, but adequate diplomatic mechanisms for dealing with these do not exist. A joint enterprise will have to be built by finding a way to encourage such steps. Declaratory policies may be one way to achieve this, in addition to establishing more effective negotiating mechanisms. For example, initially some nuclear weapons states might undertake unilateral political commitments not to increase their nuclear weapons numbers so long as the United States and Russia are reducing theirs.

A fourth imperative in moving from a limited partnership to a broad coalition of nations would be to *find a way to cooperate more effectively in realizing the benefits of civil nuclear power while removing the breakout potential of civil nuclear programs* that takes nations to the point where fabricating nuclear weapons is only a brief step from an advanced civil power program.

Shultz, Perry, Kissinger, and Nunn saw US-Russian leadership as critical to the success of the project. But they also stressed on January 15, 2008, the need to involve states that do not possess nuclear weapons: "In parallel with these steps by the US and Russia, the dialogue must broaden on an international scale, including non-nuclear as well as nuclear nations." This recognized, among other things, that civil nuclear power operations should be included in the agenda of a joint enterprise.

In the *Wall Street Journal* of March 7, 2011, they argued that "ensuring that nuclear materials are protected globally . . . is a top priority." In this area, the Obama administration's creation of the Nuclear Security Summit process in 2010 has, in effect, already created a joint enterprise in one important area of a new global security commons. While that process has made progress, the president in June 2013 wisely announced his intention to extend it by proposing a 2016 summit in the United States.

The joint enterprise process could be launched with the participation of just some nuclear-armed states. It ultimately, however, will require broader participation, including all states possessing nuclear weapons; indeed, the participation of all nations ultimately would be sought. What criteria should govern the membership at the beginning? The smaller the number of participants, the more workable the forum. But states that are not in on the takeoff may be reluctant to participate in the landing. Certain states—even if not nuclear-armed states—will need to be engaged early on to secure their ultimate buy-in to the goal as well as to the successive implementing agreements required to achieve it.

Part of the answer to this question would come from private consultations that the United States and Russia and other nuclear-armed states involved in launching the joint enterprise process would conduct with other "relevant states." The UN Security Council Permanent Five states and India, Pakistan, and Israel should be invited to join the process. The Democratic People's Republic of Korea and Iran should be involved at some point in the process after they have made convincing responses to proposals that have been put before them by the international community regarding their current nuclear programs.

A major role should be assigned to those states that renounced nuclear weapons or weapons programs and those whose advanced civil nuclear capabilities would permit them to build nuclear weapons within a very few years. This would include Argentina, Belarus, Brazil, Canada, Germany, Japan, Kazakhstan, South Africa, South Korea, Sweden, and Ukraine. Representatives of the non-aligned movement, such as Indonesia, might be added. Just this group would come close to two dozen. To provide a sustained sense of direction, a smaller and continuously operating "contact group" or "friends of the joint enterprise" would have to be established.

A direct approach to zero that has been proposed in the past is a nuclear weapons convention (NWC) modeled on the chemical and biological weapons conventions. An NWC has broad support among states that do not possess nuclear weapons and nongovernmental organizations, but not among nuclear-armed states. Although some kind of a legally binding document would likely be required to achieve a world without nuclear weapons, seeking one now seems highly premature—in part because the conditions noted above for a world without nuclear weapons have not been achieved and an NWC by itself likely would not achieve them.

The Present Approach

In the years since the advent of the nuclear age in 1945, efforts to control nuclear weapons have evolved into a system of diplomacy with clearly defined characteristics. Major reductions in nuclear arsenals have been the exclusive province of the United States and the Soviet Union/Russia. Limits or constraints on a nation's freedom of action regarding testing, development, transfer, or deployment of nuclear weapons have been the province of groups of nations, ranging in size from the United Nations, to the sixty-five members of the UN Conference on Disarmament in Geneva, to small ad hoc groups such as the Six-Party Talks on North Korea's nuclear weapons program. Russia and the United States are members of each of the groups just listed but not of the groups of nations that have negotiated on nuclear-weapons-free zones in Latin America, Africa, the South Pacific, Southeast Asia, and Central Asia. The United States and Russia, as well as China, Britain, and France, are, however, relevant to those groups as signatories of protocols that show that the nuclear weapons states support and respect the obligations undertaken by participants in nuclear-weapons-free zones.

The patterns of activities in these various forums vary. The Review Conference that monitors implementation of the NPT holds sessions every five years. Holding regularly scheduled sessions several times each year is the practice at the Conference on Disarmament in Geneva. Negotiations aimed at achieving specific objectives, like New START, the

2010 US-Russia Strategic Arms Reduction Treaty, proceed at a steady and fairly intensive pace and then conclude until a new round of negotiations is agreed upon.

Since the end of the Cold War, now nearly a quarter of a century ago, much of the urgency has gone out of the quest for nuclear arms reductions. There are reasons for this that are unrelated to the system currently in place to conduct negotiations on nuclear weapons. Some are related to the dramatic reductions in US and Soviet/Russian nuclear arsenals since 1991, some to public perceptions that a nuclear attack is no longer a serious possibility, and some to other preoccupations in the nuclear arena.

In the immediate aftermath of the breakup of the Soviet Union, Washington focused on preventing loss of control of weapons and fissile materials that Russia and the newly independent republics of the former Soviet Union had inherited from that recently defunct state. The Clinton administration enjoyed considerable success in this area. In contrast, during this same period, Moscow and Washington sparred fruitlessly over the framework for a new strategic arms reduction treaty and the question of how US ballistic missile defense efforts would be controlled, if at all.

The Bush administration withdrew from the 1972 Anti-Ballistic Missile (ABM) Treaty but put in place a series of instruments to deal with illicit traffic in fissile materials—the Proliferation Security Initiative (PSI), UN Security Council Resolution 1540, the Global Initiative to Combat Nuclear Terrorism, and the Global Nuclear Energy Partnership (GNEP), among them. A Strategic Offensive Reductions Treaty (SORT) was concluded in 2002 between Russia and the United States, which focused on limiting operationally deployed strategic warheads. Bilateral consultative mechanisms also were put in place at the same time but were sparingly used.

The Obama administration returned to negotiations with Russia on strategic arms in 2009 and produced the New START Treaty, which entered into force in February 2011. A consultative mechanism to oversee implementation was established. The administration has also used the UN

Security Council to rally support for the idea of a world without nuclear weapons. As previously noted, an innovative new forum was established, the Nuclear Security Summit, in which forty-seven heads of states or governments participated in 2010. Its mission was to tighten controls over fissile materials. Thus, a joint enterprise has been created that is a useful precedent for the future. A second meeting in Seoul, South Korea, was held in March 2012 and a third in the Netherlands in March 2014, with one more planned for the United States in 2016.

For the past few decades, the periodic meetings of the Review Conferences of the Non-Proliferation Treaty have been the center of the most controversial and intense debates about the future of civil nuclear power, nuclear disarmament, and nuclear nonproliferation. In those conferences, the question of how viable the basic bargain of the NPT really is has come to a head. That bargain—which envisaged nuclear disarmament by the nuclear weapons states, in return for which other states would not acquire nuclear weapons but would have access to civil nuclear technology—has been challenged by the non-nuclear weapons states. They argue that the five recognized nuclear weapons states have not done enough to disarm and that nuclear technology useful for civil nuclear power is being denied to the non-nuclear weapons states. The nuclear weapons states, in turn, complain that the obligations not to acquire nuclear weapons are being challenged by proliferant countries such as North Korea and Iran.

The heat generated by these conferences has been insufficient to propel the negotiating process forward. But they do pose sets of objectives that furnish a means of measuring progress and pointing to the desired direction of travel.

Not yet in the mode of a negotiating forum, but potentially so, are recent meetings of the nuclear-armed permanent members of the UN Security Council. They have dealt with verification experiences and are beginning to expand into the issue of cutting off the production of fissile material for use in weapons, including discussions with other countries.

Their statement, issued on July 1, 2011, declared that they intended to "renew their efforts with other relevant partners to promote such negotiations."

Finally, it must be said that treaties are not usually the mechanisms chosen to reflect decisions of governments. Most decisions that lead to new nuclear weapons postures by those nations that possess them are reflected in national policies, national defense budgets, and orders to various elements of national governments. That is how President George W. Bush intended to set the US nuclear arsenal at 1,700 to 2,200 operationally deployed strategic warheads. Only the insistence of Russian President Vladimir Putin led to the Strategic Offensive Reductions Treaty in May 2002, which codified the already-made US decision.

President George H. W. Bush practiced the non-treaty approach in order to induce the Soviet government under Mikhail Gorbachev in 1991 and then the Russian government under Boris Yeltsin in 1992 to reduce the number of nuclear weapons and consolidate in Russia the nuclear warheads from bases in the other republics of the Soviet Union as it collapsed into fifteen independent states. Bush announced that the United States would remove its tactical nuclear weapons from most forward bases and take other steps unilaterally, including the removal of warheads from missiles scheduled for elimination under the START I Treaty. Gorbachev and Yeltsin responded by announcing their own unilateral decisions to reduce tactical nuclear warheads and other nuclear weapons. This method is managed without the benefit of a negotiating forum and could be used by several states—not just two—to enhance the safety of nuclear weapons and provide policymakers with more time for decisions.

New Diplomatic Mechanisms

Could new diplomatic mechanisms help to make creating the conditions for a world without nuclear weapons a truly joint enterprise? That's not a foregone conclusion. But it is conceivable that one or more new mechanisms could perform this role, and these possibilities should be explored. An organizational home ultimately will be necessary to buttress and support the diplomacy of individual nations and provide at least loose coordination for efforts that may take place in a variety of forums (e.g., bilateral negotiations, the United Nations, the Nuclear Security Summit process, the International Atomic Energy Agency). No nation by itself has the solution to the question of how to move from general theory to practical methods of forming a joint enterprise. It can be found only by a coalition of nations committed to creating the conditions for a world without nuclear weapons.

In their most recent *Wall Street Journal* article, on March 5, 2013, Shultz, Perry, Kissinger, and Nunn suggested a "coalition of the willing" to establish long-term goals and near-term actions. Several coalitions of the willing, including the Proliferation Security Initiative and the Nuclear Security Summits, have been created in recent years and have had considerable success in reducing nuclear risks. A new coalition could have the advantage of lacking an overt connection to institutions and agreements that have had their legitimacy questioned by many states, including India, Pakistan, and Israel. Moreover, while a coalition invariably involves the need to find a "lowest common denominator" process that moves no faster than the most recalcitrant participant, finding a lowest common denominator may be more possible with a less-than-universal group of states.

The process of creating an ad hoc coalition would presumably begin with informal high-level consultations to find a group of like-minded world leaders. Such a group, drawing participants from the countries suggested earlier, would ideally be small enough to be agile, but large enough to allow for sufficient diversity in order to command legitimacy. At a summit-level meeting, the leaders could issue a communiqué and work plan (see below). Just as importantly, they could also commit to giving personal attention to some of the more immediate blocks in the road to zero, such as the Iranian nuclear crisis and the impasse over negotiation of a fissile material cutoff treaty. At an appropriate time, the joint enterprise might also engage regional security organizations that support the objective of creating the conditions for a world without nuclear arms.

Clearly, to reach zero (or to get anywhere near it), a universal process would eventually be needed. The coalition, therefore, would seek to gradually add new members and to formalize the process (much as the Proliferation Security Initiative has done). To facilitate further expansion, participants could, at an early stage, consider developing a statement of principles that new members would commit to upholding.

Initial Actions

The purpose of convening a meeting of heads of state or government would be to demonstrate the commitment of a sizable coalition of nations to creating the conditions for a world without nuclear weapons. The commitment would necessarily be codified in a written statement released to the public after the deliberations. Many variations on such a statement are imaginable. At the end of this chapter are a draft communiqué and work plan modeled after those issued by the Nuclear Security Summit held in Washington in 2010. Perhaps it should go without saying that skillful diplomacy would have to be deployed to produce such a document (or documents) that would present more than one nation's view of the world.

Participants in the joint enterprise might bring to the initial summit their national commitments to take immediate action to begin creating the conditions for a world without nuclear weapons. The implementation of national nuclear initiatives, examples of which are shown at the end of this chapter and which would constitute an attachment to the work plan, would be the first test of whether the joint enterprise was beginning to take off. Many of these individual national actions likely could not be exactly reciprocated, because exact analogues are not available. The important factor would be the overall balance between national actions taken by participants in the joint enterprise. Participants might bring additional national actions to review summits that might be held every two years.

Long-Term Agenda

A joint enterprise is a multifaceted movement proceeding over many years or decades in different forums in different parts of the world. It would be nothing less than an effort to construct a safer global security environment and could fit into a broader effort to build institutions to succeed those created after World War II, which built the foundations for peace, freedom, and prosperity in that era.[3]

The agreement of a coalition of the willing to a set of priorities for actions to be taken by nations that accept those commitments is just the beginning of a very complex undertaking. One of the most important features of any type of agreement that might emerge from a joint enterprise summit would be a provision that requires periodic review summits. An illustration of such a provision is contained in the draft work plan text, calling for reviews every other year—at the summit level to sustain high-level attention—and the establishment of a contact group to function in an oversight role between review meetings.

Oversight of all the activities that might be identified as potential elements of a joint enterprise would be, at best, a means of keeping governments—both those participating in the process and the majority of states, who initially would be outside of the process—informed of progress in each of these elements. Assuring the fulfillment of agreements would be another matter altogether, dependent in large measure on whether the joint enterprise gains a public identity, public support, and a sense of momentum. The early years of implementing the type of program shown in the attached model documents would be absolutely critical.

---

3. "So there's this fractured world . . . we have to come to grips with that and try to put it back together again . . . if we can create a world free of nuclear weapons . . . or as you make progress toward doing that, you are making progress toward rebuilding a security and economic commons." George P. Shultz, July 25, 2012.

Ancillary Agreements

A focus on nuclear issues alone can only go so far in creating conditions for a world without nuclear weapons. Nuclear weapons do not exist in a vacuum, and progress toward zero will require other agreements, some of them relating to international governance.

One of the more important ancillary agreements will deal with non-nuclear forces. Imbalances in conventional forces create tensions and can lead to pressures for nuclear offsets. The only way to deal with that problem is through regional negotiations of the type that took place in Europe in the 1980s and 1990s. These led to a treaty regime that limited conventional force deployments. Importantly, the talks also led to a series of confidence-building measures that were considered politically, but not legally, binding. They included:

- Exchange of information on organization, manpower, and weapons/equipment, including plans for deployments of weapons/equipment
- Exchange of information on defense planning, including defense policy and doctrine and force plans
- Consultation and cooperation as regards unusual military activities and hazardous incidents
- Voluntary hosting of military visits
- Military-to-military contacts
- Joint military exercises and training to work on tasks of mutual interest
- Prior notification and observation of certain military activities, including an annual calendar of such activities
- Constraints on size and frequency of exercises and prohibition of any large unannounced exercises
- Inspections and evaluations
- Communications networks
- Annual implementation assessment meetings

For some years into the future in regions of the world outside of Europe, confidence-building measures like these would represent an extraordinary advance. They could be developed in small groups and could be politically, rather than legally, binding. Ultimately, of course, a legally binding treaty with an array of rigorous verification measures would be required to assure that conventional force limitations were properly observed.

Countries, in particular the United States and Russia, would have to reach understandings regarding missile defense in order to facilitate offensive nuclear arms reductions. In a world without nuclear weapons, missile defense could provide an important hedge against possible nuclear cheating. While the current gap between strategic offense and defense is so large that a treaty limiting missile defense is not needed, as the number of nuclear weapons is reduced, careful attention to missile defense and possible limitations thereon might be necessary and appropriate in order to avoid potentially destabilizing combinations of nuclear-armed ballistic missiles and missile defense interceptors.

Likewise, countries may have to take up other questions, such as the potential of long-range, precision-guided conventional weapons. Some countries fear that such weapons could carry out missions that previously required nuclear-armed systems.

Concluding Thoughts

As noted in chapter 2, Winston Churchill's last great speech in the House of Commons in 1955 is famous for his prophecy that "safety will be the sturdy child of terror, and survival the twin brother of annihilation." Usually forgotten is that nuclear deterrence was not a feature of international relations that Churchill wanted to last forever. In that last speech he said that he hoped for political change among nations so that nuclear deterrence would no longer be needed. The nuclear shadow over the earth should be removed as soon as conditions permitted. Ronald Reagan felt much the same way. He said so many times, publicly and privately.

Nearly three decades after Churchill spoke those words, Soviet dissident Andrei Sakharov suggested that the time had come to ask whether nuclear deterrence had not outlived its usefulness. In a letter from Gorky, published in July 1983, Sakharov said that ". . . nuclear deterrence is gradually turning into its own antithesis and becoming a dangerous remnant of the past."[4] Now, more than three decades after those words were written, Sakharov's judgment needs to be elevated to the status of a crucial question for the survival of humanity.

By the early 1990s the Cold War had ended and the Soviet Union, whose nuclear weapons were the subject of Churchill's remarks about retaliation, had ceased to exist. Very likely this was even more political change than Churchill privately imagined in 1955. Yet two more decades have gone by since the end of the Cold War, and nuclear deterrence still has an almost mystical hold on many opinion-shapers around the world. The idea shapes force structures and dominates the thinking of security communities nearly everywhere. UN Secretary General Ban Ki-moon has said that "the doctrine of nuclear deterrence has proven to be contagious. This has made non-proliferation more difficult, which in turn raises new risks that nuclear weapons will be used."[5]

Perhaps the most important legacy of the Cold War is one we rarely think of: nuclear weapons were never used in war after 1945. Nuclear deterrence deserves a large measure of credit for that as well as for the absence of a major armed conflict directly between the United States and Soviet Union. But it is important to recall that at key points—the Cuban missile crisis, the Soviet misreading of the NATO "Able Archer" exercise, and times when computers gave false warnings—the world was awfully lucky. Can we perpetuate that legacy and good fortune indefinitely into the future—particularly if the number of nuclear weapons states continues to grow?

---

4. Andrei Sakharov's letter from internal exile in Gorky, on the occasion of being presented the Leo Szilard Lectureship Award. For full text, see https://www.aip.org /history/sakharov/essay2.htm.

5. Address to the East-West Institute, "The United Nations and Security in a Nuclear-Weapon-Free World," New York, October 24, 2008.

A further complication is that "deterrence" has been misinterpreted in recent years. It has come to be linked with nuclear weapons. It would be a huge mistake to perpetuate that misleading idea. Deterrence, through the threat of forceful actions, is an ancient and enduring concept. "Nuclear" is not an essential part of it. In a non-nuclear world, states would find non-nuclear ways to deter potential aggression. Fortunately, many leaders around the world share Churchill's and Reagan's judgment that a day might come—and should come—when nuclear deterrence will no longer be needed. And in that lies the hope that a joint enterprise can be created.

Draft Communiqué of the Summit Meeting of the Joint Enterprise

The following is the text of a draft communiqué that might be issued by summit leaders at their first meeting to launch a joint enterprise, modeled on the communiqué issued by the 2010 Nuclear Security Summit:

The world is now on the precipice of a new and dangerous nuclear era. The spread of nuclear weapons, nuclear know-how, and nuclear material, combined with national decisions to give more emphasis to nuclear weapons in defense plans, has brought us to a nuclear tipping point. A very real and increasing possibility exists that the deadliest weapons ever invented could be used in a state-to-state conflict or fall into the hands of non-state actors who would feel no political, ethical, or moral compunctions against their use. No historical experience with nuclear warfare underpins the calculations about nuclear use or nuclear deterrence. An unrestrained nuclear war could destroy in days civilized life as we know it. The steps being taken now to address this threat are not adequate to meet the danger.

A world free of nuclear weapons is like the top of a very tall mountain. We cannot see the top of the mountain; but we know that the risks from continuing to go down the mountain are too real to ignore. It thus makes sense to begin to ascend the mountain, so that we can gain a better and clearer view of the safest routes to the top.

We recognize that the security of future generations will require responsible national actions now, and sustained and effective international cooperation in the future. We recognize that a clear statement of our ultimate goal is the only way to build the kind of international trust and broad cooperation that will unleash the creativity needed to build new institutional arrangements for verification and enforcement of compliance with agreements that will be required to effectively address today's threats. We call for a global joint enterprise to create the conditions for a world without nuclear weapons. We endorse setting the goal of a world free of nuclear weapons and we will work energetically on the actions required to achieve that goal.

Therefore, we affirm that:

1. We will support the determination of the United Nations Security Council, as expressed in its Resolution 1887 of September 24, 2009, "to seek a safer world for all and to create the conditions for a world without nuclear weapons."
2. To that end, we will carry out a systematic series of agreements supplemented by cooperative national actions undertaken by many states in the coming years to approach that goal in a timely, balanced, predictable, secure, verifiable, enforceable, and sustainable fashion.
3. We will ensure that incentives for the use of nuclear weapons, as well as the possibilities for accidental or unauthorized use, are reduced and eliminated in the process of reducing and eliminating nuclear weapons, and that all arrangements related to these agreements will be configured to increase security and strengthen international stability.

In sum, we have agreed that:

A world without nuclear weapons is desirable and that each of us henceforward is under an obligation to pursue it promptly and vigorously. We will do everything in our power to cooperate in creating the conditions necessary for the global elimination of all nuclear weapons.

Draft Work Plan

The following is the text of a draft work plan that might be issued by summit leaders at their first meeting to launch a joint enterprise, modeled on the work plan issued by the 2010 Nuclear Security Summit:[6]

1. This work plan supports the communiqué of the Joint Enterprise Summit. To promote progress on sequential agreements referred to in the communiqué, the Participating States offer the national initiatives attached as Annex 1 to this document as examples of immediate steps that they will initiate to facilitate progress toward the elimination of nuclear weapons. The Participating States encourage all states to fulfill their contributions to this roster and to expand it.

2. All Participating States that have not yet done so should in the near future join the 1972 Convention on the Prohibition of the Development, Production, and Stockpiling of Bacteriological (Biological) and Toxin Weapons and on their Destruction; the

---

6. The following ideas are similar to ideas put forward by David A. Koplow in "What Would Zero Look Like? A Treaty for the Abolition of Nuclear Weapons," *Georgetown Journal of International Law* 45, no. 3 (Spring 2014): 683–781. The ideas for both this chapter and his paper came out of roundtable discussions that the authors attended with Koplow in 2012.

1993 Convention on the Prohibition of the Development, Production, Stockpiling, and Use of Chemical Weapons and on their Destruction; and the 1996 Comprehensive Nuclear-Test-Ban Treaty. All Participating States will promote universal adherence and observance of these instruments.

3. All Participating States will support the development, implementation, and widespread acceptance of regional nuclear weapons-free-zone treaties and protocols attached thereto.

4. Russia and the United States will promptly and urgently enter into negotiations and conclude an agreement for the further reduction of their nuclear weapons below New START limits, with the goal of reducing their stockpiles of deployed and non-deployed strategic and non-strategic nuclear warheads by 50 percent.

5. Once Russia and the United States have reached the above agreement, each other Participating State that possesses nuclear weapons will cap at the current level the total number of its nuclear weapons and will undertake additional measures of transparency regarding its nuclear weapons programs.

6. Participating states will begin to explore verification measures that might be needed for further reductions, as addressed further in point no. 11.

7. Each Participating State that possesses nuclear weapons or an advanced civil or military nuclear program will contribute to the cooperative development of the conditions for the prohibition of nuclear weapons by undertaking the following actions:

   a. Ceasing the production of fissile materials for use in weapons or in excess of civilian needs

   b. Enhancing the effectiveness of secure international and domestic controls over fissile materials

   c. Accepting and fully implementing the Additional Protocol with the International Atomic Energy Agency

    d. Exchanging data regarding the production and possession of fissile materials

    e. Participating in negotiations to create a comprehensive, legally binding treaty to regulate the production of fissile materials, including the institution of international control over facilities for the enrichment of fissile materials and for the storage of spent nuclear fuel and the establishment of an international fuel bank to be operated by the International Atomic Energy Agency

8. The Participating States possessing nuclear weapons will, as they reduce their nuclear forces, take steps to remove nuclear weapons from prompt launch status.

9. Subsequent to US-Russian agreement to each reduce their total nuclear warheads by 50 percent and agreement by each other Participating State to cap at the current level the total number of its nuclear weapons (see points no. 4 and no. 5 above), the Participating States possessing nuclear weapons will agree upon and implement, in a balanced and progressive fashion, deep reductions in the numbers of their deployed nuclear weapons and will disassemble the weapons. They may implement these reductions in stages. Any nuclear weapons removed from delivery systems will be stored under safeguards in conditions that would preclude them from being quickly and secretly restored to the delivery systems, and any nuclear weapons to be eliminated will be disassembled and their components will be irreversibly destroyed or stored under safeguards in conditions that would preclude them from being quickly and secretly reassembled.

10. In a final stage, the Participating States will enter negotiations to reduce their nuclear weapons stockpiles to zero. These negotiations will include all nuclear weapons, regardless of range, type, age, size, or status as deployed, non-deployed, retired, reserve, awaiting disassembly, or otherwise. These

negotiations may proceed in stages, including via regional or other groups, as well as bilaterally and multilaterally.

11. In anticipation of the sequential stages outlined above, the Participating States will meet to discuss and develop a highly effective worldwide verification system to ensure adequate monitoring of compliance with the obligations regarding nuclear weapons. This verification system will include multiple components such as: national and multilateral technical means of verification; routine on-site inspection; submission of relevant data to a global data base; and challenge on-site inspection. The verification system will be sufficiently rigorous and intrusive that Participating States will have confidence in its ability to identify violations in sufficient time to enable them to mount an effective response.

12. In anticipation of the sequential stages outlined above, the Participating States will meet to discuss and develop a highly effective worldwide enforcement system to ensure an adequate response to any violation of the agreements. This enforcement system will include multiple components such as: diplomatic measures; resort to the institutions of international law; punitive economic measures; and military measures. The enforcement system will be sufficiently rigorous and powerful that Participating States will have confidence in its ability to deter violations, to punish violators, to negate the effects of any violation, and to ensure that violations do not result in military or other gains.

13. The leaders of the Participating States will continuously monitor progress in implementation of this communiqué and its work plan and will meet every other year beginning in 2016 to review its progress and to consider additional measures necessary to promote its objectives. Participating States (to be named later) will serve as a Contact Group, to facilitate accomplishment of these objectives. (Note: these might be the UN Security Council

Permanent Five plus nations such as Brazil, Kazakhstan, South Africa, Sweden, Ukraine, and others that have given up nuclear weapons or programs that might have led to them. Japan, as the only nation to have undergone a nuclear attack, should be a charter member.)

Draft Annex to the Work Plan

A draft annex to the above work plan that might be issued by summit leaders at their first meeting to launch a joint enterprise could include a list of national nuclear initiatives, steps announced by leaders at the summit.[7] Examples of such national nuclear initiatives include:

- A declaration that fissile materials removed from nuclear weapons being eliminated will not be used to manufacture new types of nuclear weapons; that no newly produced fissile materials will be used in nuclear weapons; and that fissile material from or within civil nuclear programs will not be used to manufacture nuclear weapons
- Declarations of national fissile materials holdings in accordance with an agreed standard format
- Acceptance by nuclear-armed states of transparency measures at all nuclear test sites and declarations that none of them will be the first to break the current moratoriums on nuclear testing
- A means of ensuring that targeting codes for nuclear weapons are altered or maintained to aim only at unpopulated ocean areas
- Elimination of the requirement for prompt launch from war plans
- A freeze at current levels on nuclear stockpiles

---

7.   Ibid.

- Invitations to third-country nuclear-armed states' officials to join actual or practice inspections conducted by the United States and Russia as observers
- Verified storage of nuclear weapons designated for dismantlement at specified storage sites within the territory of their possessors with the understanding that such weapons and the fissile materials they contain will not be re-introduced into the weapons stockpiles of their possessor or of any other entity
- Confirmed dismantlement of nuclear warheads excess to national security needs under conditions of irreversibility
- Voluntary acceptance on a trial basis of additional Open Skies sensors, both in countries where the Open Skies Treaty is now in force and in areas where cooperative aerial monitoring could contribute to confidence-building, such as where nuclear-weapons-free zones are established
- Formation of a multilateral group of national experts with the assignment from governments of developing generic measures for monitoring and verifying warhead numbers and warhead elimination
- Formation of a multilateral group of national experts with the assignment from governments of developing generic measures for monitoring and verifying amounts of fissile material
- Formation of a multilateral group of national experts with the assignment from governments of developing enforcement measures and mechanisms for a world without nuclear weapons
- Formation of a multilateral group of national experts with the assignment from governments of developing rules for a world without nuclear weapons as regards (1) what former nuclear-armed states might maintain temporarily as a hedge against cheating and (2) what nuclear materials might be allowed any state on a permanent basis
- Establishment of regional forums to promote security and cooperation

- Establishment of national commissions to record histories of their states' nuclear weapons programs and collection of supporting evidence (even if such evidence were kept classified for the time being, it would be an invaluable verification resource for the future)
- Agreement by the United States and Russia to provide each other annual declarations providing, for each key element of its missile defense system, the current numbers and the maximum numbers planned in each year over the next ten years, with advance notice of any changes in those numbers

About the Authors

Nobumasa Akiyama is a professor at the Graduate School of Law and the Graduate School of International and Public Policy at Hitotsubashi University in Japan, and an adjunct research fellow at the Japan Institute of International Affairs. His other professional appointments include memberships in various governmental consultative groups and study groups at the ministries of Foreign Affairs and Defense, the Japan Atomic Energy Commission, and the Nuclear Regulatory Commission of Japan; and advisor to the Japanese delegation to the Non-Proliferation Treaty Review Conferences. Professor Akiyama has published extensively and presented papers at various conferences on nonproliferation, Japan's national security, and nuclear energy. He also worked on the review of the Fukushima nuclear accident as a leader of the working group for the Independent Commission on the Investigation of the Fukushima Nuclear Accident, initiated by a private think tank, the Rebuild Japan Initiative Foundation.

Steven P. Andreasen is a national security consultant with the Nuclear Threat Initiative in Washington, DC, and teaches courses on national security policy and crisis management in foreign affairs at the Hubert H. Humphrey School of Public Affairs, University of Minnesota. He served as director for defense policy and arms control on the US National Security Council at the White House from February 1993 to January 2001. He was the principal advisor on strategic policy, nuclear arms control, and missile defense to the national security advisor and the president. He is a member of the International Institute for Strategic Studies.

Brig. Gen. (ret.) **Shlomo Brom** is a visiting fellow with the National Security and International Policy team at the Center for American Progress. He is also a senior research fellow at the Institute for National Security Studies at Tel Aviv. He retired from the Israel Defense Forces, where he held the position of director of strategic planning in the general staff, in 1998. He was also the deputy national security advisor, 2000–2001. He participated in peace negotiations with Jordan, Syria, and the Palestinians, and in Middle East Arms Control and Regional Security talks during the 1990s. He published numerous papers on Middle Eastern national security and foreign policy issues.

Michael S. Gerson is an independent consultant in Atlanta, Georgia. He was previously a division lead, project director, and senior analyst at the Center for Naval Analyses, where his research focused on nuclear and conventional deterrence, nuclear strategy, and arms control. From 2011–2012 he was appointed to the office of the secretary of defense and in 2009–2010 he was a staff member on the Nuclear Posture Review. He has published numerous articles and book chapters on nuclear issues, co-chaired a Center for Strategic and International Studies (CSIS)-funded commission on the future of US-Russia nuclear arms control, and served as a committee member of a CSIS-funded commission on US-China nuclear relations.

James E. Goodby is an author and retired US Foreign Service officer. Highlights in his career include negotiations with NATO alliance partners as part of the Conference on Security and Cooperation in Europe to create the Helsinki Accords. He has served as US ambassador to Finland, vice chairman of the US delegation to the Strategic Arms Reduction Talks, and chief US negotiator for the safe and secure dismantlement of nuclear weapons. He is currently the Annenberg Distinguished Visiting Fellow at the Hoover Institution. In 1994, he received the first Heinz Award in Public Policy from the Heinz Family Foundation.

Karim Haggag is a career Egyptian diplomat. Throughout his twenty-year diplomatic career, he has focused on Middle East regional security, arms control and nonproliferation, Arab-Israeli diplomacy, and counter-terrorism. He has served in the Egyptian Embassy in Washington, DC, the cabinet of the foreign minister, the Office of the Presidency, the Policy Planning Division, and as director of the Counter-terrorism Unit in the Egyptian Foreign Ministry. From 2011 to 2013 he was a visiting professor at the Near East and South Asia Center for Strategic Studies/National Defense University in Washington. He is a graduate of the American University in Cairo and holds a master's degree in War Studies from King's College, London. The views expressed in his chapter are his own and do not reflect the position of the Egyptian Foreign Ministry or the government of Egypt.

Peter Hayes is a professor at the Center for International Security Studies, Sydney University, Australia, and director of the Nautilus Institute in Berkeley, California. He works at the nexus of security, environment, and energy policy problems. Best known for innovative cooperative engagement strategies in North Korea, he has developed techniques at the Nautilus Institute for seeking near-term solutions to global security and sustainability problems and has applied them in East Asia, Australia, and South Asia. He has worked for many international organizations, including the UN Development Program, Asian Development Bank, and Global Environment Facility. He was founding director of the Environment Liaison Centre in Kenya in 1975.

Peter Jones is an associate professor in the Graduate School of Public and International Affairs at the University of Ottawa. He is also an Annenberg Distinguished Visiting Fellow at the Hoover Institution at Stanford University. Before joining the academy, he spent fourteen years in government service in Canada, much of it dealing with disarmament and arms control issues. During this time he was a member of the Canadian delegation to the Arms Control and Regional Security working group (ACRS) of the Middle East Peace Process. He also served as project leader of the Middle East Regional Security and Arms Control project at the Stockholm International Peace Research Institute. He has led or participated in numerous Track 2 projects on regional security and arms control in the Middle East over several decades.

S. Paul Kapur is a professor in the Department of National Security Affairs at the US Naval Postgraduate School. He is also a visiting fellow at the Observer Research Foundation, New Delhi. Previously, he was on the faculties of the US Naval War College and Claremont McKenna College, and was a visiting professor at Stanford University's Center for International Security and Cooperation. His research and teaching interests include nuclear weapons proliferation, deterrence, ethno-religious violence, and the international security environment in South Asia. He regularly serves as a consultant to the US departments of Defense and State as well as to a range of private entities.

Katarzyna Kubiak is a doctoral candidate at the Institute for Peace Research and Security Policy at the University of Hamburg (IFSH), working on extended nuclear deterrence. Previously, she was a researcher at the German Institute for International and Security Affairs, IFSH and the German Bundestag as well as a field researcher for the National Consortium for the Study of Terrorism and Responses to Terrorism. She is an alumna of the University of California Institute on Global Conflict and Cooperation nuclear boot camp. Her research interests comprise NATO nuclear policy, arms control, disarmament, nonproliferation, and nuclear safety and security.

Li Bin is a senior associate working jointly in the Nuclear Policy Program and the Asia Program at the Carnegie Endowment for International Peace. A physicist and expert on nuclear disarmament, his research focuses on

China's nuclear and arms control policy and on US-Chinese nuclear relations. He is also a professor of international relations at Tsinghua University. He previously directed the arms control division at the Institute of Applied Physics and Computational Mathematics, where he also served as executive director of the Program for Science and National Security Studies. Li was a Social Science Research Council–MacArthur Foundation Peace and Security Fellow at the Massachusetts Institute of Technology and Princeton University. In 1996, he joined the Chinese delegation on the Comprehensive Test Ban Treaty negotiations.

Oliver Meier is an associate at the German Institute for International and Security Affairs in Berlin. Previously, he was senior researcher with the Institute for Peace Research and Security Policy at the University of Hamburg and the international representative and correspondent of the US Arms Control Association. He has also worked on the staff of Uta Zapf, who is a member of the Foreign Relations Committee and chairperson of the subcommittee on disarmament, arms control, and nonproliferation in the German Bundestag. He was also senior arms control and disarmament researcher with the Verification Research, Training and Information Centre in London and a consultant to several nongovernmental organizations.

Chung-in Moon is a professor of political science at Yonsei University in Seoul and editor-in-chief of *Global Asia,* a quarterly magazine in English. He is currently serving as a member of the Presidential Committee on Unification Preparation of the Republic of Korea. He chaired the Presidential Committee on Northeast Asian Cooperation Initiative, a cabinet-level post, and was ambassador for international security affairs at the ROK Ministry of Foreign Affairs and Trade. He has taught at Williams College and the University of Kentucky and held visiting professorships at Duke University, the University of California-San Diego, Keio University (Japan) and Beijing University. He has published over forty-five books and 250 articles in edited volumes and scholarly journals.

Benoît Pelopidas is a lecturer (assistant professor with tenure) in international relations at the University of Bristol (Global Insecurities Center) and an affiliate of the Center for International Security and Cooperation at Stanford University. He has been awarded two international prizes for his research, from the International Studies Association and the James Martin Center for Nonproliferation Studies. His research focuses on the global politics of nuclear vulnerability, cases of near-use of nuclear weapons, and lessons learned from global nuclear history and French nuclear policies. His is currently completing an edited volume on the experience of the Cuban missile crisis worldwide as an early set of experiences of global nuclear vulnerability and its implications for security, responsibility, and alliance dynamics.

Steven Pifer is director of the Arms Control and Non-Proliferation Initiative at the Brookings Institution, where he also works on Ukraine and Russia questions. He frequently comments on these issues in the media, and his articles have appeared in the *New York Times, Washington Post,* and *National Interest,* among others. He is co-author of *The Opportunity: Next Steps in Reducing Nuclear Arms.* A retired Foreign Service officer, his more than twenty-five years with the State Department included assignments as deputy assistant secretary of state with responsibilities for Russia and Ukraine (2001–2004), ambassador to Ukraine (1998–2000), and special assistant to the president and senior director for Russia, Ukraine, and Eurasia on the National Security Council (1996–1997). He also served in Warsaw, Geneva, Moscow, and London.

Pavel Podvig is an independent analyst based in Geneva, where he runs his research project, "Russian Nuclear Forces." He is also a senior research fellow at the UN Institute for Disarmament Research. He started his work on arms control at the Center for Arms Control Studies at the Moscow Institute of Physics and Technology, the first independent research organization in Russia dedicated to analysis of technical issues of disarmament and nonproliferation. He led the Center for Arms Control Studies project that produced the book, *Russian Strategic Nuclear Forces* (MIT Press,

2001). In recognition of his work in Russia, the American Physical Society awarded him the Leo Szilard Lectureship Award of 2008 (with Anatoli Diakov). He has worked with the Program on Science and Global Security at Princeton University, the Security Studies Program at MIT, and the Center for International Security and Cooperation at Stanford University.

George P. Shultz, a graduate of Princeton University and a US Marine Corps veteran, was appointed secretary of labor in 1969, director of the Office of Management and Budget in 1970, and secretary of the treasury in 1972. He served in the Reagan administration as chairman of the President's Economic Policy Advisory Board (1981–82) and secretary of state (1982–89). Since 1989, he has been a distinguished fellow at Stanford University's Hoover Institution; in 2001, he was named the Thomas W. and Susan B. Ford Distinguished Fellow. He is honorary chairman of the Stanford Institute for Economic Policy Research, Advisory Council, and is chair of the Precourt Institute Energy Advisory Council at Stanford, the MIT Energy Initiative External Advisory Board, and the Shultz-Stephenson Task Force on Energy Policy at the Hoover Institution. His publications include *Turmoil and Triumph: My Years as Secretary of State* (1993), *Issues on My Mind: Strategies for the Future (2013),* and *Game Changers: Energy on the Move* (2014).

Isabelle Williams joined the Nuclear Threat Initiative in 2007 and serves as codirector of the Nuclear Security Project, where she helps coordinate international strategy, including managing the work of NSP global partners in the areas of research, analysis, policy development, and public education. She has also helped develop the NSP analytical framework and coauthored the report "NATO and Nuclear Weapons: Is a New Consensus Possible?" Earlier, she worked at the Partnership for Global Security, where she managed the next generation nonproliferation program, which included work on Pakistan's nuclear security and US threat reduction budgets, and at the Chemical and Biological Arms Control Institute and the International Institute for Strategic Studies in London. She earned degrees from the University of Leeds, United Kingdom.

Index

Books of Related Interest

Implications of the Reykjavik Summit on Its Twentieth Anniversary: Conference Report
Sidney D. Drell and George P. Shultz, editors; 2007

Reykjavik Revisited: Steps Toward a World Free of Nuclear Weapons (Summary Report)
George P. Shultz, Sidney D. Drell, and James E. Goodby, editors; 2008

Reykjavik Revisited: Steps Toward a World Free of Nuclear Weapons (Complete Report)
George P. Shultz, Steven P. Andreasen, Sidney D. Drell, and James E. Goodby, editors; 2008

A World without Nuclear Weapons: End-State Issues
Sidney D. Drell and James E. Goodby; 2009

Toward a Diplomatic Action Plan on Nuclear Issues
Chester A. Crocker; 2009

The Gravest Danger: Nuclear Weapons
James E. Goodby and Sidney D. Drell; 2010

Deterrence: Its Past and Future—A Summary Account of Conference Proceedings
George P. Shultz, Sidney D. Drell, and James E. Goodby, editors; 2011

Deterrence: Its Past and Future—Papers Presented at Hoover Institution, November 2010
George P. Shultz, Sidney D. Drell, and James E. Goodby, editors; 2011

The Nuclear Enterprise: High-Consequence Accidents: How to Enhance Safety and Minimize Risks in Nuclear Weapons and Reactors
George P. Shultz and Sidney D. Drell, editors; 2012

Nuclear Security: The Problems and the Road Ahead
George P. Shultz, Sidney D. Drell, Henry A. Kissinger, and Sam Nunn; 2014